E G L I

The Morality
of Terrorism

Pergamon Titles of Related Interest

Alexander/Gleason   BEHAVIORAL & QUANTITATIVE
PERSPECTIVES ON TERRORISM
Cannizzo   THE GUN MERCHANTS:
Politics and Policies of the Major Arms Suppliers
Kilmarx/Alexander   BUSINESS AND THE MIDDLE EAST:
Threats and Prospects
Shultz/Sloan   RESPONDING TO THE TERRORIST THREAT:
Security and Crisis

Related Journals*

HISTORY OF EUROPEAN IDEAS
LEARNING AND SOCIETY
SYSTEM

*Free specimen copies available upon request.

PERGAMON POLICY STUDIES
ON INTERNATIONAL POLITICS

The Morality of Terrorism

Religious and Secular Justifications

Edited by
David C. Rapoport
Yonah Alexander

Pergamon Press
NEW YORK • OXFORD • TORONTO • SYDNEY • PARIS • FRANKFURT

Pergamon Press Offices:

U.S.A.   Pergamon Press Inc., Maxwell House, Fairview Park,
                     Elmsford, New York 10523, U.S.A.

U.K.   Pergamon Press Ltd., Headington Hill Hall,
                     Oxford OX3 0BW, England

CANADA   Pergamon Press Canada Ltd., Suite 104, 150 Consumers Road,
                     Willowdale, Ontario M2J 1P9, Canada

AUSTRALIA   Pergamon Press (Aust.) Pty. Ltd., P.O. Box 544,
                     Potts Point, NSW 2011, Australia

FRANCE   Pergamon Press SARL, 24 rue des Ecoles,
                     75240 Paris, Cedex 05, France

FEDERAL REPUBLIC Pergamon Press GmbH, Hammerweg 6
OF GERMANY   6242 Kronberg/Taunus, Federal Republic of Germany

Library of Congress Cataloging in Publication Data
Main entry under title:

The Morality of terrorism

     (Pergamon policy studies on international
politics)
     Bibliography: p.
     Includes index.
     1. Terrorism. I. Rapoport, David C.
II. Alexander, Yonah. III. Title.
HV6431.M66   1982   303.6'2   81-10603
ISBN 0-08-026347-X   AACR2

Printed in the United States of America

To Barbara and Miriam

Contents

Preface

In March 1979 a UCLA-SUNY Conference was held at UCLA. Its proceedings are now in the process of being published.* The discussions of the Conference made it abundantly clear that there was a pressing need for new studies which could provide both historical and moral perspectives for terrorist activities, and this volume was designed to meet that deficiency. Two of the Conference papers were suitable for this purpose, and we solicited thirteen additional ones.

Our concern is the "terrorist tradition" from its origin in the revealed religions to its present manifestations which are largely secular though not exclusively so, as the recent assassination of President Anwar Sadat by members of the Society for Repentance and the Flight From Sin indicates. The most conspicuous sources for secular terror are states and rebels, and the organization of the book reflects that fact. Important common themes running through all the essays are the moral climate that produces terrorism, the doctrines terrorists used to justify themselves and the moral predicaments terrorists create. These themes have been sadly and inexplicably neglected in the literature. The general introduction and the separate ones for each of the three sections are designed to draw out these particular themes in the articles which, of course, deal also with very different concerns.

All editors incur debts, and it is always a pleasure to acknowledge them. We want to thank the contributors. Ap-

---

*Rapoport, David C. and Yonah Alexander, The Rationalization of Terrorism: UCLA-SUNY Conference on Terrorism (Frederick, Maryland, University Publications of America) forthcoming.

preciation is also due to Barbara Rapoport who completed the index despite a very serious illness and to the secretaries in the Department of Political Science at UCLA who patiently typed, retyped, and retyped again pages of this manuscript.

David Rapoport wishes to make some special acknowledgements. The National Institute of Mental Health provided a grant several years ago which enabled him to develop an interest in religion as a source for terror and to bring "Terror and the Messiah" to completion. He is also grateful to the Reason Foundation which granted him a Fellowship during the summer of 1980 in Santa Barbara which provided some time and much stimulation.

Washington, D.C.
Los Angeles, California

Introduction
David C. Rapoport

> I will send forth My terror before you, and I will throw into
> panic all the people among whom you come, and I will make all
> your enemies turn tail before you... I will drive them out
> before you little by little, until you have increased and
> possessed the land.
>
> - <u>Exodus</u> 23:27

> Terror . . . is a consequence of the general principle of
> <u>democracy</u> applied to the most pressing needs of the father-
> land.
>
> - Robespierre (emphasis
added).

In 1969 when I accepted the Canadian Broadcasting Corporation's invitation for a series of lectures to be entitled
"Assassination and Terrorism," I discovered that it was extraordinarily difficult to assemble a useful bibliography. A
few discussions of particular events and specific campaigns
were available, but there was very little on the general
meaning and nature of the two phenomena. (1)

I was particularly surprised to find nothing in <u>the</u>
current monument to "relevant" erudition, the <u>International</u>
<u>Encyclopedia of the Social Sciences</u> which had just been pub-
lished (1968). Ironically, its predecessor (1933) did contain
two fascinating useful essays; (2) they concluded on what
seemed to me a very strange note, namely that assassinations
and acts of terror were declining so much that in the future
the subjects would be interesting to historians or antiquarians
only! What was the explanation for that development? Modern
technology had made our world so complex that we had become
largely <u>invulnerable</u> to determined actions of individuals or
small groups! In the future events would be more and more
determined by "classes" and "masses." The editors of the

second edition of the Encyclopedia apparently believed that prophecy, and when leading authorities describe their own subjects as immaterial to the concerns of the modern world, why waste valuable time, space, and money to commission new essays?

Could any estimation of "relevance" have ever been more mistaken? In the next decade great quantities of articles and books on terrorist activities began flowing out from both the popular and academic presses. A journal entitled Terrorism has been established, and a great many American colleges and universities now offer a course or two on terrorism as part of their curriculum. The reason for this interest is that terrorist activity has increased dramatically, so much so that in his confirmation hearings, Secretary of State Alexander M. Haig Jr. even described terrorism as the Reagan Administration's major international problem.

When newspaper headlines so decisively influence our willingness to accept the relevancy of an academic subject as they do today, they must also shape our understanding of how we should go about studying it. Our literature is dominated by an inclination to treat only the most recent events or to make projections about the immediate future. Of course, these concerns reflect a very practical orientation, a commitment to developing tools to control the spread of terrorism.

The purpose of this volume is to suggest other ways to approach the subject. The understanding of terrorism, we think, will be enhanced immensely by expanding our historical perspective, and by stimulating a finer appreciation of what terrorist doctrines and activities involve and why they seem to create unusual moral predicaments.

For most commentators terrorism really has no history, or at least they would have us believe that the "terrorist problem" had no significance until the 1960s, when the full impact of modern technology was felt, endowing most individuals as individuals or as members of small groups, with capacities they never had before. More specifically, weapons became more destructive, cheaper, readily obtainable, and easier to conceal: "The technological quantum jumps from the arrow to the revolver and from the gun to the Molotov Cocktail."(3) Mass communications and transport allowed insignificant individuals to travel and/or contact each other quickly and efficiently, to coordinate activities of small numbers over vast spaces. By giving extensive coverage to unusual events, the mass media completed the picture. "You can't be a revolutionary without a color T.V. set; it's as necessary as a gun."(4)

Those who subscribe to this position do not remember, perhaps, that recently distinguished academics were just as certain that modern technology had quite a different meaning. The absence of historical memory (which the juxtaposition of

these two views emphasize) not only indicates a shocking neglect of anything published on the subject before the 1960s,
but also, and perhaps even more distressing, suggests a
wholesale indifference to anything that happened before that
decade. Because we 'know' what the historical record has to
reveal, we never feel a need to scrutinize it. One can continue to ignore the past, but there surely will be a price to
pay.

The fact is that we do know very little about how deeply
rooted the terrorist phenomena is in our traditions, and we
know less about how much of a tradition terrorists themselves
share.(5) Until these things are understood better, can we
even appreciate the meaning of the information gathered about
terrorists today? Our collection of essays has only opened a
few cracks here and there; but something necessary has been
attempted, and the contributors have caught sight of some
promising possibilities.

A principal theme of this volume is that there is a sharp
distinction between violence and terror which the contemporary
literature too often blurs. Violence may well be a universal
phenomenon, as inseparable from the human condition as is the
sense of frustration and anxiety which produces that violence.
To justify violence we usually argue that the persons we want
to hurt either deserve punishment for misdeeds or that they
deserve it because they can hurt us and intend to do so. A
very different kind of logic is required to justify terror. The
victims do not manifestly threaten us; they are innocent by
conventional moral standards or by the evidence of our own
senses. Terrorists, therefore, abandon ordinary conceptions
and experiences, and they normally avoid speaking of their
victims as persons. Depending on the context, the victims
become symbols, tools, animals or corrupt beings. To be a
terrorist one must have a special picture of the world, a
specific consciousness. Terrorism, consequently, cannot be
a universal phenomenon. It must be, and the evidence shows
that it is, an historical one, emerging only at particular times
and associated with particular developments in a people's
consciousness.

Doctrine, not technology, is the ultimate source for terrorism, and the French not the Industrial Revolution should
preoccupy those interested in modern terror because it provided conceptions that made justifications of the phenomena credible. The purpose of the Reign of Terror was not to destroy
individuals but remnants of the old system, and the revolutionary government understood that system as one which, inter
alia, penetrated the hearts and minds of individuals, creating
propensities or tendencies that under appropriate circumstances could make them dangerous to the Revolution. Those
propensities existed even when they were not manifested in
action; they persisted sometimes even when individuals were

not aware of their presence, and they often remained even
when their carriers made strenuous efforts to eliminate them.
Since existing legal conventions (and indeed all acceptable
ones) refer to actions and intentions, the Revolutionary Tribunals or People's Courts operated largely without rules.
Individuals were not necessarily responsible for their potentialities or character defects; and they were dealt with much
as one might treat limbs infected with gangerene to protect an
otherwise healthy body, i.e., the rest of the community.

The Revolution established a new principle of legitimacy
("The Will of the People") which did not simply absolve its
agents from adhering to existing moral and legal rules, even
those authorized by the People; it also obligated them sometimes to do so. In the subsequent rationales for modern
terror, History sometimes supplants the People as the legitimating source; in either case, the idea of a transcendent
entity that cannot be subjected to rules in the ordinary sense
of the term, even rules that the entity supposedly creates,
remains the same.(6) Terror is always one likely expression
of doctrines which encourage antinomian behavior.

In the French Revolution, terror is not only an instrument of government; it also appears as a tactic for insurrection, particularly in the writings and deeds of Babeuf and
later Buonarotti. The views are primitive, but they become
fully developed during the second third of the nineteenth
century when the Russian anarchists, Bakunin and Nechaev,
construct a doctrine and a picture of the kinds of societies
vulnerable to rebel terror tactics. Significantly, Russian
revolutionary terrorists never refer to themselves as "guerrillas," a perfectly familiar term but one that was inappropriate then (as it is now) because guerrillas on the whole
accept the principal convention of war, which makes only the
armed forces, or persons who have the will and capacity to be
threatening, legitimate targets.

Modern state and rebel terror are two dimensions of a
single tradition, now nearly two centuries old. Often commentators have difficulty in identifying that tradition, perhaps
because terrorist activity has not been continuous; it erupts
periodically at uneven intervals. A second reason is that the
two major forms of terrorism alternatively eclipse each other -
a pattern reflected in our commentaries too. The term terrorist, for example, normally referred in the past to state
activities; now it seems that we can only visualize terrorists as
rebels. The consequence has been that one form of terror is
discussed as though it had no relation to the other. A major
aim of this collection, one that nearly all the contributors
support,(7) is to show that state and rebel terror are two
different expressions of a common ethos, and that a thorough
understanding of one helps illuminate the other.(8)

What is the terrorist experience prior to the French Revolution? Governments and rebels occasionally employed terror for <u>political</u> purposes. But in the West, at least, they did their <u>dirty</u> work in secret and kept their mouths shut afterwards. Terror was too shameful to justify as a political measure, and under those circumstances it was impossible to develop a "tradition of terror" that could be studied for lessons or inspiration.

Terrorism could be justified, however, on religious grounds, and there are some striking and enormously significant examples. No instance of <u>rebel</u> terror in the modern world has had (or perhaps even could have) the impact of the Jewish Zealots and Sicarii, known to us now principally through the spectacular mass suicide at Masada in the first century. Their earlier outrages created the conditions for the loss of the homeland, an Exile that lasted until the present century. The Jewish memory of those deeds and of their consequences had a traumatic continuing impact for two thousand years on Jewish character and institutions.

The durability or continuity of some early terrorist groups also seems quite remarkable. No group in our world has exceeded the tenacity of the Irish Republican Army (IRA) which has struggled for more than sixty years. Still, the Assassins of mediaeval Islam, who called themselves Fidayeen (the "devoted ones"), a name still used often by Moslem terrorists today, survived nearly two and a half centuries; and the astonishing Thugs of India, extinguished in the nineteenth century, apparently were in existence at least as far back as the time of Herodotus 2500 years earlier!

In the major revealed religions (Judaism, Christianity, and Islam) terror is often a particular outgrowth of Messianic or millenarian visions, of the belief that the Messiah can annul God's law or existing restraints in order to fulfill the meaning of history, or God's intention for man.(8) Messianic expectations erupted periodically, and it would seem that as long as the religious traditions that make Messianism conceivable prevail, an outburst is always possible.

Terror for revolutionary purposes has had also a cyclical character since the French Revolution. One might even argue that in our world the conditions for the specific surges in revolutionary and Messianic cult activity may be similar. At least the two often flourish simultaneously; much more often than one would expect, the membership in each overlaps sometimes. One reason may be that many radical revolutionary cults have views of the world that retain elements of the Messianic vision. In both faiths, all existing moral and legal rules will be supplanted. Human nature will be transformed, paving the way for a higher condition of moral existence where oppression, inequality, and even the state (as we know it) disappears. Finally, in both political and religious groups we often find the belief that the road to Paradise runs directly through Hell.(9)

Many of our essays are historical case studies treating issues created by terror for different secular and religious purposes. The majority confine themselves to specific time periods; others range through time more freely, searching for pertinent comparisons, and a few address the problem of historical perspective.

All the essays, historical or not, discuss moral matters, and in this respect they can be distinguished from those normally encountered in the contemporary literature. A principal theme of this volume is that no aspect of terrorism can be more important than the moral questions it raises; yet, none in the literature has been more neglected or muddled. The indifference is not simply a reflection of the lack of focus on moral issues. Much more significant than that, they are also brushed aside with the constantly reiterated, never analyzed tiresome cliche, "one man's terrorist is another's freedom fighter." What is not brushed aside is unintentionally obscured in ways that strip it of moral meaning, insofar as that is possible. The illegal, not the extra-normal, character of terrorist violence becomes then the critical defining feature.(10) Governments prefer to define terrorism in this way too, especially when rebel activities are considered. But the governments' reason is not ours. Governments want the right to treat all acts of violence (no matter what the purpose, manner, or victim) as deeds of ordinary criminals. Academics seek something else - "objectivity" - and we think that we are likely to achieve that "objectivity" if our definitions lack pejorative connotations.(11) In the case of terrorism, the search for what is believed to be "objectivity" is bound to be fruitless, because the moral feelings of the public and the participants themselves are essential aspects of the phenomena we want to understand.

There is no obvious explanation for our inability to grasp this essential point. This persistent problem is quite surprising, just because the contemporary literature is preoccupied with the rebel terrorist who more than any other depends upon generating moral sympathies to compensate for inadequate physical forces.

Any rebel may act to redress a grievance by punishing those responsible or by coercing anyone resisting his attempts. But the terrorist does something else; he designs <u>methods</u> that call attention to a moral plight, uses <u>means</u> that <u>he</u> recognizes are repulsive or shocking to others and may even be revolting to himself. Those methods <u>always</u> provoke outrage, but the paradox is that they can arouse moral support too. Outrageous actions receive more attention than those that are simply violent, and outrages are more likely to provoke antagonists to repulsive counter-responses. In the world in which we live, a

world so burdened with guilt that we are peculiarly susceptible
to terrorist appeals, when two antagonists appear to be employing similar tactics, the weaker (mutatis mutandis) is more
likely to gain the sympathies and the help of the uncommitted
because we value equality so much.

By using violence beyond the limits society thinks tolerable, or by consciously calculating atrocities to stir the
emotions of victims and onlookers despite their will, the
terrorist is distinguishable from others who seek to coerce.(12)
This is true regardless of whether the ultimate purpose is to
serve religious or political objectives and whether terrorists
are members of a rebel band or leaders of a government.
Because each action in a terrorist effort may be a violation of
a rule governing violence, it must be accompanied by new or
fresh justifications. A soldier, if pressed, may explain to his
comrades and fellow citizens why an attack may weaken the
enemy, but a terrorist who is known or wants to be known as
having committed an atrocity must explain to every one (his
comrades, the enemy, and the uncommitted) why the action
was deserved, and hence might not have been an atrocity after
all.(13)

As this very brief characterization suggests, terrorist
activity raises a wide range of moral questions, questions
pertaining to both moral fact and prescription. The term
moral fact refers here to the description of circumstances, like
the moral contexts terrorists thrive in, the moral pictures they
have of their world, the relationship between religious and
secular justifying doctrines, and to explanations of how the
process of attracting moral sympathy by committing outrageous
actions work. Questions of prescription, or moral discussions
in a more classical mode refer here to the evaluation of moral
arguments such as whether or not terrorism can ever by justified. Moral prescriptions can also refer to recommendations,
such as the kind of responses those opposed to terrorism are
entitled to take. Although that may not be their major concern, virtually all the essays touch on moral matters, especially questions of fact. Issues of moral prescription are
reserved for the final and largest section of the collection
which discusses contemporary problems.

The initial section deals with religious terror; the second
and third with the two major secular forms, state and rebel
terror. A number of the essays focus on historical events or
periods, which is why the individual sections are organized
chronologically where that has been feasible.

The separate introductions for each section describe the
individual essays in some detail and discuss their mutual
relationships. The different views expressed seem quite consistent with each other, and this fact may seem surprising
when one remembers the great range of experience considered

and that we are dealing with a subject that normally provokes very strong and very divisive emotions. Sharp clashes do occur, and although the issues raised are not always resolved, their importance at least has been identified. In the process interesting materials for further reflections have been provided.

NOTES

(1) Assassination and Terrorism (Toronto: Canadian Broadcasting Corp., 1971).

(2) Max Lerner, "Assassination" and J. Hardman, "Terrorism," Encyclopaedia of the Social Sciences (New York: Macmillan, 1933).

(3) Frederick J. Hacker, Crusaders, Criminals, and Crazies (New York: W. W. Norton, 1976), p. IX. An identical view was proposed by 19th century Anarchists who were so impressed by what they believed were the potentialties of dynamite that they developed what I would call a "weapons theory of history."

"The reign of the bourgeoise rests . . . on gun powder. It cannot survive the use by the proletariat of a weapon requiring no capital, and against which gun powder would be as impotent as armor and castles were against gun powder. Such a weapon is dynamite." C. L. James, "Tract of Time," Albert Parsons, ed., Anarchism: Its Philosophy and Scientific Basis as Defined by Some of Its Apostles (Westport, Conn: Greenwood Press, 1970), p. 162. A number of highly ranked police and military officials in the period believed that dynamite made the terrorist so potent that armies would be useless and cities made uninhabitable. For an interesting summary of the fascination which dynamite had for late nineteenth and early twentieth century terrorists, see David Ronfeldt and David Sater, "The Mindsets of High Technology Terrorists: Future Implications From an Historical Analog" (Santa Monica: The Rand Corporation, 1981).

(4) Jerry Rubin, Do It (New York: Simon and Schuster, 1970), p. 108.

(5) E. V. Walter, the first American scholar after World War II to study terrorism systematically intended to write a history of the phenomena, but, alas, abandoned the effort after developing a useful definition and showing its pertinence in some illuminating case studies, Terror and Resistance (New York: Oxford University Press, 1969). Walter Laqueur provides some interesting material too, but his promise to give us historical

depth does not go beyond the nineteenth century and pertains to rebels only. He also confounds terror with other forms of rebel violence. See Terrorism (Boston: Little, Brown, 1977).

(6) George Quester, who contributes the final essay, explicitly rejects the notion that state and rebel terror are similar phenomena.

(7) Camus [The Rebel (New York: Vintage, 1954)] traced connections between the French Revolution and modern rebel terror quite some time ago but no one paid much attention.

(8) Modern terrorism is an aspect of the "revolutionary tradition," but the dimensions of that tradition have not been treated often. The most recent examination, and one which pays special attention to the terrorist theme, is James H. Billington, Fire in the Minds of Men: Origins of the Revolutionary Faith (New York: Basic Books, 1980).

(9) For the purposes of this volume the terms Messianic and millenarian are synonyms, as they usually are in ordinary language. Scholars normally characterize Messianic movements as millenarian ones led by a divinely inspired or appointed personality. Since leadership is not a concern of this volume we have no reason to distinguish the terms. For two excellent introductions to the subject, see Yonina Talmon, "Millenarism," International Encyclopedia of the Social Sciences (New York: Macmillan, 1968) and Hans Kohn, "Messianism," Encyclopaedia of the Social Sciences (New York: Macmillan, 1933).

(10) "The basic similarities and interconnections between religious and secular revolutionism is a major theme in most recent studies of millenarism irrespective of (the author's) ideological position." Y. Talmon, "Millenarism," p. 360. Twenty-five years earlier Han Kohn ("Messianism") made the same point. Those who write exclusively on revolution are not familiar with millenarian or Messianic literature, although occasionally they feel obliged to dismiss it peremptorily. Regarding the issue of terrorism, Walter Laqueur, for example, comments "Compared with the Sicarii and Assassins . . . contemporary terrorist groups seem to belong to another species altogether," Terrorism (p. 10). No reason is given for Laqueur's assertion, and our first essay "Terror and the Messiah" attempts to demonstrate how similar the two "species" really are.

(11) In the municipal law of many states, the terrorist is indistinguishable from the ordinary criminal or from anyone else who uses violence - a fact that generates some difficult moral and political predicaments discussed in section III, "Rebel Terror."

(12) See Ambassador Anthony C.E. Quainton, "Moral and Ethical Considerations in Defining a Counter-Terrorist Policy" in D.C. Rapoport and Y. Alexander, The Rationalization of Terrorism; UCLA Conference Proceedings (Frederick, MD: University Publications of America, forthcoming).

(13) See my "Politics of Atrocity" in Terrorism: Interdisciplinary Perspectives eds., Yonah Alexander and Seymour Finger (New York: John Jay Press, 1978).

The Morality
of Terrorism

I
Religious Terror

Introduction to Part I
David C. Rapoport

I know thee by thy works, that thou art neither cold nor hot;
I would thou wert cold or hot. So then because thou are
lukewarm....I will spew thee out of my mouth.
                                    - Revelations 7:15

(F)or the godless, the time is up. . . . Even if there were
only three of you, you would be able to fight one hundred
thousand, if you seek honor in God and in his name. Therefore, strike, strike, strike! This is the moment. These
villains cower like dogs. . . . Have no concern for their
misery; they will beg you, they will whine and cry like children. Do not show them any mercy. . . . Strike, strike,
while the fire's hot. . . . Have no fear, God is on your side!
- Thomas Muntzer's call to battle during the German Peasants'
War.

Each study in the section treats a very different subject, and
that subject is the author's major preoccupation. But there is
a significant common underlying theme which I will develop,
namely that religious studies can help one understand better
the character of secular terrorist activities. This theme is
developed in two distinct ways, and it will be useful to enumerate them now before moving on to discuss the individual
contributions and pointing out some other common threads.

The first approach suggests appropriate analogies and
parallels. My essay, for example, compares actual religious
and secular terrorist movements, their political and moral
contexts, and the strategy and tactics employed. Kavolis and
Amon compare images and metaphors used to describe rebels
and their antagonists. The second approach, which is represented by Dugard and Pottenger, treats particular theological
concepts used or apparently used consciously by moderns to
justify secular movements.

(1)   "Terror and the Messiah," the first chapter, is a study
of the successful efforts of Jewish terrorists in the first
century to provoke a popular uprising. The Sicarii/Zealot
achievement merits serious attention, if only because it occurs
so rarely. No religious terrorist movement has ever been as
successful; for that matter one would be hard pressed to find
a secular movement that comes close, although ever since the
nineteenth century most have visualized terror as the means,
par excellence, of generating a revolt by the masses.
       The rebels displayed unusual abilities to invent a wide
range of shock tactics from passive resistance to terror.
Their purpose was to make Jews lose confidence in Jewish
authorities and to provoke such hatred between Jews, Greeks,
and Romans that every effort to find a political solution would
be frustrated. A moral and political environment partly created by a government anxious to avoid trouble made these tactics feasible. Parallels between this case and some modern
instances since World War II (i.e., Palestine, Cyprus, and
Northern Ireland) sometimes are so striking that the comparisons (which are developed mostly in the footnotes) help clarify
a hitherto obscure logic for actions in the separate campaigns.
In one case, that of Menachem Begin, the evidence is that his
awareness of the most serious Zealot crimes and mistakes contributed to his resolve to compel the Irgun to restrain itself in
significant ways, and that policy contributed to Jewish success
nearly two thousand years later in the insurrection against
Britain.
       Concluding themes treat Zealot doctrine and mentality.
Messianism, developed for the first time in Judaism, became
the driving force of the rebellion, leading to the dreadful
climax at Masada. This particular understanding of Messianic
deliverance nourishes an obsession with indiscriminate destruction that foreshadows views of the nineteenth century Anarchists who first constructed a doctrine for revolutionary terror.
The Zealots consciously fostered "zeal" or "righteous rage"
among their members too; this is paralleled by the "enthusiasm" of Christian millenarian movements and by modern terrorists who ever since Robespierre seek to transform the
dissatisfied into the angry (enrages) burning with "compassionate zeal."(1)
       Beyond its role in the Sicarii/Zealot revolt, the mille-
narian theme is not developed in the other essays. But it is
worth noting here that the millenarian dream (which originated
in Persian Zoroastrianism) remained an irreducible ingredient
in Judaism and its two major religious offsprings, Christianity
and Islam. Traces of the impulse exist as indigenous growths
elsewhere (i.e., Taoism and Mahayana Buddhism) but it appears as a repeated and prominent feature only in religions
professing that history necessarily has direction or purpose
which will enable humanity ultimately to perfect itself.

Obviously, most millenarian groups do not use terror. They are much more likely to be passive, even pacifist, bodies seeking separation from the greater society in order to make spiritual preparations for the day of reckoning. But withdrawn pacifist groups may, as some Jewish rebels did, turn to terror. This can happen when the possibility of an earthly paradise seems imminent, the mechanism for achieving it is visualized as a series of catastrophes, and finally when it seems necessary to participate in the events precipitating those cataclysms. The orthodox religious elements, to a large extent, have been able to discourage the Messianic imagination from becoming fixed either on one or all of these conditions.

When Messianic impulses did produce terror prior to the French Revolution, the patterns developed varied widely. In Islam, Messianic (Mahdi) inspired terror (largely confined to Shiite sources) took the form of assassination cults, the most successful and widely known of which were the Assassins or Nizaris. The terror of the Nizaris was largely directed against officials who prevented their mission (dais) from operating openly.

Christian millenarian sects employing terror developed in the late medieval period (i.e., Taborites, Waldensians, and Anabaptists), and their enthusiasms were expressed through different organizational strategies. The Zealots and Assassins fought as underground or conspiratorial groups; one desired to provoke a popular uprising and the other to destroy prominent personalities. Christian millenarians organized their communities more openly. Their armies waged a "holy war" against existing society by periodically sweeping over the countryside indiscriminately devastating, burning, and massacring. Within their own communities gruesome purges were organized to obliterate all physical and spiritual traces of the old order. A noteworthy later effort to capture government for the purpose of purifying society was contained in the abortive plans of the Fifth Monarchy Men during the Puritan Revolution. "Their great achievement," Michael Walzer writes, "is what is known in the sociology of revolution as the terror, the effort to create a holy commonwealth and to force man to be godly."(2)

Except for outbursts by tiny fragments, millenarian activity in the West after the French Revolution rarely led to terror against the greater society. A most recent bizarre illustration of one such outburst was the frenzied mutilation murders of whites in San Francisco (1973-74) by the Fruit of Islam, a Black Muslim element. The more common practice where terror is used, is to employ it against millenarian cult members themselves in order to keep them isolated from 'corrupting' contacts with the outside world, i.e., Jim Jones' People's Temple which organized a mass suicide that stunned the world in 1979.

As a direct consequence of contact with the revealed religions millenarian activity usually flourished during the late 19th and early 20th centuries in the Third World especially Asia and Africa; that activity "facilitated passage to full fledged revolutionary movements."(3)   The Indian experience was, perhaps, the most unusual.   The revival of Hinduism among intellectuals at the turn of the century contained millenarian influences, a foreign theme in the Hindu tradition, and these helped create the Bengali terrorists.   But the enthusiasm, and, indeed, the leading members of that movement eventually became absorbed with the passive resistance tactics reversing the process in the West where the failure of passive resistance more often provides justifications for terror.(4)

Vytautas Kavolis is less concerned with movements than with the striking fact that the religious myths of various civilizations portray their rebels so differently.   The unique sociological conditions which explain how a particular conception of the rebel emerges and is accepted, seem also to shape, he argues, the behavior of actual rebels so that they tend to conform to the model itself.

Prometheus and Satan are the two major contrasting models for rebellion, and in various ways both became heroes for 19th century Romantic literary figures and for authors of revolutionary and terrorist treatises.   Prometheus rebels to help others by rectifying a flawed order that still contains much good.   He accepts full responsibility for his crime, and that very fact becomes the condition for a new conception of justice.   Satan, on the other hand, rebels to create a new personal identity and is driven by resentment for having had his true nature suppressed.   He accepts no responsibility for his action, viewing himself as a blameless victim of powerful impersonal forces.   Because he understands the existing order as totally corrupt, his rebellion aims at creating a new system, one which is global.   He manipulates, debases, and destroys existing standards in the effort to create a wholly new life style based on an idea of perfect virtue.   But in the end he cannot create, only mock old values by inverting them.   Satanism requires a world whose inhabitants see good and evil represented by mutually exclusive principles of organization in deadly conflict with each other, where no reconciliation or compromise is feasible, and where evil ultimately is destined to be abolished.

"Models of Rebellion" does not treat terrorism directly, though it does seem clear from Kavolis' account why the concept of Satan must be so pertinent.   Millenarian movements, particularly Christian ones, usually believed the existing social system to be Satan's creation, a doctrine that justified their own terror.   In psychological terms, this view of Satan corrupting humans is similar to one common among contemporary rebel and state terrorists who "arm" themselves by stripping their enemies of human qualities and refer to those enemies as "symbols" of a system or "animals."

Some 19th century revolutionaries made efforts to assimilate Prometheus and Satan. But instead they produced a hero resembling Dionysus who revolts against the routines and the rationalization of everyday life, seeks temporary ecstasy in action, shuns power, and provokes cannibalism from those who oppose him.

The first two chapters discuss conceptions that lead a rebel to invoke terror against authority in the name of the very religion which established that authority. Moshe Amon reminds us once more, however, that these outbursts are exceptional and that organized religions normally exert pressures in the opposite direction. The Latin origin of the term religion is significant here, for religion initially referred to a condition of being bound by rules or law, and even now it is difficult to imagine a religion without rules. Terror, on the other hand, <u>always</u> involves going beyond the rules, and the revealed religions do have antinomian ingredients which lead them to sometimes place faith above rules or norms.

Rules command our allegiance only when we can believe in the view (or myth) of the world that gives those rules meaning. But beliefs cannot be sustained forever, and Moshe Amon examines the erosion of credibility in Western religious beliefs since the Renaissance, the genesis of a secular myth of progress, and the relationship of both to each other and to modern terrorism.

The myth of progress is one of a "continuous advance towards a future utopia." It requires that we liberate ourselves from all norms derived from preceeding myths and view <u>all</u> institutions created as tentative, having utilitarian value only. "The responsible person is no longer seen as one who wishes to preserve the social structure, but rather the one who . . . destroy(s) it in order to pave the way for an ideal future."

The periodic explosions induced by the new myth are characterized by millenarian and Satanic images which ironically seem to be inspired by the older religious myths. With each successive disruption, the separation from the past and the desire to erase historical memory becomes more intense, producing uprisings that become more formless and less restrained. This is why the classic works by terrorists since the mid-nineteenth century, like Nechaev's "Revolutionary Catechism" and Marighella's "Minimanual," are technical manuals concerned exclusively with elaborating methods of destruction.

The myth of progress necessarily atomizes society, which means that terrorist groups are attractive because they supply a sense of community-emotional satisfactions and solidarity to participants. In the language of Kavolis, terrorist groups, much more than we realize, become Dionysian cults or ends in themselves.

John Dugard and John Pottenger discuss a different set of issues, namely the extent to which traditional religious doctrines have or have not been consciously employed to support terrorist activities in the last two decades. Dugard examines the revival, misuse, and perhaps, the perversion of the Christian concept of the "just war" in United Nations debates, while Pottenger looks at the Christian sources for Latin American "liberation theology," a new philosophical development, which has encouraged clerical elements to regard revolutionary terrorist activities sympathically.

A requirement of a "just war" is that one party is believed to be morally culpable, while the other intends to rectify a wrong. The just party, consequently, is not constrained to accept some limitations on his mode of conducting war, and he has the right to destroy any person who can (but does not necessarily) bear arms against him. This view stands in striking contrast to the conventional understanding of war in the past few centuries, where all combatants who are entitled to particular rights are obliged to accept specific limitations in return, and where distinctions between the statuses of combatants, noncombatants, and neutrals are understood.

The contemporary version of the just war doctrine is that only self-defense justifies coercion, a doctrine that is incorporated in the United Nations Charter. When this view is applied to terrorist questions those subjected to "colonial" and/or "racist" governments are by definition the "victims of aggression" and consequently are not only justified in taking up arms but also free from the normal moral restraints incumbent on soldiers even with regard to neutral persons and territories. In fact, the doctrine, in the eyes of some advocates, virtually eliminates the concept of neutrality altogether. "Colonial" and/or "racist" parties, however, are expected to observe conventional moral restraints. In the context of this doctrine the terrorist can only be one whose motive is immoral or whose cause is unjust.

By shifting the criteria for culpability from action to motive, a fundamental principle of traditional international law, and one for nearly all existing domestic legal systems too, has been overturned. Dugard examines some of the moral and legal predicaments created and also shows why the just war doctrine which was devised initially for states cannot be coherently utilized or applied when one party is not a state.

John Pottenger cites the difficulty of extending just war doctrines to illustrate why "liberation theology" writers have discarded traditional mainstream Christian categories. For although just war arguments can provide moral aid, they also restrict revolutionary activities, especially with regard to ter-

ror. The immediate aim of a just war is punishment, and
punishment requires rules and limits. Moreover, the ultimate
object of a just war is to reconcile the parties so that peace
may be restored. The doctrine presupposes that the offending
party may have a right to exist after punishment and repentance, that there are universal standards for gauging actions
and infractions, and finally that there are differences between
what humans can and should do to each other and what God
will do.

The presuppositions of traditional Christian theology
(i.e., the distinction between the ordinary and divine spheres,
and the commitment to universal standards and to rules) in
effect suppresses what liberation theologians take to be the
Bible's revolutionary message, "the exhortation to side with
the poor and oppressed" and to reconstruct the world accordingly. Furthermore, since the Bible itself lacks pertinent
sociological analysis and political prescriptions, orthodox
Christians feel that as Christians they must either support the
status quo or refrain from politics altogether.

The solution of the new theologians is to combine "the
ethical implications of Christianity" with appropriate modern
sociological analysis, namely phenomenology and/or Marxism, in
order to establish and justify various approaches to politics.
The primary commitments are participation on behalf of the
poor and to a metaphysics that allows the freedom to act in
any way suitable to the concrete situation. The final intellectual step is a re-interpretation of the Bible in the light of
those commitments.

Liberation theologians provide very different political
prescriptions. Pottenger concentrates on those who endorse
violence, and compares the structure of their arguments with
ordinary ways of justifying violence. His final observation is
that liberation theologians find that the most difficult form of
violence to incorporate is terror, because the terrorist must
regard victims as objects and nothing could be more anti-
thetical to the Christian injunction to demonstrate love for
one's enemies.

To the accounts of Dugard and Pottenger, one should add
a parenthetical note. The notion of a "holy war," which was
developed in the Middle Ages to justify the crusades and also
used at the same time by millenarian sects, is probably more
appropriate to contemporary revolutionary terrorist needs and
practices, especially those of the more radical groups, than
the idea of a just war, though perhaps the associated religious
connotations are much too conspicuous for contemporary tastes.

As it was originally conceived by Christian writers, a just
war was always declared by established secular authority, and
while its aim was a restoration of the status quo ante, it could
also be terminated at whatever time and for whatever reason that authority deemed appropriate. Traditional exemptions

from military service enjoyed by the clergy and other classes prevailed, and the war was supposedly fought in the spirit of love. None of these restrictions applied to the holy war which, compared to the just war, was an unusual event or one that occurred rarely. The holy war was divinely authorized and one was obliged to pursue it until the war's object – the destruction of the enemy or total victory – was achieved. A spirit of anger, zeal, or hate was supposed to infuse the soldier who always volunteered. The fact that priests and monks participated not only indicates that all normal immunities were waived but also that the distinction between the divine and the ordinary disappeared. (5)

NOTES

(1) "When (the Parisian mobs were) let loose, when everybody had become convinced that only naked need and interest were without hypocrisy, the malheureux changed into the enrages, for rage is indeed the only form in which misfortune can become active. . . . (T)he suffering they exposed transformed the malheureux into the enrages only when the "compassionate zeal" of the revolutionaries – of Robespierre, probably more than of anyone else – began to glorify the exposed misery as the best and even only guarantee of virtue, so that albeit without realizing it – the men of the Revolution set out to emancipate the people not qua prospective citizens but qua malheureux." Hannah Arendt, On Revolution (New York: Viking 1963), pp. 106-07.

(2) "Puritanism as a Revolutionary Ideology," History and Theory, III (1963) p. 88. (Walzer's emphasis) The Zealots and the Sicarii did not stay underground. They eventually organized armies and established something like a Reign of Terror in Jerusalem during the siege; but as the initial essay will indicate, their actions were either meant to provoke rage from the enemy or to eliminate influential persons who had opposed them.

(3) An interesting discussion of Black Muslim millenarian sentiment may be found in E. A. Essien-Udom, Black Nationalism; A Search for Identity in America (Chicago: University of Chicago, 1962). The outbreak of terror is described in a reasonably true but overly gruesome bestseller. Howard Clark, Zebra (New York: Merek, 1979).

(4) Y. Talmon, "Millenarianism," E.S.S., p. 359. On the whole, the movements were not violent and certainly not prone to terror.

(5) The dilemma faced by liberation theologians has an interesting counterpart in the Reformation when Protestants
found the concept of a just war really provided an unsatisfactory ground for revolution and they began reviving the
notion of a holy war.   See Roland Bainton, "Congregationalism:
From the Just War to the Crusade in the Puritan Revolution",
The American Newton Theological School Bulletin 35, April
1943.

     The concept originates in the Old Testament, the war
(herem) Israel was commanded to fight against the Canaanites
for possession of the Promised Land, and the Bible constantly
refers to the Terror that war was supposed to produce.   The
Israelites were admonished not to let any person or his property remain in the land, lest it become a 'snare' or corrupting influence.   The term herem (which is the source of
the Arab harem) means forbidden or consecrated, and refers
to the enemy and his property and to those dedicated to God's
service as well!   It designates a sacred sphere where ordinary
rules did not apply.   Significantly, the Bible indicates that
Israelites were usually unable to live up to the requirements of
the herem, presumably because they surrendered to human
concerns and standards.   Israel was not permitted, furthermore, to sanction inhumane wars on its own.

     Note, also, the intriguing, influential, and suggestive
work of G. Mendenhall who argues that the war depended upon
appealing to the slaves already in Canaan, and that its ultimate aim was the destruction of all bureaucratic and centralized administration in order to produce a harmonious
anarchy under the direct rule of God.   Law and Covenant in
Israel and the Ancient Near East (Pittsburgh: Biblical Col-
loquium 1955), The Tenth Generation: Origins of the Biblical
Tradition (Baltimore: John Hopkins 1973)

     The war of the Zealots resembles the "herem" but certain
differences are significant.   The former was fought largely
against the corrupting influence in Israel, the notion of
Satanism was present, and it had a universal or international
significance, as the war to end all wars!   Those features are
all more clearly pronounced in the Christian versions.   Islam,
also, has its own special conception of the holy war (jihad).

1 Terror and the Messiah: An Ancient Experience and Some Modern Parallels
David C. Rapoport

> The war of the Jews against the Romans was
> the greatest of our time: greater too, perhaps than
> any recorded struggle.
>
> — Josephus(2)

While it is generally acknowledged that modern revolutionary
terrorism(3) originated in the writings and deeds of mid-
nineteenth-century Russian anarchists, no one has discussed
the relationships between modern experiences and earlier ones.
The Assassins of medieval Islam who called themselves the
Fidayeen, "the faithful ones," are the most publicized of the
early movements.(4)   But Thomas De Quincey, the English
Romantic and first student of terrorist movements, reminds us
of others.   In a bizarre essay he tells of an imaginary club
which met regularly to discuss the more "interesting" forms of
assassination and terror:

> The first official toast of the day to the Old Man of
> the Mountain [the leader of the Assassins and 'pa-
> tron saint' of De Quincey's club] was drunk in si-
> lence. . . . The next toast was the Jewish Sicarii.
> Upon which I made the following explanation . . .
> "Gentlemen, I am sure that it will interest you all to
> hear that the Assassins, ancient as they were, had
> . . . predecessors in the very same country."(5)

The Sicarii and the Zealots, another major terrorist
element, successfully induced a massive revolt against Rome in
66-70 CE.   The conflict, which ended in a spectacular mass
suicide at Masada, was recorded by Josephus, a moderate
Jewish commander who became a Roman supporter.   While often
unreliable, his narrative nonetheless contains so much informa-

13

tion that it is the most useful primary source on any terrorist
campaign prior to the nineteenth century.

When De Quincey toasts the Sicarii, he singles out their
ability to produce panic or paralyzing fear, citing Josephus'
vivid account of how the Sicarii first became known:

> When the countryside had been cleared of bandits,
> another type sprang up in Jerusalem known as the
> Sicarii who committed murders in broad daylight in
> the heart of the city. The festivals were their
> special seasons, when they would mingle with the
> crowd, carrying short daggers concealed under their
> clothing, with which they stabbed their enemies.
> Then, when they fell, the murderers joined in the
> cries of indignation and, through this plausible
> behavior, were never discovered. The first to be
> assassinated . . . was Jonathan the high-priest,
> after his death there were numerous daily murders.
> The panic created was more alarming than the ca-
> lamity itself; everyone, as on the battlefield, hourly
> expected death. Men kept watch at a distance on
> their enemies and would not trust even their friends
> when they approached. Yet, even while their sus-
> picions were aroused and they were on their guard,
> they fell; so swift were the conspirators and so
> crafty in eluding detection. (6)

The Sicarii, De Quincey noted, realized that a man is
potentially most vulnerable when he considers himself entirely
secure. They struck in broad daylight when a victim was
surrounded by witnesses and supporters and on occasions
universally regarded as sacred. Their assaults were intended
to demonstrate that no circumstance or convention could provide immunity, reducing potential victims to a state of complete
uncertainty, creating the most profound sense of terror possible.

De Quincey sees only part of the picture - the least
interesting part. All terrorist movements have aimed at
producing panic or paralyzing fear, although their abilities to
do so vary enormously. But in the modern world at least,
terrorist assaults have served other, possibly more important,
purposes too. What makes the efforts Josephus describes so
intriguing is that they foreshadow contemporary experiences.

I

> You can't be a revoluntionary today without a tele-
> vision set - it's as important as a gun.
> - Jerry Rubin(7)

> The aims of our Society are none other than the
> entire emancipation and happiness of the people.
> . . . Convinced that their emancipation and the
> achievement of this happiness is brought about only
> by means of all-destroying popular revolt, we shall
> see that society will employ all its power, all its
> resources until their patience is exhausted and they
> will break out in a <u>levee-en-masse</u>.
> - S. Nechaev(8)

Before we discuss the early experience, it will be useful if we comment briefly on the contemporary notion of revolutionary terrorism, and on the kind of situations in our world where terrorism has and has not been successful.

So often is an act of terror associated with violence that the two terms are frequently and incorrectly employed as synonyms. If a distinction is made, terror is usually understood as an "extreme form of violence."(9) More precisely understood, however, terror is violence which goes beyond the norms generally accepted as regulating violence. Attacking "innocent" or defenseless persons, mutilating prisoners, and desecrating the dead are typical acts of terror in contemporary times, for they are prohibited in war and condemned as atrocities. Knowing that others think that violence should be limited, the terrorist aims to exploit their various responses to his outrages.

Atrocities serve several principal purposes. Most obviously they can produce pure terror or paralyzing fear. But since no terrorist group has sufficient resources to maintain a condition of complete uncertainty in an entire society for long periods, pure terror has a limited role in the insurrection process. It is most effective when directed against specific critical groups. In the 20th century, for example, successful terrorist movements following the example of Michael Collins, (IRA leader after World War I) paralyzed the police early usually by systematic assassination policies.(10)

A second major purpose of atrocities is publicity to gain sympathy, and hence the Russian anarchists described terror as "propaganda by the deed." It is in the nature of an atrocity to attract considerable attention; the more spectacular the outrage the more interest it arouses.(11) Depending on the latent dispositions of particular audiences, the concern may lead one audience to supply recruits, and others material aid, and/or encouragement. The outrage also may increase the prestige of the terrorist group itself. Audacity may strengthen its claim to be the only legitimate spokesmen for the grievance, pushing others aside who have hitherto been championing it by less spectacular or by different means. The latter, in turn, may be driven against their will to emulate the terrorists in order to regain lost ground and demonstrate superior commitment.

Many potential sympathizers, however, are repelled as well as attracted by atrocities, and a terrorist movement cannot gain substantial strength until the government or its supporters are "seen" employing similar tactics. A skillful terrorist knows that those who identify most closely with his victims, may be so enraged that they are provoked into committing counter-atrocities. Hence, a third purpose of atrocities is the stimulation of indiscriminate hostility.(12)

In these last two respects, the generation of sympathy and the provocation of indiscriminate hostility, the tactics of a revolutionary terrorist campaign are sharply distinguished from those of a conventional military one. Atrocities occur in war because participants are enraged or think that their acts could paralyze or panic the enemy. But intelligent soldiers avoid atrocities, knowing that they normally strengthen the enemy's determination to keep fighting. The revolutionary terrorist wants to enrage "the establishment"; otherwise his strength cannot grow.(13) "Your operation against the terrorist," a Cypriot told an English friend, "must be conducted across the body of the Cyprus people - like a man who has to hit an opponent through the body of the referee."(14)

No terrorist can afford, however, to enrage a government too much. His initial resources are too meager, and eventually a determined government will extinguish the hope of success upon which all rebels depend. The terrorist requires ambivalent governments which in some ways recognize aspects of his cause as legitimate, and are morally or politically embarrassed by actions which they are provoked into either taking or permitting. Ambivalence breeds inconsistency, and nothing disillusions one's firm supporters or excites terrorist hopes more.

But where has this condition been fulfilled? Four generations of terrorists since the 1880s have left a record of successes and failures sufficiently clear for us to make a judgment. No terrorist campaign has succeeded in democratic, stable states and only in Nicaragua have terrorists succeeded in undeveloped, unstable ones. Often terrorist intentions were misperceived as limited protests, and consequently, inconsistent government responses gave a terrorist movement strength. But ultimately defenders of "the system" learned that the issue at stake was survival. In totalitarian states terrorist activity has rarely even been attempted, indicating that potential

terrorists are convinced from the beginning that their adversaries are determined to prevail, whatever the cost.(15)

Only in colonial territories have terrorists occasionally
been successful, not in stimulating a massive uprising but at
least in surviving long enough to induce the colonial power to
withdraw, which the latter was normally able to do without
destroying its constitutional identity in the process. Yet, with
the sole exception of Ireland after World War I, all those
successes have taken place since World War II, indicating how
much that war transformed the general political context. The
most obvious changes were increased moral ambivalence within
metropolitan populations concerning their right to retain
overseas territories, and a significant international desire to
see Western empires destroyed, a desire which could be mobilized more easily because the United Nations existed. When
legitimacy rests on such fragile grounds, the atrocities of the
"weak" seem natural, inevitable responses to oppression, and
the reactions of the strong by the same token appear morally
indefensible. The dynamics of the situation were neatly
summarized by a Cypriot who told Lawrence Durrell, "Of a
stupid man (the peasants say) 'He thought he could beat his
wife, without his neighbors' hearing.' In this case the
neighbors are your own Labour Party, the UN . . . and many
others. We are provoking you to beat us so that our cries
reach their ears."(16)

                                II

On the Roman side . . . it seemed as though [all]
concessions made to Jewish religious susceptibilities
had been interpreted as weakness and led to an even
more unreasonable demand on a potentially dangerous
occasion.
                              - S.G.F. Brandon(17)

When we glance over the history of the Roman pro-
curators [who governed] Palestine, we might readily
suppose that all of them, as if by secret arrangement so conducted themselves . . . to arouse the
people to revolt. Even the best had no appreciation
. . . that . . . the Jews required . . . consideration for their prejudices and peculiarities.
                              - Emil Schurer(18)

There are enormous differences between the position of Rome
in Judea, and those of the Western colonial empires after 1945.
But the Romans, too, experienced a basic ambivalence which
made them vulnerable to the tactics of small bands of militants

calculated to produce outrage. Rome had important international and domestic reasons for wanting to avoid trouble.
Perhaps the Romans themselves did not know how much they
would be willing to concede for the sake of peace; certainly no
one else did.

Judea was on the Roman eastern frontier next to Parthia,
the last remaining major power in the ancient world. If a
rebellion occurred, Parthia was likely to intervene. She had
done so earlier in Jewish dynastic quarrels. Parthia had also
exploited Rome's difficulty with Armenia, Rome's client state,
where as late as 62 CE (four years before the Jewish revolt),
Parthia had inflicted a humiliating defeat on Roman arms.
Even if Parthia wanted to avoid involvement, she might find it
difficult to do so. Her Jewish population was large, and
within the Parthian sphere of influence, one client state,
Adiabene (Assyria), had a Jewish dynasty which bore a special
hatred for Rome because it had been attacked several times by
Armenia. The great annual pilgrimages of the Parthian Jews
to Jerusalem and the massive flow of wealth they contributed
to build and maintain the temple gave evidence of the strength
of their tie to Judea.(19)

In the eastern half of the Roman Empire, Jews constituted
perhaps as much as one-fifth or more of the total population.
Moreover, Rome had to contend with a group of Jewish sympathizers (the sebomenoi, "God-fearers") whose size was unknown and whose influence occasionally seemed to reach
members of Rome's ruling circles.(20)

Rome had other reasons to nurture Jewish loyalties. Jews
had made significant contributions to Julius Caesar's revolution, and successive emperors found them useful supports
against restive dominant Greek elements in the eastern provinces. The Romans tried to satisfy the Jews' religious concerns wherever they settled in the Empire. Since they could
not do any work on the Sabbath, Jews were exempted from
military conscription and from answering judicial summonses on
the Sabbath. Taxes they would have been obliged to pay to
local communities throughout the Empire were remitted to a
special tax fund to maintain the temple. Jewish communities
were given a separate unique status as autonomous associations
with the right to settle internal legal controversies.(21)
Although restrictions were placed on proselytizing activity,
their right to worship was protected. Jews alone were exempted from participating in the imperial cult, the worship of
the emperor, the Empire's one common bond. By virtue of a
compromise worked out with Augustus, the temple accepted
sacrifices for the emperor instead of to him.

To avoid antagonizing Judean Jews, Romans maintained a
"low profile," and initially attempted to rule indirectly through
a Jewish monarchy. From the imperial perspective the arrangement provided the advantage of making Jewish kings bear

the immediate brunt of local dissatisfactions, thereby giving Rome time to consider appropriate policies and to assume a moderating or conciliatory role. On the other hand, unlike Western colonial powers in the 20th century, Rome did not doubt her right to rule a conquered people and was willing to expend enormous power to maintain her government. But between these two points there was much maneuvering room and considerable prospects for a political solution which the major parties could accept.(22)

Roman maneuverability, however, was hampered by the necessity of conciliating the Greeks who occasionally provoked riots to compel her to revoke the Jew's special privileges and protection. Although she held firm against Greek demands, the provocations kept Rome from moving further in the Jewish direction to eliminate what appeared to be the last source of resentment in the Diaspora, the Jewish legal status as alien resident in Greek cities.

The Judean monarchy had similar problems militating against consistent policies in crisis periods and making it likely that Rome, against her will, might have to assume direct rule. Many Judean residents were Greeks, and a significant Samaritan element was hostile to both Greek and Jew. The legitimacy of the dynasty was not fully established; an earlier one (the Hasmonean) still had Jewish supporters and most of the priests desired a return to priestly government. Finally, the dynasty had not developed a recognized principle of succession. All these circumstances were conducive to intrigues and efforts to exploit inflammatory incidents in the hopes of compelling Rome to alter existing constitutional arrangements.(23)

The movement toward revolution did not begin as a terrorist campaign; initially public opinion was shocked by a series of nonviolent acts of defiance. Always the confrontations involved religious symbols, and governments discover that willy nilly they have backed (or been backed) into situations where they must either yield to flagrant disobedience or commit actions which seem threats to the Jewish religion, the only issue which could unite all Jews. Sometimes the confrontations resulted in atrocities by governments which are made more horrifying when they occurred, as they usually did, on holy days.

The Jewish monarchy was the first institutional casualty. The initial issues involved King Herod's tendency to adopt Greek and Roman customs to mollify his Greek subjects and to strengthen his bid to convince Rome to confirm his choice for a successor. Several times he demanded oaths of allegiance, but he capitulated when Jews refused to comply, arguing that such oaths would compromise their unconditional commitment to God. The circumstances surrounding his retreat indicate that the opposition had considerable support reaching to members of the dynasty itself who seemed to be using the issue to shape the emerging succession struggle.(24)

In the last year of Herod's reign, when the king was ill,
the religious opposition took the offensive. Students who felt
that the emblem of a great eagle which Herod placed on the
main temple gate violated the Mosaic law prohibiting images
tore it down. An enraged Herod seized everyone in the area
who applauded the act, but popular pressures prevented him
from executing them. He decided to punish only those who
removed the emblem and the rabbis who incited them. The
rabbis were burnt alive; one needs no imagination to understand what effects that deed could have had.

Herod's presumptive heir, Archelaus, released the remaining prisoners, but demonstrators in Jerusalem, swollen by
the enormous influx of celebrants for the Passover holy days,
demanded that he go further and make a clear sweep of
Herod's administration. Uncertain of Rome's reaction, he
refused. When some demonstrators stoned the garrison, "the
whole army" was sent in. A massacre resulted; many victims
were killed while attending religious services.

The emotional revulsion aroused was a major factor in
Rome's decision to divide the kingdom into three realms. But
the disturbances continued for nine years and Archelaus, who
retained the major portion of the realm, was banished. Finally
yielding to Jewish demands, the Romans reluctantly assumed
direct rule.(25)

To implement direct rule the Romans took two steps which
had deep symbolic implications. A census for Roman taxing
purposes aroused an ancient Jewish sentiment that the land
belonged to God and generated violence in the countryside.
The major resistance, however, began in the cities as a response to a new policy on images. In deference to the jurisdiction of the Jewish monarchy and its concern for Jewish
religious sensibilities, Roman troops had abandoned their
traditional custom of carrying busts to the emperor. But the
new Roman procurator, Pontius Pilate, ordered standards designed in the conventional way to symbolize Judea's new constitutional status. He expected trouble (the troops came
"secretly at night"), but he was totally unprepared for the
reception he received:

> The Jews implored him to remove the standards from
> Jersualem and to uphold the laws of their ancestors.
> When Pilate refused, they fell prostrate around his
> house and for five whole days and nights remained
> motionless in that position. . . .
>   Pilate after threatening to cut them down if
> they refused to admit Caesar's images signals to the
> soldiers to draw their swords. Thereupon, the Jews
> by concerted action, flung themselves in a body on
> the ground and exclaimed that they were ready
> rather to die than to transgress the law. Overcome

with astonishment at such intense religious zeal,
Pilate gave orders for the immediate removal of the
standards.(26)

Pilate's replacement (under orders from the Emperor,
Caligula) tried again, moving slowly and with great force,
hoping thereby to give the Jews opportunity and reason to
avoid the conflict. But the results were the same. "Will you
then go to war with Caesar?" he asked an unarmed multitude
blocking his way;

> The Jews replied that they offered sacrifices daily
> for Caesar and the Roman people but that if he
> wished to set up these statues he must first sacrifice
> the entire Jewish nation; and that they presented
> themselves, their wives and their children ready for
> the slaughter. These words filled Petronius with
> astonishment and pity at the spectacle of the incom-
> parable devotion of this people to their religion and
> their unflinching resignation to death. So for the
> time he dismissed them, nothing being decided.(27)

The implications of the confrontation, especially at a time
when trouble with Parthia over Armenia was developing and a
second small autonomous Jewish state (Nebardea) was established within the Parthian sphere of influence, led Petronius to
risk his own life by refusing the emperor's order to proceed.
Fortunately for him, Caligula was assassinated, and the new
Emperor, Claudius, withdrew the standards.

To reconcile the Jews firmly, Claudius restored the
jurisdiction of the Jewish monarchy over the whole of Judea
under Agrippa I. Unfortunately, a fatal illness had terminated
Agrippa's reign three years later. While he seemed largely
successful, the problems of governing Judea began manifesting
themselves again. In cultivating Jews, Agrippa alienated
Greeks; and in the last few months of the reign his efforts to
win back the Greeks revived Jewish protests. Fearing that
such delicate political balancing was too much for Agrippa's
young inexperienced heir (Agrippa II), Claudius temporarily
resumed direct rule, confining the new king to a small territory. The decision proved to be disastrous.

In the initial instance of Roman direct rule, the tactic of
passive resistance, perhaps the earliest example recorded in
history, was employed. The development merits comment for a
similar tactic has often appeared in our world (i.e., Cyprus
and Northern Ireland) as an initial step in conflicts which later
"matured" into full-scale terrorist campaigns. In each instance, the tactic directly drew large numbers into the conflict, and by dramatizing the action raised the consciousness
level of all potential participants.(28)

Although we do not know which Jews developed the tactic, or why, its plausibility and utility (at least in retrospect) seem quite clear. In the past Rome's willingness to back down encouraged hopes that she might do so again, providing her authority was not compromised by violent outbreaks. Most Jews felt Rome's military strength overwhelming and the antagonisms had not been sufficiently developed to make them feel that they lacked alternatives to violence. Passive resistance might be a form of action, perhaps the only illegal form, which moderates would be willing to undertake. Significantly, Josephus mentions no violent activity during the relevant period. The militants probably participated in passive resistance efforts, for if Romans broke up the demonstrations, the circumstances could produce atrocities which would have played into the militants' hands.

Under any conditions it requires discipline and imagination by all participants to keep a passive confrontation from erupting into violence.(29) Those difficulties are multiplied when some participants on either side prefer violence and when passive resistance is viewed as a tactic, and, therefore, discardable because other tactics seem more productive.(30)

The imminent dangers of confrontation tactics had been clearly indicated in a dispute concerning the proper use of temple revenues. To avoid provoking the expected demonstrators, the troops were ordered to wear civilian clothes and carry wooden clubs instead of swords.(31) But many demonstrators taunted Roman officials, and when the troops were ordered to disperse the crowd, they ran amuck. In the ensuing panic many demonstrators and innocent bystanders were trampled to death in the narrow streets and alleys of Jerusalem.

The demonstrations began again in the second attempt at direct rule, but this time they always culminated in atrocities. On the Jewish side the demonstrations seemed more poorly organized and, Josephus says, they contained participants bent on violence. On the Roman side military discipline kept breaking down, partly because the emperor, under pressure from the troops, decided to keep units of Judean Greeks in the area instead of replacing them with others lacking personal interests in the struggle.(32)

The holy days of Passover, when Jerusalem was packed with celebrants massed to receive free unleavened bread, was the scene of the first clash. A guard at the temple gates suddenly "turn[ed] his backside to the Jews and made a noise in keeping with his posture."(33) The enraged crowd became abusive; some members began throwing stones. When military reinforcements arrived, the crowd panicked and once more - a pattern which was to become familiar - many were trampled to death. "The feast was turned into mourning for the whole nation, and for every household into lamentation. Such were the calamities produced by the indecent behavior of a single soldier."(34)

The Romans tried to repair the damage done by the troops. When villagers were unable or unwilling to provide information to aid a search for assassins, a soldier provoked a furious demonstration by publicly burning a copy of the Jewish sacred scriptures. The offender was promptly executed.(35) But when the political dimensions were more complex, Roman officials on the spot preferred not to take responsibility for decisions. When Samaritans, for example, ambushed a pilgrim body passing through to Jerusalem, the procurator did not punish the murderers for fear of alienating a significant group of supporters. Furious Jews responded by attacking Samaritan villages, massacring all inhabitants. Moderates led by the high priest successfully persuaded the Jewish community that Roman law could provide a remedy, and they were vindicated by the Emperor Claudius in Rome who punished his own officials savagely. But the long delay generated enough recruits to revive a flagging rural terrorist campaign.

When Claudius died, Nero initiated a "hard-line" policy which apparently restored order in the countryside. Then Rome adopted a "soft line," ostensibly believing that a secure reconciliation requires that "internment camp" prisoners be released. But, as has often so been the case, particularly in Northern Ireland, the new policy was premature; and the internees rejoined their comrades who left the rural areas to mass in Jerusalem.

Strangely, the Romans did not try to stop this regrouping, and left the terrorist forces in the city unmolested. Perhaps Rome wanted to let the Jews "fight it out." More likely, she wanted to avoid a massive struggle. Whatever her reason, the decision, like similar ones in modern campaigns,(36) proved a capital blunder for it gave the terrorists the free hand they needed to assault moderate influence there, especially the priests who were the major force restraining the nation. Initially the terrorists intimidated moderates by an extensive assassination campaign. Then, the priests undermined their own credibility as political leaders by submission in incident after incident to terrorist demands to use their influence to persuade the Romans to exchange prisoners for priests whom the terrorists held as hostages. The final blow occurred as peaceful protests organized by the priesthood against the current Roman procurator ended in massacres when militant participants got out of hand. Moderate ranks were split; some joined the terrorists, making it impossible for the rest to resist the popular demand to reverse the traditional policy of accepting sacrifices for the emperor - a decision which Josephus says was essentially a declaration of war against Rome.(37)

The terrorists then besieged the small Roman garrison in
Jerusalem, which lay down its arms for a safe-passage promise:

> So long as the soldiers retained their arms, none of
> the rebels molested them . . . but when in accor-
> dance with the covenant, they had all laid down
> their [arms, the rebels] massacred them; the Romans
> neither resisting, nor suing for mercy, but merely
> appealing with loud cries to "the covenant."   . . .
> Thus, brutally butchered perished all, save Metilius
> [the Roman commander]; he alone saved his life by
> entreaties and promises to turn Jew, and even be
> circumcised.   The whole city was a scene of de-
> jection, and among the moderates there was not one
> who was not racked with the thought that he should
> personally have to suffer for the rebels' crime.   For
> to add to its heinousness the massacre took place on
> the sabbath, a day on which from religious scruples
> Jews abstain even from the most innocent acts. (38)

Josephus does not explain the reason for the unprovoked
massacre, but, as would be expected, it compelled the Romans
to send massive military reinforcements to Judea as law and
order everywhere crumbled.   The Greeks of Caesarea, the
Roman capital in Judea, massacred its entire Jewish population
numbering "perhaps 20,000 in a single hour."   Jews revenged
themselves by indiscriminate attacks on Greeks in most cities,
and the conflict spread throughout the eastern portion of the
empire:

> [E]very city was divided into two camps and the
> safety of one party lay in their anticipating the
> other.   They passed their days in blood, their
> nights, yet more dreadful in terror.   For though
> believing that they had rid themselves of the Jews,
> still each city had its Judaisers who aroused sus-
> picion; and while they shrunk from killing offhand
> they feared these neutrals as much as pronounced
> aliens.   Even those who had long been reputed to be
> the mildest of men were instigated by avarice to
> murder their adversaries.   . . . One saw cities
> . . . full of indescribable horrors; and even worse
> than the tale of atrocities committed was the sus-
> pense caused by the menace of evils in store. (39)

> [When Jewish reprisal seekers] invaded Scythopolis
> they found . . . the Jews in this district . . . on
> the side of the Scythopolitans . . . regarding their
> own security more important than the ties of blood.

. . . However, this excess of ardour brought them
under the Greeks who slaughtered them all. (40)

A Roman army moved into Judea sacking Jewish cities,
but at the urging of Jewish moderates, its commander agreed
to send two envoys to Jerusalem to discuss a peace settlement.
"The insurgents fearing the prospect of an amnesty"
would dissolve their hold on the city, "made a murderous
assault upon his emissaries . . . before [they] had uttered a
syllable."(41)

For reasons not altogether clear, the Romans called the
siege of Jerusalem off. Their retreating forces were ambushed
at Beth-Horon and dealt a devastating defeat. This put remaining moderate leaders in a politically difficult position,
undermining their major prudential argument that Roman armies
were invincible in the field.(42)   In the flush of popular
enthusiasm for the war, they had to choose sides. Some left
Jerusalem and joined the Romans; others supported the rebellion hoping thereby to curb its excesses and to make sure that
it accepted the terms Romans would offer.(43)

The moderates did succeed in getting formal control of
the Jewish armies; the country was organized into military
commands and the victorious Beth-Horon leaders were relegated
to secondary positions subordinate to generals selected from
the priestly class.   Significantly, the "demoted" Jews were
from the Parthian Empire - a decision which might have contributed to the fact that Judeans received less-organized
support from that quarter than the militants had originally
anticipated.

Information on the objectives and methods of the moderates is scanty. Virtually all of it comes from Galilee where
Josephus commanded.(44) His charges were to restore law and
order, provide an adequate provincial administration for the
new republic, and to organize an army. Clearly the military
policy was defensive; "the army had its weapons constantly in
readiness for future contingencies waiting and seeing what
action the Romans would take."(45)   Efforts were made to
avert further atrocities against the Greeks and provocative
actions against the possessions of Agrippa II, so that he would
not be discouraged from pursuing his earlier efforts to act as
a mediator.(46)

The chances that this policy could succeed in such an
emotionally laden atmosphere were remote. Militants ignored
their orders perpetrating new atrocities, and moderate efforts
to stop them were constantly weakened by the quite plausible
accusation that moderates had always intended to betray the
revolution.   The Romans meanwhile wanted some victories to
restore their military reputation, and Agrippa II felt compelled
to put his forces at their disposal. Galilee and the remaining
provinces soon fell. Under a new vigorous commander, Vespasian, the Romans concentrated on Jerusalem which the Jews
decided would be their major resistance point.

But the attack on Jerusalem was delayed for a year. Vespasian's command automatically lapsed when the Emperor Nero was assassinated and in the ensuing confused civil war he could not get clear instructions. In time Vespasian himself became a contender for the throne leaving his son Titus to finish the war in Judea. (It is worth observing en passant that when the Parthians offered Vespasian an army of 40,000 to pursue his "candidacy," Jewish hopes in receiving Parthian aid must have been dispelled finally.)

A second compelling reason for the delay was the persistance of the conviction among Roman commanders that divisions among Jews would grow in time, and make a costly attack on Jerusalem's enormous fortifications unnecessary. At best it was thought that the "peace party" would eventually get the upper hand. At the minimum, bitter quarrels within Jerusalem would make it incapable of organizing vigorous resistance. Both judgments were sorely mistaken. The "peace party" was devastated politically by the ineptness of its military efforts in the country. Its major leaders were murdered and "executed in treason trials," leaving the Romans with no Jewish leadership strong enough to negotiate with, and the terrorists in complete control of Jerusalem. Terrorist forces did battle each other in the capital, breaching its defenses and destroying its supplies; but when Roman armies finally arrived, the terrorists unexpectedly composed their differences sufficiently to organize a ferocious, no quarter given or allowed, defense which lasted for more than half a year.

The fall of Jerusalem and the destruction of the temple virtually ended resistance in Judea. It was only a matter of time before the last stronghold at Masada fell. When the Romans penetrated its outer defenses, the most spectacular act of Jewish despair and defiance occurred. The entire garrison of nearly a thousand Sicarii, including women and children, committed suicide rather than become Roman prisoners.

III

From 160 B.C. we are in a new age, an age of extraordinary fervour and religiosity, in which almost every event . . . was seized upon . . . to discover how and in what way it represented a Sign of the Times and threw light on the approach of the End of the Days. The whole condition of the Jewish people was psychologically abnormal. The strangest tales and imaginings could find ready credence. A new pseudonymous literature came into being, part moral exhortation and part apocalyptic prophecy, a kind of messianic science-fiction. People were on edge, neurotic.

- Hugh J. Schonfield(47)

I have tried to expose parallels between an ancient experience and modern ones. The most striking resemblance is the use of atrocities to provoke a massive uprising. Consecutive atrocities keep narrowing the room for a political or mutually agreeable solution, serving to destroy the credibility of moderates on both sides while expanding the conflict which steadily enlists more and more participants. It should be emphasized, however, that in this ancient example no master hand can be detected. The terrorists reflect a bewildering assortment of forces. There are several Zealot, at least two Sicarii organizations, and many other groups whose names and activities have scarcely survived. Then, as now, the effect of such multiplicity compelled each element toward more heinous atrocities to prove the superiority of its commitment. And in time the groups turned upon and decimated each other with the same ferocity with which they assailed the Romans. As these extraordinary actions increased, these groups, like so many modern counterparts, had to keep making more unusual claims about their enemies and more radical promises about the social reconstruction which victory would bring.(48)

It would be impossible to compare the organizational structure and battle doctrines (i.e., strategy and tactics) of early and modern groups because the early source materials provide virtually no relevant information.(49) Still, particular political and ideological features of the general environment and of the terrorist groups suggest interesting analogies.

Rising expectations rather than oppression made it virtually impossible for Jews to accept any terms the Romans could offer - a circumstance which, as I have already suggested, is also generally true of the context where modern terrorism flourishes as well. Her obvious fear that a rebellion could engulf the eastern half of the empire made Rome seem less determined than she really was to hang on. Jewish moderates were encouraged to be reckless, to go much further in pushing Rome than they had originally intended. For Rome kept retreating in the hope of restricting the conflict and because numerous imperial candidates (in the midst of dynastic struggles) offered new concessions to attract firmer Jewish support.(50)

Jewish expectations were raised by the political recognition that a good possibility existed of mobilizing significant outside support. But the expectation of divine aid was most firmly entrenched among the terrorist groups, an expectation which ironically became more dominant as the real possibilities for political support outside Judea vanished. When His people demonstrated sufficient faith and commitment, God, they believed, would redeem His ancient promise by sending the Messiah to initiate the Millenium, a social condition where governments would not be needed because oppression would disappear. (In this respect, the parallel with millenarian

expectations as an element in Anarchist thought in the genesis
of modern terrorism seems instructive.)

I cannot develop here a comprehensive picture of the
particulars of the Jewish millenarian atmosphere,(51) but
certain salient features must be emphasized. As an eschato-
logical figure, the Messiah is a rather late concept in Judaism,
developed during the reign of Herod. Before that time no
messianic claims were made, and by the first century CE,
Judea lived in a feverish, almost hysterical state as new
messianic pretenders flourished everywhere.

According to the most common conceptions of the matter,
the Messiah would appear during the Last Times, an era of
titanic natural catastrophes and revolutionary cataclysms. The
forces of evil would be at their greatest height, as all hope
vanished. Apostasy would be evident everywhere, and all
would witness the "desecration of God's name" and "the up-
setting of all moral order to the point of dissolving the laws of
nature."(52) It was not known how long the Last Times would
endure, but the most popularly believed prophecies dated its
beginning with the Roman presence.

The essence of the messianic hope was a Kingdom of God
on earth, for which the prerequisite was a righteous Israel, or
at least, an elect faithful remnant. Early apocalyptic prophecies are not directives for revolutionary action; God alone
determines the timing and course of messianic deliverance.
They do suggest that prayer and fasting are appropriate, that
the righteous person who passively resists to the point of
martyrdom certainly guarantees his own immortality (when the
Messiah resurrects the dead) and may even touch God's concern to speed the redemptive process.

The contribution of the Sicarii and the Zealots to this
atmosphere was the certainty that God could be moved when
the believer's action was sufficiently resolute and spectacular.
Martyrdom was necessary but not sufficient. God would intervene only if the Jews "with high devotion in their hearts
stood firm and did not shrink from the bloodshed that might
be necessary."(53)

Sufficient information for a detailed picture of terrorist
ideology is not available.(54) We know that their inspiration
was derived from the deed of Phinehas, the high priest during
the time of Moses, whose zeal (anger) averted a plague which
afflicted Israel for acts of apostasy and "whoring with Moabite
women." Phinehas took the law into his own hands and killed
a tribal chief together with his concubine who flaunted their
contempt in a sacred site: "Phinehas . . . has turned back My
Wrath . . . by displaying . . . his passion for Me so that I
did not wipe out the Israelite people in My passion. Say,
therefore, I grant him My Covenant of friendship. It shall be
for him and his descendents after him a covenant of priesthood
for all time."(55)

Phinehas' deed had several meanings. The method he employed was important. Rabbinic commentary records that he detached the head of his spear from its shaft, using the head as a dagger, and, therefore, Sicarii (daggermen) tactics were dictated by ritual as well as by practical concerns.(56) He struck against apostasy or assimilation tendencies and hence gave warrant, the terrorists thought, for assaults against their own people. Since his principal victim was a tribal chief, Phinehas' action could be construed as having class overtones. Whether or not this was a contributing justification, the terrorist groups undeniably had pronounced egalitarian sympathies. The Sicarii often burned government records listing debts and property holdings. Modern scholars sometimes describe them as anarchists, citing Josephus' description of the Sicarii as "hav[ing] a passion for liberty that is almost unconquerable since they are convinced that God alone is their leader and master."(57) Another terrorist group linked with the Zealots and led by Simeon Bar Giora is the champion of rural masses, especially recent converts, and has as a principal aim the emancipation of slaves. The major Zealot group in Jerusalem represents the lower order of priests and wants to "democratize" the order.

Phinehas, finally, is one of the few - perhaps the only - Biblical heroes to receive a personal reward for his zeal directly from God. A conspicuous characteristic of the Zealots and Sicarii, and one that lacks a parallel in earlier Jewish tradition, is their belief that one who gives his life in the struggle on God's behalf would certainly gain immortality. The climax at Masada is only the most memorable instance in a long series where members of the group gave their lives rather than surrender, deliberately seeking death in battle or suicide. Occasionally, those options were not available. They were

[s]ubjected to every form of torture and bodily suffering that could be thought of for the one purpose of making them acknowledge Caesar as lord, not a man gave in or came near to saying it, but rising above the strongest compulsion they all maintained their resolve, and it seemed as if their bodies felt no pain and their souls were almost exhultant as they met the torture and the flames. But nothing amazed the spectators as much as the behavior of young children; for not one could be constrained to call Caesar lord. So far did the strength of a brave spirit prevail over the weakness of their little bodies.(58)

In a rough but still pertinent way, the view represented here parallels one conspicuous in the intellectual origins of

modern terrorism and is still manifested in a number of contemporary groups as well. I have discussed the issue elsewhere; it is sufficient to point out here that the Anarchists
distinguished between two functions of revolutionary action, its
political consequences and its value in itself or in the personal
benefits the actor received. As one might expect, the extent
to which action for its own sake dominates one's consciousness
affects how he assesses political or prudential significance.
(Atrocities, ultimately, may become substitutes for revolution –
a possibility suggested by slogans of many contemporary
groups which make action actually synonymous with revolution
itself.) Josephus may well have been the first – he was
certainly not the last – to stress that the concern for finding
personal fulfillment in action can lead to a wholesale disregard
for political consequences, destroying the movement and de-
cimating the people that movement was designed to serve.(59)

　　And yet, while some of the more incomprehensible actions
of the Zealots and Sicarii may be explained in this fashion,
another dimension of their outlook is also pertinent. When a
period of unimaginable "woe" is perceived as a precondition of
messianic deliverance, then it would seem natural that some
believers would take the initiative to bring about the precondition. The most flagrant action in this respect, one
recorded in all our sources, is the decision of the Zealot
leaders to burn the food supplies during Jerusalem's long
siege. In the eyes of the faithful this seemed evidence that
they had indeed placed all their trust in God, that there was
no turning back; one might even call it a kind of moral blackmail. During the conflict the most decisive disasters seemed to
create rather than extinguish hope in the breasts of the
committed. When the Temple was burning (and the war was in
fact irretrievably lost), a messianic imposter was able to use
the fact as proof that the time for deliverance had arrived,
and 6,000 recruits joined him!

　　It is quite likely (though no direct evidence exists) that
the cold-blooded massacre of the Roman garrison which had
surrendered and the murder of two peace envoys stem from
the same consideration. Whatever the reason for particular
puzzling actions, when it is believed that the fulfillment of the
"Promise" depends upon life becoming as unbearable as possible, that Hell must precede Paradise, terror can have no
limits because it cannot be associated with a principle that tells
us when to stop because we have succeeded or failed.

　　The fall of Masada signified the physical exhaustion of
one generation; the belief that a Messianic Age could be
ushered in by violence persisted, for a single storm, no matter
how catastrophic, rarely pulls up profoundly rooted faiths.
Children will always find a reason to think that they can
succeed where their fathers had failed. In the next generation when Rome went to war with Parthia, messianic uprisings

began simultaneously in various Jewish centers outside Judea (115-117) and they were savagely repressed. A third struggle (the Bar Kochba rebellion) began almost 20 years later during the reign of Hadrian, which concluded in the complete destruction of the great Jewish centers of Egypt and Cyprus and in the virtual depopulation of Judea, as the disaster of disasters, the exile itself - an exile which lasted for almost two thousand years - began.

The terror campaigns had a traumatic impact on Jewish consciousness, making it virtually impossible for Jews to justify violence for political purposes until the middle of the 20th century. That subject cannot be discussed here, but we should stress that although the expectation of a messianic deliverance (which would result in an ingathering of the exiles and a revival of political independence) survived, the rabbis convinced their people that they must wait patiently and passively for redemption, that they could only bring additional misfortune by attempting to expedite the process by political action and/or violence: "May the curse of Heaven fall upon those who calculate the advent of the Messiah and thus create political and social unrest among the people."(60)

POSTSCRIPT

It is well known, though never systematically studied, that the Rabbinic tradition transmitted a memory of how Jews lost their homeland that decisively influenced Jewish consciousness. But we seem to have forgotten entirely how the recollection of that senseless and avoidable catastrophe shaped the course of the insurrection which helped establish the modern state of Israel. A brief postscript, therefore, is very much in order.

As an avid student of the Zealot revolt, Ben Gurion, the leader of the Jewish establishment (The Jewish Agency and its military arm the Haganah) was desperately apprehensive that history might repeat itself. Another terrorist campaign, he felt, would make it impossible for the moderates again to retain control. Britain, like Rome, would become inflexible despite contrary inclinations. As the Greeks did before them, the other local residents, the Arabs, would support the dominant power, and once again terrorists would force Jews to fight each other too.

The Irgun was the modern counterpart to the Zealots and the Sicarii, and their leader was Menachem Begin. The introduction to his account of the campaign The Revolt suggests him to be totally oblivious to these fears. It heralds the collapse of the mentality which the Rabbinic tradition fostered. "Out of the blood and fire and tears and ashes a new specimen of human being was born, a specimen completely unknown to

the world for over 1800 years - 'The Fighting Jew.'" Nonetheless, many times the book speaks of a determination to
avoid a second Masada, and the Irgun's manifestos tirelessly
reiterated the slogan "No Masada."

A second Masada was avoided. The civil war did not
occur. Britain yielded, partly because the Arabs did not rally
to her side when their support could have made the difference. One essential reason, though obviously not the only
one, these things did not happen was that Begin compelled the
Irgun to remember Jewish history and accept certain restraints.

The first limit was never to attack other Jews. At least
three times the Irgun's resolution was pushed to the straining
point. In 1944 when the Haganah began kidnapping, beating,
and even turning Irgun members over to British authorities,
Begin refused to retaliate, an unusual decision in the history
of revolutionary insurrections. "We heard the echoes of those
other wars, the cursed internecine wars in dying Jerusalem
nineteen centuries before. . . . Not logic but instinct said
imperatively, 'No, not civil war. Not that at any price.' We
were spared the catastrophe of catastrophies."(61) Four years
later when the Haganah fired on Irgun members in the "Ata-
lena Incident," then kidnapped and possibly murdered an
Irgun leader, Begin refused to fight back.

Against the British the problem of how to prevent the
conflict from getting out meant restricting assaults. No
random attacks were permitted; every operation had to be
authorized by the High Command. To implement this objective,
all arms were held in central depots and issued only after an
assault plan had been approved. Begin violated a central
principle of terrorist operations in this respect that normally
allows local units great autonomy to wreak whatever havoc they
deem appropriate. The policy complicated Irgun operations but
it served an absolutely essential purpose.

The decision to restrict choices attacking the British
was also manifested in the selection of targets. With the
exception of police officers and immigration facilities, the
Irgun avoided civilian or defenseless targets and struck "hard
ones" - military personnel and positions - in the hopes of
reducing outrage. It developed, and I believe it was the first
rebel group to do so, an effective warning system that allowed
the enemy to evacuate civilians. The warning policy increased chances assaults might be foiled, and consequently the
Irgun was denounced as impossibly quixotic by the less restrained Stern Gang. In many ways, the Irgun observed the
rules of war: certainly nothing it did remotely resembled the
massacre of the Roman garrison in Jerusalem. The wounds of
captured soldiers were attended, and they were freed as soon
as the military operation was completed. A British officer was
whipped and several British NCO's hung. But in these in-

stances Irgun members had previously suffered the same fate, and when the British changed their policy, the Irgun followed suit.(62)

In view of the previous conflicts between Jew and Arab and the very different experiences in other modern terrorist campaigns where the situation is similar, it is quite remarkable that the Arabs began fighting only after Britain abandoned the Mandate. A contributing factor, certainly, was the Irgun's decisions not to provoke them and to carefully restrict assaults on British units in Arab areas. The contrast with the Zealot policy towards Greeks is striking.(63)

Finally, the Zealots refused every political solution the moderates might negotiate short of total victory. The Irgun did manage a delicate and complicated arrangement of maintaining its claim to the entire land while simultaneously laying down its aims to support Ben-Gurion's decision to accept partition. The achievement was not inconsiderable.

NOTES

(1) I am indebted to the National Institute of Mental Health for its grant (RO 1 MH 205 22), which enabled me to complete this paper.

(2) The Jewish War (hereafter cited as J.W.), transl., H. St. Thackeray, Josephus, Loeb Classical Library (London: Heinemann, 1926), 8 vols.

(3) Revolutionary terrorism here refers only to the use of terror to promote a popular insurrection. The Russians were not the first to employ terror in this way, but through them the doctrine of its potentialities was formulated and transmitted to successive generations. See my Assassination and Terrorism (Toronto: Canadian Broadcasting Corp., 1971).

(4) The most useful studies of the Assassins are Marshall Hodgson, The Order of Assassins (Gravenhage: Mouton, 1955) and Bernard Lewis, The Assassins (London: Weidenfeld, 1967). In Lewis' last chapter he offers a suggestive note on the movement's place in the history of terrorism. For brief discussions of the Assassins as the classic prototype of terrorist organizations and mentality, see Assassination and Terrorism ch. IV, and my unpublished essay "Religions and Terror."

(5) Supplementary Paper on Murder Considered as One of the Fine Arts," Works (Boston: Houghton Mifflin, 1877) XI, pp. 579-80. Much more than any other terrorist group, the Sicarii dominate De Quincey's attention. He returns to it again in "The Essenes," "Secret Societies," and "Supplementary Note on the Essenes," VIII, pp. 52-222.

(6)   J.W., II, 254-57.

(7)   Do It (New York: Simon & Schuster, 1970), p. 108.

(8)   "Revolutionary Catechism," Art 22, transl. Robert Payne, in Assassination and Terrorism, p. 83.

(9)   A more extensive treatment of the definitional problems appears in my "Politics of Atrocity," Terrorism: Interdisciplinary Perspectives, ed. Y. Alexander and S. Finger (New York: John Jay, 1977), pp. 46-61.

(10)   For a more extensive discussion of the police as target, see my "Inside the Terrorist Mind," Chicago Tribune "Perspective," November 2, 1975. The film, Battle of Algiers, offers a brilliant depiction of the process.

(11)   It is a commonplace to describe revolutionary terrorism as a phenomena unique to a world characterized by independent mass media. The confidence, it is often argued, that the media will provide them with extensive coverage encourages small groups to commit spectacular outrages to elicit attention from an otherwise indifferent world. "You can't be a revolutionary today, without a television set - it's as important as a gun."
          But the anarchist phrase, "propaganda by the deed," indicates that contemporary terrorism precedes the invention of television. To justify her assassination attempt against General Trepoff (1877) (perhaps the first violent act by a Russian terrorist), the assailant "declared in court that she had resorted to arms only when all means for bringing the affair [the flogging of a prisoner] to public knowledge . . . had been exhausted." P. Kropotkin, Memoirs of a Revolutionist (Boston: Houghton Mifflin, 1899), p. 415. The failure of the Russian and foreign press to record the flogging and the subsequent lionization of the assailant by the newspapers indicates that even a relatively primitive and controlled mass media "encouraged" terrorism. More important, atrocities always attract attention; and since no society can fully control the transmission of news, there is no reason for thinking that terror for publicity purposes requires an independent mass media.

(12)   In the writings of modern revolutionary terrorists, atrocities are seen as having value in themselves, or providing therapeutic benefits for the perpetrator. I will not be discussing this fourth purpose of terror here, but see my "Politics of Atrocity."

(13)   If the logic of revolutionary terrorism governed all acts of terror in war, we would have to argue that the horrible Dresden fire raids in World War II were undertaken to evoke sympathy for the Allied cause, or to provoke Germans to burn more Englishmen so that other Englishmen would become enthusiastic about incinerating more Germans!

(14)   Lawrence Durrell, Bitter Lemons (London: Faber and Faber, 1959), p. 224.

(15)   "Underground" activity during World War II is the major exception. But it is doubtful whether one can describe it as terrorist as I have defined the term. In any case, the hopes of the participants were fueled by the strength of the Allied armies.

(16)   Bitter Lemons, p. 224.

(17)   Jesus and The Zealots (Manchester: Manchester University, 1967), p. 83.

(18)   A History of the Jews in the Time of Jesus Christ, transl. J. Machpherson, (New York: Scribners, 1970), III, p. 166.

(19)   Micheal Grant describes Parthian Jewry "as a sort of 'reserve' Israel . . . like American Jewry in the 20th century." The Jews in The Roman World (London: Weidenfeld, 1973), p. 48. Parthian Jews aided the Judean uprising, but were unable (for reasons I shall note) to influence their government to pressure Rome, as American Jews did much later when Jews in the Mandate rebelled against Britain.

(20)   Grant estimates that seven million Jews lived in the Roman Empire, constituting between 6 to 9 percent of its total population. Two and a half million lived in Judea, one million in Egypt, one and a half million in Syria and Asia Minor, and there were large concentrations in Cyrenica (i.e., Libya and Crete) and Italy. Parthia had a million Jews.
    For an interesting discussion of the sebomenoi, see Salo Baron, A Social and Religious History of the Jews (New York: Columbia University, 1952), vol. I, ch. I. The category is a loose one, and at times it is difficult to know to whom it should be applied. Poppaea, Nero's wife, who pressures him to render judgment in favor of the Jews in a significant controversy is called by Josephus a "worshipper of God." Still she was unlikely to have been a "sympathizer" (i.e., a person who observed Jewish practices and certain Jewish beliefs without becoming a proselyte.) See Antiquities of the Jews, (hereafter cited as A.J.) XX, 193, transl. Louis Feldman. On the other hand, when Josephus described the treacherous attack on Jews by the Greeks of Damascus, he says they had to act secretly, being afraid of "their own wives who with few exceptions had all become converts to the Jewish religion." J.W., II, 559.

(21)   The unique status of Jewish communities is discussed in E.M. Smallwood, The Jews under Roman Rule (Leiden: Brill, 1976), pp. 133-38.

(22)   Although originally the Romans were welcomed in Judea, the early years were punctuated by bitterly resented events. Pompey and then Crassus plundered the temple; in seizing the throne Herod brutally decimated rivals and potential opposition.   One object of the terrorist campaign later was to demonstrate that Rome's subsequent restraint was an arbitrary decision that could be easily reversed.

(23)   The hostility between ethnic elements created impasses for the imperial power which in many ways is similar to British difficulties in dealing with terrorism in Palestine, Cyprus, and Northern Ireland.

(24)   A.J., XVII, 41-46.   The wife of Herod's younger brother paid the find levied against the "six thousand" who refused the oath, and they in turn proclaimed that the throne would be transferred to her family.

(25)   J.W., I, 648-55; See also A.J., XVII, 149-69.   The belief that Herod was on his deathbed precipitated maneuvers to influence the succession.

Rome distrusted the priesthood and ignored its request that their order be allowed to resume its rule.   She followed Herod's practice of appointing mediocrities as high priests, and discharging them whenever it suited Roman purpose.   The policy inevitably eroded priestly authority, which suited one aspect of the Roman design, but a weakened priesthood by the same token was less effective in defusing tensions, which was certainly not in Rome's interest.   Like Herod, Rome retained control of the high priest's sacred vestaments, a precaution which became a constant irritant, because Jews now could not be certain that the vestaments would remain untouched by polluted hands.

In addition to the priests, perhaps the moderate Pharisees might have been able to keep the dissidents from getting out of control, but Rome mistrusted them too.

(26)   B.J., II, 169ff; see also A.J., XVIII, 55ff.

(27)   B.J., II, 195ff; see also A.S., XVIII, 269.

(28)   T.P. Thorton notes: "If we seek an insurgent tactic that fulfills all the other criteria (except violence) for terrorism, the Ghandian non-violent movement against the British shows identical structural features."   "Terror as A Weapon of Political Agitation," Internal War, ed. H. Eckstein, (New York: Free Press, 1964), p. 75.   Grivas says that EOKA organized young "boys and girls of [high] school age . . . who love danger [and] must take risks to prove their worth" for demonstration purposes in Cyprus so that the public would be ready to support EOKA's terror later.   "The use of young people . . . was entirely my own idea. . . . In December 1954 the army opened fire on a crowd and wounded three boys.   There

were bitter feelings in Greece and Cyprus over this incident."
Memoirs of General Grivas, ed. C. Foley (London: Longmans,
1964) pp. 28-29, and Appendix I; see also his Guerrilla War
and EOKA's Struggle (New York: Praeger, 1965) ch. 1. In
Northern Ireland, extensive, prolonged, nonviolent civil rights
marches set the stage for the present IRA terror, but in this
case passive resistance was not planned as an initial stage of
the terrorist campaign.   Similarly in America, although the
terror activities of the Weathermen developed out of the civil
rights campaign in the South and passive resistance efforts
against the Vietnam War, there was clearly no "organizational
plan" linking the two forms of resistance.   Jerry Rubin's
work, tirelessly emphasizes how easy it is to provoke an
atrocity in a nonviolent demonstration.   My Assassination and
Terrorism, ch. 6, discusses the role of the "demonstration" in
the various stages of a terrorist campaign.

(29) Note the testimony of Menachem Begin concerning the
enormous difficulties in keeping his followers from retaliating
against the Haganah when it attempted to break the Irgun by
kidnapping Irgun members.   "They went to concentration
camps, were thrown into dark cellars, starved, beaten and
maligned yet not one ever broke his solemn undertaking not to
retaliate on his tormentors. . . . Discipline? What is military
discipline, discipline in action, compared with this discipline of
inaction, when your whole soul cries out for retaliation and
retribution.   A human 'order' would have been of no avail
here.   The order came from 'somewhere,' . . . and it was
obeyed.   We were spared the catastrophe of catastrophies."
The Revolt, (Los Angeles: Nash, 1972), p. 153.   The memory
of the "cursed internecine wars in Jerusalem nineteen centuries before," Begin says, made restraint possible.

(30) Only rarely is passive resistance seen as an end.
Jesus, perhaps, is the first to formulate the doctrine; and the
Gospels, of course, directly influenced the two most important
modern exponents, Ghandi and Martin Luther King.   The commitment to passive resistance as an end does not mean that
those who employ it are oblivious to its tactical value as a
method of increasing the opponent's guilt, exasperation, and in
generating doubt concerning the real victor.   Perhaps, the
recognition that nonviolence is a tactic even for those who are
most committed to it as an end explains why most of their
followers eventually abandon it to seek "more realistic" or
violent tactics.   G. Lewy points out that the examples of the
Taborites and Anabaptists during the Reformation suggest that
when passive resistance is abandoned as an end by Messianic
groups, they often turn to terrorist, as to violent activity.
Religion and Revolution (London: Oxford University, 1972), p.
121.

(31) Water cannon, night sticks, and shields to ward off rocks are now, of course, standard items of equipment to reduce the destructive capacities of troops clashing with demonstrators when, for one reason or another, the ordinary police force is no longer available. If the Romans had a police force (as we understand the term) in Judea, Josephus never refers to its presence. In the particular incident described, the troops might have been disguised as civilians, not to avoid provocation but to get the advantage of surprise. Still, Josephus makes it clear that they exceeded their instructions. A.J., VIII, 60-62 cf. B.J., 175-76. Here as elsewhere, when Josephus describes the same events in different places, the details vary.

(32) "The troops were not transferred as they had been ordered, for they sent a deputation which appeased Claudius and obtained leave to remain in Judea. In the period that followed, these men proved to be a source of the greatest disasters to the Jews by sowing the seeds of war." A.J., XIX, 366. After the war was over (and after the damage was done), the troops were removed.

(33) B.J., II, 224-28.

(34) A.J., XX, 112.

(35) B.J., II, 228ff; see also A.J., XX, 117ff. To avoid cluttering the text I have omitted citing the names of the numerous participants mentioned by Josephus, except where they might already be known to readers unfamiliar with the historical period.

√ (36) In the present struggle in Northern Ireland, when British troops replaced Irish police, the government in order to "avoid trouble" established "no go areas" in predominantly Catholic sections, particularly Londonderry. An unmolested IRA quickly took over those areas, turning them into sanctuaries, and terrorizing Catholics who wanted peace. A few years ago, Israel pursued a similar policy in Gaza, which gave terrorists a city to govern until the policy was reversed.

(37) B.J., II, 409. The Jewish Talmud suggests that priests were pushed into the decision by Roman provocateurs who fraudently offered for the sacrifice blemished animals which they knew would be rejected. See W.R. Farmer, Maccabees, Zealots and Josephus, (New York: Columbia University, 1956), p. 94. The difficulty in establishing the truth here is typical of many inflammatory incidents, and indeed is characteristic of revolutionary terrorist struggles where both sides employ double agents. The most notorious incident in the history of terrorism, of course, is the case of Eugene Azeff the Czarist agent who as head of the Battle Organization of The Socialist Revolutionary Party became the major Russian terrorist. The

shock which his exposure produced in 1909 destroyed that movement.

(38)   Ibid., II, 451ff.

(39)   Ibid., II, 457ff.   Josephus' treatment of the two atrocities is extraordinary.   Jerusalem was aware of trouble in Caesarea before the troops were massacred and the Caesareans knew that the garrison was besieged before they slaughtered the Jews.   The troops in Jerusalem, moreover, were Greeks from Caesarea.   The two atrocities, therefore, must be related; but Josephus conspicuously omits to explain why either occurred or what their mutual relationship might be.

He provides a detailed account of events leading up to the Jerusalem massacre before mentioning the Greek atrocity. But he offers no details on the events in Caesarea preceding the Greek attack and says that it was a divine punishment for the Jewish sacrilege.   One suspects that the Jerusalem massacre occurred first and provoked the other; it might even have been undertaken for that purpose.   Modern scholars generally treat the atrocity in Jerusalem as having provoked the Caesarea slaughter, even when they disagree on whether Jews or Romans are to blame for the war itself.   (See S. Zeitlin, The Rise and Fall of the Judean State (Philadelphia: Jewish Publication Society, 1967), vol. II, p. 243; and M. Grant, p. 192).   Still, Josephus insists that the two atrocities occurred simultaneously.   No other evidence exists on the matter.   But Josephus' unreliability regarding motives is well known.   His divided loyalties might have prevented him from making a judgment on what must have been a hotly disputed issue.   In his autobiography, Josephus does not mention the Jerusalem massacre but he describes Greek atrocities "to convince my readers that the war was due not so much to the deliberate choice of the Jews as to necessity."   The Life, p. 27.

(40)   Ibid.

(41)   Ibid., II, 526.   The desire to negotiate is partly attributable to the fact that the Jews commanded local mountain height making the Roman military position insecure.   Yet throughout the war when the Romans had a clear military advantage, they kept offering a settlement which by one extraordinary atrocity or another the terrorists managed to sabotage.   The news of Beth-Horon also produced at least one major atrocity - the interned Jewish population of Damascus was slaughtered.   Ibid., II. 560.

(42)   Moderates who refused to join the rebellion or leave Jerusalem were apparently murdered.   Ibid., II, 577 and IV, 40.

(43) In the debate over the decision to go to war, moderates warn that the Parthians in order to secure the treaty recently signed with Rome, would prevent their Jewish subjects from getting involved (Ibid., II, 390). Josephus says little about relevant events in Parthia, but apparently little aid got through. The "demotion" of the generals might have weakened the Parthian Jews' commitment, but equally the demotion could have signified a recognition that more aid from the east was not forthcoming anyway. In either case, it seems reasonable to think that native leadership would be needed to mobilize the Judean population.

(44) The Life, 30. Josephus describes his purpose here merely as an effort to provide civil order. But the descriptions of actions taken quite clearly go beyond that, and are consistent with his military mission described in his major work on the war. The Life was written to counter allegations that his initial sympathies were with the militants.

(45) Ibid., 29. Even when he has clear military superiority, Josephus is reluctant to attack Roman units.

(46) Tacitus, Histories, IV, 51. Had Parthia been seeking to compound Rome's difficulties, she most probably would have supported one of the several imposters claiming to be the deceased Nero, who was extremely popular in the eastern portions of the empire. Revolts in Pontus, Germany, and Gaul in 69 CE rekindled some hopes that outside support was forthcoming, though it must have been disappointing that Jews were not involved.

(47) The Passover Plot (New York: Random House, 1965), p. 19.

(48) G. Ferrero's comment on the dynamics of the Reign of Terror during the French Revolution is especially pertinent: "The Jacobins did not spill all that blood because they believed in popular sovereignty as a religious truth; they tried to believe in popular sovereignty as a religious truth because their fear made them spill so much blood." Principles of Power (New York: Arno, 1972), p. 100.

(49) Jewish terrorist operations go through two major phases. Initially they are characterized by "hit and disappear" or guerrilla-like tactics, and then a war of fixed positions ensues. The development reminds one of contemporary revolutionary war theories, but it seems most likely that unforseen circumstances determined the change. No evidence of a planned transformation, at any rate, exists.

(50) Morton Smith, "Palestine Judaism in the First Century," in Israel: Its Role in Civilization, ed. Moshe Davis (New York: Harper & Row, 1956), p. 74.

(51)   As the details of the Messianic picture vary from primary source to primary source, the picture offered here can only be a composite not a comprehensive one.   For an excellent analysis of Messianic prophecies in Jewish thought, see G. Scholem, The Messianic Idea in Judaism (New York: Schocken 1971); and for a useful effort to treat messianism as a political force, see Guenther Lewy, Religion and Revolution (New York: Oxford University Press, 1974).

(52)   G. Scholem, The Messianic Idea, p. 12.

(53)   A.J., XVIII, 23.

(54)   In recent years the literature on the Zealots and Sicarii has become quite extensive.   The most important source is M. Hengel, Die Zeloten (Leiden: Brill, 1961).   See also, S.G.F. Brandon, Jesus and The Zealots (Manchester: 1957); S. Applebaum, "The Zealots; The Case for Revolution," Journal of Roman Studies, 61 (1971): 155-70; M. Borg, "The Currency of the Term 'Zealot,'" Journal of Theological Studies, 22, (1971): 504-13; H. Paul Kingdom, "Who were The Zealots," New Testament Studies, 17 (1970): 68-72, and "Origins of the Zealots," ibid., 19 (1971): 74-81; K. Kohler, "Zealots," The Jewish Encyclopedia, (New York: Funk & Wagnalls, 1905) XII, 639-43; C. Roth, "The Zealots and The War of 66-70," Journal of Semitic Studies, 4 (1959): 332-44; M. Smith, "Zealots and Sicarii: Their Origins and Relations," Harvard Theological Review, 54 (1971): 1-19; M. Stern, "Zealots," Encyclopedia Judaica (Jerusalem: Yearbook 1973), 135-52); S. Zeitlin, "The Sicarii and The Zealots," Jewish Quarterly Review, 57 (1967): 251-70.

(55)   Numbers, 25:11.

(56)   S. Zeitlin has a different view: The Sicarii "were only a small group and, unlike the Galileans could not wage an open organized fight. . . . As a consequence, these Judean revolutionaries resorted to individual acts . . . assassination. Their weapon was a small dagger (Latin: sica), and they came to be known as Sicarii." The Rise and Fall of the Judean State, vol. 3 (Philadelphia: Jewish Publication Society, 1978), p. 6.   From the days of the Republic a sicarii referred to an action and not its political intent.   Roth, arguing largely from contemporary analogy ("The Zealots . . ."), claims that the Romans called all Jewish rebels Sicarii to emphasize their invidious nature but the rebels, like contemporary terrorists who call themselves revolutionaries, knew themselves to be Zealots, a term which specifies purpose.   The argument is interesting but not supported by the evidence.

(57)   B.J., VII, 30.

(58)   Ibid., VII, 400.

(59) A.J., XVIII, 23. I briefly discuss terror as "personal therapy" in "The Politics of Atrocity."

(60) T.B. Sanhedrin, 97a, cited by Wilson D. Wallis in Messiahs: Their Role in Civilization (Washington, D.C.: American Council on Education, 1943), p. 16.

(61) The Revolt, pp. 152-3. (reprint of 1948 edition). When Begin discusses the Zealots, he speaks both of their heroism and an inability to understand strategic considerations (p. 47). He also suggests they lacked sufficient "moral character" (p. 135).

(62) Begin describes these last two acts as consistent with the "law of reprisal" in war. This law allows one party to violate military conventions in order to compel an enemy to stop his infractions of those rules. In addition to assaults on police and immigration facilities, the Irgun violated military conventions by frequently wearing British uniforms and concealing their weapons. The attack on the King David Hotel, which caused well over a hundred civilian casualties, mostly Jewish, is often cited as an exception too, and is discussed by Tugwell below. But the hotel was the Center of British Intelligence, and a warning was given, though received apparently too late. In my view, there is no reason to think the Irgun did not want the warning to get through.

(63) EOKA made no plans vis-a-vis the Turks on Cyprus; in the effort to attack the British without providing warnings, Turks were killed producing a Turkish reaction which frustrated EOKA's objective of union with Greece. The precipitating incident is described in two accounts whose striking differences are very revealing. Cf. Laurence Durrell, Bitter Lemons (London: Faber, 1957) and General Grivas, Memoirs, ed. C. Foley (London: Longman's, 1964): p. 37. Significantly, EOKA's "Preparatory General Plan" contains no reference to the Turks (p. 204). In five conspicuous cases where two groups of local residents were implicated in a terrorist campaign against an imperial power (the two Jewish instances, Cyprus, Algeria, and Ireland), only in Palestine did one of the groups abstain from entering the conflict early. It is interesting to note that the outcome in each case was different.

One should stress that the Irgun was prepared to see its policy of restraint vis-a-vis the Arabs fail. It made backup plans to use terror, and was willing to risk a "repetition of history" in this one respect. After the British evacuated and the Arabs took up arms to frustrate the UN Partition Plan, the Irgun was involved in the "Dir Yassin Massacre," The Revolt, (pp. 76-80 and 162-165).

2 Models of Rebellion
Vytautas Kavolis

I

One enjoys an analytical advantage in seeking to understand what rebellion means not through explicit normative formulations but through mythologies in which rebellion is represented "in flesh and blood" (or at least the kind of flesh and blood that mythologies recognize). The advantage is that a mythology, at least a basic mythology of one of the historic civilizations, contains not only a normative principle, but also, and primarily (1) a model of consciousness for comprehending a particular type of human behavior, (2) a psychological theory revealing how, and of what materials, a particular cultural tradition constructs psychological theories, and (3) a suggestion of the sociological setting within which either (a) the type of <u>behavior</u> represented in the myth tends to arise, or (b) a <u>particular</u> psychological theory of its genesis and manifestations is generated.

Thus, a mythological representation reveals not only how rebellion was understood in the civilization in which the myth was created and how different understandings of rebellion arise; it also provides one of the general human (that is, intercivilizational) repertoire of models for comprehending particular kinds of rebellion in all times and places. It is in this sense that great myths are "eternally true" - though they are true as <u>theories</u> applicable to particular segments of experience, not as overarching <u>systems</u> embracing all reality.

II

These general considerations lead us to an analysis of the myths of Prometheus and Satan, both of which treat the general theme of rebellion by an individual against the supreme authority in the established order and against the rules by which this order operates.(44,47,24,33) But Prometheus rebels, in stealing fire against the prohibition of Zeus, motivated by sympathy for the sufferings of those unlike himself - people deprived of fire, and he gives them practical assistance without imposing on them either his own values or his leadership. He permits them to incorporate his technical gifts into the structure of their own life, as they themselves see fit.

Surely what might be called the "humane attachment-practical assistance mechanism" is a universal possibility, experienced and observed by people in all civilizations. But what is remarkable is that the Greeks - or some significant Greeks - have associated the humane attachment-practical assistance mechanism with what they themselves thought of as the crime of rebellion against established authority or, more precisely, against a concrete inequity in the normative order sanctioned by it. Rebellion is therefore a "noble crime"; and in the life history of the rebel (or in the historical development of his image) the substantive personal virtue of the individual overcomes the formal criminality of his act.

This is one model for conceptualizing the behavior of the rebel. The other is the Satanic model. As described in medieval Christian writings Satan rebels out of resentment. The causes of his resentment are variously interpreted by the theologians: he is the first of the angels who thinks he has been replaced in God's affection by a "younger sibling" - man or Christ; he objects to having been created by someone else and wants to be the sole maker of his own identity. But he rebels not out of sympathy for others, but from resentment of what he perceives as loss or lack of recognition of his own excellence - "pride born of envy" and "a sense of his own greatness."(26) And, while he employs wealth and power as a means for attaining control over those he seeks to corrupt, he is wholly unconcerned with meeting the practical (food, warmth or health) needs of anyone.

Indeed, both as the servant of God, in the story of Job, and as the evil one, Satan appears to find the peaceful enjoyment of material comfort intolerable. The simple felicities of ordinary life offend against Satan's single-minded pursuit of absolute "virtue" or, in his transformed state, "anti-virtue." The final goal of the resentful idealist is to create a total alternative to the divine order, an "adversary culture" and, within it, to assume God's place. But the results of his activities are wholly destructive. While Prometheus, a materialist-rationalist "partial rebel" who sought only to provide a useful service, winds up evoking a new conception of justice which even Zeus, in the lost parts of the Aeschylean trilogy, apparently comes to accept - Satan proves unable to create any value and can only mock the old by inverting them. The would be total innovator is enchained to the inverse of all of the old.

Satanic behavior can be conceptualized psychologically as governed by the resentment-destruction mechanism. Surely this mechanism, too, is a universal possibility, experienced and observed by people in all civilizations. But note that in the Judeo-Christian, and particularly the medieval Christian, tradition it is the resentment-destruction mechanism that is firmly attached to the theme of rebellion against the legitimately established power holders and the normative order represented by them. Within this tradition, there is no nobility in the crime of rebellion against the existing normative order. Rebellion is in itself evil even when its occurrence is "objectively necessary" for the completion of the larger design of God and contributes to the comprehension, by men, of this design. What is "spontaneous" in Satan is evil even though this spontaneity has been "provided for" and kept "under control" by the irreplaceable occupant of the commanding heights of "power" and "goodness."

The connection between rebellion and the resentment-destruction mechanism is much more central to the Christian tradition that the linkage between rebellion and the sympathy-assistance mechanism in the Greek civilization. Prometheus was far less important in Greek mythology than Satan in the medieval Christian. But, centrality aside, the linkage of the cultural theme of rebellion with the psychological mechanism of humane attachment resulting in practical assistance to others is, among the historic civilizations, a distinctively Greek theme. The older Plato would not have appreciated it, but in no other pre-modern civilization has this particular linkage of themes been given a mythological elaboration anywhere approaching that given to it by Aeschylus.(b) And we are concerned not only with what is central to a civilization, but also with what is unique in it.

We have, so far, two interpretative models of rebellion, both potentially applicable to the behavior of actual rebels in any civilization. The first model suggests that rebellion, ① motivated by humane sympathy for the sufferings of others and expressed through particular acts of practical assistance, results in an enduringly valuable change in the structure of the moral universe. The other model contends that rebellion② motivated by personal resentment, and expressed in global attempts to create an alternative style of life and impose it on others, is destructive in its consequences. We also have the historical fact that one of these potentially universal theories of rebellion has been created by important representatives of the Greek civilization, and the other has possessed immense influence in the medieval Christian civilization (and in some of its secular derivatives). Is the selection of the theoretical model by which to interpret rebellion a consequence of the different behavior of key rebels in the two civilizations, or is it an expression of differences in the cognitive structure of the two civilizations at the time when these models acquired their hold over the imagination?

Before addressing myself to this question, however, I wish to compare the psychogenetic theories contained, or implied, in the Promethean and the Satanic legends to account for the origins of the rebel. What is most distinctive of Satan at his earliest appearance in the Old Testament is that he is a function of God specializing in ferreting out potential transgressors and bringing them to God's attention to be punished. He is, on the one hand, an absolute servant, created by his master, who has no existence of his own, no civil rights, and no social ties except the bond of obedience against which he eventually rebels; and, on the other hand, he is the enforcer of morality, the chairman of the Heavenly Un-Godly Activities Committee. When the absolute servant rebels, he can only imagine himself replacing the despot at the peak of the power structure, without disturbing the structure itself; and he will be more merciless than his former master. He who begins as the enforcer of morality, ends as the great corrupter.

Prometheus, on the other hand, is an independent from the very beginning of his conscious existence. He has his own independent position, not delegated to him by a higher authority; he has his own relatives, wife, and children; and, above all, he has his own knowledge – the ability to predict the future – which is in fact superior to the knowledge possessed by the ruler of the gods.(c) It would have been inconceivable for Satan to have known more than God does. That is, the Satanic rebel acts out of ignorance, on the basis of an inferior, self-deceptive theory. Or so the Judeo-Christian tradition, in which, at the peak of the hierarchies of knowledge and power, knowledge tends to be identified with power, interprets the intellectual condition of the rebel. In Greece, it was possible for highest power to be perceived as deficient in knowledge (as well as in virtue).

Prometheus, then, begins as the equivalent of a knowledgeable, high-status adolescent used to making his own decisions. The first significant decision he makes is in fact one to support Zeus in his battle against the Titans, who are members of Prometheus' own family. This decision – in some ways the equivalent of Crane Brinton's "desertion of the intellectuals" in the revolutionary process(4) – proves to be a mistake, since Zeus, in power, becomes a ruthless tyrant. Rebellion, for Prometheus – if not necessarily in conscious intention, than in its objective effects - functions as an expiation for the unintended wrongs he had earlier helped to create by having aligned himself with an emergent tyranny. While the expiation motive is not specifically mentioned in the Greek texts, the logic of Promethean behavior permits this interpretation, as Satanic behavior does not. Satan could feel no guilt for what he had done in serving his master (in bringing down, for example, the undeserved misfortunes of Job), since, having been created entirely as a tool of that master, he did not develop the habit of considering himself responsible for his own actions. It is he who perceives himself as the blameless agent of a greater power - or as the necessary evil - rather than he who has reason to know he has been a fool in his own judgments, who develops into the resentful destroyer.(d)

One further element in the background of Prometheus is his part as a trickster who delights in substituting bones and fat for meat in a sacrifice to Zeus, thus deceiving the supreme authority without any motive apparent in this action other than the pure fun of it.(23) Satan, on the other hand, does not appear capable of pure fun, unrelated to his single-mindedness of his service to God (in his earlier career) or to that of his rebellion against God (in his later identity). Thus the final psychogenetic summary of the evolution of Satanic and Promethean types of rebellion: abstract justice, combined with resentment, corrupts the absolute servant; playful trickery, to which sympathetic kindness is added, permits a moral evolution in an independent mind.

We now have not only two models of rebellious behavior, but also two psychological theories of how these respective types of behavior have come about. And the civilization-comparative question may be repeated on another level: Why did the Greek and the Judeo-Christian civilizatons develop different "psychological" theories of the origin of rebellion against authority?

Two possible approaches to this question may be suggested. The first focuses on differences in the depth structure of moral thinking of the two civilizations. The dominant Judeo-Christian tendency, shaped or reinforced by Iranian influences, and surviving in a variety of secular ideologies of Western-European derivation, has been to adopt a "mobilizing," or "reifying," attitude toward moral issues. The goal implicit in this attitude is to enhance the "good" and to exorcise the "evil" in history and personality by rigidly separating them, as objects of total worship and absolute condemnation, in the mythological constructs used to comprehend historical experiences and subjective states of the personality. This attitude has also been strong in the North African and Near Eastern Islamic traditions, and has recently revived there.

The Greeks, in contrast, have sometimes been able to adopt a "developmental," or "dialectical," attitude toward moral issues, with the implicit goal of integrating a recognized "evil" (e.g., the crime of rebellion) with the presumed "good" (e.g., the authority of the legal order) in such a way that the "evil" is gradually transformed into the "good," or functions as an indispensable challenge to it, while the "good" must be exposed to a searching criticism of its claims, in the absence of which it stands in danger of revealing itself as (or degenerating into) another form of "evil."(e) This attitude is evident not only in the Promethean myth, and in the conception of Zeus, in whom, as Paul Ricoeur puts it, "the problematics of the 'wicked god,' the undivided unity of the divine and the satanic reaches its highest pitch,"(42) but also in the treatment of Dionysus, in whom Christ-like and Satan-like elements are intertwined.(21,39,43) A somewhat comparable mode of integrating the "evil" into the "good" has been evolved in Hasidism (e.g., "Use evil to do good").

Within the relatively enduring Indian and Chinese structures of moral thinking, the primary categories to which substance is attributed are not "good" and "evil," and the relationships between the fundamental opposites take the form neither of "battle" nor of "dialectical transformation." In Hinduism, dualistic categories both stand in a relationship of mutual recognition of each other (being in the world and world renunciation) and (as in the purity-pollution distinction) are used to separate hierarchically arranged entities representing phases of an interminably cyclical process.(9,37) While the categories themselves constitute a permanent structure, the particular contents of Indian categories are comparatively fluid: the ascetic becomes an erotic profligate and bounces back again; an individual moves from being in the world to world renunciation; what is "polluting" overflows and infects the "pure" (but never the opposite, thus suggesting the strength of "pollution" and the weakness of "purity," in some contrast to the powerful Chinese belief that good examples normally attract others to emulate them).

In Confucian China, polarities equal in value but unequal in power (as in the Yin-Yang paradigm) cooperate, in a rigorously defined but contextually variable manner, to sustain and develop a harmonious cosmic hierarchy.(3,15) This is less fluidity of the contents of the categories and more of a "practical" cooperation between the opposites than in the Indian structure of moral thinking.

In the medieval and early modern European tradition, polar opposites either battle energetically until the final solution the outcome of which is predetermined (the God-Satan model), or are mutually interdependent in a static hierarchical relationship, which it is impermissible to challenge (as in the notion of the "marriage" of the soul with the body, in which the "masculine" soul is entitled to the obedience of the "feminine" body).(38) The result of the concurrent presence of both of these models in the Western tradition is a constant tension between "hierarchy" and "dualism": hierarchies are always potentially threatened by a dualistic militance subversive of them, as they are not in either India or China.

In contrast to all of these conceptions of the proper relationship between polar opposites, Greek dramatists have conceived of a dialectic in which the opposites evolve, changing their own character and the structure of their setting, in the course of a battle in which the cards are not stacked in advance in favor of one participant, as they are in the God-Satan paradigm. While the image of Prometheus has appealed at various times and in various ways to European traditions of experience,(f) the Promethean dialectic has re-emerged most prominently in the Romantic imagination.(1) But the Romantics had a tendency to collapse Satan and Prometheus into one (or rather to impart the psychological qualities of the former to the imagery of the latter).(13,17)(g) Marx resonated to this ambience; Stalin remained a medieval Christian dominant with a factory for the transformation of humanity in his hands.

The second approach to explaining the differences between the Greek and the Judeo-Christian models of rebellious behavior, and between their theories of the origin of such behavior, can be made on the social-structural level. The construction of Satan has started within the general ambience of a militaristic, Persian "oriental despotism," where the obligation of everyone, including the highest officials, has been to serve the ruler in the manner of disciplined soldiers, and in which, since the judgment of the supreme power holder could not legitimately be questioned, failure to submit to him had to appear as the upheaval of primeval chaos against the righteousness of civilization. The Persian type of oriental despotism may be contrasted to the bureaucratic empire of historic China, where officials, insofar as they were "true gentlemen" (chün-tzu), adhered to generalized moral standards of their estate, by which they could define their own dignity and even judge their supreme authority, the emperor - thus retaining a certain margin of dignified moral independence relative to him.(h)

In the Chinese framework, in which supreme worldly power could legitimately be perceived as deficient in knowledge and in virtue, rebellion could not automatically be judged as arising outside of the normative order and as constituting a threat not only to the current political manifestation of that order, but to the principle of order itself. Rebellion could therefore not easily be interpreted within an imagery of the Satanic type. The most popular image of the rebel in traditional Chinese fiction is that of a trickster-monkey who, after having fought successfully against all sorts of heavenly powers

and secular sages, ends up as the defender of a Buddhist
pilgrim.(52,53) Rebelliousness, in this case, appears not as a
serious human, angelic or titanic quality, but as a playful
expression of primordial nature, capable, in the very course of
its rebellion, of rising to the level of moral responsibility.
There is a bit of Prometheus in the monkey, but nothing whatsoever of Satan. Actual rebellions tended in China to be
rationalized by the theorists as expressions of the loss of "the
mandate of heaven" and legitimated by the rebels themselves,
until the nineteenth century, in the imagery of the nature
mysticism of popular Taoism and the reassertion of traditional
peasant values.

The myth of Prometheus has been put together in a society which cultivated "individualistic heroism" in social action
and in fact provided opportunities for a privileged elite   to
seek this goal. When Prometheus first appears, in Hesiod, the
breaking down of clan controls was taking place in the absence
of both a dominant state organization and a rigorously dualistic
intellectual culture. In this setting, a mere semigod senses
the "prerogative of the privileged" - the obligation to come to
the aid of others in his own way, without waiting for legitimation by any traditional standard or a newly formulated
explicit ideology. A society which permits individualistic
practical (not merely symbolic) action for at least some of its
members is probably necessary for such trust in one's own
private moral sensitivities, not sanctioned by any imaginable
agency or tradition external to the individual. In a stable
peasant society, or within a bureaucracy such an attitude
would not be credible enough to sustain a great myth.

Yet Prometheus is not a feudal lord, or a Hegelian "honest soul," acting with the archaic directness of "honor." He
is a "subtle-spirit" (Aeschylus), a user of his mind, who has
clearly seen oppression and its limits, and it has become his
nature to "think deviously" (Hesiod): it is apparently Prometheus who has invented the deceptive sacrifice to the powerful.(22) But to invent it with full conviction in the propriety
of his act, he has not to need it for himself. He is willing to
sin, but only for the concrete benefit of others. In the
tradition in which he originates, this commitment is associated
with supreme intelligence.

Another structural characteristic of the Greek society
relevant to the Promethean theme is the presence of a body of
intellectuals, principally the dramatic poets, who were deeply
concerned with interpreting moral issues, but were not functionaries within, or tightly controlled by, a religious or
political organization. In the ancient Near East, where moral
poetry was, by and large, in the hands of organized religious
bodies, the priesthoods were organized, like the state, along
the lines of a militaristic "oriental despotism." In the Israelite
tradition, where they were not   -   and where the institution of

prophecy permitted "rebelliousness" against the established
social order in the name of a higher obedience, Satan originally did not have the character of a rebel, let alone a nihilistic
rebel.

The sense of the virulence of Satan had been taking
shape under the Seleucid conquerors of Palestine, when a
strong movement toward Hellenization in the Jewish aristocracy, ambitious to increase the scope of its power, began
seriously to threaten the cultural identity of the Jewish
community.(45) The vivid experience of this threat to national
and religious identity must have lent emotional vitality to the
elaboration of the Satanic myth from its already existing
elements into a full-fledged dramatic explanation of the meaning
of the experience (e.g., in the "temptations" of Christ).
Satan emerged as a religious interpretation of the perceived
readiness of members of a community, in which high value had
been traditionally placed on group solidarity, to abandon the
moral ties of mutual obligation in search of the recognition of
unique personal excellence. The uprisings of the period,
which reasserted collective identities and the ties of mutual
obligation, and the growth of the Satanic mythology are products of the same historical situation. And a similar situation
developed in Christian Europe at the peak of the power of the
devil and fear of witchcraft toward the end of the Middle
Ages.

III

While Prometheus has, since the nineteenth century, been
frequently assimilated to Satan, it is Dionysus - an avenger of
offenses suffered by himself, and a purely expressive actor
totally unconcerned with the practical needs of others - who is
morphologically closer to Satan. But Dionysus appears to have
been raised by emotionally deprived women in a male-dominated
society. In contrast, only the authoritarian Old Testament
patriarch and his servants are mentioned in the domestic
environment in which Satan spent the early years of his career. The "childhood environment" may help explain why
Dionysus, violent as he is, seeks temporary ecstasy rather
than permanent power, and being sacrificed or provoking
cannibalism in others are equally ecstatic fulfillments for
him.(39,43,50)

Dionysus creates resources of intense emotionality where
they are, in his absence, lacking. He does not, however,
integrate these resources with the rest of human existence.
Left in his hands, they therefore become destructive forces.
In this respect, he is like Satan: resources that might feed
life become agencies of destruction in the hands of both. And

it is in this respect that Dionysus is unlike Prometheus, who
integrates the resources he has not created - as well as the
skills he has - into the life of other people without doing
injury to the structure of existence of the recipients of his
gifts. Prometheus is a skilled inventor of useful objects and
activities. He also has the gift of prophecy - that is, a valid
theory of the future. His ultimate genius, however, does not
lie in the generation of light, but in the precise recognition of
brilliance where it exists (=fire, the source of light and
warmth) and its incorporation into the everyday life of mankind.

In contrast to both Satan and Prometheus, Dionysus is
not himself explicitly a rebel. He is rather an avenger and a
revealer of the barbaric depths suppressed by civilization.
But his actions provide stages for the unacknowledged rebellions of others - those who are subjected to suffering from the
existing structure of civilization. And it is only the others
who suffer the exhaustion and emptiness which follows, at
least in Euripides, the orgy of mad destructiveness inspired
by Dionysus; their mover, "wearing a mask with a fixed
smile," merely goes away for another travelling exhibition of
his sinister powers.(25) The Dionysian rebellion is directed
not against a power system as a whole or its specific com-
mandments, but against the ordered routine of everyday life,
against "quotidianty" or "rationalization." His rebellion - and
the kind of "significant disordering of the senses" it represents - can be used by an established power system for
strengthening its own position, if it knows how to associate
itself with or even arrange, protests against ordered routines.(49) (Even Mao has, in the "cultural revolution," sought
to employ Dionysus.)

In the emotional character of the rebellions he provokes
(and in the importance of the performing arts in these rebellions), the collectivist Dionysus is comparable to the
medieval European individualist, Tristan.(i) But there are two
differences between the cult of the Greek god and the medieval
European tale: (1) In the environment of Dionysus, normally
suppressed, powerless collectivities - women and the lower
classes - intentionally seek the intoxication of rebellion against
the routine order. Aristocratic Tristan has to be infused with
an external agent to become a rebel against the customary
roles and his own contractual obligation of fidelity to the King.
He accidentally swallows the love potion intended for the King
and is overcome by a madness he does not understand. No
longer, as in Prometheus, is rebellion the expression of
unsurpassed intelligence. The primordial romantic hero is not
the responsible agent of his own rebellion, but an "accidental
rebel" - with a cause but without his own purpose - the mechanical receptacle of an externally generated passion.(j) In
contrast to his more interesting (as well as more real) near-

contemporary, Abelard, the Tristan of the twelfth-century "canonical" version does not have mind enough to have a will of his own in his body.(2) The cult of Dionysus establishes opportunities for shared - though savage - emotional experiences in a temporary community of the intoxicated from which, in principle, no one who appears as a mindless adherent is excluded. The emotional potencies of Tristan and Iseult are withdrawn from everything else and totally concentrated in an exclusive pair relationship (as a Western ascetic might withdraw from the "world" for the sake of his "soul" alone).

The love potion was apparently lacking in the Celtic sources of the myth, in which love was initiated by a conscious agent, the king's wife. What had started as a woman's spontaneous passion in Celtic mythology became, in the hands of the courtly poets of twelfth-century France, an impersonal power overwhelming both man and woman and transforming them into sadly exalted "mechanical toys," an early version of "escape from freedom." At the roots of the "alchemy" of romantic love is the transformation into a power-driven machinery, separated from consciousness, of that activated receptivity called emotion.

Perhaps to make a historical advance in the understanding of an emotional (or intellectual or moral) quality, it needs first to be "alienated" from the organic flow of everyday existence of human beings, "constructed" as a mechanism so that it could be seen more clearly (at the risk that what is helpful as a visual aid becomes a source of corruption when literally imitated in social action). Whether this interpretation clarifies the historical function of the "objectification of love" in the Tristanic legend or not, the contents of the myth document a ritualism of mutuality without spontaneity (and hence without change) and of individualism without self-determination (and hence without responsibility). It is as if a courtly Confucian had to make sense out of the emerging emotional dynamics of modern Western civilization.(k)

The contraction of an individual's emotional life to the totalization of a passion alienates the individual not only from everyone not included in such a relationship, but also from aspects of his own self that cannot be encompassed within it and must therefore be suppressed. The Tristan story suggests that such transformation of the life world into a mechanism of private passion transforms emotion itself into a "thing," an alien substance, for the individual in whom it materializes (=the love potion, an intrusion detached from, but compelling, one's personality); and it ends up transforming the person on whom it is totally focused also into a "thing" that is programmed to perform a highly stylized ritual. In a collectivized form, this also happens in Dionysian rites.

But it has not happened to Abelard, whose intellectual rebellion preceded, and then overlapped, the unorthodoxy of his secular love for Heloise; he had purposes of his own in both, and continued to analyse and to do his work - though, as he thought, less creatively - even while he loved.(14,31,32) Hence the hypothesis on Tristanic-Dionysian (as contrasted to Promethean or Abelardian) behavior: Emotionality detached from normal everyday concerns, from ethics, and from the habit of analysis - and also from the people who do not immediately participate in its making - "freezes" both its sender and its recipient into a death-like state of compulsion, whatever their self-perceptions of "emotional vitality." The search for intensity in self-sufficient emotion transforms emotion itself into a mechanism. "Miraculous intrusion" at its purest processes its recipient to the most exact specifications. In dreams begin factories.

Yet in the Tristan legend, for the first time, mythology provides a model for man and woman to be equal fellow-rebels.(1) For Satan - as currently for the mass advertiser - woman was a promiscuously used instrument to attract other men into his field of domination. For Prometheus, she - his apparently wholly domestic wife - was an attached non-participant in his rebellion. For Dionysus, she was a temporarily self-involving mass of faceless followers.

The Tristanic model of a joint rebellion by equal individuals for the sake of an interest that they do not share with anyone else has, however, simultaneously established the Western paradigm of private suffering: the impossibility of intimacy when individuals relate to each other by that which alienates them from their own identities.

IV

The Satanic theory of rebellious behavior appears to require both a social structure built for the maximization of obedience and elimination of independence, and an intellectual tradition of rigorous (non-cooperative) dualism. A civilization like the traditional Chinese, which comes close to eliminating individual independence in politically relevant action, but does not favor rigorous dualism in thought, does not generate Satanic interpretations of rebellious behavior. And in the post-medieval bourgeois societies of Western Europe, including those of the most rigorous Calvinistic shaping - which tended, however, to legitimate individual independence (through "voluntary consent")(28,48) - the hold of Satan declined with the stabilization of the new order. Given an obedience-maximizing structure and a dualistic tradition, social strains and particularly threats to this structure and tradition increase the likelihood, and the virulence, of Satanic theories.(5,46) Thus it is when an obedience-maximizing social structure is beginning to break down - or to appear "untidy" - that Satanic theories - and revolutionary (or counter-revolutionary) movements which frequently become their carriers - emerge into prominence. (m)

If there is little culturally visible untidiness, or if one takes it for granted that there will always be untidy areas in human experience and gets used to them, Satanic theories of rebellious behavior should have a limited appeal - or Satanic rebels might be perceived in the relatively innocuous guise of merely "romantic" or "decadent" eccentrics, as they tended to be in nineteenth-century England. But with Byron we leave the realm of mythology for that of aesthetics, and with Swinburne we witness the transformation of the Satanic into the Dionysian mode of the avant-garde culture.

It is conceivable that conditions under which Satanic theories arise also favor Satanic behavior, as the twentieth-century totalitarianisms (promoted and legitimated by the rigorous dualism of racist and class ideologies) suggest. However, a mythological construct should not be seen as a reflection of observed, that is already existing behavior, but rather as a selective editing and creative elaboration of fantasy dispositions that arise in response to the conjunction of a particular organization of social relations and a particular set of basic forms for the intuitive perception of order and disorder. In imagination, alternative possibilities of behavior are actively tried out (and sometimes judged to be wanting). But the trials of what is currently experienced are conducted in the courthouse of the basic categories and formalizations explicitly provided by one's intellectual tradition or implicit in it.

Thus the analysis of the interpretations of rebellious behavior underlines the impossibility of understanding the distinctive symbolic designs of particular civilizations either without reference to their social structures or as direct reflections of their social structures. Nor, in all likelihood, should differences in symbolic designs be read as registering corresponding differences in visible behavior, or the absence of a particular symbolic design be interpreted as indicating the absence of the behavior which other peoples objectify in such designs. What symbolic designs in their totality express exists, outside of them, only in the imagination; and not all the "raw materials" of experience that exist outside of the active imagination are transmuted into its splendid and horrifying craftsmanship. (20)

V

The Greeks have provided two mythological models for rebellion: a "rational" rebellion for the privileged individual
(Prometheus) and an "emotional" rebellion for the underpriv-
ileged collectivity (Dionysus). The modern European civilization inverts the equation: an "emotional" rebellion for the
privileged individual (Tristan), a "rational" rebellion, later on,
for the oppressed collectivity (Marx). Dionysus has been
individualized, Prometheus collectivized.

Both Greece and the modern West knew morally justifiable, rational rebellions, but located them differently; and
psychologically understandable, emotional rebellions, but
conceived the emotions underlying such rebellions as divinely
inspired in one case (Greece, where it was the emotion of the
downtrodden), as artificially induced in the other (the West,
where it became the emotion of the cultivated). Only the
downtrodden need divine inspiration for their rebellions; the
cultivated hold the means to inspire themselves in their own
hands (even when they do not know what they hold).

But the medieval paradigm of the Satanic rebellion continues to insinuate itself into the modern shapes of both
Prometheus and Dionysus. Greek mythological rebels could be
exactly what they were: gods, titans. Satan (and, with him,
a multitude of nineteenth- and twentieth-century rebels) are
functionaries who seek to be gods capable of creating themselves. In our times, it has become a legitimate aspiration to
make of oneself, individually or collectively, an artificial god.
We are condemned to discover whether the Satanic rebellion is
destructive only when it is "defined as deviant" by the surrounding society, or whether it too constitutes a sociopsychological model universally valid for that which it comprehends.

NOTES

(a) Adapted version of paper published in Comparative
Civilizations Review, 8, no. 3 (Fall 1979): 13-39.

(b) "Promethean" culture heroes who have stolen,
"through
cunning or daring," fire, grain, or the sheep from
the gods are familiar to a variety of preliterate societies
above the level of archaic cultivators.(19) But the myths
dealing with these heroes constitute descriptions of the origin
of a cultural trait rather than explanations of the behavior of
an individual. In the mythology of the Dogon, personal motivation for stealing fire, by the "ancestral constructor," from
"the workshop of the great Nummo, who are Heaven's smiths,"
is replaced by an impersonal assignment: he steals because
"his future task was to teach men the use of iron to enable

them to cultivate the land."(16)   In a sense, the primeval blacksmith of the Dogon is the <u>idea</u> of Prometheus without his <u>personality</u>.

(c) Prometheus' relations with feminine figures are specifically worth noting. By some accounts, it was Athena (whom Prometheus, by splitting the skull of Zeus, helped to be born; thus a woman "of the younger generation") who taught him many of the practical skills he then transmitted to men. And it was his mother, Themis, who provided him with his ultimate resource - knowledge of the future. Prometheus not only does not misuse women to gratify his whims (as Greek gods habitually do), but he makes good use of the creative strengths women possess and willingly share with him. He is unafraid to be dependent on women at the same time that he helps them. In contrast, there are no significant women in Satan's early history, and in his later career he manipulates women to achieve his goal of seducing men to do his bidding. In this respect, he is some what comparable to Zeus who sends Pandora, the first human woman, to punish men for receiving the Promethean gift of fire. But in the Greek scheme of metaphysical sobriety it was the highest god - not an evil spirit - who both misused women to indulge himself and manipulated them to exercise his control over men.

(d) Perceptions of the individual actor as <u>either</u> a blameless agent of a greater power (who does not consider himself responsible even when he commits evil acts) <u>or</u> as an entirely independent actor who establishes his own responsibilities by his own moral decision are peculiar to the Western civilization, but they (especially the latter, "Promethean" perception) tend to be lacking in other civilizations. Both notions are alien to Confucianism.(10,12)

(e) In Christian religious thought, the evil is sometimes perceived as "objectively necessary" to enhance man's understanding of the nature of the good or as a stage in man's development, through guilt and expiation, toward proper humility. But even when necessary for the benefit of <u>mankind</u>, the evil itself, as a component of the underlying moral structure, remains evil, does not evolve into the good or fuse with the good. Nor does the good, in its perfection, need evil: it is only men, with their imperfect understanding of the moral structure, who need evil as a "visual aid." The crucial point is that, in the medieval Christian tradition, the objective moral structure within which human existence is comprehended <u>is not perceived as evolving</u> through confrontations of "good" with "evil."

(f) Social conditions favoring the original elaboration of mythical construct do not have to be exactly replicated in the historical environments in which some versions of that construct later on acquires more or less of a popular appeal.

Thus the popularity of the Promethean theme in the literature of Augustan Rome is to be explained partly by the esteem it gave to Greek culture, and in part by its need for models of secular, activistic heroism.   Once the Promethean theme is available, it lends itself to be drawn upon, in literature, by the secular humanists and, in the visual arts, by the cultists of passion and suffering, whether religious or secular.(41) The theme had considerable prominence in Renaissance and Baroque art.

(g) And Denis Donoghue sees as the Promethean "form" or "genre" of feeling what is in fact a conflation of Dionysian and Faustian themes.   It is not Prometheus who has sought "intensity and vehemence" above all else, and it is not <u>his</u> myth that can be "interpreted as testifying to the endlessness and namelessness of man's desire."(7)   Such conflations of distinctive mythological paradigms, or the appearance of one in the guise of another, seem to be characteristic of periods in which the basic symbolic structure of a civilization is undergoing a breakdown or reorganization.

(h) In China, "legitimated protest was an intellectually central and institutionally prominent aspect of the traditional political culture."(29)   "Byzantine Christian officials, much more than Chinese Confucianists, were a despot's faceless men."(27)   Karl A. Wittfogel does not recognize the importance of the "symbolic" distinction made here.(51)

(i)   Like Prometheus, Tristan started out, in the medieval Welsh tradition, as a trickster - an origin unimaginable for the ever-serious Satan.

(j)   By 1210, however, a version of the Tristanic myth appears in which love potion is but a symbol of spontaneous mutual responsiveness.(18)

(k)   In Chinese Confucian thought, strong emotion between the sexes has tended to be perceived as not originating in the internal dynamics of a personality, but as "the work of others," induced from without.(40)

(l)   The reality of man and woman as equal cooperators in an important creative task emerged almost at the same time in the movement of affective mysticism.(30)

(m) Mary Douglas points out that "when moral rules are obscure or contradictory there is a tendency for pollution beliefs to simplify or clarify the point at issue."(8)

REFERENCES

(1) Abrams, M.H. <u>Natural Supernaturalism: Tradition and Revolution in Romantic Literature.</u> New York: W.W. Norton Company, 1971.

(2) Balazs, E. Chinese Civilization and Bureaucracy. New Haven: Yale University Press, 1964, p. 165.

(3) Bodde, D. Harmony and Conflict in Chinese Philosophy. In A.F. Wright (Ed), Studies in Chinese Thought. Chicago: The University of Chicago Press, 1953, pp. 19-80.

(4) Brinton, C. The Anatomy of Revolution. New York: Prentice-Hall, 1938.

(5) Cohn, N. The Pursuit of the Millennium: Revolutionary Messianism in Medieval and Reformation Europe and Its Bearing on Modern Totalitarian Movements. Rev. Ed. New York: Harper Torchbooks, 1961.

(6) De Rougemont, D. Love in the Western World. Rev. Ed. New York: Pantheon, 1956.

(7) Donoghue, D. Thieves of Fire. New York: Oxford University Press, 1974, pp. 20, 113.

(8) Dougles, M. Purity and Danger: An Analysis of Concepts of Pollution and Taboo. Baltimore: Penguin Books, 1970, p. 168.

(9) Dumont, L. Religion/Politics and History: Collected Papers in Indian Sociology. Paris: Mouton, 1970.

(10) Eberhard, W. Guilt and Sin in Traditional China. Berkeley: University of California Press, 1967.

(11) Eisner, S. The Tristan Legend: A Study in Sources. Evanston: Northwestern University Press, 1969.

(12) Fingarette, H. Confucius - the Secular as Sacred. New York: Harper Torchbooks, 1972.

(13) Friedman, M. Problematic Rebel: Melville, Dostoievsky, Kafka, Camus. Rev. Ed. Chicago: The University of Chicago Press, 1970.

(14) Gilson, É. Heloise and Abelard. Ann Arbor: The University of Michigan Press, 1960.

(15) Granet, M. Right and Left in China. In R. Needham (Ed.), Right & Left: Essays on Dual Symbolic Classification. Chicago: The University of Chicago Press, 1973, pp. 43-58.

(16) Griaule, M. Conversations with Ogotemmêli: An Introduction to Dogon Religious Ideas. London: Oxford University Press, 1965, pp. 41-42.

(17) Guerard, A., Jr. Prometheus and the Aeolian Lyre. The Yale Review, Vol. 33, 1944, pp. 482-497.

(18) Jackson, W. T.H. The Anatomy of Love: The Tristan of Gottfried von Strasburg. New York: Columbia University Press, 1971.

(19) Jensen, A.E. Myth and Cult among Primitive Peoples. Chicago: The University of Chicago Press, 1963, pp. 112, 107.

(20) Kavolis, V. Literature and the Dialectics of Modernization. In J.P. Strelka (Ed.), Literary Criticism and Sociology. University Park: The Pennsylvania State University Press, 1973, pp. 89-106.

(21) Kerényi, C. Dionysos: Archetypal Image of Indestructible Life. Princeton, N.J.: Princeton University Press, 1976.

(22) Kerényi, C. Prometheus: Archetypal Image of Human Existence. New York: Bollingen Foundation, 1963, pp. 54-55.

(23) Kerényi, Karl. The Trickster in Relation to Greek Mythology. In P. Radin, The Trickster: A Study in American Indian Mythology. New York: Philosophical Library, 1956, pp. 180-182.

(24) Kluger, R.S. Satan in the Old Testament. Evanston: Northwestern University Press, 1967.

(25) Kott, J. The Eating of the Gods: An Interpretation of Greek Tragedy. New York: Random House, 1973, p. 186.

(26) Langton, E. Satan, A Portrait: A Study of the Character of Satan Through All the Ages. London: Skeffington & Sons, Ltd., 1945, pp. 69, 67.

(27) Levenson, J.R. Confucian China and Its Modern Fate: A Trilogy. Vol. II. Berkeley: University of California Press, 1965, p. 97.

(28) Little, D. Religion, Order, and Law: A Study in Pre-Revolutionary England. New York: Harper & Row, 1969.

(29) Metzger, T.A. On Chinese Political Culture. The Journal of Asian Studies, Vol. 32, 1972, p. 102.

(30) Moller, H. The Social Causation of Affective Mysticism. Journal of Social History, Vol. 4, 1971, pp. 305-338.

(31) Muckle, J.T. (Ed.). The Story of Abelard's Adversities: A Translation with Notes of the Historia Calamitatum. Toronto: The Pontifical Institute of Medieval Studies, 1964. Esp. pp. 26-37.

(32) Murray, A.V. Abelard and St. Bernard: A Study in Twelfth Century "Modernism." Manchester: Manchester University Press, 1967.

(33) Murray, H.A. The Personality and Career of Satan. Journal of Social Issues, Vol. 18, 1962, pp. 36-54.

(34) Nelson, B. Actors, Directors, Roles, Cues, Meanings, Identities: Further Thoughts on 'Anomie.' The Psychoanalytic Review, Vol. 51, 1964, pp. 135-160.

(35) Nelson, B. De Profundis: . . . Responses to Friends and Critics. Sociological Analysis, Vol. 35, 1974, pp. 129-141.

(36) Nelson, B., and V. Kavolis. The Civilization-Analytic Approach to Comparative Studies. Comparative Civilizations Bulletin, No. 5, 1973, pp. 13-14.

(37) O'Flaherty, W.D. Asceticism and Eroticism in the Mythology of Siva. London: Oxford University Press, 1973.

(38) Osmond, R.E. Body, Soul, and the Marriage Relationship: The History of an Analogy. Journal of the History of Ideas, Vol. 34, 1973, p. 290.

(39) Otto, W.F. Dionysus: Myth and Cult. Bloomington: Indiana University Press, 1965.

(40) Pye, L. The Spirit of Chinese Politics: A Psychocultural Study of the Authority Crisis in Political Development. Cambridge, Mass.: The M.I.T. Press, 1968, p. 156.

(41) Raggio, O. The Myth of Prometheus: Its Survival and Metamorphoses up to the Eighteenth Century. Journal of the Warburg and Courtauld Institutes, Vol. 21, 1958, pp. 44-62.

(42) Ricoeur, P. The Symbolism of Evil. Boston: Beacon Press, 1969, p. 218.

(43) Slater, P.E. The Glory of Hera: Greek Mythology and the Greek Family. Boston: Beacon Press, 1968.

(44) Solmsen, F. Hesiod and Aeschylus. Ithaca, N.Y.: Cornell University Press, 1949.

(45) Tcherikover, V. Hellenistic Civilization and the Jews. New York: Atheneum, 1970.

(46) Thomas, K. Religion and the Decline of Magic. New York: Charles Scribner's Sons, 1971.

(47) Thomson, G. Aeschylus and Athens: A Study in the Social Origins of Drama. London: Lawrence & Wishart, 1966.

(48) Walzer, M. The Revolution of the Saints: A Study in the Origins of Radical Politics. Cambridge, Mass.: Harvard University Press, 1965.

(49) Weber, M. The Sociology of Religion. Boston: Beacon Press, 1964, p. 51.

(50) Whiting, B.B. Sex Identity Conflict and Physical Violence: A Comparative Study. American Anthropologist, Vol. 67, 1965, No. 6, Part II, pp. 123-140.

(51) Wittfogel, K.A. Oriental Despotism: A Comparative Study of Total Power. New Haven: Yale University Press, 1957.

(52) Wu Ch'eng-en. Monkey. New York: Grove Press, 1958.

(53) Yu, A.C. (Tr.). The Journey to the West. Vol. I. Chicago: The University of Chicago Press, 1976.

3 The Unraveling of the Myth of Progress
Moshe Amon

In this chapter I examine the myths and fantasies in the minds of terrorists and how these myths are related to the ramshackle world of Western civilization, where religion is in a state of crisis and many established myths are losing their meaning and significance. For this purpose, I would like to posit here that religions usually operate through myths that describe the transcendental as penetrating into our world at a certain point in history. This event endows history with a special meaning, as it shapes the fate of the human race and directs humanity toward a predestined end. Each moment in history, every participant, and every occurrence are then endowed with special meaning derived from this unique event. Each myth serves as a basis for an order of things, and the laws derived from this order are therefore in accord with the initial event. Different myths will generate different laws. A myth may serve as a basis for a static social order, as in the case of those described by Levi-Strauss as societies "without writing,"(1) in which the social structure is kept stable by a continuous imitation of the prehistoric events that are believed to have shaped this structure. Other myths may allow for a dynamic type of a society by depicting, for example, a fugue-type structure in which two opposing themes, such as good and evil or light and dark, pursue each other in an incessant chase, leading eventually to a different structure and a different myth.

Social stability may be measured by the degree to which society is in tune with its dominant myth, as a society is most stable when most of the phases of life are directed according to a religious myth. The less the myth provides a rationale for all phases of daily life, social mores, or mode of government, the more secular and dynamic the society becomes. When a myth withdraws from the social scene, the religion

coupled with it loses much of its validity and vigor. Without
an accompanying myth, the religion seems to be anchored only
in institutions and suffers a decline in authority and meaning.
The more technological a society becomes, the more it "slides"
away from the sphere of the prevailing myth, until this myth
is seen as a mere superstition.

Such a withdrawal of religious myth occurred in the 16th
century and allowed for the advancement of science and the
industrial revolution, as well as for a series of social and
political revolutions. With the decline of the prevailing myths
of the Middle Ages and the advancement of technology, religion
lost much of its authority and was replaced by a new secular
myth, that of progress - the myth of a continuous advance
toward a future utopia, as opposed to the old myth of a lost
paradise. The transcendental, together with all its ensuing
functions, was removed from the historical scene. With the
new myth of progress came a shift toward technological needs,
toward a material world and material needs. The myth of
progress, which becomes a modern form of a secular religion,
tends to shape a cold, mechanical world, a world that reduces
emotions into their elementary components - love into sex, and
compassion into utility. In this situation, human beings
become alienated from their human or spiritual nature and from
the world of the spirit. Man acts upon nature but he is no
longer in a dialogue with it. Without enough external stimuli
to facilitate creative spiritual activity and sublimation, man
turns into his inner self - into the world of voices from his
subconscious. Under these conditions, the stimuli for spiritual
life emerge from the primitive, archetypal elements of his
nature. Human society reverts, then, into the primeval element of Thanatos - the myth of self-destruction.

In ancient myths and beliefs, death was signified as a
descent into the nether world. In order to reach this world,
the dead had to cross Lethe, the river of forgetfulness. On
crossing this river, one forgot one's past and was cut off from
the world of the living, thus becoming a denizen of the world
of the dead. This separation from the past is indigenous to
the myth of progress, which serves as the fundamental myth
of the modern world. It involves a continuous crossing of
Lethe and accordingly signifies a transition into the nether
world, a world without historical memory. Prior to the 16th
century, major social changes were termed renaissance, sig-
nifying a renewal of something presumed to have existed already in the past; beginning with the 16th century, similar
changes have been termed revolution. The era of revolutions
led to a process of continuous separation from the past, a
striving to erase historical memory, until, in the 20th century,
we have managed to reach the level of the subconscious, to
penetrate the precultural layers of our minds. Our thought
processes seem to act through myths that give direction to our

thoughts; the irrational reveals itself through mythological
forms and symbols.

We have to think through the myth before reaching its
borders and the return of rational thought. We should reach
the limit of the conventional before breaking out of it. But,
in the long run, the myth of progress leads the thought process to a dead end where, after eliminating all past memory,
nothing remains but the point of the beginning, where no
thought exists. The forward advance leads paradoxically into
the primitive past, into the dream world of nightmare. In this
world the handsome prince still wears the form of a frog,
Psyche is still married to a faceless Cupid who visits her only
under the cover of night, Red Riding Hood is swallowed by
the hungry wolf, and we all live snugly inside the belly of the
whale.

The myth of progress calls for liberation from the fetters
of the order shaped by old myths. The responsible person is
no longer seen as the one who tries to preserve the social
structure but rather the one who tries to destroy it in order
to pave the way for the ideal future. In the process of
destruction, everyone can take part, including the meek and
the lowly, who thus gain the respectability of belonging to the
avant garde.

As the modern myth of progress is being shaped according to technical specifications, its priests and acolytes are not
required to possess any ancient knowledge. When the social
structure no longer even attempts to reflect the transcendental
but is directed toward the satisfaction of immediate material
needs, the knowledge needed for the preservation of this
structure is of a technical and material nature alone.

The myth of progress entertains the notion of liberation
from the old social and political structure, its advance is very
often accompanied by the assassination and liquidation of the
leaders of the old regime. In the 16th century, nationalistic
movements of the time of the Reformation adopted assassination
as a common political device. The revolutions in England,
France, and Russia led to the execution of their kings. The
romantic movement of the 19th century witnessed the assassination of Lincoln in America, and of Alexander II in Russia,
and even the rise of the concept of the death of God Himself.
In Germany, the 20th century began with the Wandervoegel
youth movement seeking the joys to be found at the bosom of
nature, and continued with political assassinations, the rise of
the Nazi movement, and the installation of extermination camps.
In America, the decade that started with the assassination of
Kennedy continued not only with the movement of "flower
children" but also with bombs exploding in university li-
braries.

All myths of creation start with a state of chaos. This is
the beginning point; therefore, all revolutions claim to return

to this point in order to legitimize the new order of things. The Reformation claimed a return to the beginnings of Christianity; and the modern state is based upon theories that depict an inchoate state of nature. These theories replaced the myths that granted to each person and class a definite role and place in a more or less stable social and political order. Yet, old gods do not die with one stroke; the death of a god is a very slow process. Nor do old religions. Religions are, however, in a state of crisis as the technological society and the boundaries of the cosmos extend far beyond the limits of the myths that these religions embraced.

At the same time, those parts of society that disengaged themselves completely from religion and from myth find that they are bereft of a personal role and status in a world that no longer has an inherently defined principle of order. Hence the rise of theories that strive to reshape the social order according to a new coordinating principle – theories of natural rights, social contract, liberalism, competition, socialism, communism, and an array of social and anthropological schools. All of these are secular teachings and therefore lack the same authority and sanction that the concept of the presence of God in history imposed upon premodern social orders. This situation leads to the rise of new religious sects and of nationalism and racism, as a means of fusing the particles back into peoples and of regaining the lost feeling of fraternity.

But without the knowledge of its past, a society is doomed to a state of perdurable childhood, of perpetual desire, with no awareness of its own limitations. The content of the past is transmitted into the future through language, literature, history, philosophy, and all forms of art, and it is this content that facilitates future growth. Only the primitive lacks the knowledge of history, and modern society worships the primitive. Language, history, philosophy, and art are bridges between the future and the past, and when we no longer believe that the contents of the past are worth transmitting, we allow the bridges to collapse. With them collapse the means of communication, not only between future and past, but also between the different parts of the social body at the present time.

Society is condemned, then, to anarchy and decay. The fact that many high school graduates are practically illiterate is not so much the fault of television as it is the fault of the liberal belief that the holdings of this generation, spiritual as well as material, do not deserve to be transmitted to the next generation and so should not shape the fate and nature of the young. (It is worth noting, nevertheless, that most television "sages" are liberals.) The result is that the young generations are becoming more primitive, more barbarian, more violent, and more amenable to the beat of the tom tom than to the message of our cultural inheritance. If the social body – past, present, and future - forms in essence one organism, then severing the umbilical cord, which is the conduit of the values and the contents of the past, and without roots nothing can grow to see the future. When one generation declines to mold the shape and the nature of the next, this generation is doomed to have no future.

When different generations see no need for conversing with one another, language dies. With no medium of communication, each individual feels isolated, alienated, out of place. Without cultural nourishment, individuals feel insecure, unable to sustain themselves; they therefore seek the support of their government to shape and to secure their lives. But this situation only intensifies their feeling of insecurity, since the more a person yields of his compass of responsibility, the smaller the scope of his personal security becomes. The more a person depends on the government, the more his own personality becomes effaced. Every new law, every new form of taxation changes the situation of each individual and does not allow him, even though only for a short period, to plan and shape his own life.

Paradoxically, the more a government is busy enacting new laws, the more the individual citizen has the feeling of living in a lawless society, in a state of anarchy, where frequent changes of laws are bringing about the dissolution of the social body. Reduced to particles, driven to a state of isolation and solitude, people are looking for means to break out of the mold that forced them into such confinement. Without language and other traditional means of communication, they turn to violence. The more a free society depends upon its government - and without alternative social organizations that can check aggression, as, for example, is the case with Indian tribes on reservations - the more violent it will become. War is another means of removing the confines between individuals and between nations. War brings individuals to situations where expressions of comradeship, compassion, and mutual responsibility are quite common. Until the Vietnam War, which brought the cruel side of war into the living room of every home, war often was a means for national and social unity. Terrorism represents another, quite sophisticated, way of breaking barriers and of finding comradeship, common goals, and fraternity on an international level.

The modern terrorists are offshoots of the nineteenth-century revolutionists, of those who followed to the extreme the myth of material progress and rebelled against the religious myths at a period when society at large still supported them. As they could not find objects or symbols of identification in their own society, they looked for ideal types of periods that preceded the foundation of the myths prevailing in their own: the periods of Rome, Athens and Jerusalem. The French revolutionaries identified themselves with Plutarch's

Roman heroes, the nineteenth-century revolutionaries chose for themselves Greek pagan names like Anaxagoras and Anacharsis. James H. Billington notes that the "recurrent mythic model for revolutionaries - early romantics, the young Marx, the Russians of Lenin's times - was Prometheus."(2) Billington points also to the fact that the further they went in history to look for their "Holy Other," the more extreme they became.(3)

In the second half of the 20th century, both the myth of progress and the historical horizons from which to draw have run their course and exhausted themselves. Modern terrorists seem to be people without a knowledge of history and without a memory of the origins of their own culture. Billington notes that not only do modern revolutionaries lack a perspective on history but they also are uninterested even in the available academic literature about the revolutionary tradition.(4) Modern terrorists do not try to emulate other historical forms of organization; furthermore, quite often they have no established hierarchy of authority except that of the leader of each group. Yet, in this way of life they manage to satisfy their need for solidarity on an international scale, as well as to find a feeling of fulfillment and a common language with other groups.

The myth of material progress initiated the movement of a cyclic social whirl that shattered the foundations of a social structure with a solid center consisting of an emperor and a pope - one representing worldly power, the other spiritual power, and both together, universal order. When Luther removed the pope from the center, he also removed the authority that legitimized the power of the emperor. With this act he started a worldwide movement that led to a gradual removal of the source of authority from the center out to the periphery. From here on, the sequence of social classes that got into the center formed and shaped the character of the whole social body. In this process, every loop in the spiral, as it reached the center, adopted an ideal image from the historical periphery to support a new myth that could legitimize its claim to authority over a center that had lost its own myth and legitimacy. At the beginning of this century, with the spread of the concept of equality, the center came to adopt the most peripheral image, and consequently there were no historical horizons left to support a new myth, man himself took the place of God.

Luther removed the pope from the center by declaring him to be the anti-Christ, and thus the pope was cast into the nether world to join the company of Lucifer, Cronus, Saturn, and other fallen gods and angels who symbolize the incarnation of the cosmic blacksmith who forges the tools for the control of this world. With the transfer of authority from the center to

the periphery, the whole structure became fluid, free to move.
And move it did, driven by a messianic myth of perpetual war
between the powers of good and the powers of evil. As in the
instance of Luther and the pope, everyone ousted from the
center has been considered the embodiment of the reactionary
powers of evil, forming a threat to progress and enlighten-
ment. Humanity disengaged itself from the fetters of the past
and became free to shape its own fate and to extend its rule
over nature in accord with human will and human comprehension. But without a myth that sets common ends to nature
and to man as a product of nature, man acts upon nature
according to an arbitrary will. To allow this will a free hand,
each new group that enters the center accommodates the laws
to a social structure that changes perpetually to comply with
changing technical needs.

The modern state is in a situation that necessarily leads
to a continuous condition of antinomian revolt, as it incessantly
destroys all the elements that represent past traditions and
customs. The first target for destruction is usually the god
of the last myth that established the previous order and its
accommodating laws. This god (and in our times, at the last
stages of the myth of progress, the place of this god is always
being taken by a human being) is murdered because he allegedly represents the powers of evil that try to force the world
to implement their sinister goals. Thus, the myth of progress, coupled with messianic expectations in a secular form,
has evoked the old gnostic concept of the evil god who created
this world in his image.(5) With the death of God, man becomes free to exercise his will with no restraint, freed from
modes of thought and behavior shaped by numerous generations in order to control his social behaviour, including the
inhibition of aggression and violence.

The era of revolutions drew out the image of the Faustian
personality, the one who sacrificed his soul to Satan to satisfy
a boundless desire for the treasures of this world. Since the
16th century, the image of Satan has been evoked on the
historical scene with unprecedented intensity and might.
Revolutionaries and terrorists consider all others to be in the
service of the devil. Those in the center consider the revolutionaries to be in alliance with Satan. We have here a
concept of an inverted covenant, in opposition to the covenant
between God and man. The social contract that serves as a
basis for the political theory of the modern state represents an
attempt to steer the liberated forces and disjoined individuals
to follow a principle of order that answers to the spirit of the
people or of universal history. But in an era in which the
hero of Turgenev's Fathers and Sons (1861) chooses for himself the name Nihilist, disclaiming everything that his parents
represent, every social group can claim to be the sole representative of the Mortal God. Opposing groups are therefore

viewed as representatives of the adversary power, that is, the devil.

Since the 16th century, the images of Faust and the devil imbue all forms of Western civilization - in literature, religion, and politics. Since then, Western civilization has been in an incessant state of civil strife between those who wish to destroy the social order in anticipation of an impending messianic era, and those who consider the revolutionaries to be in league with the devil. The more society disengages itself from past traditions and institutions, the more it gets on the road leading to violence, civil wars, riots, dissent movements, kidnapping, strikes, and so on. Unbound and unchecked by traditional norms and institutions, people become more violent in their efforts to break out of their confinement. Terrorism thus serves both as a means to fight Satan who presumably has a pact with other social groups, and as a way to find human fraternity and solidarity, common to all those who serve in the front line.

Revolutionary and terrorist ideologies usually fall into a messianic, gnostic, and apocalyptic genre. They claim to represent, here and now, the attributes of the world to come, to know the nature of this ideal world, and quite often even who its "messiah" is. This knowledge stems from a conviction that they have "seen the light" and are therefore the only "enlightened" people. One sees what one is looking for, and they choose to look at the seamy side of society, which they believe to reflect the whole. With the inner certainty that this world is hopeless and cannot be mended, as it is wholly infused with evil, they propose to demolish it and to build something new out of the remains.

Their belief that they are the only ones to represent the powers of light stems from the conviction that they are the only ones who see the real world, and the only ones who are not affected by its depravity. It is their mission, therefore, to "liberate" the blind people of this world from the rule of the unjust; by this they are doing "justice" because in their opinion they are the only ones who represent a kernel of justice in an unjust world. They differ from each other in degree of inner conviction, and thus form a wide array of different movements - from liberals who seek only to initiate a change, to anarchists and nihilists who seek destruction, to communist and other millennial movements which believe that they already live in the ideal world and therefore limit their acts of destruction to the world outside their borders.

The apocalyptic and, most likely, also the gnostic trends of messianism started in Judaism in the second century BC, and were carried later into Western society by movements that deserted and rejected Judaism. It is interesting, therefore, to note that a somewhat similar phenomenon also happened in the

modern era. I tend to agree with J. H. Billington's claim that
the roots of modern revolutionary movements are to be found
more in German occultism and protoromanticism than in the rational trends of the French Revolution. Much of his evidence
rests upon the influence of the secret order of Illuminists
founded in 1776 by the Bavarian professor Adam Weishaupt,
and

> dedicated to Weishaupt's Rousseauian vision of
> leading all humanity to a new moral perfection freed
> from all established religious and political authority.
> . . . The revolutionaries' primitive vision of the
> world as a dualistic struggle between the force of
> darkness and of light may originate in the neo-
> Manichaean view of Weishaupt's followers that their
> elect group of "illuminated ones" was engaged in
> struggle with "the sons of darkness," their cate-
> gorical name for all outside the order.(6)

Illuminists and ex-Illuminists became members of different
Masonic orders and had some impact upon the formation of
their theories and mode of action.(7) Illuminists' ideas
affected the views of Count Mirabeau, Nicholas Bonneville, and
Fillippo Buonarroti - the prototype of the nineteenth- and
twentieth-century revolutionaries. Yet, nineteenth-century
revolutionists were politically oriented. Modern terrorists, on
the other hand, seem to be less politically oriented, but
manipulated much more by external political powers and cal-
culations. The Revolutionary Catechism of Nechaev, the
"founder" of modern terrorism, is concerned only with techniques of destruction, as is the most "celebrated" text of
twentieth-century terrorism, Marighella's Minimanual. Both
revolutionaries and terrorists have been recruited from among
those who feel culturally, socially, or politically alienated,
especially when they are under the impression, right or
wrong, of being powerless to influence the affairs of their
society. The differences in motivation and mode of action
between the nineteenth-century revolutionaries and twentieth-
century terrorists are, in my opinion, due not so much to
different political situations as to differences in the cultural
climate. An understanding of the cultural scene seems to be
imperative for the comprehension of the phenomena of both
revolutionaries and terrorists.
        The Reformation, which marked the beginning of the
modern era, strove to recapture the spirit of the original
Christian church. But, as we now know, this spirit was expressed not only in the New Testament but also in a great
variety of gnostic and apocalyptic schools of thought. Those
schools fit very well into the modern trend toward invalidating
all past authority, tradition and law. "The gnostic God," says

Hans Jonas, "has more of the <u>nihil</u> than the <u>ens</u> [being] in his concept . . . for all purposes of man's relation to the reality that surrounds him this hidden God is a nihilistic conception: no <u>nomos</u> emanates from him, no law for nature and thus none for <u>human</u> action as a part of the natural order."(8)

Since the 16th century, an array of variegated social and political schools of thought, as well as different religions, are competing for our souls. As the monolithic social structure of the Middle Ages was sundered, man also came to be torn between different choices and modes of action, each claiming to represent the final solution to all problems. In this situation, according to Sartre, with each decision that a person makes, he is aware that he is sacrificing all other possibilities; each choice signifies an elimination of the rest. The freedom acquired by leaving the transcendental outside one's world is a desperate kind of freedom: freedom that inspires anxiety, fear, and passivity. Orwell phrased it well in his assessment of Henry Miller and the literary history of the 1930s:

> Progress and reaction have both turned out to be swindles. Seemingly there is nothing left but quietism - robbing reality of its terrors by simply submitting to it. Get inside the whale (for you are, of course). Give yourself over to the world-process, stop fighting against it or pretending that you control it; simply accept it, endure it, record it. . . . The "democratic vistas" have ended in barbed wire. There is less feeling of creation and growth, less and less emphasis on the cradle, more and more emphasis on the teapot, endlessly stewing. To accept civilisation as it is practically means accepting decay. It has ceased to be a strenuous attitude and become a passive attitude - even "decadent", if that word means anything. . . . To say "I accept" in an age like our own is to say that you accept concentration camps, rubber truncheons, Hitler, Stalin, bombs, aeroplanes, tinned food, machine-guns, putsches, purges, slogans, Bedaux belts, gas-masks, submarines, spies, provocateurs, press censorship, secret prisons, aspirins, Hollywood films and political murders.(9)

Every revolution, social or political, gives rise to a new myth and creates a new language that draws its terminology from this myth. With the ongoing process of social dissolution, the same words no longer mean the same things for all people. Babel is thus in a state of anarchy. In the era of progress and revolution, not only myth and religion lost their rationale but also the whole weft of Western civilization. Without a knowledge of the thoughts of those who preceded us, we cannot know ourselves, as those thoughts fashioned us and molded the world we live in. It is the voice of the past which defines the present and, unable to hear this voice, we have no self-definition and no self-esteem. We are driven into a constant state of alienation. No longer do we dare to define the shape of future generations by injecting our voice into the process of education. All we dare do is to substitute real knowledge with information of the kind we consider to be relevant to the life of future generations; but in a highly technological society the scope of relevance diminishes with each moment. We presume to send the young into the future without the fetters of the past, but in reality we deprive them of the knowledge necessary to uphold a very complex structure.

As a result, modern people are being drawn to the simplest nostrums. But simple solutions cannot sustain a complex society, and simple people are unable to understand the nature of this complexity. By depriving the young generations of an education that allows them a good understanding of the process that shaped civilization, we deprive them of their future in a civilized world. The process cannot begin anew with each generation, as the point of the beginning is a point of chaos, and each beginning drives us back to that point. Nineteenth-century revolutionists differ from twentieth-century terrorists mainly in the fact that they still had enough cultural heritage to sustain them, enough cultural and historical horizons to find a model for identification and to evoke new myths from the past. Twentieth-century terrorists, on the other hand, are the product of a society weary unto death of the myth of progress, a society with no cultural background left to keep it viable.

Economics and technology are means of keeping society strong, but only culture can keep it alive. Human beings can preserve a social and economic structure, but economic factors cannot preserve humanity. When the social body is in the process of eating its own flesh, it will produce the agents that will hasten this process, and these agents are right in assuming that they represent an historical trend. The agents of destruction are nourished by putrefaction, while the antibodies that can arrest their action grow only on ground manured with the knowledge of our cultural background. The more cultural the body gets, the more strength it has for resisting all agents of doom and destruction. Just recently, Indians in Paraguay who were not allowed to observe their customs and rituals refused to eat and preferred to die, as they no longer considered themselves to be men. (10) The starving people of Cambodia have been asking Buddhist monks to renew the ritual of begging for food, wishing to share with the monks what little they have, in order to restore a sense of worth and to rebuild the entire structure of social and religious life. (11) The Jews have put a similar accent on culture during more than three millennia of continuous and viable history, and thus have preserved their identity through a history replete with hardships and persecution.

We are victims of the modern trend toward disregarding everything that is not new, but by adopting this approach we lose our own self-esteem, as by eradicating the past we get out of touch with the rationale for our own existence. By ignoring the past and drawing only on the future, the myth of progress has demolished the world of yesterday with its myths and religions; at this point in history it has exhausted itself, along with our past and the prospects for our future.

Now, as we near the end of the road, we can continue in the same direction and fall into the abyss – or we can change direction and take the opposite course. A trend common among present-day conservatives is that of fundamentalism, evident both in Christianity and in Islam; but the fundamentalists are already the product of a culture that has lost its memory. Simple nostrums offered by most unsophisticated and bathetic conservatives cannot sustain a most sophisticated and complex society. Each revolution has carried us closer toward Lethe, the river of forgetfulness. With each revolution the top of the social pyramid descended further toward the nether world until, in our age of super-accent on equality, the top is almost level with the bottom in the land of Hades.

Yet, hope for the future lies precisely in the fact that society has been reduced to individuals, since during and through this process, the individual has been discovered. Now is the time for the individual to rediscover society by plunging back into the now dark past, by relearning and reintroducing himself to history – to the rationale that erected all those institutions and values that we so readily deserted. We can overcome the past and release ourselves from its embrace only by knowing it and turning it into a part of our own conscious self. But this time the expanses of the past are much wider than those adumbrated by Western civilization alone, as on our way to self-destruction we have passed through many other cultures and religions. Now we shall have to integrate all of them in our renewed dialogue with the past. The result will be a viable society, resembling nothing in past history. In the process of adopting the past we shall most likely discover the religions and the myths of the future. We shall then be able to establish the future on a much broader, more secure, and, most likely, more viable foundation than ever before.

NOTES

(1) Claude Levi-Strauss, Myth and Meaning (Toronto: University of Toronto Press, 1978), p. 15.

(2) James H. Billington, Fire in the Minds of Men: Origins of the Revolutionary Faith (New York: Basic Books, 1980), p. 6.

(3) Ibid., p. 7.

(4) Ibid., p. 10.

(5) "Gnosticism" (a term derived from the Greek word "gnosis," knowledge), is a collective name for many sects and religions which appeared at about the beginning of the Christian era. The main features of their teaching is that our material world is the realm of darkness, created and dominated by the powers of evil, and is in complete opposition to the nature of God which is alien to this world, unknown in it, and not responsible for what happens in it:

> Gnosticism has been the most radical embodiment of dualism ever to have appeared on the stage of history, and its exploration provides a case study of all that is implicated in it. It is a split between self and world, men's alienation from nature, the metaphysical devaluation of nature, the cosmic solitude of the spirit and the nihilism of mundane norms; and in its general extremist style it shows what radicalism really is. [Hans Jonas, "A Retrospective View" in Proceedings of the International Colloquium on Gnosticism, Stockholm 1973, Brill, Leiden.]

(6) Billington, p. 94.

(7) Among the influx of former German Illuminists into Paris at the time of the French Revolution, Billington mentions the name of the Frey brothers. Now, Siegmund Gottlob Junius Brutus Frey was one of the pseudonyms used by a most fascinating personality of the time: Moses Dobruska, alias Franz Thomas von Schonfeld. M. Dobruska and his brother Emanuel came to Paris in March 1792, joined the Jacobins, and were guillotined in April 1794, together with Danton and Francois Chabot, who was married to their sister. Besides being a member of a regular Masonic group, Dobruska, known then as von Schonfeld, also belonged to the group that founded and drafted the charter of the Knights of the True Light (Ritter vom Wahren Licht), and its later derivation, the order of Asiatic Brothers (Asiatisch Brueder), and most likely also to the Illuminists. Born to a Jewish family which belonged to the Sabbatian sect, Dobruska along with other members of his

family converted to Christianity in 1775. They all changed their name to Schonfeld, and were ennobled in 1778.

His mother was a cousin of Jacob Frank, who formed his own sect within the Sabbatian movement and declared himself the last and real messiah, the incarnation of the real and "good god." After converting to Islam in 1757, Frank converted to Christianity in 1759 together with about a thousand of his followers. Like a similar Jewish-Islamic-Sabbetean sect, the Dohnmeh of Salonica, Greece, the Frankists kept to themselves and went on observing Frankish and Jewish as well as Christian customs. Frank's teaching was what Gershom Scholem calls nihilistic-antinomism with a strong Manichaean influence.

Frank's basic motif was destruction, demolition of all religions, all laws and all common values, in order to liberate the world from the dominion of what he conceived as the "three evil leaders of the world" and to pave the way for the rule of the "good god" through his incarnation Jacob Frank, and his daughter Eva. He commanded his followers, Jews and Christians, to destroy all religions from within by transgressing their laws, and to become soldiers so as to decimate and devastate all existing social and political orders.

The links of Dobruska to this sect are well established, and it is known that, after Frank's death, his followers chose Dobruska to be his successor, a position Dobruska declined. For a while, during the French Revolution and the Napoleonic Wars, the Frankists believed that their leader's vision was coming true; but during the 19th century the movement practically faded away. Yet it seems that through people like Dobruska some Frankish ideas, including the use of some inverted Kabbalistic symbols, may have penetrated movements like the Illuminists and such semi-Masonic orders as the Asiatic Brothers and through them, or in some other ways, also some revolutionary groups.

Gershom Scholem wrote an extensive essay about Dobruska, "A Career of a Frankist: the Metamorphoses of Moses Dobruska," in Studies and Texts Concerning the History of Sabbatianism and Its Metamorphoses (Jerusalem: Mosad Bialik, 1974; Hebrew); see also his "Ein verschollener juedischer mystiker der Aufklaerungszeit": E. J. Hirschfeld, in Yearbook VII of the Leo Baeck Institute, pp. 247-278. See also Jacob Katz, Freemasons and Jews (Jerusalem: Mosad Bialik, 1968: Hebrew), chap. 3.

(8) Hans Jonas, The Gnostic Religion (Boston: Bacon Press, 1963), p. 332.

(9) "Inside the Whale," in The Collected Essays, Journalism and Letters of George Orwell, ed. Sonia Orwell and Ian Angus (London, Secker & Warburg 1968), Vol. 1, pp. 526, 500, 499.

(10) In a paper read by Richard Arens at a convention on Psychology and Political Violence, Terrorism and Assassination, November 1979, at the University of Chicago.

(11) <u>Time</u>, November 17, 1980, p. 72.

4 International Terrorism and the Just War

John Dugard

While terror directed at civilian targets is widely condemned in Western countries as senseless and unjustifiable, the same acts are often viewed in many Third World countries as noble acts of "freedom fighters." Most Westerners would be surprised to learn that the Third World argument is based largely on a respectable Western philosophical tradition: that of the "just war." Like the crusader of a bygone era, the modern-day terrorist sees himself as being engaged in a just war in which right and justice are exclusively on his side and he is absolved from the customary restraints on the use of violence employed in his struggle.

This chapter examines the notion of the just war in its historical and modern setting in order to demonstrate its influence upon politico-legal thought in the Third World, and its contribution to the justification of wars of national liberation and acts of terror committed in the furtherance of these wars.

1. THE JUST WAR, ANCIENT AND MODERN

A. The History of the Just War

The idea of the just war, jus ad bellum, has been a recurring theme in Western philosophy. St. Augustine, St. Thomas

*This article first appeared in 1977 in STANFORD JOURNAL OF INTERNATIONAL STUDIES XII, 21-37. Only minor alterations have been made to the article. I am grateful to the Stanford Journal of International Law and to Fred Rothman and Company for the right to reprint.

Aquinas, Franciscus de Victoria, Gentilis, Grotius, and a host of other philosophers, theologians, and jurists sought to distinguish just wars from unjust wars and enunciate the circumstances which justify resorting to war, the ultimate means of terror.(1) St. Thomas Aquinas, for example, required both fault on the part of the attacked party and a "right intention" (recta intentio), an intention to advance good or avoid evil, on the part of the belligerent claiming a just cause.(2) Grotius was more specific: just causes were defense, recovery of property, and punishment; unjust causes included the "desire for richer land," the "desire for freedom among a subject people," and the "desire to rule others against their will on the pretext that it is for their own good."(3)

As the concept of the just war was largely a creature of Christian philosophy, it is hardly surprising that wars against the infidel non-Christians were categorized as "just."(4) Although some theologians, such as Franciscus de Victoria,(5) raised their voices against this view, particularly when it was used as a rationalization for imperialist expansion in the New World, it remained prevalent. From the earliest days, therefore, the doctrine of the just war served the cause of one faith or ideology at the expense of another.

The development of this doctrine intensified the severity of warfare's violence. When a belligerent's cause was deemed to be just, God was on its side, and military action on its behalf became the instrument of God's will and retribution. Accordingly, there was no room for a jus in bello (the humanitarian laws of war), and the most barbarous methods were permitted, and used, to subject the unjust opponent to the imputed wrath of God. This was particularly true in the case of wars in the name of Christianity, when the restraints of chivalry were jettisoned in the interests of the only "true" faith. Even so progressive a thinker as Franciscus de Victoria stated:

> Sometimes it is lawful and expedient to kill all the guilty. The proof is that war is waged in order to get peace and security. But there are times when security cannot be got save by destroying all one's enemies: and this is especially the case against unbelievers, from whom it is useless ever to hope for a just peace on any terms. And as [sic] the only remedy is to destroy all of them who can bear arms against us, provided they have already been in fault.(6)

The just war was clearly inimical to notions of equal treatment for combatants on both sides and of minimum standards of humanity in the field. Professor Draper has thus asserted that ". . . the importance attributed to the idea of the just war throughout the Middle Ages and well into the seventeenth century undoubtedly delayed the appearance of any body of rules restraining the more barbarous practices of warfare."(7)

The notion of the just war was discarded after the Peace of Westphalia in 1648, and State practices gradually came to reflect Machiavelli's philosophy that all war is necessarily just.(8) Consequently, the emphasis shifted from the justi-fication for war to the means of its regulation. This attitude was well developed during the nineteenth century which, on the one hand, was "dominated by an unrestricted right of war and the recognition of conquests,"(9) but on the other was characterized by a new concern for the regulation of hostil-ities. The Geneva Convention of 1864 (amelioration of treat-ment of wounded soldiers), the Declaration of St. Petersburg of 1868 (renunciation of the use of explosive bullets), and the First Hague Conference in 1899 (prohibition of methods of warfare that caused unnecessary suffering) all illustrate this concern.(10)

The twentieth century saw a continuation of this policy through a host of multilateral humanitarian conventions, notably the Geneva Conventions of 1929 and 1949.(11) In contrast to the method of warfare sanctioned by the doctrine of just war, the new order adopted an evenhanded approach to combatants. The jus in bello incorporated in these conventions was "based upon the principle that the law relating to the conduct of warfare and the protection of war victims [would] be neutral and that there [would] be an equality of treatment for the participants in a conflict."(12)

The twentieth century also witnessed the revival of the idea of the just war in the Charter of the United Nations.(13) In Article 2(4) of the Charter, member States undertake to "refrain in their international relations from the threat or use of force against the territorial integrity or political indepen-dence of any State." The U.N. Charter does not, however, outlaw the use of force in all cases, as it recognizes the right to use force in self-defense and specifically provides for the use of force under the authority of the Security Council.(14) By outlawing the use of force in some cases and permitting it in others, the Charter put an end to the Machiavellian phase of world order and heralded a return to the Grotian distinction between just and unjust warfare. Wars waged other than in self-defense or under the authority of the United Nations can now be categorized as unjust or unlawful, with the result that international law once again discriminates against the "unjust" belligerent.(15)

This discrimination, however, operates only in relation to third parties during the conflict and to the post-conflict settlement. During the war, both sides are bound to observe the rules of war, as the legality of the conflict cannot affect the applicability of rules designed to introduce humanitarian considerations into conflicts.(16)

B. The Modern Version of the Just War

The Charter of the United Nations clearly condemns all force
other than that used in self-defense or under the authority of
the United Nations. This severe limitation on the use of force
has not, however, proved to be universally acceptable in a
world in which the expansion of ideology plays a major role.

Not unexpectedly, new arguments have been raised in
support of the use of force. Since Article 51 of the Charter
provides the document's only justification for the use of force,
it has been subjected to very broad interpretations in order to
permit the unilateral use of force. Although Article 51 does
not explicitly encompass the vague doctrine of just war, it
does permit the use of force when the cause of a State is
"just" by virtue of its being attacked. From this has come,
by syllogistic reasoning, the argument that when the cause of
one State is "just," it is entitled to use force in the exercise
of its right of self-defense. In this way, the just war has
been resurrected to justify the use of force in situations not
contemplated by the Charter.

In the modern era, the war of national liberation is seen
by the Soviet Union and Third World countries as a paradig-
matic just war. Consequently, they reason that these wars
fall within the scope of Article 51 and are therefore not
affected by the Charter's prohibition on the use of force.

It is ironic that the Soviet Union, with its traditional
aversion to natural law theory, espouses the doctrine of the
just war. Originally, it preferred to categorize wars as
progressive (supporting socialism) and reactionary (opposing
socialism).(17) Stalin subsequently translated these terms into
the language of the just war;(18) struggles to liberate colonies
and dependent countries from the yoke of imperialism were
claimed to be both "just" and "sacred."(19) Curiously, the
rhetoric employed to justify these wars is reminiscent of that
of early Christian theologians committed to justifying the use
of force against the infidel. For example, in 1963 a Soviet
writer declared:

> With fire and sword the Western powers seized and
> kept "their" colonies. But aggression and annexa-
> tion cannot remain unpunished. . . . Refusal of the
> necessity of punishment for aggression and annexa-
> tion means the recognition of lawlessness in in-
> ternational relations.(20)

The Soviet view of wars of national liberation has been
accepted by Third World states, many of which had been subjected to colonial domination until recent times. But while the
Soviet Union couches its arguments in Marxist-Leninist language, the Third World prefers to rely upon the principle of

self-determination, recognized by the United Nations in its Charter and given sweeping endorsement in Resolution 1514 (XV) of 1960 - the Declaration on the Granting of Independence to Colonial Countries and Peoples.

This argument has been forcefully propounded by Professor Abi-Saab, who contends that liberation movements have a jus ad bellum and a jus in bello derived from the principle of self-determination as it has evolved within the political organs of the United Nations.(21) But the argument is not confined to academic journals; it is often invoked to justify the use of force in southern Africa and against Israel, which has been classified as a case of alien domination to which the newly revived doctrine of just war is equally applicable.

This just war doctrine was recently advanced by SWAPO (South West Africa People's Organization), the liberation movement for Namibia. SWAPO has argued that its war of liberation is both "morally justified," under "the modern version of the bellum justum in the old natural law ideology of international law," and "legally justified," as a defensive action under Article 51 of the Charter aimed at the assertion of the principle of self-determination.(22) The latter argument is supported by Judge Ammoun's dictum in the 1971 Namibia Opinion that:

> In law, the legitimacy of the Namibia people's struggle cannot be in any doubt, for it follows from the right of self-defense, inherent in human nature, which is confirmed by Article 51 of the United Nations Charter.(23)

It is difficult to accept the view that the Charter of the United Nations, even as interpreted by its political organs, condones the use of force in wars of national liberation.(24) The Charter is clear on the circumstances in which force may lawfully be used in international relations: in the exercise of the right of self-defense under Article 51, and under the authority of the Security Council. Not only does the Charter fail to permit the use of force to eradicate colonialism, but it expressly recognizes the legitimacy of colonialism in Chapter XI. However, since the adoption of the Declaration on the Granting of Independence to Colonial Countries and Peoples, the legitimacy of colonialism has become suspect; and the notion has developed that force may be used to destroy it.(25) This notion has been implicitly supported by General Assembly resolutions calling upon States to give "material assistance" to liberation movements(26) and to recognize "the legitimacy of the struggle of colonial peoples for their freedom by all appropriate means at their disposal."(27) The Declaration on Principles of International Law Concerning Friendly Relations and Co-operation among States in Accordance with the Charter of the United Nations encourages this argument by proclaiming that:

> Every State has the duty to refrain from any forc-
> ible action which deprives peoples . . . of their
> right of self-determination and freedom and inde-
> pendence. In their actions against, and resistance
> to such forcible action in pursuit of the exercise of
> their right to self-determination, such peoples are
> entitled to seek and receive support in accordance
> with the purposes and principles of the Charter.(28)

Further support is found in the most recent definition of aggression formulated by the Special Committee on the Question of Defining Aggression:

> Nothing in this definition [of aggression] . . . could
> in any way prejudice the right to self-determination,
> freedom, and independence, as derived from the
> Charter, of peoples forcibly deprived of that right
> and referred to in the Declaration on Principles of
> International Law Concerning Friendly Relations and
> Co-operation among States in Accordance with the
> Charter of the United Nations, particularly peoples
> under colonial and racist regimes or other forms of
> alien domination; nor the right of these peoples to
> struggle to that end and to seek and receive sup-
> port, in accordance with the principles of the
> Charter and in conformity with the above mentioned
> Declaration.(29)

Although these resolutions recognize the right of revo-lution in unequivocal terms and go a long way towards con-doning military aid to liberation movements, they still fall short of declaring that force can be used in pursuance of a war of national liberation.(30)

The argument that force may be used to implement the right of self-determination depends ultimately on whether there is a species of self-defense, recognized by Article 51 of the Charter, that permits the use of force in such circumstances. In 1967, when arguments that wars of self-determination were legitimate forms of self-defense were still in their infancy, these arguments were analyzed and disputed by this author for the following reasons.(31) Self-defense against colonial domination in the exercise of the right of self-determination has nothing to do with self-defense as it is traditionally defined or as it is described in Article 51 of the Charter. Self-defense is the right of a State to resort to force as a result of an attack by an aggressor. A sine qua non for such a right is an "aggressor State" and a "victim State."(32)

In the case of colonial domination, this necessary condition is absent. While it is possible to identify an aggressor State (the colonial power), it is not possible to identify the victim State. The victim of colonial or racist aggression is not a State, but instead the nationals of the aggressor State itself, who are attacked within the boundaries of the aggressor State. Lamentable as this may be, it does not constitute an unlawful use of force within the meaning of Article 2(4) of the Charter, which prohibits only the use of force against States.

If, despite these arguments, wars of liberation are to be classified as international wars, then it is both logical and desirable that the rules of jus in bello should apply with equal force to both the colonial power and the national liberation movement. Third World jurists(33) and national liberation movements have pleaded for the extension of the rules of war to wars of national liberation,(34) and there are a number of General Assembly resolutions calling for the application of the Geneva Convention to conflicts of this kind.(35) In 1977 Additional Protocols were attached to the Geneva Conventions of 1949 which seek in Protocol I to extend the Geneva Conventions to

> include armed conflicts in which people are fighting against colonial domination and alien occupation and against racist regimes in the exercise of their right of self-determination, as enshrined in the Charter of United Nations and the Declaration on Principles of International Law concerning Friendly Relations and Co-operation among States in accordance with the Charter of the United Nations.(36)

This extension, promoted largely by Third World States, has not received wide acceptance and there is little likelihood that South Africa and Israel, against which such wars of national liberation are being waged, will accept this Protocol.

Unfortunately, it is not generally agreed that colonial powers and liberation movements should be bound by the same rules of warfare. Some commentators contend that national liberation movements, because of their jus ad bellum, should be treated as privileged belligerents and absolved from the normal restraints of the humanitarian rules of war. Others argue that because of the superior military might of colonial regimes and their imperialist Western supporters, liberation movements are entitled to resort to unorthodox methods of warfare.(37) Arguments of this kind have given rise to the claim that liberation movements are above the laws of war.(38)

The logical extension of this argument is that groups fighting against colonial or racist regimes are permitted, indeed encouraged, to commit unconventional acts of violence, viewed by many as acts of terrorism.(39) Nor does there appear to be any logical reason why these acts of terrorism should be confined to the territory in dispute. Colonial and racist powers have diplomats and citizens living abroad, and will, in most instances, have the backing of foreign governments and multinational corporations with headquarters in foreign countries. Ideological claims will inevitably be made that they ought to be held subject to the same retribution meted out to modern-day "infidels" who oppose liberation movements.

II. INTERNATIONAL TERRORISM

A. Defining Punishable Terrorism - The U.N. Debates

If the modern just war thesis is accepted, along with the corollary that those "in the right" are released from the rules of warfare, it is difficult to outlaw the activities of modern international terrorists. Acceptance of this belief was the main reason for the failure of the international community to achieve an agreement in 1972 designed to prevent and punish terrorism.

In 1972, following the Lod Airport massacre in Tel Aviv, the Munich Olympic Games disaster, and a wave of letter bombs directed at Israeli diplomats, the Secretary-General of the United Nations requested the General Assembly to consider "measures to prevent terrorism and other forms of violence which endanger or take human lives or jeopardize fundamental freedoms."(40) The item was referred to the Sixth Committee in an amended form which directed the Committee to include within its field of concern a study of the causes which lead to international terrorism.(41) The amendment to the original request resulted from a coalition of (1) some States that wished to exclude wars of self-determination from the ambit of terrorism and (2) Arab nations which claimed that terrorism was a response to "government terror" and injustice.

The item was thoroughly debated in the Sixth Committee, which had before it a Draft Convention for the Prevention and Punishment of Certain Acts of International Terrorism(42) submitted by the United States and a study on international terrorism prepared by the Secretariat.(43) The United States insisted that its draft convention would not "adversely affect the right of self-determination."(44) The debate revealed a clear determination by Third World countries to resist any international restrictions on the methods of violence open to liberation movements.(45) For example, one of the most articulate presentations of their argument occurred when Mr. Joewono of Indonesia stated that:

[A] distinction should be drawn between terrorism perpetrated for personal gain and other acts of violence committed for political purposes. Although recourse to violence must ultimately be eliminated from relations between peoples, it must be borne in mind that certain kinds of violence were bred by oppression, injustice, the denial of basic human rights, and the fact that whole nations were deprived of their homeland and their property. It would be unjust to expect such peoples to adhere to the same code of ethics as those who possessed more sophisticated means of advancing their interests. It was unacceptable for acts committed by common criminals to be identified with acts committed by those who resisted oppression and injustice by all possible means in order to achieve independence and regain their dignity. Such acts could not be classified as terrorism; on the contrary, they were to a certain extent to be regarded as anti-terrorist acts aimed at combatting a much more repulsive kind of terrorism, namely colonialism and other forms of domination. These forms of violence were legitimate, being founded on the right to self-determination proclaimed in the Charter and often reaffirmed by the United Nations. (46)

Following this Committee debate, the General Assembly rejected an American resolution calling for "a plenipotentiary conference in early 1973 to consider the adoption of a convention on the prevention and punishment of international terrorism." (47) Instead, the Assembly invited States to make proposals on the matter, to be considered by an Ad Hoc Committee of 35. This resolution (adopted by a vote of 76 in favor, 35 against, and 17 abstaining) received its strongest support from Arab, African, and East European countries, and showed more concern for the legitimization of wars of national liberation than for the suppression of international terrorism. In its third paragraph it:

reaffirms the inalienable right to self-determination and independence of all peoples under colonial and racist regimes and other forms of alien domination and upholds the legitimacy of their struggle, in particular the struggle of national liberation movements, in accordance with the purposes and principles of the Charter and the relevant resolutions of the organs of the United Nations. (48)

The Ad Hoc Committee of 35 met in July and August of 1973, but was unable to agree on a common approach to the

problem of international terrorism.(49)   The opposing coalitions
which had emerged during the debates in the General Assembly
and the Sixth Committee also divided this committee and obstructed its work.(50)   In the concluding statement, the
chairman of the Committee merely declared that international
terrorism was a "delicate and complex problem" and acknowledged that there had been a "frank and extensive exchange of
ideas" on the subject.(51)   These views were then presented
to the General Assembly, which declined to take any further
action.(52)

Two important conclusions can be drawn from the 1972-73
debates on international terrorism.   First, many States are
unwilling to confine the actions of liberation movements to the
territory in dispute or even its immediate precincts.   Second,
the political motive of an international terrorist is seen as a
factor directly relevant to his guilt.

B.   The Export of Terrorism

The United States Draft Convention for the Prevention and
Punishment of Certain Acts of International Terrorism(53) made
no attempt to interfere with the normal activities of liberation
movements, but sought instead to localize conflicts and prevent
wars of national liberation from escalating.(54)   It prohibited
only those acts of terrorism with "international significance,"
acts which occurred outside the territory of the target State
or which were directed at foreign nationals.(55)   This goal was
supported by several delegates who argued that the rules of
neutrality should apply to wars of national liberation.   For
example, the Swedish delegate in the Sixth Committee argued
that:

> [E]very country should enjoy a right to neutrality
> not only with regard to belligerents in war situ-
> ations, but also with regard to acts of violence
> committed by individuals as a result of the internal
> political tensions of foreign countries.(56)

As this was the cardinal principle of the Draft Convention, it is possible to interpret its rejection as a refusal to
accept the principle of neutrality in wars of national liberation.
This is hardly surprising; the Third World has made it very
clear that there are no neutrals in their ideological struggle
against colonial and racist regimes.   They argue that violent
acts that are justified when aimed directly at one of these
regimes within the terrority of conflict are equally justified
when aimed at the regime's representatives abroad or at targets in States which give express or tacit support to these
regimes.   Ideological conflicts of this kind know no frontiers,

and no one is safe from international terrorism in pursuance of a supposedly "just war."

C.   The Motive of the Offender(57)

The introduction of the notion of the just war into international terrorism makes the terrorist's motive directly relevant to his culpability. If an offender's motivation is personal gain or advancement of an "unjust" (i.e., reactionary) political cause, he becomes an international terrorist, a hostis humani. If, on the other hand, his object is to oppose colonialism, racism, or alien domination, and to assert the principles of self-determination, then he is not a criminal, but an heroic figure engaged in a just struggle against the twentieth century infidel.

This is a recent development in the field of international criminal responsibility which, until now, has focused primarily on the act of the offender and, as in domestic systems of criminal justice, left the issue of motivation for consideration only in the determination of sentence. Motive may also become relevant in extradition proceedings if the State of incarceration considers that the political nature of the crime precludes extradition. This is, however, a matter generally left to the discretion of the courts of the State of incarceration and not one regulated in a treaty dealing with international criminal responsibility.

The 1937 Convention for the Prevention and Punishment of Terrorism(58) (which was signed by 24 countries, but did not come into force)(59) was prompted by the assassination of King Alexander I of Yugoslavia and Louis Barthou, President of the Council of the French Republic, in Marseilles in 1934 by persons who would be described today as Yugoslav "freedom fighters."(60) Despite the fact that the assassins had legitimate political grievances,(61) the International Conference on the Repression of Terrorism,(62) which produced the Convention, paid little attention to the causes of the act;(63) terrorism was defined in a way that took no account of the actor's motive. Acts of terrorism were defined as "criminal acts directed against a State and intended or calculated to create a state of terror in the minds of particular persons, or a group of persons, or the general public."(64)   Specific examples of acts of terrorism were then enumerated in the Convention. In addition, there was a concerted attempt by several Eastern European States to make the extradition of political offenders compulsory.(65) This attempt was, however, successfully resisted by the Western Powers led by the United Kingdom,(66) and the final convention recognized the right of States to grant asylum when they considered the offense to be of a political nature.(67)

The Convention to Prevent and Punish Acts of Terrorism Taking the Form of Crimes Against Persons and Related Extortion that are of International Significance,(68) adopted by the Organization of American States in 1971, is similarly unsympathetic to the motive of the actor and to the causes of terrorism. This Convention provides that certain acts of violence directed at persons "to whom the State has the duty to give special protection according to international law" shall be considered as "common crimes"(69) under the Convention "regardless of motive,"(70) (emphasis added). Moreover, in the resolution which initiated the Convention, the General Assembly of the O.A.S. declared that:

> The political and ideological pretexts utilized as justification for these crimes [acts of terrorism] in no way mitigate their cruelty and irrationality or the ignoble nature of the means employed, and in no way remove their character as acts in violation of essential human rights.(71)

Although Article 6 declares that "[n]one of the provisions of this Convention shall be interpreted so as to impair the right of asylum," Poulantzas has suggested that "Article 6 does not refer to the perpetrators of terrorist acts described in the Convention. It aims rather at reaffirming the institution of diplomatic asylum, prevalent in Latin America, which is granted to political offenders."(72)

The three conventions aimed at the crime of hijacking - the Tokyo,(73) Hague,(74) and Montreal Conventions(75) - likewise make no exculpatory exception for the actor inspired by a just cause. Instead, they define the acts prohibited in objective terms. Member States, however, retain their traditional right to grant asylum to political offenders.(76)

The Convention on the Prevention and Punishment of Crimes against Internationally Protected Persons, Including Diplomatic Agents,(77) initiated before the 1972 debate on international terrorism and finally approved by the General Assembly in December 1973,(78) also adopts the traditional view. This treaty provides for the extradition or prosecution of persons alleged to have committed certain offenses against diplomatic agents.(79) Article 2(1) declares that the intentional commission of certain enumerated acts are offenses under the Convention and rejects motive as an exculpatory factor. This provision was clarified in the International Law Commission's Draft Article 2(1),(80) which stated that these offenses were committed "regardless of motive." This language was explained as follows:

> While criminal intent is regarded as an essential element of the crimes covered by Article 2, the

> expression "regardless of motive" restates the
> universally accepted legal principle that it is the
> intent to commit the act and not the reasons that led
> to its commission that is the governing factor. . . .
> As a consequence, the requirements of the Conven-
> tion must be applied by a State Party even though,
> for example, the kidnapper of an ambassador may
> have been inspired by what appeared to him or is
> considered by the State Party to be the worthiest of
> motives.(81)

The phrase "regardless of motive" was omitted from the final
Convention on the ground that it was superfluous,(82) but it
is clear that the meaning of Article 2(1) remains unaffected.

When the Draft Convention came before the Sixth Committee for the final time in 1973, an eleventh-hour attempt was
made to grant immunity to the actor in a war of national
liberation. At that time, an article was proposed which provided that:

> [n]o provision of the present articles shall be
> applicable to peoples struggling against colonialism,
> alien domination, foreign occupation, racial dis-
> crimination and apartheid in the exercise of their
> legitimate rights to self-determination and inde-
> pendence.(83)

This article proved unacceptable to many delegates. A compromise was reached(84) under which the General Assembly
resolution approving the Convention was amended to read that
the provisions of the Convention "cannot in any way prejudice
the exercise of the legitimate right to self-determination and
independence . . . by peoples struggling against colonialism,
alien domination, foreign occupation, racial discrimination, and
apartheid."(85) Although this resolution was published with
the text of the Convention, it is a separate instrument and not
an actual part of the Convention. Consequently, if an internationally protected person is kidnapped or murdered by a
member of a national liberation movement, the crime will fall
within the Convention and the actor will receive no immunity
on account of his motive.(86)

III. CONCLUSION

The present trend in favor of the legitimization of all methods
of violence used in pursuance of a just war is extremely
dangerous. The "just war," or the war of national liberation,
is incapable of precise definition. At present it appears that a

cause is "just" only if it enjoys the support of two-thirds of the United Nations.(87)   The language used by the General Assembly to describe the just war reflects the vagueness of the concept.   While "colonialism" and "racism" have a relatively unambiguous meaning, the terms "alien occupation" (used to describe Israel's position) and "self-determination" are incapable of exact definition and may be invoked to cover almost any situation.   Professor Baxter's comment on the term "self-determination" clearly illustrates the problem:

> The right of self-determination can . . . mean different things in different contexts.   It is all very well to speak of anti-colonialist struggles in Africa, but does a similar right of self-determination exist in the metropolitan territory of other countries?   Was Biafra exercising a right to self-determination during the tragic Nigerian civil war?   Was Bangladesh in its revolt against Pakistan asserting a right guaranteed it under the Charter?   . . . It is quite clear that one man's war of national liberation is another man's war of national secession.(88)

If States are released from their commitment to abstain from the use of force in the case of "just" wars, there is a substantial danger that these wars will proliferate, since it is much easier to justify the use of force in terms of this vague doctrine than in terms of the more restrictive Article 51.

The revival of the concept of the just war not only poses a threat to the Charter's prohibition on the use of force in international relations, but also presents serious implications for the protection of human rights under international law.   If the most brutal acts of terrorism directed at innocent civilian targets are permitted when committed by members of a "liberation movement," human rights will suffer a severe setback at the hand of international law.

In an ideologically divided world, only an ideologically neutral approach to the laws of war can maintain order and prevent needless suffering.   This goal is the basis of the modern humanitarian law of war and of multilateral conventions which outlaw hijacking and terrorism directed at international agents.(89)   Any convention which seeks to prohibit international terrorism in general must follow the precedent set by these conventions and enumerate those acts which are judged to have international significance without regard to the motive of the actor.   Motive should be considered as a mitigating factor in the imposition of punishment in individual cases, but it is impossible to provide an escape clause for the actor engaged in a war of national liberation without reinstating the just war in international relations.   Actors engaged in a war of national liberation must not be granted immunity from the

normal restraints of humanitarian law. The statement by the
Jordanian delegate in the Sixth Committee debate on international terrorism reflects the desirable approach. He stated
that:

> [Jordan] believed in the legitimacy and dignity of
> national resistance against alien domination and
> oppression and also believed that the ethical rules of
> national resistance should be strict and humane; in
> this way, it would be possible to distinguish the
> national struggle and resistance from the spirit of
> hate and violence which was the motivating force in
> all colonial and oppressive enterprises. It was
> imperative, in the interests of all movements of
> national liberation, to draw up and abide by a
> humanitarian code of ethics dissociated from any form
> of indiscriminate violence against innocent civilians
> or third parties.(90)

The proposal that certain forms of violence should be prohibited, even when used in a war of national liberation, is in
full accord with the modern approach of international law
concerning the use of force and acts of terror. But is is not
enough to adopt this firm line towards international terrorism.
Third World countries have a number of legitimate grievances
which must be heeded.

It must be frankly acknowledged that many States, including the major Western powers, have on occasion engaged in
acts of terror against civilian populations which completely
overshadow the acts of terror committed by national liberation
movements. It is true that international instruments already
exist that seek to curb State terror (e.g., the Genocide Convention, the Nuremberg principles, the Geneva Conventions for
the protection of war victims, and a number of human rights
conventions), but it is equally true that these conventions are
inadequately enforced.(91) While these conventions remain
unenforced, it is asking too much of Third World countries to
collaborate in the suppression of the most effective means of
counter-terror available to national liberation movements.

In addition, the Geneva Conventions of 1949 do not extend to wars of national liberation, but instead categorize them
as internal conflicts to which only the minimum safeguards of
Article 3 are applicable.(92) Thus, according to these conventions, many of the armed conflicts in the modern world fall
beyond the scope of the applicability of the humanitarian laws
of war. Although the 1977 Protocols do seek to extend the
protection of the 1949 Geneva Conventions to such conflicts,
there is little prospect that they will be accepted by those
countries fighting against national liberation movements, namely
South Africa and Israel.

The dictates of humanity require that all forms of terrorism be subjected to international legal regulation, irrespective of whether the terror emanates from a State or from a liberation movement. Precise rules, with adequate machinery for enforcement, are the ultimate goal. This goal will not be furthered by a return to the medieval doctrine of the "just war," and the corollary that no holds are barred for the "just" combatant.

NOTES

(1) For accounts of the history of the just war, see Von Elbe, The Evolution of the Concept of the Just War in International Law, 33 AM. J. INT'L L. 665 (1939); WILLIAM S. HOLDSWORTH, 5 A HISTORY OF ENGLISH LAW 29-35 (London: Methuen & Co., 1924); IAN BROWNLIE, INTERNATIONAL LAW AND THE USE OF FORCE BY STATES 3-18 (Oxford: Clarendon Press, 1963).

(2) ST. THOMAS AQUINAS, SUMMA THEOLOGICA Secunda Secundae, Question 40.

(3) HUGO GROTIUS, DE JURE BELLI AC PACIS Bk. II, Ch. I sec. ii, 2; Ch. XXII sec. viii-xii. Translated in No. 3 vol. 2 THE CLASSICS OF INTERNATIONAL LAW 172 (Oxford: Clarendon Press; London: Humphrey Milford, trans. Francis W. Kelsey, ed. James Brown Scott, 1925).

(4) Von Elbe, supra note 1, at 672; WILLIAM S. HOLDSWORTH, supra note 1, at 31.

(5) de Victoria, De Indis Noviter Inventis Sec. II (11), translated in JAMES BROWN SCOTT, THE SPANISH ORIGIN OF INTERNATIONAL LAW: FRANCISCO DE VITORIA [sic] AND HIS LAW OF NATIONS i, xxix (Oxford: Clarendon Press; London: Humphrey Milford, trans. John Pawley Bates, 1934); de Victoria, De Jure Belli 10, translated in id. at xivii, liii, 152.

(6) de Victoria, De Jure Belli 48, id., at lxvi.

(7) Draper, The Idea of the Just War, 60 THE LISTENER 221, 222 (Aug. 14, 1958).

(8) NICCOLO MACHIAVELLI, THE PRINCE 117 (London: Alexander Moring, trans. Edward Dacres, 1929).

(9) IAN BROWNLIE, supra note 1, at 19.

(10) For a description of these treaties, see L. OPPENHEIM, II INTERNATIONAL LAW 227-39, 340-42 (London, New York, Toronto: Longmans, Green & Co., ed. H. Lauterpacht, 7th ed., 1952).

(11) For a comprehensive list of these treaties, see id.,at 230-31.

(12) Baxter, The Geneva Conventions of 1949 and Wars of National Liberation, 57 RIVISTA DI DIRITTO INTERNAZIONALE 193, 199 (1974).

(13) Miller, The Contemporary Significance of the Doctrine of Just War, 16 WORLD POLITICS 254, 259 (1964); YEHUDA MEL- ZER, CONCEPTS OF JUST WAR (Leyden, Netherlands: A.W. Sijthoff, 1975).

(14) Lauterpacht, The Grotian Tradition in International Law, 23 BRIT. Y.B. INT'L L., 35-59 (1946).

(15) Kunz, Bellum Justum and Bellum Legale, 45 AM. J. INT'L L. 528 (1951).

(16) L. OPPENHEIM, supra note 10 at 218.

(17) Ginsburgs, "Wars of National Liberation" and the Modern Law of Nations - the Soviet Thesis, THE SOVIET IMPACT ON INTERNATIONAL LAW 66, 88 (Dobbs Ferry, New York: Oceana Publications, ed. Hans W. Baade, 1965).

(18) Id. at 89-90.

(19) Id. at 76, 92, 95.

(20) Tuzmukhamedov, Mirnoe Sosushchestvovanie i Natsional- no- Osvoboditelnaya Voina (Peaceful Coexistence and National Liberation Wars), quoted in id. at 84.

(21) Abi-Saab, Wars of National Liberation and the Laws of War, 3 ANNALS INT'L STUD. 93, 99-101 (1972). See also UMOZURIKE OJI UMOZURIKE, SELF-DETERMINATION IN IN- TERNATIONAL LAW 80-84 (Hamden, Conn.: Archon Books, 1972).

(22) Namibia and the International Rule of Law, Conf. Dakar (NDH 76) IV a, 9 (Strasbourg: The International Institute of Human Rights, 1976) [hereinafter cited as Conf. Dakar]. See further, Dugard, SWAPO: The Jus ad Bellum and the Jus in Bello, 93 SOUTH AFRICAN L.J. 144 (1976).

(23) Legal Consequences for States of the Continued Presence of South Africa in Namibia (South West Africa) notwithstanding Security Council Resolution 276 (1970), INT'L COURT JUST. REP. 3, 70 (1971).

(24) Schwebel, Wars of Liberation - as Fought in U.N. Or- gans, LAW AND CIVIL WAR IN THE MODERN WORLD 446, 457 (Baltimore & London: Johns Hopkins U. Press, ed. John N. Moore, 1974) [hereinafter cited as MOORE].

(25) Dugard, The Organization of African Unity and Colonial- ism: An Enquiry into the Plea of Self-Defense as a Justification

for the Use of Force in the Eradication of Colonialization, 16
INT'L & COMP. L. Q. 157, 172 (1967).

(26) See, e.g., General Assembly Resolutions 2945 (XXVII) &
3031 (XXVII) (U.N. Doc. A/8730, 1972).

(27) Id. Resolution 2936 (XXVII) at 6. See also id. Resolutions 2908, 2923 (E), 2955.

(28) General Assembly Resolution 2625 (XXV) (U.N. Doc.
A/8028, 1970).

(29) Definition of Aggression Article 7 (U.N. Doc. A/AC
134/L 46) (reprinted in 13 INT'L LEGAL MATERIALS 710).
This definition of aggression was adopted by consensus on
April 12, 1974.

(30) Schwebel, supra note 24, at 457.

(31) Supra note 25.

(32) Article 51 of the Charter recognizes that a right of
self-defense arises "if an armed attack occurs against a
member of the United Nations." As the membership of the
United Nations is restricted to States, in Article 4 of the
Charter, it follows that the attack must be against a State.

(33) Abi-Saab, supra note 21, at 102-07, 116-17.

(34) Conf. Dakar, supra note 22, at 12. SWAPO claims that
"the Namibian Liberation Army must - and does - comply with
the laws of and customs of war as set out, in particular, in
the Geneva Conventions of 1949 and South Africa's armed
forces are also bound by these provisions."

(35) In 1973 the General Assembly adopted Resolution 3103
(XXVII), entitled Basic Principles of the Legal Status of the
Combatants Struggling against Colonial and Alien Domination
and Racist Regimes, in which it declared that "the armed
conflicts involving the struggle of peoples against colonial and
alien domination and racist regimes are to be regarded as
international armed conflicts in the sense of the 1949 Geneva
Conventions and the legal status envisaged to apply to the
combatants in the 1949 Geneva Conventions and other international instruments is to apply to the persons engaged in
armed struggle against colonial and alien domination and racist
regimes." For further resolutions of this kind, see Secretary-
General, Second Report on Respect of Human Rights in Armed
Conflicts, (U.N. Doc. A/8052, 1970, sec. 195-203); see also,
Resolutions 2621 (XXV) and 2674 (XXV) (U.N. Doc. A/8028,
1970).

(36) Article 1 (4). The text of these Protocols appears in 72
AM. J. INT'L L. See further on this subject, Ribeiro, International Humanitarian Law: Advancing Progressively Backwards
97 SOUTH AFRICAN L. J. 42 (1980); Baxter, Humanitarian

Law or Humanitarian Politics? The 1974 Diplomatic Conference on Humanitarian Law, 16 HARV. INT'L. L.J. 1 (Wint. 1975); Forsythe, The 1974 Diplomatic Conference on Humanitarian Law: Some Observations, 69 AM. J. INT'L L. 77 (1975); Graham, The 1974 Diplomatic Conference on the Law of War: A Victory for Political Causes and a Return to the "Just War" Concept of the Eleventh Century, 32 Washington & Lee L. Rev. 25 (1975).

(37) This accords with Marx's view that "[a] people resolved to be independent should not be satisfied with conventional methods of warfare, Riots, revolt and guerrilla tactics are the ways by which a small nation can overcome a large one. It is the only way a weak army can resist a large, well-trained army." Cited by Firmage, The "War of National Liberation" and the Third World, in MOORE, supra note 24, at 314-315.

(38) Soviet legal theory, while maintaining that liberation movements need not comply with the rules of warfare because of the justice of their cause and the difficulties of compliance, nevertheless insists that colonial or racist powers are them-selves bound by the entire body of the jus in bello. Unfor-tunately, some Third World States also incline towards this double standard. Ginsburgs, supra note 17, at 72-74, 90-92.

(39) Professor Abu-Lughod prefers the term "unconventional violence" to terrorism" because of the tendency to label only the actions of liberation movements as terrorism. This is a valid objection as the major powers have undeniably engaged in acts of military terrorism on many occasions. Abu-Lughod, Unconventional Violence and International Politics, 67 AM. J. INT'L. L. 100 (No. 5, Proceedings of the Sixty-Seventh An-nual Meeting of the American Society of International Law, Nov. 1973).

(40) See generally Request for the Inclusion of an Additional Item in the Agenda of the Twenty-Seventh Session Measures to Prevent Terrorism and Other Forms of Violence which Endan-ger or Take Innocent Human Lives or Jeopardize Fundamental Freedoms (U.N. Doc. A/8791, 1972).

(41) The item was finally placed on the agenda in the fol-lowing form: "Measures to prevent international terrorism which endangers or takes innocent human lives or jeopardizes fundamental freedoms, and study of the underlying causes of those forms of terrorism and acts of violence which lie in misery, frustration, grievance and despair and which cause some people to sacrifice human lives, including their own, in an attempt to effect radical changes." 27 U.N. GAOR, Sixth Committee, Agenda Item No. 92 (1972).

(42) Text of Draft Convention, 67 DEP'T STATE BULL. 431 (Oct. 1972).

(43) U.N. Doc. A/C.6/418, 1972.

(44) U.N. Doc. A/C.6/SR 1357, 1972.

(45) See, e.g., statements by Yugoslavia (U.N. Doc. A/C.6/SR.1357, 1972). Pakistan (U.N. Doc. A/C.6/SR.1357, 1972).

(46) U.N. Doc. A/C.6/SR, 1368, 1972.

(47) Supra note 42, at 433.

(48) General Assembly Resolution 3034 (XXVII) (U.N. Doc. Supp. No. 30, A/8730, 1972).

(49) Ad Hoc Comm. on Int'l Terrorism, Report of the Ad Hoc Comm. on Int'l Terrorism, (U.N. Doc. A/9028, 1973).

(50) Dugard, International Terrorism, Problems of Definition, 50 INT'L AFFAIRS 67, 74 (1974).

(51) Ad Hoc Comm. on Int'l Terrorism, supra note 49, at 7.

(52) This matter was deferred annually by the General Assembly for further consideration. See U.N. Doc. A/PV.2197, Dec. 12, 1973; U.N. Doc. A/PV, 2319, Dec. 14, 1974; U.N. Doc. A/PV.2441, Dec. 15, 1975.

(53) Supra note 42.

(54) See Dugard, supra note 50, at 78-81; Dugard, Towards the Definition of International Terrorism, 67 AM. J. INT'L L. 94, 98 (No. 5, Proceedings of the Sixty-Seventh Annual Meeting of the American Society of International Law, Nov. 1973).

(55) Supra note 42, at 431.

(56) U.N. Doc. A/C.6/SR. 1355, 1972.

(57) See generally Frank & Lockwood, Preliminary Thoughts Towards an International Convention on Terrorism, 68 AM. J. INT'L. L. 69, 78-80 (Jan. 1974).

(58) Convention for the Prevention and Punishment of Terrorism, LEAGUE OF NATIONS (Doc. C, 546. M. 383, 1937); (the text also appears in U.N. Doc. A/C.6/418, 1972). See generally Sottile, Le Terrorisme International [International Terrorism], 65 RECUEIL DES COURS [Collected Courses] 87 (No. 3, 1938).

(59) It was ratified by only one State.

(60) See ARNOLD J. TOYNBEE, SURVEY OF INTERNATIONAL AFFAIRS 1934 at 566-71 (London: Oxford U. Press, 1935).

(61) See id. at 540-43.

(62) For an account of the deliberations of this Conference, see Proceedings of the International Conference on the Repression of Terrorism, LEAGUE OF NATIONS (Doc. C. 94. M. 47, 1937).

(63) One of the only references to the causes of terrorism was a statement by the Finnish delegate that his Government "would find it very difficult to extradite a person who had met terrorism in his country by an act of desperation." Id. at 103.

(64) Convention for the Prevention and Punishment of Terrorism, LEAGUE OF NATIONS art. 1 (Doc. C. 546. M. 383, 1937).

(65) The States which adopted this approach were Poland, Czechoslovakia, Rumania, and the USSR. Mr. Pella, the Romanian delegate and rapporteur, favored the inclusion of a clause to the effect that terrorism could never be a political offense. See id. at 67, 99.

(66) Id, at 99.

(67) Although Article 8(1) describes the offenses under the Convention as "extradition crimes," Article 8(4) provides that "the obligation to grant extradition under the present article shall be subject to any conditions and limitations recognized by the law or the practice of the country to which application is made."

(68) 10 INT'L LEGAL MATERIALS 225 (1971). For an analysis of this Convention, see Poulantzas, Some Problems of International Law Connected with Urban Guerrilla Warfare: The Kidnapping of Members of Diplomatic Missions, Consular Offices and other Foreign Personnel 3 ANNALS INT'L STUD. 137, 154-67 (1972); Brach, The Interamerican Convention on the Kidnapping of Diplomats, 10 COLUM. J. TRANSNAT'L. L. 393 (1971).

(69) The phrase "common crimes" is of importance as a distinction is generally drawn between "common crimes" and "political crimes" for the purpose of asylum and extradition.

(70) Convention to Prevent and Punish Acts of Terrorism, supra note 68, at art. 2.

(71) Resolution of 30 June, 1970: 9 INT'L LEGAL MATERIALS 1084 (1970).

(72) Supra note 68, at 159; Brach, supra note 68, at 404-05.

(73) Convention on Offences and Certain other Acts Committed on Board Aircraft, 1963, 2 INT'L LEGAL MATERIALS 1042 (1963).

(74) Convention for the Suppression of Unlawful Acts against the Safety of Civil Aviation, [Seizure of Aircraft] 1970, 10 INT'L LEGAL MATERIALS 133 (1971).

(75) Convention for the Suppression of Unlawful Acts Against the Safety of Civil Aviation (1971), id. at 1151.

(76) Article 7 of both the Hague and the Montreal Conventions oblige States to submit offenders "without exception whatsoever" to their competent authorities for the purpose of prosecution. Commentators are generally agreed, however, that this does not exclude the right to grant asylum. See Mankiewicz, The 1970 Hague Convention, 37 J. AIR L. & COM. 195, 204-06 (1971); Lissitzyn, International Control of Aerial Hi-jacking: The Role of Values and Interests, PROC. AM. SOC. INT'L. L. 80, 81-83 (1971).

(77) The text of this treaty is annexed to General Assembly Resolution 3166 (XXVIII). See also 13 INT'L LEGAL MATERIALS 41 (1974).

(78) For the history of this Convention, see Kearney, The Twenty-fourth Session of the International Law Commission, 67 AM. J. INT'L. L. 84 (1973).

(79) For general comments on this Convention, see Rozakis, Terrorism and the Internationally Protected Persons in the Light of the ILC's Draft Articles, 23 INT'L & COMP. L.Q. 32 (1974); Wood, The Convention on the Prevention and Punishment of Crimes against Internationally Protected Persons Including Diplomatic Agents, 23 INT'L & COMP. L. Q. (1974).

(80) 11 INT'L LEGAL MATERIALS 977 (1972).

(81) Id. at 985.

(82) See Wood, supra note 79, at 804.

(83) U.N. Doc. A/AC.6/L.951/Rev. 1, 1973.

(84) See, Wood, supra note 79, at 795-97.

(85) General Assembly Resolution 3166 (XXVIII) (U.N. Doc. 30, A/9030, 1974).

(86) Wood, supra note 79, at 797-98.

(87) Graham, supra note 36, at 53.

(88) Baxter, supra note 12, at 195; Baxter, supra note 36, at 16.

(89) Professor Baxter states that, "[i]f separate bodies of law are created for the just and for the unjust, for those who fight lawful wars and those who fight unlawful wars, the whole fabric of the humanitarian law of war can be brought tumbling down." Baxter, supra note 12, at 203.

(90) GAOR, 27th Session, 6th Committee (U.N. Doc. A/C.6/SR. 1368 § 54, Nov. 21, 1972).

(91) Frank and Lockwood, supra note 57, at 74.

(92) Abi-Saab, supra note 21, at 94.

5 Liberation Theology: Its Methodological Foundation for Violence
John R. Pottenger

The existence of pervasive social injustice in Latin America raises serious ethical questions for contemporary Christians. In the face of such injustice, many believers attempt to maintain their traditional religious values of assisting the poor and oppressed by actively working for social change. Often such activity runs afoul not only of government policies but of policies of the established Church as well. A spiritual dilemma for many individuals occurs when, out of a desire to fulfill a Christian duty to alleviate the afflictions of others, their attempts to press for profound social changes encounter an ecclesiastical structure which is reluctant to become involved in politically sensitive social issues. The established Church usually counsels obedience toward, instead of confrontation with, secular authorities and passive acceptance of, rather than active rejection of or even revolt against, oppressive social conditions. In fact, members of the clergy are often discouraged from seeking political positions, elective or appointive, in government. Given, then, the often accommo-dating stance of ecclesiastical Christian authorities toward status quo politics in Latin America, disillusioned individuals frequently eschew all pretense of religious obligations and endorse more narrowly focused political movements to effect social change. It is largely this phenomenon - oppressive social conditions with no religious approach which can ade-quately deal with them - which has given rise to theologies of liberation in Latin America.(1)

The religious dimension of Latin American culture makes the Church an important, if not crucial, factor in social and political issues. When faced with poverty and political oppression, many Christians look to the Church for moral guidance. As one aspect of this religious dimension, liberation theology presents alternative attitudes toward social injustice

and addresses more favorably ethical attitudes toward political
action, including the moral problems of revolution and violence.   The encouragement to political action that finds its
justification in liberation theology may assume a variety of
forms from educating and organizing the illiterate on the
nature of their rights under various regimes(2) to support for
political participation that often culminates in revolutionary
activity.(3)   Given the social turmoil in Latin America, a
proper understanding of liberation theology is paramount to
comprehend fully the religious dimension at work in society.
     Many theologians of liberation, both Catholic and Pro-
testant, are now attempting to provide explanations for understanding the nature of social injustice and appropriate ways to
deal with it without rejecting faith in God.   In fact, it is
through faith in God and His active participation in history as
demonstrated by the scriptures - for example, the liberation of
the ancient Israelites from bondage in Egypt(4) - which provide hope for an improved temporal existence through some
form of active participation in social change.   Theologians of
liberation claim to provide a clearer understanding of scriptural values as well as a powerful analytical critique of the
current structure of society.   Although still viewing the world
from the perspective of the biblical heritage, liberation
theology revised that heritage to take contemporary needs into
account and to insist that revealed sources provide relevant
guidance for modern dilemmas.   As critical theory, it recognizes the reality of the pronounced social injustice enmeshed in
developing political economies of Latin America and has incorporated contemporary approaches to social analysis to
grapple with them.   Liberation theology, then, combines the
ethical implications of Christianity with modern social analysis
to establish and justify various approaches to political action.
This combination is the essence of the methodology of liberation theology.   And it is this methodology which must be
grasped to comprehend contemporary radical Christian attitudes
toward revolution and violence fully.
     Liberation theology is not a homogeneous body of doc-
trines but rather a broad philosophical movement comprised of
diverse arguments on theological and social issues, such as the
meaning of redemption, the role of women in the Church, and
the propriety of various political activities.   Hence disagree-
ments occur occasionally as theologians arrive at conflicting
conclusions on critical issues.   Such is the case in devising
appropriate ethical responses that may be translated into
political action to eradicate social injustice.   Many theologians
rule out revolutionary violence as an appropriate method to
effect social change, opting instead for nonviolent approaches
as an appropriate response to social injustice.(5)   Others
present differing arguments on the nature of violence and its
potentially legitimate use.   And it is this latter group which

currently commands the most attention and profoundly influences the general direction of liberation theology on questions
of social change. More notably, Gustavo Gutierrez, Juan Luis
Segundo, Hugo Assmann, Jose Miguez Bonino, and Jose Comblin present the major arguments on revolution and the nature
of violence.(6)

This chapter will focus first on the methodology of
liberation theology as understood by those theologians mentioned above. Various key aspects - for example, the understanding of the nature of truth, the importance of the
historical situation - will be contrasted with other theological
approaches - that is, traditional theology and political
theology. This is followed by an in-depth discussion of the
methodology's critical approach toward theological and social
reality which will set the stage for considerations of the nature
of violence, revolution, and terror and their justifications, if
any, within the literature of liberation theology. The methodology provides the foundation for resolving moral questions
within liberation theology and hence must first be comprehended.

To understand how various theologians can potentially
accept violence as a proper response to oppression, the essence of liberation theology must be understood. This essence
is comprised of a methodology that allows the meanings of
religious truths to be expressed in a way that effectively
meets the needs of the poor and oppressed. Liberation theology begins with a commitment to human liberation from social
injustice and then develops a theological foundation which
considers various forms of political action for effecting social
changes to be morally correct. Such a commitment emerges
from an individual's own experiences in conditions of poverty
and political oppression. "Poverty is a central theme both in
the Old and the New Testament," notes Gutierrez, "a scandal-
ous condition inimical to human dignity and therefore contrary
to the will of God."(7) Gutierrez then provides scriptural
references wherein God condemns such activities as fraudulent
commerce and exploitation, the hoarding of lands, dishonest
courts, the violence of the ruling classes, slavery, unjust
taxes, unjust functionaries, and oppression by the rich.(8)
These early gospel themes find expression in contemporary
Church documents that condemn extreme economic class distinctions, the implementation of unjust laws and decrees, the
genocide against Indian tribes, and the random assassinations
and tortures of peasant union leaders, urban community leaders, students, professionals, and priests throughout Latin
America - e.g., Oaxaca, Mexico; San Salvador, El Salvador;
Lima, Peru; Sao Paulo, Brazil; Santiago, Chile.(9) All of
which, according to Gutierrez, must be eliminated to bring all
of humanity closer to God.(10)

After receiving the scriptural exhortation to side with the poor and oppressed, the faithful then commit themselves to human liberation from social injustice. In traditional theology, the next step would be to find scriptural propositions to guide ethical behavior. In this way, an individual can know whether a particular form of political action meets biblical standards. But to theologians of liberation, the search for biblical standards of moral conduct yields unsatisfactory political results. According to Segundo, any socially viable theology must deal with two crucial questions:

> With what means or scientific instruments can the church determine when a system has ceased - once and for all, presumably - to promote the common good? And how can it be scientifically sure of the existence of another system that is more just before coming up with such proof.(11)

Traditional theologians have come to the conclusion that the Church must refrain from taking explicit and particular stands on political activities since an adequate approach to social analysis cannot be deduced from revealed precepts. Arguing against any theological support for violent revolution as a proper response to social injustice, traditional theologian Alfonso Lopez Trujillo maintains that

> The political neutrality of the Church is a mandatory condition for protecting pastoral independence. The main mission of announcing the Gospel will not be chained by the ambiguous, changing, unsteady and whimsical procedures in the political arena.(12)

In traditional theology, then, normative exhortations for personal improvement lack any specific prescriptions for social change. Thus the transcendental nature of objective certitudes relegates particular social needs to a position of secondary importance. In fact, the emphasis on other-worldly concerns usually limits secular concerns to those of social stability, thus offering little incentive to become directly involved in issues of social injustice. Hence Segundo finds that the non-political stance of academic theology invariably becomes "bound up with the status quo" in politics.(13) Furthermore, the traditional approach assumes a discontinuity between the realms of heaven and earth, the divine and the profane. But in Gutierrez' theology, the human desire to know God in fact indicates that the "natural and supernatural orders are therefore intimately unified."(14) In this way, Segundo too distinguishes traditional theology from liberation theology by noting the emphasis in the former on its universal character and the denial of any association with particular politics, while the latter "consciously and explicitly accepts its relationship with politics."(15) In fact, Assmann maintains that "all human actions have a political dimension" and that discussion of abstract theological concepts is useless without a commitment to political action.(16)

Another theological approach with similar concerns for social injustice as liberation theology is European "political theology." However, it also suffers from the problem of first looking to revealed propositions for guidance. Segundo criticizes political theologians, such as Jurgen Moltmann,(17) for misunderstanding the nature of the revelatory process. Both exegetical and phenomenological analyses of scripture demonstrate the existential basis of the development of theology and thus the prime importance of human participation.(18) Hence a crucial difference in methodologies between the two theologies occurs because liberation theology reverses the usual theoretical development by placing the commitment to liberating humans from social injustice prior to the development of the theological position. Segundo explains that

> human options depend upon an understanding and appreciation of the surrounding context and must be taken before the scientific certitudes of theology have anything to say.(19)

Because theology can have meaning only after an option within a particular historical situation has been taken, any theological certitude "is at best instrumental in nature and it does not say anything about the decisive value of what we are doing." Thus liberation theology preserves the preeminence of subjective human participation which is lacking in both traditional and political theologies.

Since theologians of liberation rule out the existence of universal propositions to guide ethical action, the traditional criteria for a "just war" cannot be offered as a pattern for developing criteria for a "just revolution" or especially a "theology of revolution" as is often mistakenly assumed.(20) Comblin emphasizes that

> the subject matter of a theology of revolution is sometimes misunderstood. Its problem does not consist in determining the legitimacy or illegitimacy of a revolution itself. Neither does it consist of a search for abstract conditions of a right revolution; it is not an attempt to develop a theory of "just revolution," like the "just war" theory.(21)

But the lack of a propositional approach to ethical behavior indicates that liberation theology must then emphasize another aspect of its methodology to provide a coherent, consistent,

and stable approach to the ethics of political action. As
Segundo notes,

> Our theory, in other words, assumes that there is
> an empty space between the concept of God that we
> receive from our faith and the problems that come to
> us from an everchanging history. So we must build
> a bridge.(22)

Segundo begins the bridge building by recognizing the
importance of the socialization process that selects and instils a
particular set of values in each individual. A set of values
initially emerges through trust in other human beings. The
child, for example, begins by "identifying himself with the
values of his parents"; later this human trust may develop into
theological faith. The particular set of values then becomes
the focal point for faith.(23) Yet with changing historical
situations, the meanings of scriptural values also differ. And
the solutions to problems of social injustice will differ as well.
Religious faith, however, continues unchanged. And it is this
unchanging faith that provides the stability for liberation
theology. Hence Segundo must explicate the nature of faith in
his theology to avoid both its identification with particular
ideologies and the epistemological problems associated with
existentialist ethics.(24)

The nature of absolute faith in liberation theology is not
the same as that of traditional theology. In traditional
theology the notion of absolute truth provides a clear delin-
eation between the values of good and evil, and faith is placed
in the truth of these values as unchanging. As Miguez Bonino
explains the traditional notion,

> Truth belongs, for this view, to a world of truth, a
> universe complete in itself, which is copied or re-
> produced in "correct" propositions, in a theory . . .
> which corresponds to this truth. Then, in a second
> moment, as a later step, comes the application in a
> particular historical situation.(25)

Freedom, then, is defined in terms of the constraints imposed
by the values of propositional truth.

The conception of freedom in liberation theology is such
that "our freedom is precisely the capacity to absolutize what
nature and history always present to us as something relative."(26) Since Segundo views a set of values as relative to
the particular historical situation from which it originated, at
any given time, through a commitment, an individual can absolutize a value - e.g., liberation - by merging it with
objective reality - e.g., the oppressed - and then declaring
the merger unconditional.   The individual must entrust his or

her commitment to liberation with complete hope regardless of
the probability of success. Segundo refers to such subjective
absolutization as "faith"; thus,

> the process of faith begins by absolutizing persons
> rather than disembodied or abstract values. How-
> ever, it does not absolutize a static person.
> Instead, it attributes value to the person as a
> companion in existence, as a guide through the
> wilderness of the unknown and the unexperi-
> enced.(27)

Miguez Bonino states that only through proper activities can
"correct knowledge" be known.(28)   And Assmann stresses
that faith has a political dimension of its own.   Hence one
cannot "live a life of faith in isolation from daily life."(29)
    Segundo points out that the absolutization of individuals
with particular social needs instead of abstractions attributes
"absolute value to a person as educator."(30)   The process of
learning itself alone transcends historical situations and can
alone claim ontological status as abstraction; although it manifests its quality conditionally:

> Thus, in and through faith, we absolutize one con-
> crete pedagogical process in history, placing it
> above and before any other such process.(31)

Therefore absolutization is a subjective and free act of the
individual's will, although it is an objective process in history
"directed by God himself . . . an absolute educator."   This
objective process for liberation indicates that faith is
"converted into freedom for history, which means freedom for
ideologies."(32)   A logical relationship exists between the
object of faith and the argument for political action.   Segundo
refers to this relationship of interconnected values as "ideology," where means-ends arguments are advanced.(33)   The
"foundation stone" of ideology, then, is faith.   The complementary relationship between the two provides the bridge
between a "conception of God and the real life problems of
history."   Faith exists as an absolute educational process
subjectively applied to problems of social injustice; while
ideology represents possible explanations and solutions relative
to the historical situation.
    Following the scriptural examples of "critical reflection"
on ancient social conditions, liberation theology attempts to
retain and strengthen the role of critical reflection on
contemporary social conditions as well.   The scriptural emphasis on a critical stance toward social injustice assists the
individual's comprehension of his or her own social situation
and gives relevant meaning to revealed gospel themes.   Thus,

explains Gutierrez, an "historical praxis" develops; that is, a practical implementation of scriptural meanings which can be modified with changing social conditions. Joining Assmann, Segundo, and Miguez Bonino, he asserts that

> In this light, the understanding of the faith appears
> as the understanding not of the simple affirmation -
> almost memorization - of truths, but of a commit-
> ment, an overall attitude, a particular posture
> toward life.(34)

After the individual's initial commitment to liberation, "theology follows; it is the second step."(35)

As mentioned above, a thorough critical reflection on one's position in life must address itself to all that is subject to scriptural comment, including social conditions. To be effective, then, a comprehensive theology must act as a critical theory of society; it must be able to analyze and explain the conditions under which those willing to live Christian lives must exist. Theologians of liberation, however, claim that scriptures do not provide any sociological framework necessary to analyze the complex economic and social arrangements of contemporary societies. In his introductory work on liberation theology, the North American theologian Robert McAfee Brown notes that until recently "theological tools have usually come from philosophy," with theological systems being based on Plato, Aristotle, and Hegel.(36) But this results in theol-ogies, like their philosophical counterparts, that "tend to justify the status quo rather than challenge it." As political scientist Michael Dodson notes, a theology of critical reflection requires something more:

> Clergy radicalized by direct involvement with the
> poor required tools for explaining the social re-
> lationships they encountered and for justifying some
> form of political action to ameliorate those con-
> ditions.(37)

Both Brown and Dodson support the contention made by the-ologians of liberation, such as Assmann, that

> a political theology cannot become truly aware of
> critical aspects of faith as a liberating historical
> process without using analytical language. This
> brings about a new relationship between theology
> and the secular sciences.(38)

The "secular science" most often employed by libera-tion theology is some version of Marxist class analysis. But according to the North American theologian Arthur F. McGovern, in his investigation of the relationship of Marxism to various forms of Christian theology, "liberation theologians have not, as a group, made Marxism an exclusive or necessarily privileged tool of analysis."(39) Yet he then states,

> On the other hand, given liberation theology's conviction about underdevelopment, and given the pervasiveness of Marxist ideas in Latin America, one could hardly analyze the problems of Latin America without at least implicit use of Marxist ideas.(40)

Comblin, however, asserts that the incorporation of Marxism is only partial since the elements of atheism and totalitarianism are rejected. Liberation theology does accept the Marxist criticisms of capitalism, the criticisms of alienation, and "the class struggle as a way to revolution."(41) Thus Marxist class analysis most often provides the analytical tool necessary for the critical reflection of society demanded by liberation theology.

The combination of social analysis with contemporary implementation of scriptural themes provides the moral foundations for liberation theology. Upon this methodological foundation, theologians of liberation construct ethical arguments for political action. Through an exposition of Segundo's "hermeneutic circle"(42) as an example of the methodology of liberation theology, the relationship between religious values and political action can now be more clearly demonstrated. Segundo's circle begins with an "act of will" as the first of four steps. An individual must make an act of will toward seeking solutions to problems of social injustice. As mentioned earlier, it is the individual's experience and religious orientation that determine the impetus and direction of the will toward any particular set of problems and possible solutions. For Segundo, the commitment to human liberation emanates from his own experience with social justice in Latin America.

This experience with its attendant act of will or commitment to liberation also involves an attitude of "ideological suspicion" with respect to current explanations of and justifications for existing political institutions, social policies, and economic conditions. Such suspicion introduces the reflective individual to the second step of the circle which calls for a critical analysis of the ideological superstructure that defends the current social policies and of the institutions that participate in their defense. The use of Marxist class analysis serves this purpose. The critical evaluation of all aspects of social existence then leads the individual to experience a new theological understanding of scriptures which leads to "exegetical suspicion,"(43) the third step. This suspicion results in a critical analysis of the prevailing interpretation of scripture with respect to current social conditions. The recognition of current sociological factors, such as the vast inequality of wealth distribution and the suppression of individual civil liberties, are now included for scriptural reflection. With the inclusion of such sociological factors that had been traditionally ignored or unknown, scriptural passages take on renewed relevance.

Finally, within the context of social injustice, a "new hermeneutic" (44) can proceed. New ways of interpreting scriptures can now be applied to give meaning to and justify political activities to fulfill the original commitment to liberation. The more relevant interpretation of scriptures, then, provides the ethical basis for political action. This completes the circle while still retaining the continual suspicion which sustains its dynamic approach to critical analysis at both the sociological and theological levels. Thus the methodology of liberation theology, as demonstrated by this example, relies not on abstract universal propositions but on a process of learning through the experiences of the people. And this process of learning reveals particular attitudes toward the ethics of political action, especially revolution and violence.

The use of social analysis by liberation theology provides a strong basis from which far-reaching critiques of current social conditions in Latin America can be produced. The results of such powerful critiques indicate that the blame for social injustice cannot be leveled simply at one individual or ruling junta but is found in the structure of social and economic institutions. Thus social injustice originated in "institutionalized violence." Such critiques have had tremendous impacts on official Latin American Church positions. According to the documents issued by the Conference of Latin American Bishops at Medellin, Colombia in 1968, the social injustice of institutionalized violence occurs

> because of a structural deficiency of industry and agriculture, of national and international economy, of cultural and political life, "whole towns lack necessities, live in such dependence as hinders all initiative and responsibility as well as every possibility for cultural promotion and participation in social and political life," thus violating fundamental rights. (45)

The Bishops warned against abusing the patience of a people suffering under such conditions and the likelihood for violence if changes were not forthcoming. Ten years later, at Puebla, Mexico, the Conference of Latin American Bishops issued a stronger appeal:

> From the depths of the countries that make up Latin
> America a cry is rising to heaven, growing louder
> and more alarming all the time. It is the cry of a
> suffering people who demand justice, freedom, and
> respect for the basic rights of human beings and
> peoples.(46)

More recently the late Archbishop of San Salvador, Oscar
Arnulfo Romero, along with present acting Archbishop Arturo
Rivera Damos, issued an appeal which contained a description
of the social pathology of violence.(47) The deprivation of the
basic necessities of life to a majority of the population occurs
as a result of the monopoly of economic power held by the
small privileged class in society - e.g., while fourteen families
control most of the wealth in El Salvador, only two countries
in Latin America had a lower per capita GNP in 1980.(48)
This in turn spawns various movements and institutions which
attempt to organize the poor economically and politically, to
assist them in meeting their needs and protecting their human
rights. This threat, however, to the economic and political
power of the elite triggers a more vicious form of violence.

> Alongside institutionalized violence there frequently
> arises repressive violence, that is to say the use of
> violence by the state's security forces to the extent
> that the state tries to contain the aspirations of the
> majority, violently crushing any signs of protest
> against the injustices we have mentioned.(49)

There are no limits to the use of repressive violence
against those attempting to ameliorate the effects of the
institutionalized violence. A prominent active leader among the
poor, Archbishop Dom Helder Camara, earlier documented the
abuses by government authorities of Brazilian clergy involved
in movements toward easing the burdens of the oppressed.(50)
The number of victims, including Romero and other clergy,
has been well documented in the recent campaign of repressive
violence in El Salvador,(51) as well as other Latin American
countries.(52) Latin American specialist Brian H. Smith
describes the violent reaction of Latin American governments to
various human rights movements within the Church:

> A major reason for their being attacked, claim
> the bishops, is their demand that society meet
> the basic needs of their people in a more just
> fashion - employment, housing, education, and
> health care.(53)

In fact, the government justifies its use of violence by
invoking national security concerns as its defense. And the

underlying values of such national security ideologies include
"anti-Marxism, patriotism, technocratic value-free planning,
and the subordination of personal rights to the interests of the
state." (54)

The escalation from institutionalized violence to repressive
violence creates an atmosphere wherein self-defensive "spontaneous violence" erupts.   Romero and Rivera Damos defined
the nature of this violence:

> We call violence spontaneous when it is an immediate,
> not a calculated or organized, reaction by groups or
> individuals when they are violently attacked in the
> exercise of their own legitimate rights in protests,
> demonstrations, just strikes and so on . . . a group
> or an individual repels by force the unjust aggres-
> sions to which they have been subjected. (55)

But with counter-violence from the government, social stability
deteriorates even further, yielding revolutionary violence and
terrorism. (56)   Thus a virtual "spiral of violence" occurs as
each side attempts to use greater force to overcome the force
of its opponent. (57)

The assumption, then, is that violence in society begins
with the nature of its institutionalization.   Thus, the impov-
erishment of the majority of the inhabitants in Latin America
represents a form of violence embedded within the very structure of current economic practices.   The economic practices,
however, are themselves a form of government-sponsored capitalistic economics interconnected with and dependent upon
other more industrialized countries for their own development.
Using analyses from dependency theories, Gutierrez feels
that the present state of underdevelopment in Latin America
"is only the by-product of the development of other countries." (58)   For Segundo, "The empty promises and the minimal realization of development help to make bearable an
order that, under the appearance of law, hides an inhuman
violence." (59)   A comprehensive move is necessary, then, to
break the dependence of Latin America on foreign industrialized nations and to break the oppressive structural violence
that maintains social injustice as a result of the foreign
dependency relationship.   As the Spanish theologian Alfredo
Fierro explains in his philosophical analysis of various forms of
political theologies, "the theology of liberation is grounded on
a social experience, lived in and with faith, wherein a colon-
ized people feels it must be liberated externally from the
forces of imperialism and internally from the grip of domestic
oligarchies." (60)

For many theologians, then, the existence of violence is
pervasive.   Yet the nature of violence is such that no social
situation can dispense with it entirely.   In fact, for Segundo,

the problem is not so much one of choosing violence or nonviolence but one of emphasizing the degree of violence permitted and to what or to whom it is directed. With regard to
love, generally assumed to be the opposite of violence, an
"economy of energy" exists.(61) Each individual has a finite
amount of available energy to expend on concern for others.
Thus, only a certain number of persons can be truly loved.
If an individual includes more persons the necessary energy
for loving the first group dissipates; and if humanity in
general is included, the individual's love becomes "vague and
ineffectual":

> Thus the economy of energy in the process of love
> implies that there is some mechanism whereby we can
> keep a whole host of people at arm's length so that
> we can effectively love a certain group of people.
> . . . This mechanism is not precisely hatred, it is
> violence - at least some initial degree of vio-
> lence.(62)

Miguez Bonino also sees the use of violence as an inherent aspect of all human action. The individual is, in fact,
"a project of liberation that constantly emerges in the fight
against the objectifications given in nature, in history, in
society, in religion."(63) In this fight with the social
environment, the individual is a creator as well as a defender.
And as creators, human beings employ some measure of violence.

To segregate those who are loved more entails a mechanism of treating others as functions. According to Segundo,
"our inclination is to treat them in terms of the role or
function they represent and perform."(64) Such a mechanism
does violence to the notion that all of humanity is equally
deserving of each individual's love. "Furthermore, even
though this violence begins as an internal thing, the need to
make this segregation and economy effective means that the
underlying violence soon surfaces directly."(65) The social
mechanism that reifies the existence of others as functions is
"law"; "Law constitutes the most generic expression of these
functional, impersonal relationships with other human individuals." And the existence of laws requires that society
possess and threaten the use of "physical violence" to exact
citizen compliance.(66)

Since all societies employ structural violence to maintain
the efficacy of law, the problem is ascertaining the degree
to which love guides the use of violence. The real antithesis
to love as love of others is "egotism" or self-love which
involves prejudices and other irrational attitudes. Egotism is
also subject to the economy of energy and thus also uses violence.(67) A society that enforces its laws through love is

to be preferred to one that does so through egotism. A critical analysis of Latin American political economies quickly
confirms the degree to which the violence of egotism dominates
social policies, policies that exacerbate poverty and maintain
political repression. For example, Latin American specialist
Roberto Calvo describes this tendency in Chile under General
Pinochet wherein national security policies primarily benefit the
military and take precedence over general concerns for human
rights.(68)

As a result of a critical theoretical analysis of social
injustice, the individual recognizes the reality of oppressive
structural violence, the violence that serves egotism. The
Christian heritage, however, exhorts all individuals to love
their enemies as well as their neighbors. But Gutierrez warns
that love remains "an abstraction unless it becomes concrete
history, process, conflict."(69) Universal love becomes
concretized by opting for the oppressed - the commitment to
human liberation - and by seeking also to liberate the oppres-
sors from their own mistaken path, "by combatting the oppressive class":

> In the context of class struggle today, to love one's
> enemies presupposes recognizing and accepting that
> one has class enemies and that it is necessary to
> combat them.(70)

Thus, in harmony with Segundo, to love one's enemies is to
"combat against them."

Combat is violence. In moral philosophy the problem of
violence is typically a problem of justification in the first place
and then a problem of its limits once justification is found.
But following the logic of Segundo's analysis wherein violence
is a necessary aspect of love and Gutierrez's exhortation to
demonstrate love for one's enemies by combatting them, it
follows that the problem of violence then becomes a problem of
historical circumstances; that is, "the problem of violence,
within a given civilization, consists precisely in the introduction of it."(71) The very nature of liberation theology's
methodology has "ruled out any possibility of a gospel-inspired
ethics or morality deciding in advance whether some line of
action is consistent with divine relevation or not."(72)
Segundo's hermeneutics reveal that the scriptures contain no
universal injunction against violence absolutely, but may be
justified depending on the situation - for example, he claims
that the scriptures exhibit the violent aspect of love in Jesus'
use of a whip to drive the merchants from the temple and in
Jesus' parable of the wealthy Samaritan who passed up a number of needy individuals before finally choosing one to assist.(73) Miguez Bonino concurs in his exegesis of the
scriptures that violence does not appear "as a general form of

human conduct which has to be accepted or rejected as such.
. . . Thus, the law forbids certain forms of violence to persons and things and authorizes and even commands others."(74)
    In traditional moral philosophy, violence itself is never
considered a moral good; only an unjust situation may require
violence as a necessity to remedy the situation in the name of
justice.   Given the conditions of social injustice in Latin
America, Miguez Bonino believes that class struggle is inevitable.   In fact, under conditions of poverty and oppression,
God requires the creation of a new society.   Hence, through
class struggle, the oppressed must gain the power to reshape
the economic and social institutions along different lines.
Unfortunately, he notes, history has shown that those with
power rarely yield their power voluntarily.   The use of violence will then be necessary to attain "a new and more just
situation."(75)   But apparently for Segundo, the amount of
violence must be limited to achieving the just goal of the
revolution.   He stipulates that

> [One should] use the least amount of violence com-
> patible with truly effective love.   The proper
> proportion, then, must be figured out in the context
> of each different historical situation.(76)

    As noted earlier, many theologians of liberation accept the
necessity for a class struggle as revealed through the use of
Marxist class analysis.   Comblin maintains that it is this
encounter with Marxism that has forced theologians to define
Christianity with regard to revolution.(77)   For Assmann, the
economic institutions in Latin America can only be changed
through revolution.   To be effective, Christians must be open
in stating their revolutionary objectives.   A revolutionary
theory must be developed.   But more importantly, they must
involve themselves with other revolutionary groups and influence the direction of the revolution as "the true theorists of
the aims and methods of the process of liberation."(78)
Segundo also recognizes the differences in intellectual capabilities and spiritual perceptiveness and realizes that there
will always be the dichotomy between "the minorities and the
masses - the former to lead the latter."(79)   Both Segundo
and Assmann agree that Christians should form the vanguard
of the revolution as a result of their commitment to the
liberation of the poor and oppressed.   In fact, Assmann stipulates that "Christians will more easily become authentic revolutionaries the more they identify their way of life with that of
the exploited."(80)   Yet, in a less elitist bias toward revolutionary leadership, Miguez Bonino feels that "there is no
divine war, there is no specifically Christian struggle."(81)
In their identification with the oppressed, Christians will
participate in class struggles.   They have, however, nothing
unique to contribute to the revolution.

Many clergy have indeed come to the conclusion after experiencing political repression while attempting to help the poor that revolutionary violence is the only recourse to effect social change. The case of Camilo Torres presents the classic example of a Catholic priest committed to the liberation of his people from social injustice in Colombia. After unsuccessful attempts to effect social change nonviolently, and after much mental anguish, Torres embraced violence as the only means to install social justice in Colombia. He maintained that "in Catholicism the main thing is love for one's fellow man. . . . For this love to be genuine, it must seek to be effective."(82) He found that one could not count on the "privileged minority" to assist in meeting the needs of the "poor majorities." Thus the political and economic power of the minority must be transferred to the majority for social injustice to cease. If the wealthy minority were not to resist violently, such a revolution would be peaceful; but a revolution was necessary just the same:

> Revolution will produce a government that carries out works of charity, of love for one's fellows - not only a few but the majority of our fellow men. This is why the revolution is not only permissible but obligatory for those Christians who see it as the only effective and far-reaching way to make the love of all people a reality.(83)

Thus, Torres was committed to revolution - nonviolent or violent - because "Christians can and must fight against tyranny." He joined a small guerrilla organization, the Army of National Liberation, and was killed by government troops.

More recently the internal strife in El Salvador has demonstrated the brutal reality of the repressive violence by government security forces. After noting many peaceful attempts at social reform that resulted in government-sanctioned tortures and deaths, a large group of Salvadorean Christian organizations, both Catholic and Protestant, issued a declaration of support for "the insurrection of the people."(84) The group referred to the encyclical letter of Pope Paul VI, Populorum Progressio, wherein revolution is condoned in situations of tyranny that "do great damage to fundamental personal rights and dangerous harm to the common good of the country."(85) The Salvadorean Christians called for "internal liberation" from tyranny as well as "external independence" from foreign powers.(86)

Given an appeal to violent revolution, what are the implications for using terror as well? The explicit issue of terror is noticeably lacking in the literature of liberation theology. How can an emphasis on the violence of love to restore human dignity rule out terror as a viable tactic to

effect social change? In fact, Segundo's position appears to
raise the specter of bestowing legitimacy under the banner of
Christianity on any means, perverse or otherwise, to achieve
any capricious end. Segundo claims that while "Christian
morality is precisely a <u>morality of ends</u>," those ends refer to
the achievement of a just society,(87) and such an achievement
can be wrought only through the liberation of the oppressed.
The context within which liberation must be achieved, then,
determines the morality of any apparently distasteful act -
such as "the use of violence against the police"(88) - necessary for liberation. As Segundo reflects: "I must admit that
such a consequence does not frighten me, nor am I disturbed
by the possibilities that certain situations can turn stealing
and killing into licit actions."(89)

Yet this is not an automatic endorsement of the use of
terror to assist the liberation effort.(90) While the "real
violence exercised by the unjust established order justifies in
principle a massive violent revolution," Segundo is not certain
what means can justifiably be used to bring about the revolution.(91) He looks at the example of a gunman who, in the
course of self-defense, may claim justification for killing his
violent assailant. But would it be legitimate self-defense for
the gunman, if he were slower at the draw than his attacker,
to kill him in an ambush? Furthermore, "would it be self-
defense if, realizing the circumstances and unable to take his
enemy by surprise, our gunman kills one of his own friends
and lays the responsibility and guilt on the enemy?"(92) This
last approach is often used by both government forces and
guerrillas to terrorize local populations and to force them into
submission through fear. Segundo seems to hesitate in accepting such terrorist tactics as a justifiable form of violence. Yet
he emphasizes again that the key to a proper understanding of
ethical questions with respect to violence is the methodology of
liberation theology, a methodology that allows the historical
situation in light of a contemporary understanding of scriptural
themes to determine moral behavior.

Miguez Bonino also apparently shies away from a complete
endorsement of the use of terror. While violence is necessary
for certain social changes and the creation of a new environment, this conception of violence as necessary to creation,
according to Bonino, "can also be escalated to the extreme,
elevating violence as an ultimate principle of creation, valid in
itself because it is, par excellence, the destruction of all
objectification."(93) But he then insists that only through the
total destruction of all limits on the individual - i.e., "nature,
social order, ethical norm, divinity" - can total freedom, even
humanity, be discovered.(94)

The reasons for the differences in attitudes toward terror
vis-a-vis other forms of violence in liberation theology appear
to center on the Christian emphasis on love as superior to

egotism in guiding ethical questions. While both love and egotism contain dimensions of violence, terror alone reduces the human being from a subject of love to an object of instrumental value. A state run by egotism tends to use violence in the form of terror to stymie efforts at social reform and to reduce sympathy for popular revolutionary organizations.(95) The methodology of liberation theology indicates that the use of violence by the oppressed as a last resort in conditions of social injustice actually represents a manifestation of love toward the oppressor as well as the oppressed. The use of violence only out of necessity to remedy unjust situations acts as a constraint on its potential elevation as a good in itself to serve egotism, not love. It appears from liberation theology that the Christian must be motivated by love not egotism and although he may be forced to use violence, he should never choose to employ terror as a response to social injustice. In their declaration of support for the revolution, the group of Salvadorean Christian organizations also stated their desire that "the uprising be as human as possible and that it not degenerate into a dynamic that is destructive."(96)

To appreciate the dimension of revolutionary activity in Latin America fully, the religious dimension must be taken seriously, especially the extensive influence of liberation theology. To comprehend fully the attitudes toward violence and terror within liberation theory, the methodology must be understood. And it is the methodology of liberation which identifies the causes of social injustice and provides the moral justification for political action. Thus, the existence of social injustice and the individual's commitment - out of love - to human liberation demand "such a radical change in our existing societies that they turn the Christian into a revolutionary vanguard."(97) Perhaps this is the impetus behind the assertion of Guillermo Ungo, leader of the Democratic Revolutionary Front in El Salvador, that the alliance of the guerrilla factions and various political groups is built on "a foundation of love."(98)

NOTES

(1) For an introduction to the primary concerns of liberation theology, see Robert McAfee Brown, Theology in a New Key: Responding to Liberation Themes (Philadelphia: Westminster Press, 1978). A deeper philosophical treatment of liberation theology along with other similarly concerned theological positions can be found in the work by Alfredo Fierro, The Militant Gospel: A Critical Introduction to Political Theologies, trans. John Drury (Maryknoll, New York: Orbis Books, 1977).

(2) See, for example, Thomas C. Bruneau's article on "base communities," "Basic Christian Communities in Latin America: Their Nature and Significance (especially in Brazil)," in Churches and Politics in Latin America, ed. Daniel H. Levine (Beverly Hills: Sage Publications, 1980).

(3) A recent example is the clergy support for and participation in the successful revolution in Nicaragua. See Christianity and Crisis, 40 (May 12, 1980), with various discussions on this topic.

(4) Exodus, 13, 14. This is a frequent image invoked by theologians of liberation to demonstrate that God not only intervenes in human history but He does so on the side of the oppressed. For a criticism of the use of this image, see William K. McElvaney, Good News is Bad News is Good News (Maryknoll, New York: Orbis Books, 1980), pp. 121-123.

(5) Perhaps the best-known Latin American religious leader who espouses nonviolence as the proper approach to social change is Dom Helder Camara. Among his many works are Revolution through Peace, trans. Amparo McLean (New York: Harper and Row, 1971), and Spiral of Violence (Denville, New Jersey: Dimension Books, 1971). A theologian of liberation in the same nonviolent style is Leonardo Boff, who is a prolific writer as well. See Liberating Grace, trans. John Drury (Maryknoll, New York: Orbis Books, 1979) and A Vida Religiosa e a Igreja no Processo de Libertação (Petropólis: Editora Vozes, 1975); also see "Christ's Liberation via Oppression: An Attempt at Theological Construction from the Standpoint of Latin America," Frontiers of Theology in Latin America, ed. Rosino Gibellini (Maryknoll, New York: Orbis Books, 1975), pp. 100-132. And an important historian and lay theologian is Enrique Dussel, Ethics and the Theology of Liberation, trans. Bernard F. McWilliams (Maryknoll, New York: Orbis Books, 1978).

(6) See especially Gustavo Gutiérrez, A Theology of Liberation: History, Politics and Salvation, trans. and ed. Caridad Inda and John Eagleson (Maryknoll, New York: Orbis Books, 1973); Juan Luís Segundo, The Liberation of Theology, trans. John Drury (Maryknoll, New York: Orbis Books, 1976); Hugo Assmann, Theology for a Nomad Church, trans. Paul Burns, with an introduction by Frederick Herzog (Maryknoll, New York: Orbis Books, 1976); José Miguez Bonino, Doing Theology in a Revolutionary Situation (Philadelphia: Fortress Press, 1975); and José Comblin, The Church and the National Security State (Maryknoll, New York: Orbis Books, 1979). Two very good collections of essays by the leading theologians of liberation are Rosino Gibellini, ed.; Frontiers of Theology in Latin America, trans. John Drury (Maryknoll, New York: Orbis Books, 1979) and Claude Geffré and Gustavo Gutiérrez,

eds., The Mystical and Political Dimension of the Christian
Faith: Concilium 96 (New York: Herder and Herder, 1974).

(7) Gutiérrez, A Theology of Liberation, p. 291.

(8) See "Violence in Oaxaca," LADOC, 10 (January-February
1980): 32-45; "Salvadoran Archbishop Romero's Epiphany Ser-
mon," LADOC, 10 (May-June 1980): 41-47; "Evangelization and
Liberation: São Paulo," "Southern Andean Church Denounces
Injustices," and "Chilean Episcopals on 'Detained-Disappear-
ed,'" LADOC, 11 (May-June 1979): 41-45, 46-54, 31-35.

(9) Gutiérrez lists the following scriptural passages to
support his categories: Fraudulent commerce and exploitation,
Hos. 12:8, Amos 8:5, Mic. 6:10-11, Isa. 3:14, Jer. 5:27, 6:12,
hoarding of lands, Mic. 2:1-3, Ezek. 22:29, Hab. 2:5-6; dishonest courts, Amos 5:7, Jer. 22:13-17, Mic. 3:9-11, Isa.
5:23, 10:1-2; the violence of the ruling classes, 2 Kings
23:30,35; Amos 4:1, Mic. 3:1-2, 6:12, Jer. 22:13-17; slavery,
Neh. 5:1-5, Amos 2:6, 8:6; unjust taxes, Amos 4:1, 5:11-12;
unjust functionaries, Amos 5:7, Jer. 5:28; and oppression by
the rich, Luke 6:24-25, 12:13-21, 16:19-31, 18:18-26, James
2:5-9, 4:13-17, 5:16. See A Theology of Liberation, p. 293.

(10) Gutiérrez, A Theology of Liberation, p. 293.

(11) Segundo, The Liberation of Theology, p. 72.

(12) Alfonso Lopez Trujillo, Liberation or Revolution?: An
Examination of the Priest's Role in the Socioeconomic Class
Struggle in Latin America (Huntington, Indiana: Our Sunday
Visitor, 1977). Also supporting this position is another Latin
American theologian, Roger Vekeman, Caesar and God: The
Priesthood and Politics (Maryknoll, New York: Orbis Books,
1972).

(13) Segundo, The Liberation of Theology, p. 74.

(14) Gutiérrez, A Theology of Liberation, p. 70.

(15) Segundo, The Liberation of Theology, pp. 75-81.

(16) Assmann, Theology for a Nomad Church, pp. 32, 145.

(17) See, for example, Robert C. Freysinger, "The First
Revolution of Modern Christian Radicalism," Contemporary
Crises, 4 (1980): 353-366. Freysinger presents an explanation
of how radical Christian positions - including liberation
theology - combine appropriate aspects of the philosophical
writings of Augustine, Aquinas, and Marx to support a position of "just revolution." Liberation theology should not have
been included. Also, for a discussion of the contemporary
criteria for a "just war" as influenced by Augustine and
Aquinas and their possible use as a model for a "just revolution," see Robert McAfee Brown, Religion and Violence: A
Primer for White Americans (Philadelphia: Westminster Press,

1973), pp. 19-20, 58-61. And J. G. Davies provides an analysis of the responses of various Christian positions to the use of violence and revolution in Christians, Politics and Violent Revolution (Maryknoll, New York: Orbis Books, 1976). See p. 166 in Davies' book for the standards of a just revolution. Neither Brown nor Davies, however, refers to liberation theology as using such criteria.

(18)   Segundo. The Liberation of Theology, p. 75.

(19)   Ibid., p. 76.

(20)   One of Jürgen Moltmann's more important works is Theology of Hope: On the Ground and the Implications of a Christian Eschatology, trans. James W. Leitch (New York: Harper & Row, 1967). A critical assessment of Moltmann's position with regard to his call for "permanent revolution" can be found in Jon P. Gunnemann, The Moral Meaning of Revolution (New Haven: Yale University Press, 1979). Gunnemann, however, confuses European political theology with Latin American liberation theology by mistakenly assuming their methodologies are identical.

(21)   Comblin, The Church and the National Security State, p. 29.

(22)   Segundo, The Liberation of Theology, p. 116.

(23)   Ibid., pp. 104-105.

(24)   Discussed in my unpublished paper "Sartre, Fanon and Value Concerns" (1979), in which I analyzed the problems that ethical theory construction encounters when founded on an existentialist commitment to political action.

(25)   Miguez Bonino, Doing Theology in a Revolutionary Situation, p. 88.

(26)   Segundo, The Liberation of Theology, p. 176.

(27)   Ibid., pp. 176-178.

(28)   Miguez Bonino, Doing Theology in a Revolutionary Situation, p. 90.

(29)   Assmann, Theology for a Nomad Church, pp. 34-35.

(30)   Segundo, The Liberation of Theology, p. 179.

(31)   Ibid., pp. 178-180.

(32)   Ibid., p. 110.

(33)   Ibid., pp. 102, 105. See Chapter 4 for the explanation of the relationship of faith to ideology.

(34)   Gutiérrez, A Theology of Liberation, p. 7.

(35)   Ibid., p. 11.

(36)   Brown, Theology in a New Key, p. 64.

(37)   Michael Dodson, "Liberation Theology and Christian Radicalism in Contemporary Latin America," Journal of Latin American Studies, 2 (May 1979): 206.

(38)   Assmann, Theology for a Nomad Church, p. 38.

(39)   Arthur F. McGovern, Marxism: An American Christian Perspective (Maryknoll, New York: 1980), p. 184.

(40)   Ibid.

(41)   Comblin, The Church and the National Security State, p. 47.   Alfredo Fierro, however, is critical of political theologies that claim to accept only certain aspects of Marxism while rejecting others.   If Marxism were fully grasped, he maintains, then at best only a secular, not a spiritual, Christianity could exist.   See The Militant Gospel, pp. 110-120.

(42)   Segundo, The Liberation of Theology, Chapter 1.   In this chapter, Segundo outlines the essential aspects of his hermeneutic circle and uses it to analyze the theoretical effectiveness of four social critics: Harvey Cox, Karl Marx, Max Weber, and James Cone.   See also Alfred T. Hennelly, Theologies in Conflict: The Challenge of Juan Luis Segundo (Maryknoll, New York: Orbis Books, 1979), pp. 108-115.

(43)   Segundo, The Liberation of Theology, p. 9.

(44)   Ibid.

(45)   "Medellín Documents: Justice, Peace, Family and Demography, Poverty of the Church (September 6, 1968)," The Gospel of Peace and Justice: Catholic Social Teaching since Pope John (Maryknoll, New York: Orbis Books, 1976), p. 460.

(46)   John Eagleson and Philip Scharper, eds., Puebla and Beyond: Documentation and Commentary (Maryknoll, New York: Orbis Books, 1979), p. 134.

(47)   Oscar Arnulfo Romero and Arturo Rivera Damos, "The Church, Political Organization and Violence," Cross Currents, 39 (Winter 1979-1980): 385-408.

(48)   World Development Report, 1980 (Washington, D. C.: The World Bank, 1980), p. 110.   El Salvador had a per capita GNP of 660 U.S. dollars in 1980 while Honduras had 480 and Haiti 260.

(49)   Romero and Rivera Damos, "The Church, Political Organization and Violence," p. 403.

(50)   Paulo Schilling, ed., Helder Câmara: Escritos (Buenos Aires: Schapire Editor, 1972), pp. 60-66.

(51)   See, for example, Raymond Bonner, "The Agony of El Salvador," The New York Times Magazine (February 22, 1981), pp. 26-46.

LIBERATION THEOLOGY   121

(52) See, for example, "Pain and Hope for Guatemalans,"
LADOC, 10 (May-June, 1980): 33-40.

(53) Brian H. Smith, "Churches and Human Rights in Latin
America: Recent Trends on the Subcontinent," Churches and
Politics in Latin America, ed. Daniel H. Levine (Beverly Hills:
Sage Publications, 1980), p. 184.

(54) Ibid., p. 187, n. 1.

(55) Romero and Rivera Damos, "The Church, Political Organization and Violence," p. 404.

(56) Ibid.

(57) This phrase is usually attributed to Dom Helder Câmara,
Spiral of Violence (Denville, New Jersey: Dimension Books,
1971).

(58) Gutiérrez, A Theology of Liberation, p. 26.

(59) Segundo, "Christianity and Violence in Latin America,"
Christianity and Crisis, 4 (March 1968): 32-33.

(60) Fierro, The Militant Gospel, p. 190.

(61) Segundo, The Liberation of Theology, p. 157.

(62) Ibid., p. 159.

(63) Miguez Bonino, Doing Theology in a Revolutionary Situation, p. 115.

(64) Segundo, The Liberation of Theology, p. 160.

(65) Ibid.

(66) Ibid.

(67) Ibid., p. 157.

(68) Roberto Calvo, "The Church and the Doctrine of National
Security," Churches and Politics in Latin America, ed. Daniel
H. Levine (Beverly Hills: Sage Publications, 1980), pp. 135-
154.

(69) Gutierrez, A Theology of Liberation, p. 275.

(70) Ibid., pp. 275-276.

(71) Segundo, "Christianity and Violence in Latin America,"
p. 32.

(72) Idem., The Liberation of Theology, p. 165.

(73) Ibid., pp. 158-159, 162-165.

(74) Miguez Bonino, Doing Theology in a Revolutionary Situation, p. 117.

(75) Ibid., pp. 118-120. For Segundo, the just society must
be constructed on a socialist foundation; see his article,

"Capitalism Versus Socialism: Crux Theologica," Frontiers of Theology in Latin America, ed. Rosino Gibellini (Maryknoll, New York: Orbis Books, 1979), pp. 240-259.

(76) Segundo, The Liberation of Theology, p. 166.

(77) Comblin, The Church and the National Security State, p. 48.

(78) Assmann, Theology for a Nomad Church, pp. 141-142.

(79) Segundo, The Liberation of Theology, pp. 224-225.

(80) Assmann, Theology for a Nomad Church, p. 142.

(81) Miguez Bonino, Doing Theology in a Revolutionary Situation, pp. 124-126.

(82) John Gerassi, ed., The Complete Writings and Messages of Camilo Torres (New York: Random House, 1971), p. 367.

(83) Ibid., p. 368.

(84) Archdiocesan CARITAS et al., "Christians in the Face of the Insurrection of the Salvadorean People" (San Salvador, January 1, 1981), pp. 1-5.

(85) Pope Paul VI, "Populorum Progressio: On the Development of Peoples," (March 26, 1967), The Gospel of Justice and Peace: Catholic Social Teaching Since Pope John (Maryknoll, New York: Orbis Books, 1976), p. 396.

(86) "Christians in the Face of the Insurrection," p. 3.

(87) Segundo, The Liberation of Theology, pp. 171-172.

(88) Ibid., p. 173.

(89) Ibid., p. 175.

(90) This was one of the points stressed in a personal conversation with theologian Alfred T. Hennelly at the Woodstock Theological Center, Georgetown University, February, 1981.

(91) Segundo, "Christianity and Violence in Latin America," p. 33.

(92) Ibid., pp. 32-33.

(93) Miguez Bonino, Doing Theology in a Revolutionary Situation, pp. 115-116.

(94) Ibid., p. 116.

(95) Raymond Bonner, "The Agony of El Salvador," pp. 26-46.

(96) "Christians in the Face of the Insurrection," p. 4.

(97) Segundo, The Liberation of Theology, p. 55.

(98) Reported by Christopher Dickey, "Prelate Says Church Must Remain Neutral," The Washington Post, 104 (March 9, 1981): A19.

II
State Terror

Introduction to Part II
David C. Rapoport

> When it is a question of annihilating the enemy, we can
> just as well do without a trial. - Andrei Vishinsky.

Since the French Revolution, terror for secular purposes has
eclipsed terror for religious ends. The state and rebels, who
strike against the state as the embodiment of a "repressive"
order, are the two major organizers of the new terror. State
terror is the most important of the two phenomena. Certainly,
it is responsible for more casualties, and it has probably also
produced greater political consequences. State terror, it is
worth noting, bears some affinity to practices of Christian
millenarian sects which often attempted to establish or capture
governmental machinery to create the new world. Indeed,
although published too late for use here, James Rhodes' study,
The Hitler Movement; A Modern Millenarian Revolution, is quite
suggestive on this point.
    The next four chapters deal respectively with Revolu-
tionary France, Fascist Italy, Nazi Germany, and the Soviet
Union. The instances examined are classic ones, and each
essay treats selected different aspects of terror. The convenience or interest of the individual author determined which
aspect of terror he would highlight, and there is no suggestion that similar features cannot be observed either in the
other cases in this volume or elsewhere. In fact, the Revolutionary Tribunals or People's Courts which appeared in France
under Robespierre also emerged in Germany under Hitler, the
Soviet Union under Stalin, China under Mao, Cuba under
Castro, and most recently Iran under Khomeini.
    The idea of the People's Courts, an instance of hostage-
taking, and a concept grotesquely identified as "enlightened
terror" (named so because the state conceals its responsibility)
are the principal examples analyzed.   Obviously, they do not

provide a comprehensive view of the forms state terror takes. We do not discuss terror as an instrument of foreign policy, a 19th century phenomena that is widely used today by Moslem states, and probably also by Marxist ones, as Claire Sterling's recent book The Terrorist Network indicates. It would appear, however, that actions of this sort would be understood as a variant of "enlightened terror." State terror as a consequence or as a condition of rebel terror is not explored, though Shlomo Aronson and others in the volume (Amon, Pottenger, Ivianski, Louch, and Tugwell) make clear that one who uses terror must believe, or at least publically justify himself by insisting that the enemy used terror first and cannot be checked without similar methods. Today, self defense, of course, is the most universally accepted rationale for violence, but perhaps the public normally finds terror so outrageous that one cannot employ it without this justification at all.

In Chapter 6 Michael Carter provides a detailed account of the French Reign of Terror, discussing its character, purposes, administrative methods, and consequences from inception to destruction. For our purposes, perhaps, the Terror's most distinctive and radical innovation occurred in the legal sphere where two classes of persons were distinguished: citizens and "Enemies of the People." Citizens enjoyed a traditional conception of legal rights and obligations, in that their offenses were actions that violated specific laws, and offenders were entitled to judicial procedures where ordinary rules of evidence were employed to help determine guilt and innocence. Enemies of the People were considered dangerous to the Revolution, not simply because of what they did but more fundamentally because of who they were and what they might do. A citizen could be deterred or made better by punishment, but the character or behavior of an enemy of the People could not be altered; he or she was simply destroyed.

The traditional reluctance of European courts to consider motivation as the primary issue, a reluctance that still characterizes all Western jurisprudence, came partly from a recognition of the difficulties of determining the offender's purpose and more from the Judaic-Christian belief that God alone was capable of assessing the human heart. But the distinction between secular and divine spheres was an anathema to the Revolution, as its attempt to destroy Christianity makes clear and its consequent construction of a new calender symbolizes.

In principle, it may be impossible for a legal system to make the character of offenders the principal issue because of the vast, probably inseperable, opportunities for judicial arbitrariness created. Moreover, in the French case, and in all others where revolutionary tribunals are established, there is no effort to check capriciousness. On the contrary, ordinary courts are abandoned because they work too deliberately, rules of evidence are scrapped <u>because</u> they impede the decision process, and the public is g<u>iven an</u> important role in the tribunal's work just <u>because</u> it is more likely to be guided by emotions than by <u>rules of</u> consistency or precedence. Hence, Carter characterizes the tribunal's task as "identifying" rather than trying those brought before it.

The term Enemy of the People was, therefore, a political not a legal category; it referred to persons outside the law in virtually every sense of that word. The words of Andrei Vishinsky, who administered the Soviet's People's Courts during Stalin's purges, are quite apt, "When it is a question of annihilating the enemy, we can just as well do without a trial."(2) It is worth noting that the French category of persons whose dispositions deprive them of legal and moral protection and Dugard's description of "liberation fighters" whose purpose entitles them to be free from restraint derived from rules, are opposite sides of the same coins, the heads depict victims and the tails assailants.

The concern for pure motives is natural when the object is to destroy a <u>system</u> that is perceived as penetrating the minds of persons <u>despite</u> either their knowledge or will. In the efforts to create a new world and a new kind of human, the terror had in Carter's words an "exemplary" function. The Revolutionary Government used terror to identify the vices it wished eradicated as well as the virtues it wanted inculcated. The architects of the Terror, clearly, meant it to be a temporary instrument, one which would be laid aside when the Revolution was secure and when the moral basis of the new system was finally established. The Terror did disappear quickly, but not for those reasons. When no relationship exists between the persons executed and the qualities identified as exemplary, a truly dreadful unanticipated insecurity and hypocrisy emerges, which may (and certainly in this case did) destroy those who introduced the notion that the People's servants carry a responsibility so awesome and sacred that they need not be bound by rules.

"Fascism's Philosophy of Violence and the Concept of Terror" represents the most explicit effort in this collection to provide a definition of terror that comprehends both state and rebel forms. Its utility is demonstrated by a comparison of Italian, German, and Russian practices. Gregor develops his argument from distinctions made by Sergio Panunzio, who later became one of Mussolini "principal ideologues."

To Panunzio force and violence are similar phenomena. Curiously, both are legitimate, though not necessarily just, forms of coercion; both are radically different from terror which Panunzio regards as so irretrievably immoral that it can not be legitimized. Governments use force by punishing those who have violated its laws and by making war against those bearing arms against it. Rebels use violence to introduce a

new order, but that violence is limited by the same considerations that restrain government. When violence or force is
used, the behavior of the persons who are its object is decisive in determining culpability. Government or rebel spon-
sored terror, by contrast, does not make action relevant: in
principle nothing the victims have done or can do reduces
their culpability. What happens to them, happens simply
because the event affects others in ways the terrorists imagine
are advantageous to their cause. For Panunzio, a government that uses weapons of indiscriminate mass destruction is
engaged in terrorist behavior in exactly the same sense that a
rebel who blows up a bus-load of children is, because both are
treating their victims as "proximate ends."(3)

The rebellion or insurrection that the Fascists waged to
achieve power, Gregor contends, recognized the moral necessity of these restraints though numerous instances of abuse
were obvious. The Special Tribunal for the Defense of the
State established later by Mussolini to intimidate political
opponents can be characterized in the same way. It punished
behavior; one could escape its jurisdiction by not committing
certain acts or in some cases by promising to desist from
repeating them. Fascist Italy was a "repressive" state, not
one that deliberately used terror. The contrast with Nazi
Germany and Stalin's Soviet Union is striking because in the
latter two instances the People's Courts followed the precedents established in the French Revolution by concerning
themselves with ascriptive traits, traits individuals were not
responsible for and could not conceivably eliminate. An
implicit conclusion of the Gregor essay is that persons or
movements should be called terrorist when they recognize no
principle by which any of their actions could be considered
arbitrary.

The theme of regarding victims as proximate ends, of
believing that they deserve to be treated in expediential terms
only is continued in Shlomo Aronson's extraordinary (and
likely to be controversial) study of the Nazi government's terrorist policies. Aronson pays special attention to the audiences the terrorist seeks, audiences who sometimes may
never understand or believe his intent toward the victim, or
who at other times may respond with moral feelings which the
terrorist plans to manipulate.

Hitler regarded the Jews as sub-human terrorists(4) and
believed that the Jews abroad misled Germany's principal rivals to believe that Germany's limited political and military aims
were a bid for world dominion. Through a policy of forced
Jewish emigration, he hoped to create anti-Semitism abroad
in order to break Jewish influence over the major powers.
When this failed, he held the Jews as hostages, in the literal
sense of that term, in the hopes that Jews abroad would force
the Allies to change their definition of the war. Instead, the

uncomprehending Allies demanded unconditional surrender and embarked on massive air-raids (Bombenterror), whereupon Hitler began exterminating the European Jewish population knowing that the Allies would ultimately charge the German people as moral accomplices. The unforgiveable crime would make the Germans themselves hostages and prevent them from abandoning the Nazi government as they deserted its predecessor during World War I, only to fall once again under Jewish domination.

The "Document on Terror" is a chilling discussion of two fundamental kinds of terror - "general" and "enlightened" - their organizational bases, particular manifestations, political, psychological, and moral consequences. The author is unknown. Initially, it was described as a manuscript found in 1948 on the body of a dead Soviet official.(4) That account was not entirely persuasive, even to the original publisher, which is probably why the "Document" never attracted much attention.

For the purposes of this volume the precise question of its origin (it may have been written by a Western intelligence officer) is not critical, because the text is a theoretical discussion and should be judged by standards normally applied to such works. Most examples are hypothetical, and even if one eliminated the few historical illustrations because they deal with incidents that cannot be documented, the strengths and weaknessess of the general thesis would, I think, be unaffected. Certainly, the author reflected a good deal on his materials; the problems formulated and specific practices enumerated are familiar elsewhere.

A "general terror" policy is initiated openly in the name of the Revolution against the whole population. Although acceptable and often indispenable in the early phase of a revolution when enthusiasms are still hot and governments seem threatened by powerful forces, "general terror" if not terminated in time produces unhealthy effects. Political judgement is corrupted as terror is believed to be the solution for every problem. The population becomes partially "immune" and hostile. Simultaneously, the international world becomes antagonistic; as the "moral isolation" of government becomes more apparent, the population sees every enemy of its own government as a potential liberator.

A policy of "enlightened terror" enables government to avoid these problems (the "Document" is much too facile here) because government's role is concealed, and the government might even be able to make a credible case that its opponents are really responsible. Characterized by intermittent selective actions, the policy is directed towards specific groups. Its effect is to manipulate the moral rage of the population in the right direction, and at the same time attract whole-hearted commitment.

The "Document" does not discuss the differences between rebel and state terror. The distinctions made and the problems developed are obviously pertinent to both, but it is also true that the same circumstances which compel government normally to conceal responsibility operate to make rebels normally "claim credit."

NOTES

(1) For a discussion of assassination as an instrument of foreign policy, see my Assassination and Terrorism, ch. IV.

(2) Quoted by Gregor, infra.

(3) For a convenient summary of the Nazi understanding of the Jew as both a sub-human and a supra-human creature, see Yehuda Bauer, "Genocide; Was It the Nazis' Original Plan? The Annals of the American Academy of Political and Social Sciences 450, (July 1980): 35-46. Bauer concludes by noting the bizarre millenarian element in Nazi consciousness which led them to see the Jew literally as an instrument of Satan: "The Holocaust was . . . a sacral act. . . . By destroying the Jew he would be doing the will of God. It was in Nazi eyes a fight against Satan. It had cosmic importance . . . a quasi-religious act" (p. 44). The argument reminds one that Crane Brinton, historian of the French Revolution, considers the use of theological images and metaphors so compelling, that he lists Satanism as the first of several indispensable ideological components for those who introduced the Reign of Terror. A Decade of Revolution (New York: Harper, 1934) p. 158.

(4) Total war, re-introduced in the West by the French Revolution which reached its present climax in World War II, should be considered a form of state terror. Burke made the point originally. "If ever a foreign prince enters into France he must enter it as into a country of assassins. The mode of civilized war will not be practised; nor are the French, who act on the present system entitled to expect it." Lord Acton even argued that the threat inherent in revolutionary wars by the state suggested "the use to which terror may be put in revolutions." Lectures on French Revolution (New York: Macmillan 1959), Lecture XIV. Michael Walzer describes rebel terror, moreover, as a totalitarian form of war. Just and Unjust Wars (New York: Basic Books, 1979).

(5) The account of the manuscript's origin is reproduced with the "Document of Terror."

6 The French Revolution: "Jacobin Terror"

Michael Phillip Carter

The terror which was inaugurated by the revolutionary government of France on September 5, 1793 lasted only until the following summer. It was sanctioned by a National Convention which had been elected to give France a constitution, and organized by committees appointed to ensure national security while foreign troops and domestic rebellion threatened. Justified in the name of the sovereign people, the terror was rooted in the fears and suspicions of that people and made them its victims. In the course of the terror some 500,000 of the 25 million citizens of France were jailed as political suspects. Over 15,000 of these were condemned to death and 12,000 more were executed without trial. Uncounted thousands died in the prisons of the new republic.(1)

In the year of the terror France was peopled by citizens who only four years before had been subjects of a Bourbon monarch who ruled as his ancestors had for centuries, absolutely. In those times the prelates of the gallican church and the titled nobility largely controlled the wealth and productivity of the realm while yielding the influence which was traditionally theirs as offspring of the founders by cross and sword of feudal France. The state developed by the Bourbons since their accession in 1589 was designed to divert the local, estate-based power of this aristocracy toward the greater glory of France and especially of its monarch. Subject to this king and his aristocracy were the millions of commoners whose role in the order of things was stated quite simply as "to toil."

In 1789 thousands of these subjects asserted a sovereignty of their own and reduced Louis XVI to the status of a constitutional monarch who ruled not by the grace of God but by the will of the people. In 1792 others exercised that will in order to depose their king and declare a republic. In 1793 they intimidated the National Convention into purging itself and declaring terror as the official policy of the French state.

Throughout this era revolutionary initiative was centered in Paris. When Louis XVI summoned the Estates General for advice and consent to a tax reform program designed to rescue the monarchy from impending bankruptcy, propaganda emanated from liberal groups in Paris, asserting new rights for commoners and raised political expectations throughout the realm. Though it was at the Estates General in Versailles that the commons declared itself an assembly representing the nation and resisted royal attempts to obstruct their efforts to establish a written constitution for the realm, it was the shopkeepers, craftsmen, and workers of Paris who rose in July to arm themselves against the troops summoned to defend royal prerogatives. Though it was the assembly which abolished feudalism and promulgated a Declaration of Rights of Man, it was the market women and militia of Paris who marched to Versailles in October to demand the king's return on the capital where they, and not the aristocrats at court, could influence his decisions.(2)

Paris was the site of demonstrations demanding the king's deposition when, in the summer of 1791, he attempted unsuccessfully to escape the revolution. A year later, shoulder to shoulder with provincial volunteers mustered to defend the capital from approaching Prussian troops, the sans-culottes, the ordinary citizens of Paris, chased the Bourbon monarch from his throne. Attempts by members of the new national government to control political activity in the capital sparked yet another insurrection in the spring of 1793, when the silence of 80,000 Parisians and the cannons of their National Guard directed the Convention to order these members' arrest. The succeeding autumn delegations from the ward assemblies of the capital invaded the Convention hall to demand that terror be placed on the order of the day.

These citizens acted not just from dreams or desperation, but from fear and suspicion as well. The old fears of famine and suspicions that speculators would starve Paris for profit gave way to the fear of royal and aristocratic reprisals, suspicion that revolutionary gains would be wiped out by conspirators bent on reestablishing monarchical sovereignty. The July revolution had shed blood to revenge presumed conspiracy and treachery. The Bastille fell to arm the capital against the king's apparent intention to prorogue the new assembly. Its commander, the Marquis de Launay, was slaughtered for having fired on its besiegers. The intendant of Paris, the royal official responsible for the capital, was dragged from hiding, hanged, and decapitated by an angry crowd who paraded his head about on the end of a pikestaff.

News of the insurrection in Paris spread to the cities and villages of France where bourgeois and peasant alike struck at the powers and privileges of traditional elites. Municipal councils were set up to ensure the security of towns. Feudal contracts were burned and with them the occasional chateau. Peasants in much of France then armed and awaited the assaults rumored to be in preparation by aristocrats and brigands paid to wreak vengence for their revolt.(3)

In 1792, the failure of the armies of France to win the war she had declared revived rumors of royal treachery and aristocratic complicity. When threats of military repression issued by the commander of the Prussian forces were published in the capital on the first day of August, the wards of Paris and delegates of the provincial volunteers responded with an ultimatum demanding the king's deposition, then organized vigilance committees throughout the capital, established a special tribunal for crimes of treason, and ordered the arrest of all political suspects. In the first days of September over two thousand of those incarcerated were dragged before makeshift courts and slaughtered lest they conspire to reestablish the dethroned king while troops fought at the front.

The end of the monarchy and the institution of a republic in France did little to quiet Parisian agitation or to quell rumors of treachery. When the National Convention convened in late September to prepare a new constitution for France its members were conscious of the scrutiny of the Parisians and the shadow of the recent massacres. Informal parties began to emerge at the meetings held in the former riding school, and to the higher seats gravitated those deputies who echoed Parisian sentiments.

Dominating that high ground - "the Mountain" as it soon came to be called - were the representatives who in the evening frequented the Jacobin Club of Paris. Little more than a deputies' caucus in the early days of the revolution, the Jacobin Club had been transformed into a center for public debate and political agitation for the capital, and current propaganda for the provinces. Below the Mountain sat "the Plain," that majority of deputies whose votes the Jacobins sought to influence. The Convention quickly inaugurated the republican era, but approached the problem of disposing of the monarch who had been deposed more gingerly.(4)

Among the first questions taken up by the Convention were whether and by whom the king could be tried for his alleged crimes against the nation. To this debate on fundamental issues of legitimacy, royal and revolutionary, the deputies brought positions colored by their attitudes toward Parisian militancy. Those who came to be known as Girondins objected strongly to Parisian domination and were outraged at the blood that was shed in September. They resisted a trial from the outset, then labored to prevent the execution which was its outcome. The deputies from the Jacobin Club of Paris, which had increasingly adopted the language of Paris' agitators, argued that the people had in insurrection handed down their verdict on the monarch's guilt; to the Convention remained but the task of carrying it out. The youngest among them, Louis Antoine Saint-Just, declared the king an enemy alien to society, a tyrant who must reign or die.(5)

The majority in the Convention carefully adopted a policy by which they, as the "entire and perfect representation of the French republic," could accuse, judge, and punish the king. Unimpressed by the deliberation with which the deputies of the Convention were determining the king's fate, citizens of Paris spoke out in pamphlets and journals and the ward assembly meetings which met nightly, attributing to the monarch all the ills with which they were beset. The judgment and execution of Louis in January of 1793 was by then insufficient evidence of the Convention's loyalty to the capital. The Girondin's efforts to win a reprieve by appealing the verdict to a nationwide referendum marked them indelibly for Parisians. Food shortages, high prices, and military reverses were the backdrop against which the Jacobins in the Convention and militants of Paris began a campaign in earnest to proscribe the more prominent Girondins as sympathizers of the fallen regime. On June 2, 1793, the Convention, surrounded by the armed militia of Paris, acceded to these demands and arrested those deputies in the name of the people.

This attack on the national representation was received in much of France as an indication that the Convention had surrendered all right to govern. The revolts in western France and in Lyons were added uprisings throughout the nation. The Jacobins who composed the dominating minority in the Conventions rushed through the text of a republican constitution and submitted it to a national referendum. The new charter was celebrated in a lavish festival in the capital to which representatives from the electoral assemblies of all France were invited.

These gestures were not effective in redeeming the allegiance of the rebels. The elections that were guaranteed by the new constitution were not held. The Convention prepared military expeditions against the centers of provincial rebellion. Parisians clamored for radical measures to ensure the security and welfare of the capital and the nation. On the 5th of September, 1793, demonstrators occupied the Convention hall. In their presence, those deputies whose claim to be the entire and perfect representation of the French republic had been all but entirely eroded, acclaimed the proposition introduced by a delegation from the 48 ward assemblies and the Jacobin Club of Paris that from that day forth, terror would be the order of the day.

The revolutionary government moved swiftly to implement the order which it had adopted, and in this mobilization the Convention's Committee of Public Safety took the lead. On the evening of the fifth the special tribunal for political crimes was reorganized and expanded into several courts. These courts

were assured a steady flow of cases by the Law of Suspects
passed on the 17th of September which determined who was apt
for internment.   With definitions as vague as "those who,
either by their conduct, relationships, suggestions or writings, have shown themselves to be partisans of tyranny," law
supplied the vigilance committees which had been formed in the
wards of Paris and the communes of France with reason for
frequent action.(6)

Among the measures which had been demanded by the
demonstrators on the 5th was a "revolutionary army," a force
composed of citizens of Paris with a mandate to spread revolutionary principles to the provinces they would scour for
food for the capital.   Recruitment soon began in earnest.(7)

To carry the terror even farther afield, deputies were
selected as special representatives on mission for the government.   Some were dispatched to the centers of rebellion.
There they purged local administrations, besieged rebellious
towns, and directed the punishment of defeated rebels.   At
Nantes, hundreds of rebels were drowned on the orders of the
representative Carrier; hundreds more were shot in front of
mass graves dug at Lyons while the representative Fouche was
in charge.   Other representatives were sent to the front to aid
the republican commanders chosen to replace the aristocrat
generals of the old regime who had fled, surrendered, or been
fired as the revolution progressed.

The revolutionary tribunal, the Law of Suspects, the
vigilance committees, the revolutionary army, and the representatives on mission were instruments of repression similar to
those which had been employed by the Commune of Paris after
the king's downfall the preceding year.   In the autumn of
1793, however, they were used by the Committee of Public
Safety, and operated on a nationwide basis.

The ascendancy of the Jacobin-dominated Committee of
Public Safety as chief architect of national policy did not go
unchallenged in the Convention.   In late September the committee was simultaneously attacked for ineffectiveness in
organizing military victory and for the summary replacement of
unsuccessful generals.   The reply of Maximilien Robespierre, a
former small town lawyer and one of the dozen members of the
committee, both enumerated the responsibilities which Public
Safety had acquired and suggested the vision with which it
shouldered them:

> To direct eleven armies, to carry the weight of all
> Europe; to unmask traitors everywhere, to foil
> emissaries bought with foreign gold, to monitor and
> prosecute unfaithful administrators; to overcome
> everywhere obstacles, hindrances to the execution of
> wise decrees; to fight all the tyrants, to intimidate
> all the conspirators. . . . These are our func-
> tions.(8)

Less than a month later, on the 10th of October, Public
Safety further cemented its position as de facto executive when
the Convention approved Saint-Just's report for the committee
on "The Necessity of Declaring the Government Revolutionary
until the Peace." By this single declaration, the committee
and the convention simultaneously asserted the necessity for,
and the provisional character of, their collective dictatorship.(9)

In the autumn of 1793 the Convention followed the Committee of Public Safety's lead in attempting to transform both
state and society in France. A ceiling was imposed on wages
and prices, a special commission made responsible for controlling provisions, and trade restrictions introduced. A new
calendar was created to emphasize the novelty of the republican era and to undermine the rhythms of the Catholic litur-
gical cycle. Over a hundred more deputies were expelled from
the Convention for protesting the course which the revolution
had taken.

At the beginning of December, after the Girondins who
had been arrested the preceding June, and the queen who had
been widowed in January had mounted the scaffold, the organizational structure of the terror was established. Dated 14
Frumaire by the new calendar, the law reordering the organs
of the revolutionary government was introduced by Jean Nicolas Billaud-Varenne, a radical lawyer and writer, for the
Committee of Public Safety. It affirmed the Convention's role
as the sole center of power in France. Directly subordinate to
the Committee of Public Safety, however, were not only the
representatives on mission but also the executive council to
whom reported the criminal and political tribunals, the de-
partmental administrations, the general staff and the military
courts. Public Safety reported only to the Convention, and
shared its hegemony only with the Committee of General Security, which directed the national agents in the districts and
the communes, and policed the nation with the help of local
vigilance committees everywhere. Robespierre, Saint-Just,
Billaud-Varenne and nine colleagues were effectively empowered
with the direction of the war and the enforcement of all civil,
criminal, and administrative measures passed by the Convention.

The power concentrated by the Committee of Public Safety
in the decrees which it submitted to the Convention was applied all the more effectively through the enlistment of the
popular societies of France in the campaign of terror. These
clubs, most often modeled on the Jacobin Club of Paris, numbered in the thousands in the second year of the republic,
and were actively recruited by Public Safety and its agents.
Representatives on mission used the local clubs not only as a
base of operation but also as a core of patriots through whom
to identify and attack administrators reluctant or unwilling to

apply and enforce the policies emanating from Paris. Even
when the representatives on mission had come and gone, the
clubs were encouraged to monitor closely the activity of local
citizens and officials, and to send denunciations directly to the
committee in Paris.(10)

The evening meetings of the Jacobin Club of Paris were
used by the members of the committee as a forum to promote
examples of suitable republican behavior for imitation by
clubmen throughout France. Reported in detail by their newspaper, the Journal of the Mountain, the Jacobin debates most
often centered on issues outlined by those members who sat on
Public Safety. On the 1st of November, for example, Robespierre spoke of a foreign plot which obstructed the revolution's progress, and launched the Jacobins on a public purge
of its membership. This "purifying scrutiny" continued
throughout the terror and was imitated in form and content by
clubs all over France. Few members were actually ousted in
this purge. All, however, were subjected to a series of
probing questions and exposed to the accusations of their
fellow members. Exclusion and denunciation served not only to
advertise the tested purity of the Jacobins but also to raise
them up in their follower's eyes as paragons of republican
orthodoxy.

The Journal of the Mountain was, like many newspapers
during the terror, subsidized by the government as a means of
building morale among the armed forces and forming public
opinion in the countryside. Editorials iterated the theme of
foreign conspiracy which was so popular in reports and petitions to the Convention. Speeches of particular import were
reprinted in their entirety. Gestures of individual citizens or
patriot groups were advertised and praised, be they contributions to the war effort, or songs, poems, and plays portraying the virtues of the new republic and its sovereign.

Although Saint-Just and Billaud-Varenne had presented
and justified the reorganization of the government to the
Convention, Robespierre assumed for himself the job of justifying the program of terror which that government had implemented. In two speeches delivered during the second
winter of the republic Robespierre outlined the principles by
which he conceived the revolutionary government to be operating.

In the first of these speeches, delivered on the 25th of
December, 1793, Robespierre elaborated on the distinction
between revolutionary and constitutional government which had
been operative since the suspension of the constitution and
been formally introduced in Saint-Just's report declaring the
government revolutionary until the peace. The purpose of a
constitutional government, argued the orator, was the preservation of the republic. The end of revolutionary government, to the contrary, was the foundation of the republic.

While under a constitutional regime it was enough that the government protect the rights of the individual against the abuse of public power, under a revolutionary regime public power was obliged to defend itself against the factions which attacked it.

Robespierre also echoed that polarity which Saint-Just had offered a year before to deny the king a trial by contrasting the citizen to the enemy of the people: "To good citizens the revolutionary government owes the nation's every safeguard; to enemies of the people it owes only death." So that good citizenship might be unambiguously identified with allegiance to the policies of the revolutionary government, Robespierre gave warning to those who might deviate to either left or right. The revolutionary government "must sail between two reefs, weakness and rashness, moderatism and excess; moderatism which is to moderation what impotence is to chastity, and excess which resembles vigor as dropsy does health."(11)

On the 5th of February Robespierre borrowed freely from Montesquieu in outlining the "Principles of Political Morality which Should Guide the National Convention in the Internal Administration of the Republic." He declared that while in peacetime the principle and mainspring of popular government was virtue, "in revolution it is simultaneously virtue and terror: virtue, without which terror is fatal, and terror, without which virtue is powerless." He defined terror as "nothing other than prompt, severe, and inflexible justice," and as such an emanation of virtue. Terror, for Robespierre, was "a consequence of the general principle of democracy applied to the most pressing needs of the fatherland," not a principle unto itself.(12)

At the end of February Saint-Just introduced legislation designed to confiscate and make available to the ordinary citizen of the republic lands formerly belonging to suspects. Designed to create a new class of property holders with an interest in the future of the republic, these Ventose decrees did little to satisfy those for whom the cost of the revolution in high prices and shortages of goods was again reaching an intolerable level.

The "justice" of which Robespierre spoke in February was soon brought to bear on the "factions" which he had warned in December. When the call for a new insurrection was voiced at a Paris club, the committee chose the occasion to lash out at the left. It arrested the popular radical journalist and national agent to the Commune Jacques-Rene Hebert, along with a curious amalgam of militant officials and miscellaneous aliens. This clump of victims was described to the Convention by Saint-Just in his report "On the Factions of Foreign Inspiration and on the Conspiracy Plotted by them in the French Republic to Destroy Representative Government by Corruption, and to Starve Paris." Eighteen were guillotined on the 24th of March. A week later Georges-Jacques Danton, one of the most popular revolutionary leaders and proponents of restraint, was arrested with several of his associates who had been critical of Jacobin policy, tried with others imprisoned for graft, and executed as part of "the plot hatched to effect a change of dynasty."(13)

The Committee of Public Safety then moved on the neighborhood political clubs which, since the beginning of the terror, had operated as the loci for Parisian agitation. Within weeks each of the clubs had announced its dissolution, and the citizens who had frequented them withdrew to their ward assemblies which were restricted in their meetings and closely surveyed by the Committee of General Security. Paris would never again dictate policy to the Convention.(14)

This further consolidation of the Committee of Public Safety's power was accompanied by new visions of the task at hand and new ways to accomplish it. The foundation decrees passed by the Convention in the fall and winter were supplemented in the spring by the reports on the factions and addresses delivered to the Convention by the members of the Committee of Public Safety. On the 1st of April, the Convention voted to abolish its Provisional Executive Council, streamlining the exercise of power to the convenience of the Committee of Public Safety. In mid-April Saint-Just delivered that committee's and the Committee of General Security's joint report "On General Police, Justice, Commerce, Legislation, and the Crimes of the Factions." Three weeks later, on May 7, Robespierre delivered his report "On the Relationship between Religious and Moral Ideas and Republican Principles, and on National Festivals." On the 10th of June, Georges Couthon delivered the report on justice, honing the revolutionary tribunal as an instrument for the mass production of convictions.

Saint-Just opened his report on police, justice, commerce, legislation, and the crimes of the factions by reminding the citizen-legislators that "It is not enough that we have destroyed the factions, we must repair the damage that they have done to the fatherland." Asserting that it would be easy to retrace the famine plot hatched to agonize the republic all the way back to the days before the revolution, Saint-Just contented himself with a brief sketch of only the most recent counter-revolutionary tactics. He then traced a portrait of the "revolutionary man," listing the virtues which such a man possessed: inflexibility tempered with judiciousness, frugality, simplicity without false modesty. Saint-Just's revolutionary man was the "irreconcilable enemy of every lie, every indulgence, every affectation." The sketch and portrait took the report out of its way to justify, for the Convention, the new General Police Bureau which was established on the committee's recommendation, and the ceding of police powers to the Committee of Public Safety by the Committee of General Security. (15)

The report of Robespierre, however, was less an act of faith in the revolutionary man than a leap of faith in the power of religious ideas over would-be republicans. As had Saint-Just, Robespierre once again rewrote the history of the revolution, highlighting the perfidy of the recently purged. The report culminated in a decree by which "the French People recognize the existence of the Supreme Being and the immortality of the soul." Each year the people were to celebrate before that deity the great days of the revolution, enumerated as 14 July 1789, 10 August 1792, 21 January 1793, and 31 May 1793 (the days the Bastille, the monarchy, the king's head, and the Girondins, respectively had fallen). A liturgy was also developed wherein each of the weekly holidays of the revolutionary calendar was given its own themes, such as Truth, the Freedom of the World, Glory and Immortality, or simply Happiness. Though the freedom of worship was confirmed in the decree, Robespierre's remarks made it clear that neither "fanaticism" (meaning Roman Catholicism) nor atheism would flourish under the new regime of the Supreme Being.

Couthon's report began with the news of naval victories but ended less auspiciously with a decree designed to step up yet again the pace of the revolutionary tribunal. As described by the reporter for the Journal of the Mountain, Couthon "directed the attention of the Assembly toward certain false notions which had survived the revolution on the correct means of rendering justice." Having set things straight, Couthon introduced the Committee of Public Safety's decree by which the revolutionary tribunal was reorganized for efficiency, and the principles governing its procedures were changed. Article IV of the decree stated quite simply, "The Revolutionary Tribunal is established to punish the enemies of the people."

In the nine months since the Convention had designated those persons who were to be presumed a potential threat to the republic and therefore subject to incarceration for the duration as "suspects," the Committee of Public Safety had made substantial progress in the development of a justification for the near total implementation of nationwide terror. The escalation from a law which identified those suspects to be incarcerated to a law identifying the enemies of the people who were to be summarily tried and executed was, if not inevitable, certainly integral to the progress of the terrorist campaign.

So it was that Article V of the Law of Prairial enumerated just who the enemies of the people might be, in terms so ambiguous as to exclude no one, to include whomsoever might need to be so identified. "Identified" as enemies of the people

were such clearly distinguishable offenders as those who
libeled patriots, who spread false news, who abused the principles of the revolution, who led opinion astray, who depraved
morals, or who "By whatever means and covered by whatever
mask, have made an attempt upon the freedom, unity or security of the Republic." The sole penalty which awaited these
enemies of the people was death. Every citizen was mandated
to denounce such enemies, and empowered to seize them and
drag them to justice. (16)

    By virtue of the decree on justice passed that day by the
Convention, the trial process was simplified to little more than
a procedure of identification. The prerogatives of the accused
in their defense were severely limited and the jury was empowered to hand down its verdict at any time in the trial. It was
this decree, the Law of Prairial, which marked the beginning
of the period known as "The Great Terror." In June and July
alone, over 2,500 death sentences were executed.

    The program of the revolutionary government successfully
suppressed rebellion in much of the republic and turned the
tide of the foreign war in France in her favor. The economic
policy was less effective in controlling prices and inflation,
and had little positive effect on production outside the realm of
musketry. The most widespread products of the campaign of
the Committee of Public Safety were fear and suspicion.

    Within the revolutionary government itself the exercise of
the power entrusted to the committees began to generate its
own brand of mutual mistrust. Members of the Committee of
General Security resented Robespierre and the new police
bureau recommended by Saint-Just. Within Public Safety the
clashes among Robespierre and Saint-Just and the other members of the panel were beginning to obstruct the smooth workings of the committees. Billaud-Varenne was one of those who
sought some sort of reconciliation among the twelve committee-
men, but failed in his attempts.

    When, on the 26th of July, Robespierre rose to address
the deputies of the Convention, he delivered a two-hour
speech on the state of the revolution. In it he defended
himself and his intimates against the charge of dictatorship,
against the "web of terror and calumny" he saw which was
being woven to ensnare the leaders of the revolutionary government and to divide the republic.

    "They call me Tyrant!" lamented the orator, attempting
once and for all to explain away the accusation which to this
day clings to his rule. Robespierre would not list all the
causes of the perfidy which threatened the revolution, but
pointed his finger unmistakably at one source, the offices of
the Committee of General Security. From there he went on to
offer what he considered a prima facie case of a conspiracy
within the government itself to discredit him and destroy the
revolution. He called upon his fellow deputies to declare op-

enly the existence of that plot and take the necessary steps to
purge the Committee of General Security of the destructive
elements which dominated it. He concluded with a plea: "I am
made to fight crime, not to govern. The time has yet to come
when good men can serve the country with impunity. Defenders of freedom will be proscribed so long as that band of
rogues stays in power." When challenged on his accusations
by a member of the Committee of General Security, Robespierre
denied any intention of inculpating the committee as a whole in
the conspiracy. When challenged to name those whom he accused, Robespierre refused.(17)

It may very well be that this refusal was Robespierre's
greatest political error. It was most certainly his last. That
night, while Robespierre was being acclaimed at the Jacobin
Club, the conspiracy which had festered in his vision met to
make plans in reality. Several of his colleagues on the
committees agreed to prevent him access to the podium of the
Convention the next day. Before he or his supporters on the
committee would be allowed to speak, they would be denounced.(18)

On the morning of July 27, 1794, the 9th of Thermidor by
the revolutionary calendar, the Convention ordered the arrest
of Robespierre, Saint-Just, Couthon, and Dumas, the president of the revolutionary tribunal. That evening they escaped
and made their way to the City Hall, Paris' "traditional" center
of insurrection. Some guardsmen were mustered from the
wards to protect these leaders from the conspiracy they had
denounced and to rally a new insurrection. No effective action
was taken.

The Convention, on the other hand, was quick to outlaw
the deputies they had had arrested as well as any who might
come to their aid. Early the next morning soldiers under the
Convention's orders arrived at the City Hall. Meeting no
resistance, they recaptured the one-time leaders who, battered
and abandoned, were executed that very night. The Jacobin
terror had come to an end.

The terror which had been assembled in the autumn of
1793 was rapidly dismantled by the Convention after the fall of
Robespierre. The great committees were renewed, and
changed again by quarters on the monthly basis. The committees of the executive were taken out from under Public Safety's purview and made to report once again directly to the
Convention. The Law of Prairial was repealed and the operation of the revolutionary tribunal curtailed.

There are nearly as many versions and interpretations of
the Reign of Terror as there are commentators. Not unexpectedly, positions frequently polarize around the figure of
Robespierre and his Jacobin colleagues on the Committee of
Public Safety. Those for whom the terror was a defensive
reaction of the revolutionary government either to war and

rebellion or to Parisian mobs give credit to the terrorists for their success but blame them for their excess. Those for whom the terror was a form of paranoia, which led to a purge of France's finest, attribute its impetus to the Jacobin leaders. Current historians often substitute classes or forces for leaders and motives, retelling the conflict as "bourgeois versus sans-culottes" or "order versus anarchy."(19)

Since it was the official spokesman for the militants of Paris and the Jacobin Club who took the cry "Let terror be the order of the day!" to the Convention of the 5th of September, it seems appropriate to consider how that terror might reflect not only the chronic suspicions of Parisians but also the few skills which the Jacobins had acquired in their four years as men of politics. In that short time the Jacobins had distinguished themselves both as exemplary patriots and as masters of expediency - exemplary in that the collective orthodoxy toward which their discussions tended was tailored for exportation to the clubs of greater France for imitation; expedient in the ease with which they not only recovered from political defeats in the assembly but rallied their rationalist approach to policy to the fears and armed might of Parisians. Those two characteristics of Jacobin politics served them well and made them the ideal auxillary when their leaders gathered power as the Committee of Public Safety.

The terror created by the Jacobins was exemplary. Exemplary not as an archetype for future revolutionaries or terrorists, which indeed it later became, but in having as its goal a model of behavior for imitation by the citizens of the new republic. The revolutionary government took upon itself the task of creating out of a population of ex-subjects with scarcely five years political experience a society of republicans who were to exercise their rights as the new sovereign of France. Public spirit and public instruction were central to the revolutionary government's campaign to consolidate the revolution and establish the republic. Their terror therefore took on the aspect of teaching patriotism by way of example - example both negative and positive.

The types of suspect defined by the Law of September 17, the categories of those who were excluded from the Jacobin rolls, the list of activities which were taken as identifying an enemy of the people - all these enumerations served as a warning to the newly constituted citizenry of what in the past and present was considered unacceptable as republicanism. The active pursuit of these suspects and enemies of the people, and the incarceration and execution of a relatively small number of Frenchmen served to advertise as well as to enforce the lines between orthodox and deviant behavior. The overweening statements of the revolutionary government and the Jacobin Club on the crimes of the conspirators, the crimes of the monarchy, the crimes of the British government, all played on the mistrust of French men and women to drive home lessons of how republicans should live by pointing out how other creatures acted.(20)

This is not to say that the executions ordered by the revolutionary government were nothing more than didactic acts, but neither were the victims of the terror simply scapegoats. The unrelenting pursuit of the chimerical "conspiracy" served both as justification for eliminating the revolutionary government's opponents and as an example to others of the pitfalls to be avoided in the exercise of sovereignty.

The characteristic of the terror most universally recognized is expediency - expediency of the sort which had served the Jacobins well even in the earliest days of the revolution. In the deadlock of the orders in the spring at Versailles, in the clash between the Court of Louis and the National Assembly, in the impasse over the Declaration of Rights, and in the passage and publication of the decrees abolishing feudalism, the deputies who were to gather at the Jacobin Club had played to the audience at hand. When the more conservative faltered and when Paris rose, and rose again, the Jacobins rode with aplomb the wave of popular revolutionary initiative, repeating again and again that "the people had spoken."

Whether one consults the grievances of those who agitated for the terror or the justifications of its architects, allusions to the urgent need for, the temporary necessity of, and the immanent end to repression abound. The Legislative Assembly itself had declared, on July 11, 1792, that "the fatherland is in danger." The organs hastily set up by the Commune of Paris were the forerunners of the instruments of the terror of 1793-94. All of the measures for which the citizens of Paris and the representatives from the provinces clamored in the summer of 1793 were proposed as imperatives forced upon France by the war and dearth which plagued the republic, by the ever-present threat of a counter-revolution from within.

From September 5, 1793, until the last oration of Robespierre on the 26th of July 1794, virtually every statement, official or unofficial, on the subject of the repressive policies of the revolutionary government stressed the transitory nature of the terror. The address of September 5th began by affirming that "the danger to the fatherland is extreme; your remedies must be equal to it." The Law of Suspects of September 17th ordered the incarceration of thousands, for the duration. On the 10th of October the Convention declared that the government of France would be "revolutionary until peacetime." Robespierre's reports on the principles of the revolutionary government and of political morality emphasized the distinction between the goals of constitutional government and the means proper to a revolutionary government whose end was the solid foundation of constitutional rule. For Saint-Just, terror was but a temporary substitute for the institutions which would ensure the survival of a republic properly constituted. In his report on justice and police on April 15, 1794, he evoked the old myth of a plot to starve France to explain the need for order.

It is symptomatic, if not ironic, that the revolutionary government stands virtually alone among the regimes of revolutionary France in asserting its temporary quality. Both before and after the era of terror each successive leadership emphasized that with them, at last, the revolution was over. The revolution "ended" with the abolition of feudalism, then "ended" again with the Constitution of 1791. The revolution was "over" when the king had fallen and the republic was declared. The revolution was once again "finished" with the purge of Robespierre and "complete" when a constitutional regime was established in 1795. The revolution was "fulfilled" with the crowning of Bonaparte as emperor. By contrast, the terrorists were the architects of a temporary rule, not a permanent or completed revolution.

The end of Robespierre and of his colleagues is often explained by an escalation of the terror so inappropriately coincident to military successes which undermined these justifications of temporary measures. It may be more useful to consider instead how the drive toward attaining a complete transformation of France as necessary to the establishment of the republic ended that campaign. Robespierre's refusal to name those he accused still retains the importance that has always been cherished by his commentators, sympathetic or not. But it was not simply that Robespierre's denunciation of another conspiracy threatened too many powerful people in the Convention and its committees. In the terror of 1793-94 no place could be reserved for deviation from the project of the whole, from the narrow path of orthodoxy in which alone was sought the salvation of the republic. His refusal to identify those whom the terror threatened left all or no one as his victim, made him yet another sort of enemy of the people.

The terror should be characterized as total primarily because it aimed at nothing less than the complete transformation of the social and political order. For that reason it is not sufficient to recount the history of the revolutionary government's consolidation of power in the capital, its organization of the instruments of repression in the provinces, its successes in developing the wartime economy which led to military victory, and its effective repression of political opposition. To comprehend the terror fully one should take into account the necessity imposed upon the revolutionary government by its own theory of legitimacy, its own justification for existence: purging every vestige, physical and moral, of the France of old. The revolutionary government set as its task the complete re-creation of France in a republican mold, the creation of the republican citizen.

The correlate and consequence of the revolutionary government's all-out stance was exclusion, the excision from the
body politic of those elements which had no place in the new
republic. Whether grouped under the rubric "suspect" or
dispatched as "enemies of the people," all those who could not
be counted upon to assume the role of good citizen in the new
society were by that fact excluded from it. The purge of the
Jacobins acted this out dramatically for the Club's imitators.

It was no coincidence that Couthon's prologue to the
Prairial Law began with an extended reflection on the mis-
conceptions of justice. It is not surprising that that law
reduced the revolutionary tribunal to determining whether or
not an accused could be identified as an enemy of the people
instead of judging on the balance of the evidence for and
against, that is, to arbitrating accusations rather than facts.
One's guilt or innocence with respect to any given act were
really not at issue. What was of concern to the tribunal, to
the state, and to the revolution was whether someone fell
sufficiently under the pale of suspicion as to lie beyond the
pale of justice. Justice did not extend to those outside the
confines of purest republicanism. Terror, not justice, was
their due. In the same way the lists of the accused and
condemned served in the Bulletin of the Revolutionary Tribunal
to define by exclusion the virtues which were expected of the
true republican, defined them as effectively as had Saint-Just
in his report on justice.

These characteristics of terror are perhaps peculiarly,
or, better, originally Jacobin. While the exploitation of the
coactive force of the populace to seize power is in no way
special to the time, the place, or the leaders, the transformation of that force, and the fears and suspicions which drove
it, into a nationwide and self-legitimizing campaign define and
delimit the Jacobin terror. By adopting proscription as the
means for prescribing republican behavior the Jacobins came
not only to enforce but also to create orthodoxy in broadcasting political deviation. By setting completion as the goal
of their task the Jacobins attempted to legitimize the use of
tyranny in the name of the spirit which had recently over-
thrown it and the virtue which in the end they destined to
supplant it.

But most significantly, by marching toward an order
that was whole and pure the Jacobins created a domain from
which these very exercises of power (not their excesses) were
to exclude them. As measures adopted collectively for the
self-defense of a community (or even a commune the size of
Paris, as in the summer of 1792), the instruments which the
Jacobins employed for repression were not beyond the bounds
of behavior traditionally tolerable in the exception, they had
been absorbed into the life of the community as necessary at
that time. The imposition of those measures by the state

strained the allegiance of the very communities in which they had sprung forth during the days of the old regime as reaction and the days of the revolution as the first acts of the people now sovereign.

In this context the measures adopted by the Jacobin state appear extraordinary in more than one sense. They are not simply aberrant extensions of the power which that state wielded, though they are remarkable in that regard - the absolutism of the monarchy which preceded them and the empire which followed legitimized their own excesses as consistant with their mandate, a circle never completed during the terror. The terrorists' vanity and justification - namely, that they were founding a whole new society of virtue - could account for the revolutionary army and tribunal as well as the direct control of the economic and political life of the citizenry only insofar as that vanity was shared, that justification was accepted on a daily basis by the populace against whom they were directed. In the one and the same program the Jacobins created and destroyed the political process within which they could reign. It is this circle which they drew for and about themselves, and which in its singularity of purpose set them apart in their time and has since given them their place.

NOTES

(1) The most reliable accounting of the terror was made by Donald Greer in The Incidence of the Terror during the French Revolution: A Statistical Interpretation (Cambridge, Mass.: Harvard University Press, 1935).

(2) Georges Lefebvre's The Coming of the French Revolution (Princeton: Princeton University Press, 1967) is still the most accessible account of the revolution of 1789.

(3) Lefebvre's The Great Fear of 1789: Rural Panic in Revolutionary France (New York: Pantheon Books, 1973) treats not only the revolt in the French countryside but also the more localized phenomenon of the Great Fear, in which peasants acted with certainty that brigands hired by the aristocrats were on their way.

(4) Both Alison Patrick, in The Men of the First French Republic: Political Alignments in the National Convention of 1792. (Baltimore and London: John Hopkins, 1972), and Michael J. Sydenham, in The Girondins (London: Athlone Press, 1961) have dealt in detail with the formation of parties in the Convention and the personal ties which gave them a substance so often distorted by commentators.

150   THE MORALITY OF TERRORISM

(5) Michael Walzer has analyzed in detail and reprinted at length many of the more critical arguments for and against the king in Regicide and Revolution: Speeches at the Trial of Louis XIV (New York and London: Cambridge University, 1974).

(6) Translated from the Réimpression de L'ancienne Moniteur (31 vols., Paris: Hiplon, 1858-70), XVII, 680-81.

(7) The campaign for and campaigns of the revolutionary army are treated exhaustively in Richard Cobb's two volume Les Armées Révolutionnaires: instruments de la terreur dans les départements avril 1793 - Floréal An II (Paris and The Hague, Mouton, 1961-63).

(8) Translated from the Oeuvres de Maximilien Robespierre, X, (Paris: Société des Etudes Robespierrestic, 1968), 117.

(9) Reprinted in the Ouvres choisies of Saint-Just (Paris: Gallimard, 1968), 168-182.

(10) One of the better portraits of a representative's mission is Colin Lucas' The Structure of the Terror: The Example of Javogues and the Loire (London, Oxford University Press, 1973).

(11) Robespierre, Oeuvres, X, 274-275.

(12) E.V. Walter convincingly argues against the mainstream of interpretation which would have Robespierre as Rousseauist-turned-pragmatist by tracing the terms of these speeches back to the work of Montesquieu in the Policies of Violence: From Montesquieu to the Terrorists," in The Critical Sprit: Essays in Honor of Herbert Marcuse, edited by Kurt H. Wolff and Barrington Moore (Boston, Beacon Press, 1967), 121-149. Citations from Robespierre, Oeuvres, X. 350-367.

(13) Reprinted in Saint-Just Oeuvres choisies, pp. 207-250.

(14) This conflict between the committee and the "popular movement" is central to the account given by Albert Sobout in Les Sans-culottes parisiens en l'An II: Mouvement populaire et gouvernement révolutionnaire 2 juin 1793 - 9 Thermidor An II (Paris, Clavreuil, 1959).

(15) Translated from Saint-Just, Oeuvres choisies, pp. 251-265.

(16) Journal de la Montagne (Paris: 1793-94), III, pp. 358-360.

(17) Robespierre, Oeuvres, X, pp. 542-576.

(18) An introduction to the conspiracy is provided by the collection of documents edited by Richard T. Bienvenu under the title The Ninth of Thermidor: The Fall of Robespierre (New York and London: 1968).

(19)   The works of Albert Soboul and Richard Cobb, professors of the French Revolution at the University of Paris and Oxford University, respectively, tend in these latter directions.

(20)   "Relatively small number" may seem to some a rather callous way to describe the hundreds of thousands of suspects imprisoned, and the thousands of French men and women executed.   While I think it silly to try to put such numbers in the context of traffic deaths or other famous purges, I do consider the numbers of the victims of the terror, if not modest, in some real sense small when compared with the size of the population from which they were drawn and to whom the lessons of the terror were directed.   Were they referred to by "victims versus target population," the disproportion would seem not at all unusual.

7 Facism's Philosophy of Violence and the Concept of Terror
A. James Gregor

More than half a century ago, Sergio Panunzio, who was to serve for the major part of his life as one of the principal ideologues of Fascism,(1) put together a rationale for political violence.(2) Given the contemporary preoccupation with political violence, that rationale seems to have particular immediate relevance. Our political universe is peopled by groups and fragments of groups committed to political violence as a revolutionary strategy, and the number of commissions and conferences devoted to the current problem of contemporary violence and terrorism is legion. To date, all those conferences and commissions have had little success in formulating a definition of violence and terrorism that might serve as the basis for either academic review, theory generation, or effective intervention and legislation.(3)

The first Fascists felt compelled by moral and pragmatic considerations to articulate a rationale for political violence as ancillary to their revolutionary enterprise. By the time Panunzio published his "defense of violence" in 1921, Fascism had fanned out from Ferrara to envelop the whole of Northern Italy in that political violence that marked the penultimate stage of Mussolini's succession to power. To the best of my knowledge, only Fascism, of all the revolutionary movements prepared to employ violence in the pursuit of power, provided an argued distinction between "violence" and "terror" that might be of some contemporary cognitive significance.

---

*The author would like to acknowledge the support and assistance of the Institute of International Studies, University of California, Berkeley, in the preparation of this chapter.

Neither Karl Marx nor Friedrich Engels were particularly scrupulous about their use of the term "terror." On one occasion Marx insisted that there was only "one way" to shorten the "agonies of the old society and the birth pangs of the new - revolutionary terrorism."(4) Elsewhere he insisted that "force is the midwife of every old society pregnant with a new one,"(5) as though both terror and force might well be the same thing. Engels' discussion of force in his Anti-Duehring takes us not a whit further in attempting to distinguish violence from terror.(6) In 1872, Marx spoke of force as necessary for revolutionary change, while a commentator on his delivery speaks of Marx's advocacy as an appeal to violence, again as though both terms referred to the same acts.(7)

In a variety of places, both Marx and Engels made reference to "terrorism," sometimes using it as a synonym for individual acts of violence.(8) There are instances when Engels came close to making a significant distinction between violence and terror, but those distinctions were not systematically pursued. Lenin, in turn, seemed to characterize terrorism as "single combat," individual acts of violence "unconnected with the mass of the people."(9) After Lenin, in the exacerbated polemics of Karl Kautsky and Leon Trotsky, written about the time that Panunzio was completing his Diritto, forza e violenza, one finds both authors moving artlessly between violence and terrorism as though both terms refer to the same behaviors and the same phenomena.(10)

Even the contemporary academic literature available to us is characterized by a wide variety of usages.(11) E. V. Walter speaks of terror as an emotional state caused by specific acts or threats of violence, and terrorism as a compound of three elements: the act or threat of violence, the emotional reaction, and the social effects.(12) Barrington Moore refers to violence and terror as "negative compulsions," and at times seems to equate violence with terror.(13) In 1934, J. B. S. Hardman spoke of terrorism as activities involving a "systematic use of violence," but somehow sought to distinguish between "mass insurrection" and the "terrorist method."(14) David Rapoport, on the other hand, speaks of terrorists and terrorism as involving individuals and acts bent on injury and unconstrained by "moral limits," and consequently argues that a moral distinction can be made between acts of political violence in general, and terrorism per se.(15)

Given all this, Panunzio was singularly modern in terms of his analysis. He advanced an account far more sophisticated than any found in Marxist and much of the contemporary academic literature. In the first place, he attempted to formulate an analysis that distinguished between the exercise of force, and the employment of violence. Force, for Panunzio, was a generic term that referred to what we now identify with power, the ability to alter individual and collective

behaviors in the service of given purpose. Alterations of such
behaviors can be the function of either normative, material, or
coercive force (or power).(16) $\underline{A}$ can alter $\underline{B}$'s conduct by
persuasion, by primary or secondary socialization, by restrict-
ing his access to some one or another welfare benefit, or by
the threat or reality of coercion.

Normative, material, or coercive force manifests itself via
socially   sanctioned   ("legitimate")   instrumentalities: the
communications media, the schools, rule-governed codes of
conduct, entrance criteria into the professions, the legal
system, the armed forces of public security, and the institutions of detention and punishment, among others. Positive
law holds all of this together and constitutes the sinews of
institutionalized force.

Violence, in turn, is the perfect analogue of force except
that its activities do not possess established social sanction
and its behaviors do not represent positive, but potential,
law. The distinction between force and violence, for Panunzio, rests in the fact that force represents the interests of the
present social system, while violence is the cutting edge of an
alternative system.(17) Like force, violence seeks to alter
individual and collective behaviors through the employment of
normative persuasion, material sanctions and incentives, and
coercive disincentives. Revolutionary propaganda attempts to
influence rational calculation and moral deliberation. Revolutionary trade and political organizations attempt to provide
the incentives that prompt men to accord their behaviors to
those of the revolutionary collectivity. Coercion is directed
against the "counter-revolutionary enemy," against whom the
revolution undertakes "internal war."

Panunzio conceived of force and violence as perfect ana-
logues. Established society makes war, uses coercion, against
criminals, subversives, and external enemies. Revolutionaries,
similarly, make war against counter-revolutionaries, the agents
of governmental despotism, and all declared "internal enemies."
For Panunzio, both force and violence were sanctioned by
moral principles. Force is employed to assure a common un-
animity of opinion concerning certain group-sustaining values -
the security of life, possessions, national integrity, continuity
of government, and the provision of necessary welfare. Violence appeals to an alternative set of priorities, an alternative
future, a potential reality, more capable of providing the
creature and moral satisfactions than the present social system
is. In substance the difference between "force" and "violence"
(a difference first suggested by Georges Sorel(18)) is the
difference between alternative social futures. The justification
for either must necessarily be the consequence of rational
calculation.

Just as external wars are never (or should never be)
undertaken without the most rigorous factual and moral cal-

culation, internal wars,(20) coercive power, can only be employed in the service of ends that promise the realization of some ultimate good unattainable by any other means.(21) Wars, the employment of coercive and deadly force, and coercive and deadly violence, are undertaken for just such moral ends. Only enough coercive power can be employed that will secure such ends.

In this sense, Panunzio, like the Marxists, in general, makes ultimate appeal to an anticipated future ("history") as providing the moral justification for the use of coercion. Thus, Trotsky sought to justify Bolshevik violence by an appeal to "the fact that the proletariat [was] the historically rising class," and that the "bourgeoisie is a falling class." The bourgeoisie was the proper object of violence, since it was "destroying the economic structure of the world and human culture generally."(22)

Unlike Trotsky, and like Karl Kautsky, Panunzio rejected the notion that any means are justified by a good end. Panunzio, like Kautsky, insisted that moral ends cannot justify immoral means.(23) Given this caveat, Panunzio, like Kautsky, was prepared to attempt to draw a line between "licit" and "illicit" individual and collective coercion. Panunzio's arguments were more rigorously developed than those of Kautsky. Panunzio sought to define violence in such a fashion that criminal and morally objectionable acts might be distinguished from those licensed by some moral precept or some effective procedural rules.

Panunzio argued that there could be crimes committed in the course of both external and internal war. Individuals who, in war or revolution, take advantage of unsettled circumstances to employ force and violence for personal advantage threaten both the moral integrity of their enterprise and the viability of the community itself. Both governments at war and revolutionary leadership have been historically prepared to recognize the existence of such criminal behaviors, and both (ideally) punish offenders in their own ranks. Rape, looting, and murder have always been recognized as punishable offenses by governments, the organized military, and the leadership of revolutionary forces. These constitute, for Panunzio, "criminal acts in war."

Panunzio was prepared to recognize another class of criminal acts in war, acts he identified as "war crimes," and their perpetrators as "war criminals." Those acts are calculated behaviors, ordered by an established leadership, that wreak havoc, death, and injury on innocents, noncombatants, women, children, the old, the unarmed, and the generally helpless. The aim of war is to bend the enemy to our will. For that purpose deadly force is employed. The enemy takes up arms in his own defense, and in the effort to bend us to his will. Against such an enemy, deadly force is appropriate. All

modern nations, on the other hand, recognize that an unarmed
enemy can no longer be the object of deadly force (just as the
police recognize that an unarmed fugitive, no matter how
heinous his crime, is no longer the proper object of deadly
force). Enemy soldiers are not "innocent." They have made
it their sworn intention to use deadly forces against our
soldiers similarly sworn. But an unarmed enemy, like an unarmed murderer, is no longer the proper object of deadly
force. He may be guilty, but he is helpless. He is a prisoner of war, or a police captive, and expects every protection
that status accords. By extension of these principles, Panunzio argued that unarmed civilians, the old, infirm, the
children, because of their innocence and helplessness, cannot
be the proper objects of deadly force.

When such deadly force is directed against such victims,
the act, for Panunzio, was an act of terror.(24) The act of
terror, in its most manifest expression, is an act of severe
coercion, frequently an act of deadly force, directed against
an innocent victim or victims (hence arbitrary), in which the
victim or victims is instrumental (a means) to the furtherance
of some proximate end (for example the generation of fear or
intense anxiety on the part of others). Panunzio seems to
have felt that only acts that satisfy these conditions can be
identified as acts of terror, morally proscribed acts of
coercion.

Thus the employment of means for indiscriminate destruction, such as poison gas, saturation bombing, and shelling of
population centers of no appreciable military significance,
biochemical and mass destruction devices, would qualify by
such criteria, as "terroristic," and constitute "war crimes."
Panunzio identified such acts with illustrations from this
contemporary experience. The long-distance and indiscriminate
shelling of Paris by German artillery, the Zeppelin bombing of
London, and the use of asphyxiant gas on the Western Front,
were all condemned by Panunzio as criminal acts of terrorism.

According to his account, Panunzio would not characterize
the public and often brutal execution of criminals in time of
peace as terroristic even if at least part of the intention was
to deter such acts, that is, even if such public executions
were employed to instil fear and anxiety among the general
population. The criminal, in such an instance, although
helpless, was not an innocent. He was (presumably) guilty of
a crime. (The circumstances provided for establishing that
guilt is a separate issue.) Similarly, the use of deadly force,
no matter how brutal, against enemy soldiers in time of war, is
not terroristic because soldiers are not innocents. The sworn
duty of a combatant involves the use of deadly force against
us. Moreover, the combatant can abandon his purpose by
surrender, and then, once helpless, is accorded whatever
protection the rules of war provide.

By implication, the use of deadly force against noncombatants in time of war is an act of terror. The victims of such deadly force are innocents. There is no specific piece of voluntary behavior on their part that would reduce the probability of their death or injury. In such cases, the use of deadly force is indiscriminate - the deaths of some innocents would do as well as the deaths of others - and its victims are used as means to the accomplishment of proximate ends: demonstrative or illustrative effect.

When Panunzio became involved in the violence of the Fascist revolution, as that violence radiated out of Ferrara, he forever attempted to characterize that violence in terms of his analysis.(25) Similarly, when Curzio Malaparte, years later, attempted an analysis of the Fascist revolution, he characterized it as an "internal war," governed by the strategy, tactics, and moral scruples of such wars. Whenever Mussolini referred to instances of Fascist and non-Fascist violence, he regularly invoked distinctions made by Panunzio.(26)

At the commencement of hostilities in northern Italy, Fascist apologists insisted that an "internal war" had been declared against their political opponents. Their enemies were armed and committed opponents lodged in Socialist and Communist organizations - the Leagues, the Chambers of Labor, the fighting squads, and the political organizations of the Socialist and Communist Parties. Their enemies had chosen to be members of such associations, and consequently were identified as "soldiers" in the enemy camp and the proper objects of revolutionary violence, including (under appropriate circumstances) deadly force.(27)

What resulted was very much like a civil war. From the 1st of January through April 7th, 1921, for example, violence in Italy claimed 102 lives, among them 25 Fascists and 41 Socialists. There were 388 wounded, 108 Fascists and 123 Socialists. The violence was neither one-sided nor directed against unarmed opponents. When the Socialists documented Fascist violence, that violence was almost always directed against victims and institutions that the Fascists had identified as "culpable": determinate political opponents and the specific political institutions that housed them.(28) The acts of terror identified by the left-wing opponents of Fascism in 1924, were almost all not acts of terror, but (by Panunzio's definition) criminal acts undertaken in the course of insurrectionary violence by individual Fascists in the pursuit of selfish ends, personal profit, the discharge of personal grievances, and simple acts of vengeance.(29) All were equally culpable by Fascism's own announced standards of conduct.

The point here is not that Fascists satisfied the requirements of the rationale concerning violence that presumably subtended their activities. It is that their violence was possessed of principles they themselves had formulated.

Although those principles were probably more honored in the breach than in the observance, the fact that those principles were bruited distinguishes Mussolini's Fascism from the acts of deadly force perpetrated by the terrorists with which we have become increasingly familiar. Thus, when Carlos Marighella spoke of "terrorism [as] an arm the revolutionary can never relinquish," he meant precisely that.(30) In this regard Marighella spoke of kidnapping "personalities who are known artists, sports figures, or are outstanding in some other field, but who have evidenced no political interest," in order to make their suffering "a useful form of propaganda." Thus, he spoke of kidnapping, and if necessary "executing," "North American residents," innocent and unarmed, to make some point or another, or to achieve some advantage in the "war of nerves" against the "establishment."(31)

What Marighella clearly advocated was terrorism: the use of severe sanction or deadly force against innocents for the express proximate purpose of bending others to his will. Given this strategy, terrorist bands commit themselves to the indiscriminate bombing of public buildings, the random downing of civilian aircraft in transit, the kidnapping of innocents to serve as hostages or examples. The difference between Mussolini's Fascists and terrorists is that while Fascists may have undertaken such acts, those acts were understood, by their own standards, as prima facie criminal. For terrorists such a distinction does not obtain. Thus Franz Fanon could advocate the murder of any "colonialist," presumably man, woman, or child, in order to restore the impaired self-esteem of an oppressed colonial: deadly force exercised against an unarmed innocent for proximate purpose.

The distinction between Fascist acts of violence and a strategy of terror seems reasonably clear. The members of the Socialist Leagues, the Chambers of Labor, or the Socialist and Communist Parties in Northern Italy during the wave of Fascist violence in the biennial 1921-22 could avoid violence by abandoning the Leagues, the Chambers, and the infrastructural institutions of Socialism and Communism. Their compliance with Fascist demands could make them reasonably confident that their immediate security was assured. Their "guilt" was a function of their voluntary behavior. They had chosen to behave in a proscribed manner. Their rehabilitation would turn on a specific schedule of compliance behaviors. Similarly, their "innocence" would have been the consequence of a voluntary avoidance of prohibited conduct. In effect, Fascists were prepared to operationalize "guilt" and "innocence" by providing a guide to prescribed conduct. Both "guilt" and "innocence" involved some determinate voluntary acts on the part of the individual or individuals.

Thus, the threat of violence might intimidate in order to bend a "guilty" individual, or individuals, to our will - when that individual or those individuals are aware of what specific behaviors will reduce the threat of injury or loss. Terrorism, on the other hand, does not intimidate its victims because it offers them no escape from deadly coercion or loss. There is no schedule of behaviors to which the prospective victim might conform. The victim is an "innocent" - he has neither done anything proscribed nor can he undertake compliance behaviors to avoid threat.

In the course of political revolution, one may intimidate those whose behaviors one wishes to modify. Terror, on the other hand, is not employed to alter the conduct of its victims. It is employed to influence others. Innocents are used as means to proximate ends.

Thus, severe coercion, even deadly force, on this analysis, used against individual landlords, capitalists, or leaders of Socialist or Communist organizations during insurrectionary phases are acts of political intimidation. By some standard, known to all parties, revolutionaries, landlords, capitalists, and political opponents, some voluntary behaviors are proscribed and other voluntary behaviors are prescribed. Compliance behavior is the saving response to such intimidation. Individual behaviors are conceived as relevant to the onset and termination of real or potential sequence of violence.

The circumstances are entirely different in the case of terror. In such cases, there is no voluntary behavior that makes the individual the proper object of terror. Any individual or individuals, irrespective of anything they may or may not choose not to do, can become the objects of terror. Nor is there any compliance behavior that would reduce the probability of their falling victim to terror. The object of terroristic violence is not a select and proper object. Terroristic violence has as its purpose not coercive sanction directed against culpable parties, but some proximate end. Instrumental terror is employed to impair the functioning of some system or institution. Demonstrative terror is used to bend entire populations to the purpose of others. Prophylactic terror is employed in anticipation of resistance or rebellion. Incidental terror involves those criminal acts - assaults, armed robbery, kidnapping, and so on - that impact upon innocent victims in the service of the perpetrator's pathology, profit, or advantage.

One of the most salient traits of terrorism is its indiscriminate and arbitrary character, in the sense that there is no piece of voluntary behavior that would increase or decrease the probability of finding oneself the object of terror. Terrorist acts are like natural catastrophe - they strike anyone, the guilty and the innocent alike. There are few precautions that one might take to avoid becoming the object of terror. Its onset is incalculable, and its termination unpredictable for those who are its victims.

A revolutionary movement or an institutionalized regime may use political intimidation on a small or a large scale. In this respect a measure of the safeguards protecting dissidence, and political opposition, might serve as an index of intimidation, and aid in characterizing a movement or regime as repressive or nonrepressive. In a repressive regime, individuals or groups of individuals can successfully avoid severe sanction by compliance behavior. For example, political anti-Fascists could avoid violence during the wave of Fascist intimidation during the biennial 1921 and 1922 by abandoning the Leagues, the infrastructural institutions and political associations of Socialism and Communism. Subsequently the institutionalized regime proceeded to intimidate Catholic and liberal interest groups and political associations. The range of intimidation that typified the political system under Fascist rule would identify it as repressive, but not terroristic. The victims of repression reduce their exposure to violence by compliance behavior. The victims of terror can do nothing to reduce the probability of their involvement in arbitrary and indiscriminate violence. Instrumental, prophylactic, and demonstrative terror uses its victims for proximate ends. It does not select its victims, nor can their behavior influence terrorism's course or termination.

The distinction has clear implications. In a regime of repression victims must evidence at least the semblance of probative guilt. Every system, no matter how libertarian, reserves the right to employ some form of repression, the suppression of dispositions or indispositions to behave in proscribed or prescribed political fashion. What distinguishes one from the other are the effective statutory and traditional restraints upon its exercise. Thus, on the 25th of November 1926, a Special Tribunal for the Defense of the State, whose transparent purpose was the intimidation of political opponents, was instituted in Fascist Italy. Its victims were given perfunctory trials with few of the legal and procedural safeguards afforded defendants in pluralistic environments. But for all that, each victim was conceived of, in some diffuse sense, as guilty of having undertaken some reasonably specific behaviors, known to all, that the regime considered inimical to its interests. From 1926 until 1943, with the collapse of the regime, the Special Tribunal meted out 47 capital sentences, beginning in 1928 with the sentence of death for Michele Della Maggiora, who was charged and convicted of assassinating two members of the Fascist militia. Not all of the capital sentences were in fact carried out. From 1928 until 1932 seven death sentences were executed.

Of the lesser sentences, of the 5,619 defendants bound over to the Tribunal between 1928 and 1943, 4,596 were found guilty in varying degrees, and 998 were exonerated. With the advent of total war, the charges and the sentences became

increasingly capricious and onerous. By 1941 a number of
persons were charged with "defeatism," that is, with the
voicing of sentiments contrary to the war then in progress.
The sentences meted out to such persons were evidently instances of demonstrative intimidation.(32)

For all that, the Tribunal, which clearly violated the
procedural rules of justice prevalent in liberal democracies,
was qualitatively different from institutionalized terrorism. In
this respect, Hannah Arendt spoke of the "surprisingly small
number and the comparatively mild sentences meted out to
political offenders" in Fascist Italy as evidence of the absence
of terror.(33) However repressive such a system might have
been, it did not qualify as a system of terror.

In order to establish the evident distinction one need only
review the circumstances involved in Soviet and National
Socialist terror systems. In the Soviet Union, for example,
severe punishment, including "corrective labor," which for all
intents and purposes meant death in a labor camp, could be
meted out by the administrative organs of the state, in effect,
the NKVD. Thousands, hundreds of thousands of persons
passed through the Special Boards in the Soviet Union. Before such boards defendants had no right whatsoever to defense and cases were brought in absentia and against entire
groups of persons. Those who could be charged included
"members of the family of a traitor to the fatherland," and
others who were "suspected of espionage." It was not necessary to establish that defendants had done anything specific,
only that they were members of a "tainted" family or were
suspected of espionage. Thus, the Basic Criminal Code, Article 22 of the Principles of Criminal Jurisdiction of the Soviet
Union of 1937, in a clause unique in international jurisprudence, reads: "Punishment in the form of exile can be applied
by a sentence of the State Prosecutor against persons recognized as being socially dangerous, without any criminal proceedings being taken against these persons on charges of
committing a specific crime or of a specific offense and, also,
even in those cases where these persons are acquitted by a
court of the accusation of committing a specific crime."(34)

By 1937 about 10 percent of all those charged by the
extrajuridical administrative bodies were receiving death
sentences. Andrei Vyshinsky, in charge of the system during
the period, maintained that "When it is a question of annihilating the enemy, we can do it just as well without a trial."
In Gorki alone it is estimated that from 50 to 70 persons were
executed each day without the semblance of a trial and for the
most obscure reasons. By 1938, 5 percent of the total population was involved, and arrests and punishments were applied
indiscriminately. By 1938 there was a call for a systematic
attack on the "silent," those who had not taken any actions
during the events of the preceding years. Relatives of "trai-

tors," sometimes singularly remote, were often arrested and
shot. There was never any suggestion that they had participated in any way in counter-revolutionary or antigovernment
activities. The characteristic question asked by victims of the
Soviet terrorism was "Why?"(35) The arrests and punishments
meted out by the administrative organs and special tribunals
under Stalin were not undertaken to identify and punish those
who had been guilty of any specifiable offense, no matter how
innocuous. Often officials of such organs were simply in-
structed to arrest a given number of counter-revolutionaries,
members of the bourgeoisie, or "kulaks." They were often not
given the least indication of the criteria by which such arrests
should be undertaken, or on what evidence punishment should
be accorded.

Soviet terrorism was clearly demonstrative and prophylactic in intention. Its victims were indiscriminately selected
from ill-defined classes of Soviet citizens. They were either
known to be innocent of any crime (having been found not
guilty by a duly constituted Soviet court), or they were never
charged with any offense. There was nothing potential victims
might do in order to increase their security against arrest.
Soviet terrorism in the military involved leaders down to
regimental command. Most of the men who became its victims
were men known to be loyal and patriotic Soviet citizens.

There was nothing like this in Fascist Italy. Fascism was
not a terroristic but a repressive political system. Its victims
were the objects of intimidation, not terror. Only with the
anti-Semitic campaign of 1938 did Fascist Italy give evidence of
a disposition to employ anything like terror as a political
instrumentality.

Racial discrimination harbors some of the principal species
traits of terrorism. In general, victims of such discrimination
are subject to social sanction without regard for personal
culpability. Since racial traits are ascriptive, there is nothing
in principal that an individual can actively do to avoid social
and political sanction once such traits are used to identify
those subject to differential treatment. Fascist legislation in
1938 identified anyone, born of Jewish parents, a Jewish
father, or of mixed parentage who professed the Jewish religion as a member of the Jewish community and hence subject
to discriminatory treatment. Particularly painful was the
treatment accorded "Jewish Fascists," those Jews who had been
loyal Fascists during the regime but who found themselves
threatened by anti-Semitic legislation.(36)

Action was undertaken against an entire category of
persons, identified only by ascriptive traits - traits for which
they could not have been responsible. Such persons were
subjected to economic and professional deprivation, and to
public and personal humiliations of a variety of sorts.
Whether such acts involved "severe coercion" depends on how

one chooses to distinguish between "severe," "onerous," or "burdensome." Such racial legislation, of course, is not unknown to democratic systems. Legislation against the Japanese on the west coast in the United States, and legislation against blacks, was indiscriminate, and produced "burdensome" and even "onerous" disabilities for its victims. Clearly unjust, such legislation may or may not qualify as terroristic when compared with the National Socialist treatment of Jews.

In the case of Fascist Italy such legislation was clearly directed against innocents in order to effect proximate purpose (most probably to cement the alliance with National Socialist Germany). The question remains whether such legislation qualified as severe coercion.

As a matter of act, Fascist anti-Semitic legislation did not produce the mass executions that are now identified with National Socialist persecutions. When the Fascist persecutions were at their climax, 7,495 Jews were deported from Italy. Of that number 6,885 perished at the hands of the National Socialists.(37) None was executed by Fascists, and the question of Fascist complicity in the deportations has not itself been resolved.(38)

In substance, Fascist treatment of the Jews was always attended by some restraint (given the example of Soviet and National Socialist practices). Because Fascist legislation allowed for "mitigations," involving voluntary acts on the part of Jews, discrimination actively fell upon about 20 to 25 percent of those potential objects of anti-Semitic legislation. Those Jewish families, for example, who had lost a member or who had a relative who was a volunteer in the First World War, or who had received decorations for bravery during that conflict, or those who had relatives who had fallen in the cause of Fascism, or had taken part either in the Fiume expedition or the March on Rome, or who had been members of the party before 1924, were relieved of many of the disabilities.(39)

Furthermore, many Jews were "aryanized," declared protected against discriminatory legislation because of some collection of personal behaviors. Conformance behavior could, as Paolo Orano early suggested,(40) provide some small measure of security against political oppression. The number so "aryanized" constituted about 75 percent of those requesting such dispensation. Although the numbers were small (148 in 1941, 163 in 1942, for example), there were provisions for the recognition of voluntary behaviors in the determination of "culpability."

The distinction between Soviet and National Socialist terror, and the oppressive system employed in Fascist Italy, hinged on the recognition that voluntary behaviors had some influence on the treatment of victims. While it is transparent that the treatment of an entire class of persons as guilty, with "innocence" established by some determinate set of compliance behaviors, is clearly in violation of our standards of justice, the fact that voluntary behaviors, in however peripheral a fashion, entered into the meting out of sanctions seems to have mitigated the Fascist system, allowing Fascist anti-Semitism to fall somewhere between terrorism and oppression.

It is interesting to note that the entire racist policy of Fascism was the object of considerable reservations on the part of some of the principal ideologues of the movement. Giovanni Gentile, often identified as the "philosopher of Fascism," clearly objected to its provisions.(41) Panunzio himself left little that was specifically addressed to anti-Semitic legislation, although he did speak of "racism" as a political policy with some approval.(42) In fact, Fascist racist policy could be incorporated into Fascist ideology only with considerable conceptual, theoretical, and moral tension.(43) This was particularly true with respect to Fascism's treatment of the Jews.(44)

It seems reasonably clear that for all its stupidities, bestialities, and injustices, Fascist anti-Semitism only approximated a policy of terror. The system remained by and large repressive and oppressive rather than terroristic. Its principal negative controls were exercised through intimidation and manipulation. This could be said of its entire insurrectionary program before its advent to power, as well as the operation of the system once ensconced.

All of this argues for a distinction between Fascist repression and oppression, however unjust and barbarous, and consciously undertaken policies of terror in which the purpose of the act is to inflict severe coercion on innocents for some proximate target purpose. In general, Fascist repression was designed to effect changes in conduct on the part of specific individuals adjudged guilty by some reasonably specific criteria. Its purpose was to compel conformity on their part and secondarily on the part of the general population. A terrorist act pursues the same secondary goal but uses innocents as its victims. The distinction between victims can be clearly discerned between the torture of an editor of an opposition newspaper, and the death of a housewife in the commission of a terrorist bombing. For the terrorist anyone who is a member of society, and not a member of his "revolutionary community," is "guilty" of "complicity" with the "establishment," and hence exposed to his violence. Given this characterization, no compliance behaviors can insulate the potential victim from the outrages of the terrorist. Given the latitude, terrorists will often make their own members the objects of terror for some obscure purpose.

Guerrilla attacks on military personnel and military bases can be taken as acts of "internal war" and at best understood as instances of revolutionary violence. But there is every difference between a selected military target, however remote from any "battle line," and the downing of a civilian aircraft carrying women and children. There is every difference between assassinating a representative of an "oppressive" regime (an eventuality Umberto of Italy once called a professional risk of the trade) and the shooting of hostages who just happen to be available to the terrorist.

Governments, armies, and revolutionaries are all capable of committing harrowing criminal acts, but only terrorists explicitly espouse terror tactics, and undertake them with easy conscience. Even Fascists were prepared to make the requisite distinctions. That they failed to honor those distinctions does not relieve us of the responsibility of pursuing them. Terrorism is a tactic that exposes innocents to unpredictable attacks. The extraordinary violence which is its species trait is indiscriminate. Whether employed by Fascists, Stalinists, the Irgun Zvai Leumi, El Fatah, Black September, the Red Guards, the Strategic Air Command, or whomever, terrorism seeks to effect its purposes over the bodies of innocents, to achieve some proximate end that can never justify its means.

NOTES

(1) See A. J. Gregor, Sergio Panunzio, il sindacalism ed il fondamento razionale del fascismo (Rome: Volpe, 1978).

(2) The principal work by Panunzio devoted to Fascism's conception of political violence is Diritto, forza e violenza (Bologna: Cappelli, 1921). Some relevant discussion is found in Panunzio's pre-Fascist work, La persistenza del diritto (Pescara: Abruzzese, 1910) and a work published after his adherence to Fascism, Lo stato di diritto (Ferrara: Taddei, 1922).

(3) See C. Johnson, "Perspectives on Terrorism," in W. Laqueur (editor), The Terrorism Reader (Philadelphia: Temple University, 1978), pp. 267-285.

(4) K. Marx and F. Engels, "Sieg der Kontrerevolution zu Wien," Werke (Berlin: Dietz, 1959), V, 457.

(5) K. Marx, Capital (Moscow: Foreign Languages, 1954), I, 751.

(6) F. Engels, Anti-Duehring: Herr Eugen Duehring's Revolution in Science (Moscow: Foreign Languages, 1962), pp. 219-254.

(7) See M. Evans, Karl Marx (Bloomington: Indiana University, 1975), p. 137.

(8) See the collection, "Marxism and Terrorism," in Laqueur, Terrorism Reader, pp. 198-223.

(9) V. I. Lenin, "Why the Social-Democrats Must Declare a Determined and Relentless War on the Socialist-Revolutionaries," Collected Works (Moscow: Foreign Languages, 1961), VI, 175.

(10) See K. Kautsky, Terrorismus und Kommunismus (Berlin: Berger, 1919); and L. Trotsky, Terrorism and Communism (Ann Arbor: University of Michigan, 1972. The original appeared in 1920).

(11) See, for example, M. Merleau-Ponty, Humanism and Terror (Boston: Beacon, 1969), in which "violence" is frequently used as a synonym for "terror." The treatment in P. Wilkinson, "Pathology and Theory," in Laqueur, Terrorism Reader, p. 237, is similar.

(12) E. V. Walter, "Violence and the Process of Terror," American Sociological Review, 29, 2 (April, 1964): 248; and E. V. Walter, Terror and Resistance (New York: Oxford, 1969), p. 5.

(13) Barrington Moore, Jr., Terror and Progress - USSR (New York: Harper, 1954), p. 11.

(14) J. B. S. Hardman, "Terrorism," in Encyclopedia of the Social Sciences, ed. by E. R. A. Seligman and A. Johnson. (New York: Macmillan, 1934), XIV, 575, 576.

(15) D. Rapoport, "The Politics of Atrocity," in Terrorism: Interdisciplinary Perspectives, ed. Y. Alexander and S. M. Finger (New York: John Jay, 1977), p. 47.

(16) See the distinctions drawn by A. Dallin and G. Breslauer, Political Terror in Communist Systems (Stanford: Stanford University, 1970), p. 2.

(17) Panunzio developed this distinction in Diritto, forza e violenza, chap. 5. The concepts of what is now called "normative" and "coercive" power were developed in La persistenza del diritto.

(18) See. G. Sorel, "Osservazioni intorno alla concezione materialista della storia," in Saggi di critica del marxismo (Milan: Sandron, 1903), pp. 38-40.

(19) Panunzio, Diritto, forza e violenza, pp. 55f.

(20) Panunzio makes the distinction between "internal" and "external" wars in several places. See ibid., pp. 75, 90.

(21) Ibid., pp. 190-194.

(22) Trotsky, Terrorism and Communism, pp. 63f.

(23) Panunzio, Diritto, forza e violenza, p. 146; Kautsky, Terrorismus und Kommunismus, p. 139.

(24) For the distinction see Panunzio, Diritto, forza e violenza, pp. 132-134.

(25) See the entire discussion in S. Panunzio, Italo Balbo (Milano Imperia, 1923).

(26) C. Malaparte, Tecnica del colpo di stato (Florence: Vallecchi, 1973).

(26) For instances of such use, see Mussolini, "Non subiamo violenze," "Parole Chiare," in Opera omnia (Florence: La fenice, 1964), 64-69; "Guerra civile? violenza contro violenza!" ibid., XIV, 101f.; "Dopo i tumulti. Coccodrilli!" ibid., XV, 57-59; "Discorso di Bologna," ibid., XVI, 239-246.

(27) In this regard, see the contemporary Fascist account in R. Forti and G. Ghedini, L'avvento del Fascismo: cronache ferraresi (Ferrara: Taddei, 1922).

(28) Fascismo: Inchiesta Socialista sulle gesta dei Fascisti in Italia (Milan: Avanti!, 1963. A reprint of the edition of 1921).

(29) F. Rapaci, Terrorismo fascista (Turin: Eclettica, 1945. A reprint of the 1924 edition.).

(30) C. Marighella, Minimanual of the Urban Guerrilla (Berkeley: Long Time Comin', n.d., but probably 1969), p. 35.

(31) Ibid., pp. 32f., 36.

(32) C. Schwarzenberg, Diritto e giustizia nell'Italia fascista (Milan: Mursia, 1977), chap. 6.

(33) H. Arendt, The Origins of Totalitarianism (New York: Harcourt, Brace, 1951), p. 303, n. 8.

(34) See R. Conquest, The Great Terror: Stalin's Purge of the Thirties (New York: Macmillan, 1968), pp. 423-425.

(35) Ibid., p. 638.

(36) See D. Sanzò, Il fascismo e gli ebrei (Rome: Trevi, 1973).

(37) R. De Felice, Storia degli ebrei italiani sotto il fascismo (Turin: Einaudi, 1961), p. 524.

(38) See G. Pisano, Mussolini e gli ebrei (Milan: FPE, 1967), pp. 117ff.; L. Poliakov and J. Sabille, Gli ebrei sotto l'occupazione italiana (Milan: Communità, 1956).

(39) L. Preti, Impero fascista, africani, ed ebrei (Milan: Mursia, 1968), p. 155.

(40) P. Orano, Gli ebrei in Italia (Rome: Pinciana, 1938).

(41) H. S. Harris, The Social Philosophy of Giovanni Gentile
(Urbana: University of Illinois, 1960), pp. 244f.

(42) See S. Panunzio, Teoria generale dello stato fascista
(Padua: Milani, 1939), pp. 31-36.

(43) See A. J. Gregor, The Ideology of Fascism (New York:
The Free Press, 1968), chap. 6.

(44) Ibid., pp. 260ff.

8 Nazi Terrorism: The Complete Trap and the Final Solution
Shlomo Aronson

INTRODUCTION

Various aspects of modern terrorism were introduced to international affairs by a state, rather than by state-supported or independent organizations. Nazi Germany used a variety of terrorist methods against the Jews. The "final solution," or mass extermination, only represents the last phase of this campaign.

The first phase might be called a form of indirect terror. German and European Jews were taken hostage to ensure the "good conduct" of the Jews abroad and of foreign governments. In addition, deportation was consciously used to ensure the rise of anti-Semitism abroad and, hence, weaken "Jewish world influence."

The second phase was a policy of direct anti-Jewish persecution that took place in Germany and in her conquered territories. The Nazis made Jewish leaders hostages (Judenrate) to ensure collaboration by Jews in German territories, inflicted physical torture, created hunger and the fear in the ghettos, and implemented the Aktinonen (kidnapping for slave labor and the death camps). These terror practices were meant to break normal and free people in order to make them instruments of their own destruction.

The "final solution" itself resulted from the failure, in Hitler's eyes, of these two previous phases of Nazi terror. It required the execution of the hostages, not only as a "positive" act of "solving" the "Jewish problem" once and for all, but also as an enormous act of revenge for Hitler, who believed that the Jews had induced the Allies to wage a war of annihilation upon Germany.

The "final solution" seems to have had a third purpose, that of making the German people (particularly the non-Nazi conservative circles, the labor movement, and the churches) accomplices in the eyes of the Allies when the news of the annihilation became known in the West in 1943. The mass of Germans, many unwittingly, were thus held hostage in an unforgivable crime so that they would have to support Hitler's regime to the bitter end.

The Allies' recognition of the enormity of the "final solution" did not lead to active support to the dying Jews because Hitler's anti-Jewish propaganda made the Allies fear that any direct aid to the Jews might harm their own popular war effort. The Allies had justified the war successfully as one to preserve Western civilization and they were apprehensive of doing anything that might lend credence to Hitler's claims that they were fighting to save the Jews. The fate of the Jews, thus, was sealed off from every direction, not merely by Hitler's initial campaign of terror but also by third party reaction to it.

HITLER'S CONCEPT OF JEWISH POWER

To substantiate these arguments I must first discuss Hitler's so-called Weltanschauung, which was an admixture of a kind of philosophy of history, biology, and understanding of contemporary economics and politics and also a program for action. His master variable for understanding history was race, and his racial perception was mixed with a decisive notion of power and violence. Recovering from his temporary blindness, following the November revolution and the armistice of 1918, Hitler perceived himself and his nation - the political-historical framework of his race - as having been victimized, raped, almost murdered by domestic and foreign powers who were dominated by a common sinister racial influence: "The Jew" from within and "The Jew" from without. German Social Democrats and Spartakists, Jewish liberals, and foreign liberal-democratic ideologies and governments, Bolshevist Russia and German Communists - all of them were racially the same even if their ideologies took different forms.

To expose liberal capitalism and communism, to fight them as a seven-headed hydra was not just an intellectual task as many anti-Semites had thought since 1848.(1) For Hitler the Jewish menace was a concrete political network of a decisive strategic-tactical significance which had to be met with a special counter-strategy and counter-tactics. He understood the world as a set of concrete power structures, based on race, fighting each other. Since November 1918, the struggle on the Aryan side had been virtually given up owing to the

blinding effects of modern capitalism and democracy combined
with Bolshevism and social democracy.   Hitler's basic "Mission," which induced him to "become a politician," was to
resume the struggle, to expose the menace which threatened to
dominate Germany's destiny and that of the Nordic race and
"humanity" as a whole.   To deal with it effectively one had to
use the enemy's own methods, which included human trade,
hostage taking, war, and total destruction.   The methods of
Nazi terror were methods which Hitler insisted that "the Jew"
himself had been practicing.

Hitler feared his people's decay and lack of will power to
assume the necessary struggle against the modern forces of
egoism, hedonism, false moralism, and racial degeneration.
The "positive" aspect of his desire to create a new Nazi Reich
was combined with the negative aspect of domestic terrorism,
concentration camps, and Gestapo violence implicating the
German people in the "final solution," thereby making any deal
between it and foreign powers, comparable to that of November
1918, very unlikely.

Vis-a-vis his enemies, Hitler's basic violent negativism
was clear and deadly from the beginning.   But being a "politician," a shrewd and responsible statesman, as he proclaimed
himself to be in his Second Book,(2) he undertook a strategy
of driving a wedge, if possible, between the real enemy (i.e.,
the Jew) and his "tools" - collaborators or clients who had the
capacity to liberate themselves from Jewish influence.   He
would use the Jew himself to put constraints on Jewish influence and promote friendship between Germany and racially
closer, legitimate world powers by spreading anti-Semitism
abroad.   At the same time he would perceive domestic and
foreign political developments always as defeats or victories for
Germany (and the Aryan race) or for the Jews.   Thus, if his
domestic or foreign political programs were stalled or resisted,
this actual political development was seen as a "Jewish victory"
that would require "counter-measures."

Hitler was careful, in his own words, not to draw Germany again into an unnecessary multifront war on side issues,
as had happened in the past.   He glorified war and saw in it a
normal, rather natural form of relations among struggling
racial and cultural entities but as a "statesman," he was
interested in the "right" or the "relevant" struggle, to be
conducted by a combination of peaceful, ideological-political,
and military means to achieve real sovereignty and hegemony
for Germany in Europe.

Hence, a more detailed inquiry into Hitler's concepts of
hegemony and sovereignty, his understanding of different
forms of wars is required to understand his role, in his own
eyes, as a "statesman," trying to execute a political strategy
of driving a wedge between "the Jew" and possible allies
during Germany's struggle for sovereignty and hegemony in

Europe. This "political strategy" assumed, among other
things, the form of hostage taking and deportation at the same
time vis-a-vis the Jews, but fell short of a "final solution."

HITLER'S FOREIGN POLICY 1938-1941: SOVEREIGNTY AND HEGEMONY

As a "statesman" Hitler did not simply carry out his private
wish to destroy the Jews physically. His modus operandi
between 1933 and 1941, especially between 1938 and 1941,
suggests a more complex, paradoxical approach to the "Jewish
question" in Central and Eastern Europe, and to "Jewish influence" outside it, including Soviet Russia.

In Mein Kampf(3) and in the Second Book(4) Hitler outlined a strategy to establish a Third Reich and maintain it by
acquiring a racial Lebensraum in Central and Eastern Europe.
The meaning of a geopolitical, racial German Lebensraum im
Osten is to be understood in connection with Hitler's perception of German sovereignty and hegemony in its "natural
space."

Both terms were referred to the exercise of ultimate
power over Germany's destiny at home and in its strategically
and economically important vicinity in Central and Eastern
Europe; otherwise the Nordic race was in danger of extinction.
For Hitler there was always an immediate linkage between
domestic order and foreign policy, or rather control over
foreign land and resistance of foreign threats. Sovereignty,
real sovereignty, in this sense, required hegemony.

In actual terms, "hegemony" was initially related to
Poland, the Balkans, the Baltic states, and possibly also to
most of Scandinavia, the low countries, and a weakened
France Sovereignty required the direct absorption of Austria,
the German speaking parts of Czechoslovakia and then, the
establishment of German hegemony over the rest of the country
in the form of a protectorate.(5) The sovereignty of this
empire had for Hitler a built-in logic of a biological-historical
and moral "right" that should have been understood and recognized as such by others to pursue its "natural" destiny.

By "others," Hitler meant in his Second Book and Table
Talks, Great Britain, the United States, and Soviet Russia
under Stalin,(6) but not France or the other European nations
which he perceived as future vassals or slaves. In the British
and the Americans Hitler saw legitimate powers, racial "relatives," whose great power role would be recognized, though
reduced, following Germany's successful emergence as a hegemonial power in Europe. Both "sovereignty" and "hegemony"
for Germany were limited in the framework of a staged master
plan to Central and parts of Eastern Europe. This initial,

absolutely vital stage was none of the business of the British, the Americans, and the Soviets, who seemingly were ready to cooperate, following the Hitler-Stalin Pact. To acquire this vital space, without which Germany was neither sovereign nor hegemonial, an anti-Semitic common denominator might have to be invoked to persuade outside powers to accept Germany's vital amibition.

Following the bloody purges of 1936-1938, Stalin was perceived by Hitler with growing admiration as one who purged his Jewish-Bolshevik elite who might become a highly nationalistic, grand reformer in the style of Peter the Great, and therefore would limit his ambition to spaces outside of Germany's vital Lebensraum.(7) International Communism in this sense might not be a tool in the hands of the Jewish-Bolshevik element in the Soviet elite and the Jewish masses in Russia who produced that elite. Instead, Communism would become a limited political instrument of a highly nationalistic Russia. Likewise, Great Britain and the United States could liberate themselves from the Jewish yoke and cooperate, or at least stay neutral during Germany's vital effort to achieve sovereignty and hegemony in Europe. In this phase Hitler would use the Jews against themselves by deporting some and by taking others hostage.

HITLER'S ANTI-JEWISH TERROR AS A DOMESTIC AND FOREIGN POLICY MEASURE

Many scholars assume that Hitler's anti-Semitic policy from the beginning involved a sinister desire to destroy the Jews while serving as a political weapon as well.(8) Hitler is supposed to have used it to unify Germany or to distract Germans from their internal difficulties after World War I and thus avoid the task of transforming Germany socially, as many of his followers had expected him to do.(9) The "final solution" is deemed inevitable once Hitler had a free hand to transform his Third Reich to a Juderein European empire.

These arguments cannot be fully denied. Still, Hitler's anti-Semitism was more than just an "anti-Jewish revolution" in order to create and lead a new Third Reich. In my view, Hitler's anti-Semitism remained the ideological-psychological-political framework for everything he did, and therefore changes within Germany during the 30s and foreign political developments later on were understood by him always in terms of the Jewish master variable. The above-mentioned scholarly school is static and perceives Nazism as a constant preconceived idea fully unveiled at the end of 1941 in Auschwitz. I maintain, on the other hand,(10) that Hitler saw himself actively fighting the Jew, responding to his "challenges,"

engaging him in a giant battle almost as a modern Siegfried,
while trying to sustain his Third Reich and give it its natural
- initial - space in Europe. The dynamism of Hitler's actual
anti-Semitic policy suggests, paradoxically enough, self-
imposed constraints on an initial desire to kill them all, and
also explains his peculiar use of terrorism before the "final
solution." Otherwise we have difficulties explaining the
different phases of Hitler's anti-Jewish policy between 1933-
1941, and mainly the sharp turn, the vehement radicalization
of both his foreign policy and anti-Jewish policy by the end of
1937, which was not followed by a "final solution" but by an
official policy of forced emigration by the so-called "Nisco
Plan" and the "Madagascar Plan," which remained in force until
mid-1941 at least. Until then, Hitler's anti-Jewish policy was
clearly divided into two periods. There was an initial anti-
Jewish economic boycott which was given up quickly and was
followed by the removal of the Jews from public life (1933-
1935). Then, the legal degradation of the Jews from citizens
to subjects began, as a consequence of the racial legislation
stemming from the Nuremberg party rally (1935-1937).

Economic discrimination, "Aryanization," and the use of
terroristic methods such as deportations to concentration camps
were seldom used against large numbers of Jews just because
they were Jewish, before the Anschluss of Austria and the
Kristallnacht, both in 1938. On the other hand, forced organization or an early Judenrate for German Jews (many of
whom did not emigrate and would not identify with a Jewish
leadership) did take place and created the impression later
that the Gestapo and the Security Service (SD) of the SS had
planned in advance the instrument of future collaboration by
the Jews to help deport themselves to preplanned death camps.

Many Holocaust historians see here a gradual, linear
process, which gathered momentum when Hitler established
himself in Germany in 1938 and reestablished Germany internationally as an armed great power.(11) The violent change in
Hitler's anti-Jewish and foreign political behavior is ascribed to
his success, following a period of power consolidation at home
and abroad, which necessarily constrained his initial plans for
the Jews. This argument cannot be fully invalidated. There
is enough evidence, however, to argue to the contrary, that
by the end of 1937 Hitler saw his regime in a serious im-
passe(12) owing to a "Jewish threat" which required strong
"counter-action," including the introduction of forced emigration and hostage taking.

A careful study of SD Lageberichte (SS security service
situation reports) reveals, that in the eyes of Hitler's racial
guard, his regime was in serious domestic crisis by the end of
1937:

> Two main enemies of the N[ational]-S[ocialist] ide-
> ology and of the state have developed [during the
> recent period]: the political churches, and the
> reaction . . . the planning of the higher priesthood
> of both Evangelical and Catholic parties is directed
> toward active resistance against the state. . . . the
> Reaction, at the same time, has assumed an unprece-
> dented active role, pursuing with all its energy [the
> goal of] destroying the party and its components,
> especially the SS, in order to transfer the [political-
> military] power to the Army, and the ideological
> power to the churches. . . .
>   The pro-Jewish approach of the churches,
> which makes every anti-Jewish propaganda effort
> among the masses of the church useless . . . is
> effective as never before, since the takeover [by
> Hitler]. Therefore it must be calculated . . . that
> Jewish emigration would be seriously reduced.(13)

Hitler read these situation reports - his only channel for
following public opinion in his totalitarian state - and attached
to them supreme importance. This very report was quoted
publicly by him almost verbatim in early 1938 when he set
forth to eliminate the army's non-Nazi command under General
von Fritsch, while establishing an <u>Oberkomando der Wehrmacht</u>
under his direct control. Moreover, his fear of the old army
(which was manifested again and again during the war) was
mixed with contempt - a typical lower-middle-class syndrome
vis-a-vis the aristocracy and the grand bourgeois which produced the military class. This traditional right could, in
Hitler's eyes, combine again with the German middle class and
the farmers, that old Bismarckian coalition, to return an old
regime of sorts, dominated by the military and the church.
Hitler feared that this coalition - which since Bismarck
experienced decay and degeneration - was basically incapable
of leading Germany as it had demonstrated during WW I, and
would if returned to power produce an eventual "Jewish triumph." Not only because of the supposed "pro-Jewish approach" of the two German churches alone, but mainly because
of the inevitability, as Hitler saw it, of Jewish predominance in
a traditional, capitalistic, bourgeois- conservative Germany.
       Hitler never trusted the working class either. It did not
give him enough support during most of the 20s and was traditionally affected by leftist, internationalist propaganda.
Timothy Mason(14) may be right when he argues that the
regime was forced to assume a much more radical foreign policy
because Hitler's rearmament program endangered his popular
base among the workers. My view is that the danger, as the
regime documented it in the <u>Lagebericht</u>, lay more in the

churches and the conservative forces ("Reaction") - whose "Judeo-Christian morality" and sheer egotism, profit seeking, and individualism could have "infested" the German people despite the party's efforts since 1933, especially after the Olympiad of 1936 when the regime achieved virtually nothing new. Militancy in foreign policy could have been perceived by the conservatives as an interim requirement helping to undo the Versailles restrictions and giving Germany a new pride. The government, however, should not be given a chance to pursue unnecessary risks abroad. Hitler indeed knew some of his generals, such as Ludwig Beck,(15) better and he decided to impose his politics and his dynamism on them, rather than become their tool. Here again we can observe Hitler's extreme sensitivity to the power game - who controls whom - which he perceived to be the essence of politics in different and yet complementary dimensions. If he "surrendered" to army professionals, traditional conservatives, the churches, he would not only fail to accomplish his positive mission, the establishment of a continental hegemonial Reich in Europe, but he also endangered Germany's sovereignty which would be turned over in due course to the Jew.

This belief in the "Jewishness" of capitalism, of socialism, of some traits of the German urban middle class, of the decaying Wilhelmine empire which lost WW I, and, of course, the very essence of the Weimar system led now to a direct anti-Jewish campaign of a distinct terroristic nature. By the end of 1937 Hitler indeed felt secure enough and threatened to start a campaign abroad to establish German "hegemony" in continental Europe while taking Jews hostage in order to ensure the good conduct of Jews abroad. Priority was given between 1938 and 1940 to deportation, and much internal debate among SS officials was devoted to the issue of whether deportation did not reinforce world Jewry and should therefore be limited to "remote places" such as Palestine.(16) Jewish refugees from Europe, however, were supposed to promote anti-Semitism abroad to create an ideological common denominator between Germany and their host countries.

Following the Munich Agreement Hitler publically made the Jews under his control hostage - i.e., responsible for the outbreak of a "world war" in which case "the Jewish race in Europe will be exterminated." This "prophecy" of January 30, 1939(7) is regarded by many scholars as a verbal proof of Hitler's initial intention to destroy the Jews; and when WW II broke out in September of the same year he finally had the opportunity to pursue his preconceived plan. This view does not explain the official continuation of the forced emigration policy well into 1940 and the above-mentioned "Nisco Plan" - a "Jewish reservoir" in the Lublin area in Poland, nor the "Madagascar Plan" of late 1940, following the fall of France. Nazi intentions with regard to Madagascar were documented by

Franz Rademacher, a high-ranking foreign office official, who stated that the European Jewry must be deported to the big island off the short of East Africa (which would be placed under Nazi control) in order to free Europe of their presence; "moreover," stated Rademacher,(18) "the Jews will remain in German hands as a pledge for the future good conduct of the members of their race in America." Hence, already envisioning a "comprehensive solution" to the Jewish question that included their physical removal from a German-dominated Europe, the policy of deportation was transformed into the policy of hostage taking. Indeed, all it required was that a submissive France (which governed Madagascar at the time) and a willing Britain, who controlled the sea routes to Africa, cooperate with a triumphant, hegemonial Germany to implement the plan, and the European Jews would have been saved to ensure the good conduct of America.

The Allies, however, did not behave in the way Hitler expected them to; nor did they share his Weltbild regarding the supremacy of the Jewish factor in international affairs. Slowly after 1938 they were pushed by Hitler's increasing pressure, and by the barbaric way that he treated his Jewish victims, to protect themselves and Western civilization against a German onslaught that seemed to be even more serious and demanding than the struggle of 1914-1918. Still, Hitler made no direct effort to conquer Britain or to break up its world empire altogether, though he perceived her interference with his European hegemonial plan as unwanted aggression and as a Jewish triumph over London's own best interest, which was to cooperate with him or to stay neutral(19). The USSR did stay neutral and we have evidence to support the argument that territorially Hitler indeed declared himself satisfied by March of 1940.(20) Stalin, however, remained an enigma to Hitler. Was the Soviet ruler indeed a Russian nationalistic despot who could in principle cooperate with the other despotic regimes of Germany, Italy, and Japan, or was Moscow a strategic, "Jewish-infested" threat to the newly conquered Lebensraum that required appropriate treatment, i.e., occupation of European Russia? During 1940, in a meeting with Mussolini, Hitler was still rather confident of Stalin. Before and mainly after the French campaign, Hitler returned to his hope of coming to terms with the British. During 1940 and 1941 he observed with restraint - straining his temper to the breaking point - growing support for the Allies, and he authorized the "Madagascar Plan," rather than give orders to organize a "final solution" for the Jews. Even the war itself and Nazi control over more and more Jews as a result of Germany's military success, which prevented a meaningful conventional forced emigration, did not induce Hitler to start destroying them en masse. Terrorism, i.e., hostage taking, on a grand scale in order to clean up Europe from Jews was now on the

agenda (Madagascar). For Hitler the war was still a limited
war, not world war, the subject of his "prophecy" of September 30, 1939. Since he still hoped to persuade the British and
the Americans to keep out, watching the Russians with growing suspicion, no plans were made beyond the concentration of
the Jews in ghettos, forced organization (Judenrate) and slave
labor on a large scale.(21)

The ultimate survival of the European Jews became con-
ditional on the outbreak of a world conflict which threatened
the very survival of Germany. Their fate may well have been
different if the European conflict had been limited to short
campaigns, such as the Polish and the French, which were
scheduled to end when Hitler's hegemony in Central and Eastern Europe was established.

Molotov's visit to Berlin following the French campaign,
during which the Soviet Union expressed territorial demands
and a desire for a comprehensive division of spheres of interests in Europe, seems to have alarmed Hitler no end, or (as
I do not venture into a psychological explanation of his inner
mechanism of challenging others and responding to outside
challenges) triggered in him an excuse, a rationale, to attack
and occupy vast parts of Russia, following his enormous successes and the obvious weakness of the Red Army as demonstrated in the Finnish War.

The perception of Stalin's Russia as a "Bolshevik-Jewish"
threat again came after Molotov's visit when he sensed a renewed Jewish influence on Stalin.(22) It was accompanied by
the first step of the "final solution" i.e., the systematic
annihilation of "Jews and commissars" in Russia by mobile
killing units (Einsatzgruppen) attached to the German army.

The "logic" of this decision seems to have been military;
"security" demanded the complete removal of racial-political
enemies such as Red Army commissars and the Jewish masses
of Russia, who supposedly maintained the regime. The means
were "military" - mass shooting and later, mobile poison gas
units - owing to the "security" nature of a war against a
"subhuman threat," which would be treated as outside the
rules of normal warfare.

The decision to round up all Central and West European
Jews and send them to factory-like death camps came a little
later, probably in the Winter of 1942.(23) Hitler's "prophecy"
came true first when the British continued to fight, a decision
attributed to Churchill's manipulation of the British people for
Jewish purposes, and started bombing German cities. According to Albert Speer,(24) Hitler attributed British Bombenterror
to the Jews, and swore revenge. Thus, Nazi Blitzkrieg terror, which brought about British aerial bombing, became one
more nail in the Jewish people's coffin. The final decision to
implement the "prophecy" of September 1939 came when the
United States joined the Allies following a German declaration

of war. Now that his hostages lost their value and "World
Jewry" at the same time was taken to be responsible for involving Britain, Russia, and the United States in a world war
to destroy Germany, the initial desire to destroy the Jews
physically, which no doubt always existed, triumphed over
Hitler the "statesman," who no longer had to pursue what he
perceived to be a clever political campaign against the Jew.
    Yet one more act of hostage taking did remain, even if it
is very difficult to prove Hitler's intentions in this regard.   I
have mentioned Hitler's basic suspicion and permanent fear of
his army's professional leadership, the conservative elite of the
"church-going masses," and of the working class.   The generals, almost enthusiastically, cooperated with the SS to
implement the "final solution" from its beginning in Russia to
the end. (25)   Neither the military, however, nor the conservatives and the working class could be completely trusted in
the event that the war dragged on for years, and occassional
defeats occurred.   By putting the Jews to death, Hitler made
his own people hostage to his policy of victory or complete
defeat, foreclosing the option for a negotiated peace such as
the "November crime" of 1918.   The logic of this hostage
situation is rooted in Hitler's bid to arrest the decline of his
domestic situation in 1937 by adopting a much more radical
foreign policy and by involving the whole German nation in a
growing anti-Jewish terrorism, which many Germans regarded
as basically irrelevant to their real interests.

THE WEST AND THE GERMAN NON-NAZI CIRCLES

Did the leadership of the West, in particular the British and
the Americans, really understand Hitler's mind?   Was his
perception of Germany's hegemonial role in Europe combined as
it was with his anti-Semitic "master key" clear enough?   Did
they understand that the issue for Hitler was either "Jewish
victory" or "Jewish defeat" when they followed or rejected his
seemingly concrete foreign policy and territorial demands?   Did
they understand his bids and overtures, his "bargaining"
methods regarding colonies outside of Europe (which he was
ready to drop) in order to achieve the main thing: Western
acceptance of a German hegemony in Europe? (25)
    His plan, according to Mein Kampf and the Second Book,
called for the division of the world into three or four blocs to
include a sovereign-maritime British empire and a main sphere
of interest for the United States in the Americas.   In his own
eyes Hitler did not seek "world domination" but a rearrange-
ment of the global order.   Even Stalin's Russia would have
found her sphere of interest here if Moscow was ready to
focus her attention on the East, possibly on India.   A Soviet-

British clash there would have been a "normal" feud between two legitimate great powers. A British, Soviet, or an American intervention in Hitler's initial - absolutely essential for him - bid to establish German hegemony in Central and parts of Eastern Europe would be "illegitimate." That would have been clear to them if they were prudent and if they could free themselves of "Jewish influence" to pursue a wise policy.

This degree of primitive flexibility - almost "generosity" - on Hitler's part must have been perceived in the West as a fusion of a new and terrible German prejudice, the Teutonic barbarism, known to them from World War I, and of a traditional German quest for world domination. The old image of Germany as an expansionist imperial latecomer striving for a "place in the sun," seeking world domination while glorifying its own Kultur, Ordnung, and political system, was dangerously intertwined with Nazi racist barbarism. The West learned its lesson from Hitler's lies and threats; after Munich, it decided to defend itself. Germany had to be stopped once more; appeasement did not work.

This decision must indeed have been interpreted by Hitler as a major Jewish victory; Western leaders, however, viewed the "Jewish" aspect of his policy as irritating and to a large extent irrelevant to their main concern: the defense of Western interests and values against a barbaric and expansionist Germany.

In refusing Hitler's assumptions of anti-Semitism and racism as the master key to understanding and reorganizing the world, the West was certainly not ready to respond positively to his "Jewish politics," by absorbing Jewish deportees and "releasing" Germany from her responsibility toward her Jewish citizens. Jewish support for the Allied cause could be taken for granted; the Jews had no chips for bargaining with the British government. Furthermore, the general nationalistic, antiliberal onslaught of Fascism and Nazism on the world's democracies paradoxically generated an aversion to Jewish nationalism in conservative British circles. Zionism was particularly suspect, as the British needed Arab support; and Jewish support was again taken for granted. Jews' pleas for help as a group in danger of extermination were, by virtue of the same liberal, antinationalistic reasoning, rejected.

Thus, during the period of forced emigration, the Jews found themselves in a triple trap: Nazi racial antisemitism, combined with Hitler's policy of forced emigration made them refugees, and at the same time, bearers of the responsibility for Allied behavior. The Allies refused to absorb many Jews, refraining from relieving Germany of her responsibility. The West had not fully recovered from the Great Depression. An anti-immigration policy was adopted in Britain and the United States earlier in the century and this mitigated against large-scale rescue. Indeed, the absorption of possibly millions

of Jews might have complicated efforts, Western leaders
thought, to mobilize resources and public support against the
Fascist threat, an effort which had to be given top priority.
The absorption of many Jews may very well have been perceived as disruptive in this regard, an exacerbating influence
on existing domestic anti-Semitism. Western (mainly Anglo-
American) determination to defend itself against the strategic
and cultural threat inherent in Nazism relegated the "Jewish
question" to a minor position; and the much greater threat to
world order and Western civilization posed by Nazi military
expansion took prominence.

Hitler ascribed all this to "Jewish influence"; the Jews
under his control had to pay the ultimate price, while he
pursued his "positive" effort to "clean up" that part of Europe
under his hegemony. At the same time, the "Jewish question"
seemed to many conservative, middle-class and upper-middle-
class Germans a marginal issue. They disliked Jews but they
also disliked the regime that deported and persecuted them.
Yet they failed to draw the obvious conclusion, and as far as
the West could see, they also were implicated, as Hitler wanted
them to be, as accomplices in a bloody plot against humanity.
The immediate victims were Jewish, whom it was impossible to
aid. An immoral Germany, however, had to be stopped in her
bid for world dominance.

For the Jews themselves, this nightmarish double trap
became a triple trap when Hitler accused them of having drawn
the West into an unnecessary world war against the West's best
interests. The Western response, especially among higher civil
servants, Foreign and Colonial Office members, and State
Department officials, was to "refuse to play Hitler's game."
They refrained from any specific response to Jewish requests,
and played down, at first, early reports on the "final solution." They regarded any specific efforts to stop the machinery of destruction as not only impractical, but also
possibly damaging from an Allied, and even from a Jewish,
point of view. The main, indeed, perhaps the only effort was
to be directed toward a unified Western struggle in defense of
its values and very existence.

Thus, the Jews, Hitler's only victims whose very existence was indeed at stake, were left outside; their reputation
as trouble makers, their "self-pity" and complaints since the
early '30s in some British and American officials' ears became
an unwanted, disturbing pressure that might have an adverse
effect on the Allied domestic determination to fight a long cruel
war which requires an overwhelming national consensus. After
an age of pacifism, isolationism, the growing influence of the
masses, and the perception of society as a democratic, volatile
structure, the image of a "Jewish war" had to be averted.
Specific efforts to punish Germany for genocide, the diversion
of war material or the war effort in this direction, could have

been very damaging. Accordingly, the only way to save Jews was to win the war while publicly declaring Germany responsible for its war crimes. One might thus arrive at the bleak conclusion that by publicly making Germany and its leaders responsible for what they called "war crimes" the Allies had in fact played into Hitler's hands, at the same time exacerbating the situation by demanding Germany's unconditional surrender. "The Jew" - this time the murdered Jewish people - became a guarantee for an enhanced German war effort - total war, since only "irresponsible fools" such as Colonel Count Stauffenberg (who plotted against Hitler in June, 1944) and his accomplices could hope for reasonable terms from the Allies.

CONCLUSION

What could the victims do in this trap from which there seemed to be no escape? To begin with, the victims did not and could not perceive themselves as hostages because they did not understand themselves as an organized nation, let alone as a race with distinctive biological and political traits as Hitler perceived them. Nor were they objectively such an entity. The truth was that patriotism (or identification with their respective European homelands), economic and cultural difficulties, and inadequate outlets for emigration prevented very many victims from reading the writing on the wall. The "objective truth," however, did not prevent the Allies from responding to Hitler's challenge in a way that sealed off the fate of the victims and rendered any possible effort by the organized Jewish leadership useless, until it became too late. The tragedy of a nation that many of its members did not believe was a nation was that Jewish rescue efforts were counter-productive. At least with regard to Great Britain, Jewish pressures and petitions after Hitler's rise to power contributed to the British decision to resist Hitler and that produced, unexpectedly, a fourth trap for the Jews: the practical denial of Palestine to Hitler's victims. Jews driven out by Hitler had immigrated in large numbers to Palestine. An open Arab rebellion there (1936-1939), in protest against the growing Jewish presence, eventually resulted in a royal commission suggesting, for the first time, the partition of the country into an Arab and a Jewish state. This was accompanied by severe British military measures against the rebelling Palestinians, whose leadership established itself firmly through domestic terror. When the British later realized that they would have to fight Hitler, and probably also Italy, whose expansionist ambitions could include the Middle East, London moved toward the Arabs, dropped the partition plan, and met most of the Arab demands regarding the preservation of the

Arab character of the country. The Jews were trapped again,
excluded from the only country in the world that had been
recognized by the League of Nations as "a Jewish Homeland."
Could the Zionist leadership effectively put pressure on Great
Britain after the proclamation of its policy vis-a-vis Palestine
once the war had started? Indeed, documents do provide
proof of some effective Jewish pressure within the British
political system, e.g., on the part of a Jewish M.P. named
Silverman, who managed after some time to help examine and
accept the cumulative reports on the Holocaust that eventually
led to a declaration of intent regarding Nazi war crimes. In
this sense, the Zionists worked outside the system even if for
Hitler they and their fellow Jews were the system. Moreover,
Hitler mentioned in his Table Talks Haim Weizman's declaration
of support to the Allies in the war against Germany, as making
him "enemy number one" of the Reich while this statement was
later quoted by Nazi officials to support the claim that "the
Jew has declared war against Germany." In fact, Zionist
influence was rather limited; but they made enough noise after
Hitler's take-over to exacerbate his rage. A kind of adverse
cumulative effect was also created by them with regard to the
British, who had their own priorities and different moral and
cultural obligations; indeed, the cry "wolf" sounded since
Hitler's take-over and the extensive use of the term "Holocaust" by Jewish and Zionist leaders even before the Holocaust
itself may have influenced those who did not care to begin
with to become bored, and to turn a deaf ear later when the
"real thing" finally happened.

NOTES

(1) Both Richard Wagner and H. S. Chamberlain spoke of
the necessary intellectual awakening of the German people
against the Jewish challenge and of the necessity to remove
Jews from German family life, politics, and culture. See G. L.
Mosse, The Crisis of German Ideology (New York: Grosset and
Dunlap, 1964), pp. 93-97.

(2) Hitler's Zweites Buch, ein Dokument aus dem Jahr 1928
ed., Gerhard L. Weinberg (Stuttgart: Deutche Verlags-
Anstalt, 1961), pp. 46-51.

(3) Mein Kampf (Munich; 1934) pp. 699-705, 721.

(4) Ibid., pp. 161-176.

(5) My argument with regard to Poland as the main territorial object of Hitler's expansion in Eastern Europe is
substantiated by his later conversation with Mussolini (see note
20 below), and by the usual pre-World War I German national-

istic reference to Congress and East Poland, the Baltic states (and Finland), as "Russland."

(6) Hitler's Table Talk, 1941-1944; His Private Conversations, translated by Norman Cameron. (London: Weidenfeld & Nicholson, 1973), pp. 11, 39, 59, 63.

(7) The notion is repeatedly mentioned in Hitler's Table Talk, pp. 7, 22, 31, 150, 343, 476, 504, 507, 512, 534, 555.

(8) See George L. Mosse, Nazism (New Brunswick: Transaction, 1978), p. 78; Gerald Reitlinger, The Final Solution (London: Valentine, 1961); Leon Poliakov, Harvest of Hate (Philadelphia: Jewish Publication Society, 1954); Lucy C. Davidowicz, The War against the Jews (New York: Holt, Reinhart, 1975).

(9) Mosse (Crisis of German Ideology) coined the term "Anti-Jewish Revolution."

(10) See my Reinhard Heydrich and die Fruengeschichte von Gestapo und SD (Stuttgart: Deutche Verlags-Anstalt, 1971), conclusion.

(11) See Poliakov, Harvest of Hate, pp. 2-3; Davidowicz, War against the Jews, pp. 106; and Karl E. Schleuns, The Twisted Road to Auschwitz (Urbana: University of Illinois Press, 1970) p. 265.

(12) See Otto D. Kulka, "The Jewish Question in the Third Reich," (Ph.D. dissertation, Hebrew University, Jerusalem, 1975), p. 329a.

(13) The national report for January 1938, doc. SDHA, ZA II/1 (1.1-31-1-38) R58/999, in my personal possession (U.S. Document Center, Berlin). The quotation is on p. 5.

(14) Timothy W. Mason, Arbeiterklasse und Volksgeminschaft (Opladen Westdeutscher Verlag 1975).

(15) Chief of Staff of the Army, deposed shortly before the outbreak of World War II.

(16) Kulka, "The Jewish Question," p. 402.

(17) Volkischer Beobachter, Munich edition, October 1, 1939.

(18) Documents on German Foreign Policy, series D., Vol. I, p. 114.

(19) See reference to Churchill as a "Jewish tool," Table Talks, and also pp. 216-217, 224 and 226. There is, of course, a vast historical debate on these issues; Klaus Hildebrand's The Foreign Policy of the Third Reich trans. A. Fothergill (London: B.T. Batsford, 1973) and Andreas Hillgruber, Hitler's Strategie, Politik and Kriegsfuehrung (Frankfurt/M: Bernard and Graefe Verlag, 1965) agree, at least, that

NAZI TERRORISM   185

Hitler wanted initially to cooperate with Britain and the United
States or to neutralize them.

(20)   See Documents on German Foreign Policy, vol. XIII, no.
663: (Hitler): "Germany had, after all, achieved her territorial
objectives. He [Hitler] would need up to 50 years to develop
the territories that now belong to him again. . . . In contrast to this the war aims of England and France were the
annihilation of Germany, and he, therefore, did not see any
other possibility of ending the conflict - than by taking up the
struggle." Soviet Russia is not seen here as a threat to Nazi
Germany. For a detailed discussion of the contemporary
sources in the spirit of my argument, see Bernd Stegemann,
"Das Ziele im Ersten Kriegsjahr 1937/1940," Militargeschicht-
liche Mitteilungen, 1/80 S 93-103.

(21)   This refers mainly to Heydrich's order of September 21,
1937 to the security police chiefs in Poland regarding the
concentration of Jews in ghettos as a measure toward "a final
arrangement yet to be announced." Nuremberg Trials Document, PS 3363.

(22)   Hitler's Table Talk, p. 26; and Hitler's Monologe im
Fuhrer-Hauptquartier (a more detailed edition of the Table
Talks) Hamburg: A. Kraus, 1980) p. 14.

(23)   The Wannsee Conference of January 20, 1942 is regarded
as the official (secret) proclamation of the "final solution."
This, too, is contested among historians, but the date seems
to be close enough to Pearl Harbor to justify this assumption,
even if the details were probably worked out later.

(24)   In a conversation with the author, July 1975, Heidel-
berg.

(25)   Professor Gerard L. Weinberg of the University of North
Carolina (Chapel Hill) drew my attention to the enthusiastic
response by generals to Hitler's explicit discussion of the
"final solution" with them as late as Autumn, 1944 (Bundesar-
chiv - Militararchiv - the documents remained unpublished).

(25)   Hildebrand, The Foreign Policy of the Third Reich, pp.
52-53.

9 Document on Terror

The "Document on Terror" was first published in News From The Iron Curtain I, 3 (March 1952), and the following description introduced the piece:

> [It] came to the National Committee for a Free Europe from a former Baltic cabinet minister, favorably known to us. This man received the document in 1948 from a Ukrainian refugee in Germany. According to the Ukrainian, the document, printed in Polish, had been found on the body of a dead NKVD officer in Poland in 1948. It was smuggled into Germany where it was lent to the Ukrainian for 24 hours. During this period the Ukrainian made a shorthand copy of the document, later translated into German. The man who lent the document to the Ukrainian has disappeared. All subsequent efforts to find him have failed. The Baltic minister describes the Ukrainian (with whom he had spent several years in a Nazi concentration camp) as "wholly reliable."
>
> . . . Certain facts support the belief that the document is a genuine product of Communist theory. First, the trend of thought and method of presentation are typical samples of dialectical materialism. Second the application of a pattern of terror methods similar to or identical with those described in the monograph did in fact occur in widely separated countries in Eastern Europe as well as in China.

---

*The editors gratefully acknowledge permission from Radio Free Europe to reprint the "Document on Terror".

The theory has been put into practice by the Communists. Third, the integrity of the man who gave it to us is of the highest order.

. . . Unfortunately, it is incomplete, lacking a title page and ending so abruptly that it seems almost certain that certain pages are missing. In addition, the German translation itself is poor, although it does have the advantage of being a literal translation, even to the extent of following the Polish syntax. The English translation has retained the style of the German except where this would promote misunderstanding. A few obvious inaccuracies have been corrected.

It is not without misgivings that this manuscript is being made available . . since the question of authenticity is by no means resolved. It is our feeling, however, that the document is of such interest and potential importance that it warrants publication.

PART I

GENERAL TERROR

The Concept of General Terror

General terror, also called mass terror, is an act based on violence. With its aid, the subject of terror destroys the most active part of the object of terror. The subject enforces its will on that part of the object of terror which has not been destroyed. Violence, in regard to general terror, means any willfull act of the subject directed against the object with hostile intentions. The only defense open to the object is self-help.

The Elements of General Terror

1. The subject

The subject is an organization of persons and of materials. This organization must be a physical and spiritual entity, aware of its aims. It must also have sufficient materials at its disposal.

The subject is generally in the minority, as compared with the object of terror. What percentage ratio must exist between subject and object in order to ensure victory to the subject, cannot be stated in advance, because the ratio depends on a number of uncertain factors. Nevertheless, this percentage ratio must be taken into account and plans must be laid accordingly.

2.   The executors of terror

In addition to the subject, there is an organ partially or entirely charged with executing the terror acts by the subject. This organ is a separate unit only as far as the actual performance of its acts is concerned. In all other respects it is an inseparable part of the subject.

3.   The object

The object of terror is the entire people, and within the people, every class, level, or group of the population. An individual group of opponents can never be called the object of general terror. The object is always the broad masses among whom the opponents live and act. From this point of view, we can speak of the blindness of the object of general terror. The theoretical reason for this blindness is found in the principles of general terror, namely. . . .

First, the entire population must be subjected to terror in order to establish the conditions for the destruction of one part of the population. Second, whoever is not in the ranks of the terrorists is either an actual or a potential opponent, or creates favorable conditions for the opponent by his passive attitude. The former two must be destroyed, the latter must be dominated: i.e., the entire population must be terrorized. Third if it is probable that a certain group contains one single enemy who cannot be identified, the entire group must be wiped out to make sure that he is destroyed.

The Weapon of Terror

The weapon of general terror is violence. In order to achieve one's aim by means of violence, and to obtain the planned results, violence must be applied at the proper time, in the proper strength, and in the proper form. The proper time is that at which the wave of terror will be a surprise both to the object and to the outside world. The proper strength is that which will disrupt even the most resistant and the strongest group among the object of terror. The proper form is that which will have the most damaging psychological effect on the object. . . .

The Phases of General Terror

A terrorist action which is well prepared and proceeding according to plan will have a normal course consisting of five phases of development, which can be described and classified in terms of the opponents' typical reactions.

1. The first phase is that of increased vitality of the object of terror. When he is struck by the first wave of terrorism, the psychological shock will cause him to go into frantic action. This is shown by the great interest in public meetings and by the overcrowding of places of entertainment. At the same time, morale is lowered.

2. The second phase puts the terror object into a shaky frame of mind. The object of terror feels instinctively that he is in the center of a storm whose extent and violence he does not know. This phase is marked by increased plotting activity, by attempts at organized defense, and by attempts to negotiate with the terrorists. There is also flight to regions not affected by the terror.

3. The third phase is that of fear psychosis. The extent of terror has reached its maximum. The object is dominated by a feeling of increasing fear. This phase is marked by uncoordinated attempts at defense, and by the obvious slowing down of public and social life.

4. The fourth phase is the decisive one for the success of the terrorist action. It is characterized by the paralyzing of the object through fear. The object is no longer capable of offering any practical resistance. This period is the most favorable for forcing the terrorists' will and conditions upon the object.

5. At the beginning of the fifth phase we reach the period in which both parties make efforts to attain a certain equilibrium. The aim has been achieved - the terror decreases. This is the phase in which the terror subject strengthens the position he has won. At the same time, the mentality of the object becomes stabilized at a new level.

Chronic Terror

Looking at it from a sober point of view, the use of terror should be stopped after the fifth phase, if the main aims have been achieved. It should not be applied any longer, while the memories of the population are still fresh. However, the amazing results which can be achieved with terror become a permanent stimulus to the terror subject. He will tend to consider it the universal solution for all problems and difficulties. If he gives in to this temptation, general terror reaches a new and different phase, that of chronic terror. It is based on the steady, repeated application of terror, in the idea that it will lead to the fulfillment of the same aims as a single application of terrorist methods. This, however, is an error, and the terror subject may have to pay dearly for it. For general terror, in this new phase, undergoes a fundamental change, and while it brings certain benefits, it also has unfavorable consequences which react against the terror subject.

The Effects of Chronic Terror

1. Positive effects of chronic terror

Application of chronic terror has a positive effect. It makes it impossible for the object of terror with his own powers to oppose the subject of terror. If terrorism is conducted according to plan, the object will have only those psychological and physical powers left which are necessary for the performance of the functions which the terror subject has forced upon him. Any excess powers must be liquidated, because they represent a danger to the subject and are not indispensable to the life of the object. This is the positive principle of chronic terror, called the principle of the lowest level of powers.

2. Negative effects

We know from the definition of general terror that it serves to achieve two aims; the destruction of one certain portion of the terror object, and the imposition of the will of the terror subject upon the part of the object which has not been destroyed. Obviously, the first task of terror is to absorb the most active part of the object, to destroy it, or at least to injure the central organs of the object effectively. But there remains the part of the object which has not been destroyed, and which, as a rule, is the largest part of the object. The will of the terror subject must be imposed upon it. This can be done by putting the object into a state of impotence, by paralyzing his will to resist. This paralysis is a psychological effect, caused by sudden fear, the fear being created by the use of concentrated force. But the terror object is a living organism with a tendency and a capacity to adapt himself to all conditions and to survive them if biological conditions permit. Chronic terror causes chronic fear, but this does not halt life as such. Thus, by the laws of nature, the terror object will become used to living in constant fear and will therefore become immune to it. Thus repeated terror can no longer achieve the effect of paralyzing the will to resist. It does create something else however, namely hatred of the terror subject. This again has effects which are called the negative

effects of chronic terror. From these, we can derive four
further principles of chronic terror; the principles of internal
intervention, of moral isolation, of unforeseen effects, and of
deception.

a.   Principle of internal intervention.   The terror object
cannot loosen the stranglehold of the terror subject, and for
that precise reason he becomes filled with the will to resist,
the feeling of hatred, and the wish for revenge. He creates a
state of potential revolt, a readiness for every action which is
directed against the terror subject, and also the willingness to
consider every enemy of the terror subject his liberator. This
attitude of the terror object creates a dangerous situation for
the terror subject; for over a period of time it forms, in the
field of force of the terror subject, a basis for the internal
intervention of the current opponent of the terror subject.
The internal intervention will be successful; that is, it will
interrupt the condition of passive conduct in which the terror
object exists, and will mobilize the terror object to the
struggle with the terror subject. When a third factor, taking
account of the positive principle of chronic terror, raises the
force of the terror object to such a level, with the aid of its
own means, then it is possible to start the struggle. So long
as this condition remains unfulfilled, the status of passive
conduct is not interrupted - and all hope of drawing the
terror object to the level of a struggle with the terror subject
is without foundation.
   No exceptions to the above rule are known. . . .
   This rule forms the first negative principle of chronic
terror, and is called the principle of internal intervention.
However, one must always consider that so-called wars of intervention, carried out around the periphery of the field of force
of the terror subject, have nothing to do with internal intervention and should not be identified with it.

b.   Principle of moral isolation.   The tool of terror constitutes force in its original form.   The continued application
of terror in this form arouses hate and aversion, not only in
the terror object, but also in the outside world, which finds
itself in constant fear that sooner or later it must share the
fate of the terror object. Masses of people exposed to terror
but so far spared by it feel this readily and very radically.
Behind them follow the objects which are not affected by the
terror but which are already threatened by it. Finally come
those who are not already threatened, and who even sympathize with the terror subject, but who are, so to speak,
"swallowed up" by the masses which are inimical to the terror
subject. In this way there forms around the terror subject a
void which becomes the more complete the longer the period of
terror domination continues, the more ruthless the terror is,

and the greater the number of victims is. The final result of the application of chronic terror is always a complete moral isolation of the terror subject.

c. Principle of unforeseen effects. The application of chronic terror isolates the terror subject morally. But along with the process of isolation another process develops in the outside world which is no smaller in extent and no less significant. The spectre of terror unites the enemies of the terror subject and forms automatically a certain enemy coalition, which grows constantly and constantly threatens to strangle the terror subject. Independent of this, and despite outward appearances, the number of opponents is not lessened even in the internal field of force of the terror subject. On the contrary, the number of opponents grows steadily, disproportionately to the strength of the terror and to the number of opponents destroyed by the terror. . . .

d. Principle of deception. The positive effects of the application of terror do not become evident and understandable until some time in the future. But it is certain that the bitter fruits of these effects are not experienced by the terror subject until after the period of the first triumph and successes.

This sly, crafty action of the negative effects of chronic terror often becomes the source of dangerous deception on the part of the terror subject. The terror subject deceives himself that the most difficult and most complicated problems can most easily be solved with the aid of force. Strengthened in this conviction, the terror subject does not look for any other solution, and finally ends up thinking only in terms of force. Under such circumstances, the problem of how one should deal with a thing is not important. A solution to the problem is always ready, although it is not always in harmony with logic and healthy understanding. For the terror subject, the main consideration is what sort of force is necessary to force upon the outside world the ideals, desires, and will of the terror subject. The effects of such a train of thought are always the same - poorly solved problems do not keep pace with life; they pile up, and once set in motion they roll like an avalanche and crush everyone who tries to restrain their natural progress. This phenomenon is constant to the extent that every subject of chronic terror has a great inclination to solve current problems with the aid of force. The extent of this inclination is an indication of the degree to which the terror subject is under the influence of this deception. Because these phenomena are constant, they form the principle of chronic terror called the principle of deception. To be sure, this principle applies only to those changes which take place under certain conditions in the psyche of the terror subject, but its general significance is so great that it would be an error not to mention it.

The Methods of General Terror

In order to attain its goal, general terror has worked out or adapted certain methods of fighting. These methods may be divided into psychological methods and direct action methods.

1. Psychological methods

The psychological methods coupled with intimidation, are aimed at forcing the terror object to behave in a manner most favorable for the terror subject. These methods have an indirect, preventive character, and are intended to produce a psychological effect. Direct attack on the opponent and his destruction are either completely ignored or are of only secondary importance. The following psychological methods are known and applied.

a. The method of intimidation through publishing of lists of persons sentenced to death, with the notation that the sentence will be executed if the terror object attempts resistance in certain fields.
This method is ineffective and must remain so, because it is a method of individual, not mass, terror. This method can be used with good results as a tool for individual terror. But in any case where the attempt to exert pressure cannot lead to the desired end, it fails. For example: I tell "N," a person who is in opposition to me, that "Z," who is in my hands, will be executed if "N" behaves in a manner disloyal to me. I can count on a positive result of the pressure if "Z" has close connections with "N." But I cannot count on such a result if "Z" is a person about whom "N" cares nothing, unless "N" is a person with very high moral principles and the causes of his opposition to me are quite a serious matter. This method is unfavorable for the terror subject if there is still a third person concerned who takes an interest in the struggle. In order to prevent any positive effects from being attained by this method, he will incite an act of terror and will thereby force the subject to carry out his threats. If the threats are realized, conditions will necessarily become more tense, and the number of opponents will necessarily increase.

b. The method of intimidation by publishing lists of persons against whom the death sentence has been carried out. This method has only one positive effect: it terrifies the uncertain element which does not possess adequate ideological strength. In addition to the general negative effects, this method also gives rise to the following supplemental effects:

(1) This method terrifies the idealistic element in as small a way as the spectre of death terrifies a volunteer in a war.

(2) The application of this method causes a qualitative selection on the part of the opponent, because only the qualitatively strongest element, the one most dangerous to the terror subject, will then volunteer for the revolutionary organizations. Thus, whatever these organizations lose in quantity is made up for in quality.

(3) This method creates a nimbus of martyrdom around the opponents and their families, and makes heroes of them. Thus this method does not achieve its aim; because the terror subject is not using it with the intention of adding high-grade human material to the resources of the opposition organizations or of creating martyrs and heroes on a production-line basis.

c. The method of intimidation through the public execution of death sentences.

This method has no positive effects. On the contrary, it increases the tension of all negative effects to a pathological degree. It amounts to planting a time bomb among one's own ranks. It can be recommended if one desires to increase the resistance of the terror object at any price, or wants to provoke the terror object to acts of active resistance.

d. The method of hostages.

This method consists of taking a number of persons in an area prisoner and publicly announcing that all these persons will be executed if there are any acts of active resistance in this area. This is a method of individual terror, and it is a mistake to use it as a tool of mass terror. It is successful if one desires to force loyalty from those persons for whom the hostages have a considerable personal significance. It would be effective as a method of mass terror if:

(1) all inhabitants of the area were agreed that they would maintain peace in exchange for the lives of the hostages; and also if

(2) there were no faction outside this area which was interested in the struggle.

In case the threat is carried out, the negative effects become more concrete because the hostages are usually prominent people and as a rule are not guilty of any offense.

e. The method of joint responsibility.

This consists of carrying out minor or major reprisals against a group of people from whose midst the executor of an act of force originated, either in fact or in supposition. Even if this method has positive effects, it does not achieve its aim, because it is directed against a group which has no influence in the matter. The negative effects of this method are identical with the effects of the hostage method.

f. The method of intimidation by bad treatment in public (striking in the face, kicking, beating with rifles, etc.).

This method is used in two cases: first, as prime punishment for infractions of regulations; and second, as initial punishment for serious offenses. This method is considered here not because of the fact that when it is once introduced it is always later misused, but because the reason for giving it attention goes much deeper. This method must be noted because, although it appears quite harmless, it actually has far-reaching effects.

2. The method of direct action

The methods of direct action are generally known and are of historical value only. However, the mechanics of the methods of direct action are always reliable from the standpoint of general terror and bring good quantitative results. The aim of these methods is: to render the active opponent harmless; to render suspected elements harmless; and to maintain the balance between the quantitative strength of the terror object and that of the terror subject, through systematic destruction of the human potential of the terror object. Finally, these methods aim to create a psychosis of "white fear," the purpose of which is to cripple the terror object's will to resist.

Neutralizing the Negative Effects of Terror

So far, this survey has been an analysis of general and chronic terror (the latter cannot be regarded as an independent type of terror, as, for example, destructive or individual terror). The purpose of this analysis is to explain the structure, the nature, and the spirit of this fighting tool, with its good and its bad properties. The analysis has shown that general terror, used once, can render excellent service. It makes it possible in one fine stroke to destroy the leading group of the terror object, to cripple his masses, and to impose the will of the terror subject. There is no doubt that even in this case the negative effects of the terror are also observable. But these effects do not become evident immediately and it is possible to suppress them and deprive them of the climate which favors their development before they mature. In view of this fact, one may risk making the statement that a single application of general terror is useful and without undesirable consequences.

The situation is different when it comes to chronic terror. To be sure, the terror object only vegetates, but the relentless laws of chronic terror are operating and are making the terror subject ripe for destruction, although the destruction can be caused - this must be specifically emphasized - only by a third external factor. Thus chronic terror is dangerous also because it promises a great deal and justifies the hopes only under conditions of isolation, when there is no danger of internal intervention. If, however, this danger exists, the application of the terror is unfavorable. But the danger of internal intervention should not be overestimated, because history shows that successful internal intervention is an exceptional case. Generally it fails because of basic errors which are in the very fundamentals of the planned action. Still more often it never actually takes place, because the leading group of the potential interventionist is incapable of the action. But in every case the application of chronic terror involves a great number of dangers. In order to minimize these dangers, other means may be used.

In the internal field, the best defense is terror itself - well organized, naturally. . . . In the external field, the best protection consists of taking proper steps to isolate the terror object and the territory which is dominated by the terror from the rest of the world. Such measures are the more successful the more complete the isolation. But one must emphasize in advance that in the times in which we live such tactics are successful only to a degree, because the development of the means of transportation makes absolute isolation impossible.

In the last analysis, those measures can be recommended which serve to strengthen the internal and external conflicts which already exist in the camp of the potential opponent. Potential opponents who are occupied with their own troubles are naturally not in a position to direct additional attention toward even an important development if it is of minor interest to them, because it does not involve their interests directly.

But all these methods are only apparent. They reduce the force of the undesirable developments, but basically they do not offer protection to the terror subject. When unfavorable conditions coexist (and one cannot deny that unfavorable conditions often have a tendency to exist simultaneously), nothing is of any avail, and in spite of all efforts the terror subject will suddenly find himself faced with a coalition of internal intervention.

PART II

ENLIGHTENED TERROR

The Concept of Enlightened Terror

The fact that a weapon has a deficiency does not mean that it is of no value as a fighting tool. In order to avoid the dangers which are connected with its utilization, it is sometimes sufficient simply to know what the shortcomings of the weapon are and to see under what conditions one can apply it not only without damage but even to advantage. Thus there is no doubt that under certain circumstances general terror (regardless of its shortcomings) can be used repeatedly as well as a single time. But the consciousness that a deficiency exists is disturbing. For this reason an effort is made to improve the structure of general terror. The result of this attempt is the concept of enlightened terror.

The Basic Principles of Enlightened Terror

1.   Camouflage maneuvers

The application of terror is dangerous for the terror subject because the terror subject acts against the terror object, and before the world at large, in its own name. For this reason the negative effects of the terror are directed against the terror subject itself. In order to avoid this danger, in the concept of enlightened terror, the terror subject remains concealed. But naturally, concealment of the fact that the terror subject exists does not alone solve the problem. Even when the best means of concealment are used, the question of who is applying the terror can not long remain unanswered. For this reason, in the concept of enlightened terror the terror subject not only remains in the shadows, but acts and applies terror not in his own name but in the name of his opponent. This principle is called the "camouflage maneuver."
       Now one must observe whether and on what bases measures will have an effect, that is, to what degree the terror subject can count on being able to deceive the opponent, his natural environment, and the rest of the world.
       From outward appearances one might assume that both measures are naive and predestined to failure. Actually the reverse is true. The possibilities of deceiving all three factions are very great, provided that the terror subject fulfills only one condition, the condition of probability. This means that the plans for the action must contain certain

elements which indicate that the execution of the action by the opponent is a probability. . . .

Two examples illustrate the truth of these "camouflage maneuvers."

From 1942 on a mighty struggle raged between the Poles and Ukrainians in the Polish-Ukrainian border regions. Its reverberations have not died out to this day. This fight was started and conducted according to the rules of enlightened terror, on the initiative of the competent Bolshevist organs. These Bolshevist elements decided to strike the three opponents, the Germans, the Poles, and the Ukrainians, in a single action and with a single stroke. This is indicated by the aim of the action, which was as follows:

> a. to bring the German hinterland to a status of "Balkanization,"
> b. to disclose the elements with nationalist leanings on both the Polish and the Ukrainian sides,
> c. to prevent any attempt at Polish-Ukrainian cooperation,
> d. to weaken Poland's position in the international field (in case the Polish government should demand the restitution of the eastern border as of 1939).

The means with which this action was carried out may be regarded as classic. Two fighting groups were formed, Polish and Ukrainian. Both groups were numerically weak and consisted of only a few people, who, however, were distinguished by special abilities. The two groups started the action simultaneously, but independently, in the sectors assigned to them (in Wolhynia). The Polish group attacked the Ukrainians, the Ukrainians, the Poles. The actions were particularly ruthless, and at first glance appeared to be completely senseless, because the objects of the action on both sides were persons who enjoyed the authority of the two groups of peoples. The actions were carried out ruthlessly and at short intervals, always in the name of the loudly proclaimed national interests, either Polish or Ukrainian.

Both Poles and Ukrainians are distinguished by the relative speed with which they can be aroused. For this reason the mass reaction occurred very quickly. In a short time the true avengers and defenders of the national interests appeared on both sides, and they continued the actions tirelessly and enthusiastically, along the lines determined in the beginning by the two operational groups.

Then the two groups were suddenly diverted to other fields, and finally completely withdrawn, because it had quickly become evident that they were no longer needed. The machine of enlightened terror was already operating automatically.

A few months passed and it became clear that the goal of the action had been attained. But the characteristic thing – and from the standpoint of enlightened terror, the important thing – is that the actual subject of the terror remained concealed and must remain concealed in the future, even from the eyes of the historians. All those affected by the action believe that it was of the nature of a spontaneous movement, and differences of opinion exist only concerning who was to blame. For the Poles blame the Ukrainians and the Ukrainians the Poles. But both sides, and also the outside world, are mistaken.

The burning of the Reichstag is the second example. The National-Socialists planned and executed the burning of the Reichstag. The act was attributed to the German Communist Party, in order to indicate and to justify the persecution of the members of this Party. The burning of the Reichstag may be regarded as a typical example of enlightened terror, mainly because of the use of the camouflage maneuver. As is well known, the effects of this maneuver have never fulfilled the hopes of those who perpetrated it, because only a very small section of world public opinion was deceived by the suggestion. This fact must be interpreted to mean that the National-Socialists did not pay adequate attention to the condition of probability when they made up their plan of action. For although the German Communists could indeed have had a certain amount of interest in the destruction of the National-Socialist elite, they could certainly have had no interest in burning the building where that elite helds its meetings.

2. Dualism of the subject

The logical extension of the principle of the "camouflage maneuvers" forms the basis of the dualism of the subject of enlightened terror. Dualism consists of the fact that the subject of enlightened terror shows himself in one form before the outside world when he appears in public, and in a different form when the conditions of the struggle necessitate it.

The first form represents openly the creative power of the terror subject; the second, his destructive power. For this reason the latter is supposed to appear outwardly, before the world at large, as the personification of the opponent. In this connection the scope and the sphere of activity of the two forms should be very carefully limited. The limits of these assignments can be described as follows:

  a. The scope of action of the public organs of the subject of enlightened terror includes all actions

which have to do with the execution of government
(power) in its classic form. On the other hand, no
action which is in any way connected with the
execution of the terror should be included.

b. The sphere of action of the concealed
organs of the terror subject includes all activities
which are based on terror.

In conjunction with the basic principle of dualism the
problem arises as to whether the responsibility of the opponent
for the actions of the concealed organs of the subject of the
enlightened terror must be based on proof, or whether it can
be based on suspicion only. . . .

To make a person suspicious is an assignment which is
easier than one might think. The wheels of terror never
operate blindly. There is always a terror object, the opponent. And the opponent can act, although, of course, he is
not supposed to. But if the opponent is capable of action, the
terror subject can assert that he actually did act. Then it
becomes very easy to establish the statement that a certain act
was done by the opponent. This sort of suspicion can always
be created.

3.   Psychological effect

The activities of general terror, independent of surprise
effects, are also designed for the psychological effect. But in
spite of this, nothing in the system of general terror is
usually given less thorough consideration than the human
being and his psyche.

In principle, knowledge of human beings and of the laws
which govern human beings is superfluous in the system of
general terror, and may perhaps be harmful for the executor
of the terror. This develops from the nature of general
terror, from its structure, and from the mechanics of its
activities, which are more than simple. It is sufficient simply
to set the mechanism in motion and to shove a portion of the
terror object into its jaws to destroy a certain number of the
opponents, a number which in certain cases can be recorded
statistically, in percentage terms, and calculated.

The system of enlightened terror is based on quite different principles. The terror subject and the opponent both
live and operate in natural environments, in a group of
people. These environments sometimes assume a friendly
attitude toward the terror subject; more often they are
neutral; and very often they are inimical. Thus in the system
of enlightened terror nearly all the efforts of the terror
subject are directed at converting the environment into a
spontaneous assistant and accessory, in ignorance of its role.
For this, a knowledge of human psychology and mass psychology is necessary for action.

There is a good example of such action. Many sections in the Lublin district through which important German communication lines ran were especially suited for the execution of diversion actions because of their very favorable topographic conditions. It was almost impossible for the irregular Bolshevist units to penetrate them, because the indigenous population, who had not been too much disturbed by the German authorities, had taken a very neutral attitude, and had in general become inimical toward the Bolshevists and would not give them the necessary support. In this situation, the Bolshevist commander ordered a small fighting group formed, and at its head he executed a few actions which were quite drastic in their planning and execution. In a short time many Germans had fallen victim to these actions. The local commander of the German security service reacted quickly and ruthlessly; in many villages he ordered several persons shot without any investigation whatever; many others were sent to concentration camps, and farm buildings were burned. But at the same time the reaction of the masses of the people was exactly as the Bolshevist commander had calculated. In a previously peaceful area there developed a ferment. The formerly peaceful people rose up and swelled the numerically weak fighting group into a large fighting unit. As a result, the Red commanders who led the action found obedience, loyalty, and support primarily among the ranks of those who suffered from the increasingly frequent, but increasingly stupid, stereotyped punitive actions carried out by the German commands. Thus, the Bolshevist commander based his action upon an excellent knowledge of the psychology of individual persons (in this case, the mentality of the German commander in question) and also of mass psychology. He recognized the basic law of psychology, that under certain definite conditions a certain definite incitation must give rise to a certain definite reaction - and he acted in accordance with this law. . . .

4. Original reaction

The system of enlightened terror is also based on the basic principle of original reaction, that is, on such a reaction as is psychologically typical of a certain person. . . . It is not a product of the conscious thought process. It develops spontaneously, almost automatically, and appears in each person in a psychologically typical form. Unexpected or undeserved censure as a rule develops in the individual a feeling of anger and then a desire for revenge. If the person gives in to the feeling of anger or revenge, he acts according to his typical original psychological reaction. If he dominates his feelings, he acts consciously, and his action appears as a conscious act of will. On the basis of experience, it has been determined that such conscious action is a very rare phenomenon. The average person, as a rule, or a mass of people, will always and without exception act in accordance with original reaction. This is a permanent, immutable phenomenon, which operates with the same intensity in any circumstances, and therefore in the system of enlightened terror it forms one of the main basic principles.

The following example illustrates the meaning of this basic principle.

During the first few months of the German-Bolshevist war, evidences of demoralization appeared among the ranks of the Red Army. This resulted in mass desertions which reached threatening proportions. One of the causes was the fact that the German command in the beginning had treated Soviet Army prisoners in general in a humane fashion. Observing this situation, the appropriate Soviet circles took draconian measures. They ordered that all Germans captured on the front or in the German hinterland, whether they fell into the hands of regular troops or of guerilla units, were to be ruthlessly and terribly mistreated.

These measures were applied systematically and over a fairly long period of time, until the order was rescinded. They produced an immediate counter-reaction on the part of the Germans. The Germans instituted reprisals, and began to shoot captured Soviet Army personnel, and additional prisoners were destroyed in the prisoner-of-war camps through hunger and infectious diseases. This action on the part of the Germans had the desired and expected reaction in the Soviet Army. Desertions ceased, and morale and fighting spirit improved notably. . . .

5. Infiltration

The basic principle of infiltration forms an organic entity with the above-mentioned basic principles. The concept of this principle is known, but it is almost always not properly understood. The idea is to fill the ranks of the opponents with qualitatively highly efficient personnel of one's own. But those who believe that the main objective of this action is vigilance, with a source of constant and reliable information are deceived. There is no doubt that this should also be given consideration, but it is only in the background of the plan and is certainly of only secondary importance. The primary mission of the persons who have penetrated is to become assimilated by the opponent, even to the point where there is no longer any doubt about the person's belonging to the enemy camp. His rightful duty, regardless of this position, is to create a focus of chronic internal and external conflict within the enemy camp. He operates dogmatically and with ruthless fanaticism, in the name of the well-being of the

opponent, supporting himself on the opponent's ideological
principles.

The Communist Party in Germany utilized this basic
principle on a historic scale after Hitler came to power. After
being declared illegal, the Communist Party ceased to operate
legally. In fact, it gave up almost entirely illegal activities.
It kept up a few of the latter only for appearances, almost
solely "as a matter of form." This was done in order to lull
the vigilance of the National-Socialists to sleep, to convince
them completely that the danger of Communism in Germany had
disappeared once and for all. Instead, all attention and all
efforts were devoted to the "Trojan horse." One may well say
that nothing in Germany remained unaffected by this unob-
served flood of Red infiltrators, who shouted the fanatic
concepts of Hitler and wore the uniforms of the National-
Socialists. Neither the National-Socialist Party and its
organizations, nor the government apparatus, nor the army,
nor even the immediate circles surrounding Hitler, Himmler,
Goebbels, or any leading person in the so-called Third Reich,
remained free of infiltration. The elite of the Communist
Party sacrificed all its forces, not to break through the
wall of defense around Hitlerism, but to undermine it.

Structural Elements of Enlightened Terror

1. The terror subject

The terror subject as known in the concepts of general terror
also exists in the structure of enlightened terror. But the
differences between the subject of general terror and the
subject of enlightened terror are of an organic character.

In the structure of general terror, the terror subject
forms a palpable open organization. The number of members
may be small, but a certain ratio relative to the quantitative
potential of the terror object must be maintained. In order to
overcome the difficulties of terror, the members of this
organization must be kept under iron discipline, and the
leaders must always be concerned with instructing their men,
with maintaining their fighting power and their unshakeable
spirit. This is the weak aspect of general terror and shows
its shortcomings. To be sure, a strong organization develops,
but the world sees it. The members are revealed to the
world. And the worst of it is that the entire world is
mobilized against the subject. The world, depending upon the
magnitude of the stated intentions, which are quite strange to
it, feels itself threatened, and with justification. As a result,
the road to the goal does not become smoother. Everything
puts obstacles in the road, and forces the use of the most
severe and the most radical fighting methods.

In the structure of enlightened terror the situation is quite different.

Upon closer examination, it is seen that the art of applying enlightened terror is the clever fabrication of outward appearances, and this knowledge forms the actual weapon of enlightened terror. Because of the nature of this weapon, the best conditions for its use are created by a group which remains concealed, and which is so small that it does not have to make known its plans and explain them openly. A large number of visible organs is not a help, but a ballast and a hindrance. For this reason a special separate group, which does not even exist so far as the outside world is concerned, becomes the subject of enlightened terror, creating the power and the assistance for the realization of its plans from the reserves of the already existing organization of the community within which it operates. In such a situation it is not necessary to maintain an open organization, and furthermore there exists a possibility of camouflaging the actual plans with those ideas which at this time are particularly desired by mankind. Both these developments are extraordinarily favorable for the terror subject, because world opinion then is not in a constant state of alert, or readiness for combat. And this excellently helps to attain the planned goal.

2.   The executors

In the structure of general terror the executors are the elite. In the structure of enlightened terror, the situation is different.

The executors are a separate entity isolated from the terror subject. Their only connection with the terror subject is their will and the logic of the mission offered or forced upon them. Other than this, there is no visible connection between the terror subject and the executors. This isolation must be maintained. The necessity of maintaining this isolation develops from the nature of enlightened terror, which consists of throwing the responsibility for every act of force executed onto the opponent. Thus the executors must represent to the outside world the object, not the subject, of enlightened terror.

The executors fall into four groups of people, depending upon how they were recruited.

The first group includes persons devoted to the cause. The terror subject accords them special confidence. They form the nucleus and the skeleton, that is, the leading group, of the executors.

The second group includes co-workers who act knowing the true state of affairs only within the limited boundaries of the missions assigned to them. But their idealistic value, their devotion, and experience have not been proved beyond doubt. Persons near to them guarantee their work, and have the same value as hostages so far as the terror subject is concerned.

The third group includes co-workers who act in the erroneous conviction that they are working for the terror object or for some other, unknown faction. Their recruitment and their work are based on the principle: deceive, and utilize the deception.

The fourth group includes chance co-workers whose assistance has been bought under some pretense or has been obtained under false pretenses.

3. The terror object

The terror object naturally also has its place in the structure of enlightened terror. But it differs basically from the object of general terror. The object of general terror is always the mass of the active opponent, a more or less passive group, and includes even the mass of the nonactive sympathizers with the terror subject. Basically, therefore, the object of general terror consists of all who are not within the ranks of the terror subject. However, the object of enlightened terror consists exclusively of the active opponents, regardless of whether they have been singled out as individuals, or whether they are still unknown. . . . A difference exists only in the method which one must use to destroy them. In the first case, when one has determined who the opponent is, he is destroyed by direct means. In the second case, when the opponent is unknown, he must be separated from the environment in which he lives. To this end, one uses direct action.

4. Resonant mass and instigation object

In the concept of enlightened terror two new factors evolve which are not known in the structure of general terror. These are the resonant mass and the instigation object. Both these factors in general have an exceptional significance. Their significance increases especially when it is impossible to destroy the terror object through direct action. If the factors are to fulfill their assignments successfully, one must separate them from the mass of the subject or the object of the action.

a. Resonant mass.   The resonant mass is the natural environment of the terror object, that is, the mass of people with which the terror object lives and acts. The resonant mass may yield more or less to outside influences, or it may offer resistance to the process of being molded, but regardless of that it always forms a plastic mass which the terror subject can adapt to its own plans, naturally under the condition that

the appropriate means are employed.   It is of no significance
whether the terror object acts openly or remains concealed.   If
the terror object develops any action whatever, it must
connect itself with its natural environment, that is, with the
resonant mass, in order to fulfill its mission.   Therefore, since
the active opponent must support this connection, the terror
subject can turn over to the resonant mass the mission of
destroying him.   In order to achieve this, it is not necessary
to dominate the resonant mass physically; nor is it necessary
to dominate its "soul."   It is sufficient if the terror subject is
able, by means of appropriate measures, to cause the resonant
mass to assume an attitude inimical to the terror object.   If
this is successful, then the opponent is no longer a component
part of the resonant mass.   He will be rejected by it as a
foreign body.

b.   The instigation object.   As is well known, the system of
enlightened terror is based, among other things, on the
principle that a single, precisely determined incitation under
definite conditions must give rise to a predetermined reaction.
For example, if I step on someone's corn, it will certainly
cause him pain.   He may cry out; he will almost certainly
become angry.   If I should purposely repeat such an act, each
of these reactions which have been described and anticipated,
will certainly appear, and their intensity will increase.   If I
carry out the act cleverly and direct suspicion at someone
else, my victim will turn around and vent his anger not on me
but on this third person.   In this example I am the terror
subject and the executor, the inciter of pain to the corn,
which is the instigation object.   The man with the corn is the
resonator, and the third man is the terror object, because the
reaction, that is, the anger of the resonant mass, is directed
toward him.
     In this text-book example the true role played by the
instigation object in the structure of enlightened terror is
described clearly and graphically.   The instigation object can
be any material object (that is, any animate or inanimate
object) or any spiritual object, provided it has a close
connection with the resonator.   It would be impossible to
survey the total number of different instigation objects.   The
choice of one type or another depends upon conditions and
circumstances in the particular case.   No less important
considerations are the terror subject's degree of culture,
intelligence, knowledge of psychology, and powers of observation.

5.   The tool of enlightened terror

The only tool which general terror knows and uses is force.

In the system of enlightened terror, force is still an important tool, but only when it is necessary to destroy the active and individually indicated opponent, or when it is necessary to produce a definitely planned and precisely defined psychological effect.

Thus the limits within which enlightened terror may permit the use of force are not only very rigorously defined but also very restricted. They are incomparably more limited than in the case of general terror, and much more limited in comparison with the ways which force can be used during armed conflict, because one does not need to kill people in order to achieve a psychological effect. The same effect is achieved by other means. Therefore the tool used by enlightened terror is any means which is able to produce the planned psychological effect.

Methods of Enlightened Terror

In the system of enlightened terror every action forms a complete whole composed of the investigation activity, the executor activity, and the amplifying activity.

Each action is based on a different method of fighting. In the system of enlightened terror a division between offensive and defensive fighting methods is unknown. All methods are equally aggressive, and all are aimed directly or indirectly at the destruction of the opponent. Therefore, from the standpoint of the subject of enlightened terror, the fighting methods are divided into methods of internal and external conflict. The methods of internal fighting have as their aim the destruction of an enemy who has penetrated into the field of force of the enlightened terror. The methods of external fighting attempt to destroy the enemy in his own or in an outside field of force.

The Methods of Internal Conflict

The aim of the activity of investigation is the identification of the opponent, the determination of his point of support, the processing of the plan of action for his destruction, and the distribution of the personnel and the material means for the execution of the action. The positive results of the investigation activities depend primarily upon the industry and the quality of the information service. In the system of enlightened terror the information service is based on the following principles.

1. The principle of infiltration

On the basis of the infiltration principle, the system of
enlightened terror can build up various organizations which
operate under other auspices, sometimes even under enemy
auspices.   In this way the terror subject builds the information organizations in his field of operations, their nature
and membership corresponding as well as possible to the local
conditions.   The terror subject recommends to a potential
candidate that he work with whatever organization best suits
him in spirit.   In this respect the system of enlightened terror
can satisfy even very capricious or special inclinations.   In
this way information from various observation points and from
various sectors should be able to give a full and graphic
picture of the corresponding field of operation.

2. The principle of free choice

The principle of free choice is based on the fact, which is
confirmed by experience, that the best information is brought
by someone who does it voluntarily, because of his feeling of
belonging to this or that group, which is determined by the
feeling of solidarity.   The feeling of this duty stems from a
consciousness of belonging to a racial, national, class,
professional, religious, or ideological group, which often
includes a very broad field.   The information network which
operates according to the principles of free choice works very
skillfully in strange, irregular terrain.   Especially to be
noted is the complete helplessness of the object whose name
the terror subject uses for his own purposes.

3. The principle of personal danger (threat)

Because in many cases the principle of free choice cannot be
applied, and in many other cases it is inadequate, the information service of enlightened terror often is supported by
the principle of personal danger (personal threat).   The
beneficial properties of personal danger derive from the fact,
well-known to every lawyer, that the defense counsel learns
more from the defendant in the period of a few minutes than
the police and the court learn during a long investigation.
This phenomenon may be easily explained by the psychological
status of the defendant.   Rightly or not, the defendant feels
that his most cherished possessions are threatened, and in the
person of the defense counsel he sees his only trustworthy
adviser.
    In the system of enlightened terror use is made of this
phenomenon to draw certain persons into the network of the
information service, particularly when one can use these
persons for procuring information only without their knowl-

edge. The process consists of putting the person into a position of personal danger which is best suited to the existing circumstances. The conditions must at the same time mean that the only trustworthy defender of the person threatened is the terror subject. The above-mentioned principle renders good service, particularly in one's own sphere of operation when setting the scene for the threatening situation.

4. The principle of retaliation

The necessary amplification of the two above-mentioned principles is the principle of retaliation. This is based on the phenomenon that every official who is connected with some shady business is particularly ready to aid the police to catch criminals. In the system of enlightened terror this phenomenon is utilized with the aim of drawing certain persons who actually, or even only apparently, are employed by the opponent of the terror subject into the information network as conscious or unconscious assistants. Naturally, in certain cases the terror subject is forced to create the crime himself.

If the conflict takes place within the scope of one's own forces, the introductory activity can determine the following situations: first, that the conditions exist for direct action by the open public organs of the terror subject; second that conditions exist for direct action by the executors; and third, that conditions exist for indirect action by the executors.

1. Direct action by the open organs of the terror subject

The conditions for direct action by the open organs of the terror subject exist in a case where either the opponent has been unmasked and identified and failure appears to be impossible, or where the opponent's support point has been discovered . . . and the extent of the action demands unequivocally the terror subject's open appearance on the scene.

Enlightened terror permits direct action by the open organs of the terror subject only in these two cases. There are very important motives underlying this limitation.

The structure of general terror not only permits, but even forces, mass arrests and raids. Statistical reports on such actions are always impressive. But the actual results are minimal, because the actual opponent generally falls into the trap of such an action only by chance. The natural environment of the terror subject knows about this. It also knows that the action involves and destroys persons who are blameless. Thus in time the natural environment becomes convinced that the terror subject is acting blindly and is wandering astray in the dark. And such a state of affairs causes the prestige of the terror subject to diminish gradually in his natural environment. In the end, the natural environment fears the terror subject in the same way that one must fear a madman. The environment avoids the terror subject, but at the same time loses all respect for it.

In the structure of enlightened terror such a development is not permissible. The open organs of the terror subject must enjoy full respect. Immunity to all blows, and manifest knowledge of how to find a way out of any situation, create this respect. For this reason, in the structure of enlightened terror the open organs of the terror subject appear only seldom, and then with an assurance that commands authority.

2. Direct action by the executors

The conditions for direct action by the executors exist in cases where the administrative authorities are competent to destroy the opponent, where there is doubt concerning the culpability of the opponent, and where important motives (for example, of a political nature) militate against open action.

In all the cases mentioned above the executors carry out the action, destroy the opponent, and create "appearances" which seem to implicate the opponent. One must specifically underline the term "appearances," which is not identical with proof. Because in this case it is simply a matter of creating the impression, enlightened terror leaves to its opponent the problem of destroying the impression and the unsuccessful efforts to prove its improbability.

In this way general terror again goes into action, but in the service of enlightened terror. Therefore the effect of its action is greatly increased. It acts like a pair of scissors, the one blade of which is formed by direct action, the other by the secondary effects of the terror. The destructive effect of this pair of shears is more rapid and radical when the opponent is more dangerous in numbers. The opponent is more vulnerable not only as the result of the direct action, but also because of the forces of the energy which is released during the process of his destruction.

Here one should also mention the secondary effects of enlightened terror. These effects, unlike the secondary effects of general terror, are positive. Only the executors act in the name of the opponent. As a result, the open representatives of enlightened terror, are regarded as the personification of good.

3. Indirect action by the executors

The conditions for indirect action by the executors exist when the information service has not fulfilled its mission, when it has not been able to identify the opponent, and when it has been determined in what vicinity the opponent is to be found.

Indirect action is based on the fact that the opponent will be forced to attempt to establish contact with the environment, in order to build up his strong points, without which an action planned for an extended period of time would be impossible. There is only a single way left open to combat the internal danger successfully. This way is to make the environment immune to the influence of the opponent, to make it adopt an attitude inimical to the opponent, and finally to force it into conflict with the opponent. Such a situation can be attained only if one infects the environment with the bacilli of fear, aversion, and hate of the opponent.

Actually all previous attempts to combat internal danger have been on the trail of this truth. But for some reason, even starting with the proper premises, false conclusions are attained. This false reasoning follows:

The opponent finds support and aid in a certain environment. Primarily responsible for this is the environment itself, for the reason that it permits itself to be persuaded by the opponent. It is necessary to wean the environment away from this influence. The more severely, the more ruthlessly, and the more horribly all cooperation with the opponent is punished, the more successful the action will be. Thus, the environment must be frightened into desisting from any co-operation with the opponent.

It may appear that such a line of reasoning is quite correct, and that from the standpoint of logic it is irre-proachable. However, the incorrectness of the reasoning is proved by the effects which it gives rise to. Such action is always severe, often ruthless, often horrible, and its tool is always the whip, the fire, the sword. The environment, which is the mass of people, is incapable of a complicated study of the situation. Therefore, this environment does not look for the causes of this treatment, but it feels and sees their effects. It does not hold responsible the persons who were the cause of the use of the whip, but the persons who actually use the whip. Therefore the environment turns against the latter persons. It learns to despise them, to feel revulsion and hatred toward them. The more severe the lashes of the whip, the more they are hated. When these reactions of the environment become visible even to the sympathizers of the whipping method, they are astonished and disappointed. Indeed, they have good reason to be. The environment has not been cowed into abandoning the opponent; on the contrary, it regards him as its defender, and it feels an elemental hatred toward the terror subject.

In the system of enlightened terror, things are done differently. The whip is given to the executors, and with their assistance, the environment is infected with the con-viction that the only cause of the evil, and especially of the lashes which it is receiving, is the opponent. The only source of good appears to be the subject of the enlightened terror.

Within the framework of indirect action, this mission is carried out by six methods, each of which aims at a different effect.

The first method aims at creating and implanting in the opponent's natural environment the conviction that simply the appearance of the opponent signifies a still unknown but approaching misfortune.

The second method aims at creating and implanting the conviction that any personal contact with the opponent involves personal danger.

The third method aims at creating and implanting the conviction that constant contact with the opponent will lead to the destruction of most of one's personal possessions, or even to loss of life, money and family fortunes.

The fourth method aims at creating and implanting the conviction that under certain circumstances contact with the opponent, although it is not the source of direct danger, brings about misfortune which affects relatives, friends, and acquaintances and others in the immediate environment of the person who maintains the contact.

The fifth method aims at creating and implanting the conviction that although contact with the opponent often brings personal benefit, it must always and without exception lead to a conflict in some respect.

The sixth method aims at creating and implanting the conviction that the only protection against the misfortunes which the opponent causes is offered by the terror subject, who spreads his protective wings over the harassed terror object.

The terror subject must always remain hidden and camouflaged. . . . His indirect action must not be improvised but always carried out according to a plan, systematically and with ruthless consistency. . . . This indirect action is always carried out by the executors, never by the open organs of the terror subject, not even by members of these organs. Naturally, the executors will carry out their assignments better if they resemble the opponent in external appearance.

If the terror is to fulfill its mission, it must have a strong psychological effect. It is already known from the analysis of general terror that any terrorist action is successful only if it is carried out at the proper time, in the proper strength, and in the proper form. The leadership of the terror subject is responsible for determining the time for the action. The executors are primarily responsible for the strength of the action and particularly for its form. If the strength of the action and its form are disproportionate, the effects of the action will be negligible.

Whether the resonant mass will fulfill its mission depends exclusively upon the terror subjects, the executors, and their ability and thoroughness. The resonant mass will respond if it is shaped by the will of the subject and by the act of the executors. The mass of people is only one element. It is an element just like air, water, or fire. The elements will serve anyone who knows how to control them. . . .

As a result of the indirect action a process involving the opponent takes place. It consists of two phases. The first phase is the period of isolation and atrophy, and results in the destruction of the minimum requirements for existence. It is reinforced by the destruction of the basis of support in the natural environment of the opponent. The second phase is the period which is characterized by the exclusion of the opponent from the environment of the resonant mass.

Providing certain conditions are kept constant, this process is invariable, and the opponent is not able to slow it down or interfere with it. Even the cleverest efforts of the opponent will be unsuccessful.

The opponent can concentrate all his efforts on propaganda action in order to try to explain his role and his aims to the resonant mass, and especially to explain that he is only the victim of provocation. These efforts will remain unsuccessful. For even if the conviction of the truth of the opponent's statements should win out in the resonant mass, no one will be in a position to distinguish between the opponent and the camouflaged terror subject. For this reason the resonant mass, led by the instinct of self-preservation, will have the greatest distrust of everyone who appears under the opponent's flag.

The opponent may concentrate all his efforts against the terror subject. The losses of the terror subject may be great and painful. But as a result the action of the subject of enlightened terror acquires outstanding characteristics which attract attention to the fact that the action is being conducted to the advantage of the opponent, that is, of the terror object.

Aroused by the unfriendly attitude of the resonant mass, the opponent may also strike at it. In this way he will only intensify the effects of the action and speed his own downfall. The opponent can avoid his own destruction only if he withdraws quickly or if he relinquishes the entire activity carefully camouflaging his tracks.

Only those methods have been mentioned which are typical and comparatively easy to use. During peace time they should be used only with great caution. In time of war, in time of internal unrest, or in periods of transition, especially in foreign terrain, they can be used with great effect.

As has already been frequently emphasized, the aim of any action in the system of enlightened terror is to evoke a psychological process and implant and amplify its effects in the consciousness of the resonant mass.

This goal can be attained if one repeats the same action constantly and systematically. But naturally such a method - the repetition of the action - is uneconomical. It involves many sacrifices, and a great deal of time, force, and energy.

The same goal can be attained if one is able to cause the resonant mass to experience the same action repeatedly through clever propaganda. The name of this method is "the stage method." It consists of executing a typical, planned action in classic form. Subsequently this action is brought home to the resonant mass through printed statements, the radio, the motion picture, the press - in short, through all the means of propaganda available. Naturally such propaganda cannot be dry and factual reports. That type of propaganda would never attain its goal, because factual propaganda does not give the resonant mass any reason to become involved in the action. Thus the propaganda of enlightened terror cannot be of a statistical nature. Its propaganda must be lively, colorful, dramatic - that is, dynamic. But it is not important that it follow the truth in details. The system of enlightened terror leaves it up to the opponent to take the trouble and effort to collect the proofs that the propaganda does not correspond to facts. This effort will be unsuccessful, any way, because in the meantime the propaganda will already have attained its aim. Furthermore, the collection of material for proof is always tiresome, and there is seldom anyone who is ready to give it any attention.

Repetition should be used widely in foreign terrain during the external conflict. On the other hand, in internal conflicts the "stage method" can be used with success. But one must note that this method has centrifugal tendencies. Its intensity diminishes the farther one gets from the large cultural centers. Therefore even in internal conflicts one must use the method of repetition, and its intensity will be greater the farther we get from the center of a given operational field. The strength of an action which is based upon the repetition method will be greatest around the periphery.

Thus the aim of the amplifying activity is the utilization of the effects of the executor action for propaganda purposes. In order to attain a further aim of the amplifying activity, the public organs of the object of enlightened terror must expand the network of the information service through the practical and proper utilization of the basic principle of personal danger (threat) and the basic principle of retaliation. . . .

Furthermore, if the terror subject strikes a blow against an object which is a part of the resonant mass, the government fighting against the terror subject cannot be indifferent. Such conduct is disadvantageous because then the resonant mass becomes convinced that there is no connection between its good and the good of the terror subject. The resonant mass feels then that the terror object must have sufficient power to guarantee assistance. Thus in the system of enlightened terror one should sooner make an attack on an object of one's own than on an object of the resonant mass. As long as the conflict continues, losses of one's own are unavoidable. It makes no difference on which front they fall, the external or the internal, although every loss on the internal front appears abnormal and therefore is almost always overvalued. Thus the preparation of the resonant mass for participation in the action directed at the destruction of the opponent is the most important function of the open organs of enlightened terror.

On the basis of the principles of general terror, the secondary effects of terror will strike back at the terror subject. In the system of enlightened terror these effects are directed against the terror object. As a result, the terror object undergoes the stage of atrophy which develops automatically by itself. Therefore the main task of the open organs of the terror subject is the creation of the conditions which will then precipitate the terror object into the next phase. From the general principle of chronic terror known by the name of "internal intervention," it is seen that a terror object can enter into conflict with the terror subject only when a third factor intervenes in the terrorist action and forms the backbone of the resistance action. In the structure of enlightened terror in the field of an internal conflict, this third factor consists of the public organs of the terror subject itself. It becomes their duty to create, through the effects of the propaganda action, such objective conditions as will give the resonant mass an opportunity to take up an active struggle with the opponent. These conditions are of an economic and political nature, and as such will not be discussed here.

The Methods of External Conflict

All methods of external conflict are called by the general name "disintegrating action," because this action is aimed at breaking up and disintegrating the opponent's gravitational field with the aid of the forces which exist within this field. All methods of disintegrating action, indeed all methods of enlightened terror, are based on similar premises. . . .

By the term "gravitational field" is meant the internal sphere of influence of a given organization of persons. This organization may have various aims, especially governmental, but also including social, economic, and cultural. Thus there exists a governmental gravitational field of superior order, and within its framework the gravitational field of subordinate organizations. As a result, both the form and the extent of the gravitational fields are varied. The form and extent of the gravitational field of the government are the largest and the most complicated, because this gravitational field unites all members of social, economic, and cultural institutions.

Every organization of persons, regardless of the scope of its activities, forms a certain situation of power, order, and government, which, in order to simplify the logical concept, will be referred to here as "the system." Any system means that the mass of the members (participants) of the given organization are divided into three groups. The characteristics of these groups are their various attitudes both toward the prevailing system and toward one another.

The first group includes the positivists. The members of this group are directly or indirectly interested in having the existing system continue to exist. They regard this system as their own and strive to strengthen it. Therefore, their psychological attitude toward the prevailing system is positive.

The second, and largest group, includes those who are indifferent. This group agrees to the fact of the existence of the prevailing system and subordinates itself to it, although its opinion concerning the value of the system may be different from that of the positivists. Thus the psychological attitude of this group toward the system is indifferent.

The third group includes the antagonists. They are against the prevailing order, are more or less indirectly interested in having the desired and planned changes carried out, and make an active effort to execute changes. Thus their attitude toward the system is negative.

There are various reasons for the antagonism. The cause may be their envy or personal sympathies, or social, ideological, money, or class differences. The strength and the effects of antagonisms which are based on personal reasons may often be greater than the effects of antagonisms which develop from ideological considerations.

The structure of the gravitational field of the basic organizations of people is simple. The positive pole of the field is the group of positivists, who try to maintain the existing system and to combat oppositional efforts and tendencies. After the collapse of their organization this group may also represent the radical, or even extremist, opinions. . . .

III
Rebel Terror

Introduction to Part III
David C. Rapoport

> The horror of deliberate murder, of ambush or
> grenade, is at least purging - the pity and the
> terror are in them, and the conciseness of actions
> which can be met. But the evil genius of terrorism
> is suspicion - the man who stops and asks for a
> light, a cart with a broken axle signalling for help.
> . . . The sudden pealing of a doorbell in the night.
> The slender chain of trust upon which all human
> relations are based is broken - and this the terrorist
> knows and sharpens his claws precisely here; for
> his primary objective is not battle. It is to bring
> down upon the community in general a reprisal for
> his wrongs, in the hope that that the fury and
> resentment roused by punishment meted out to the
> innocent will gradually swell the ranks of those from
> whom he will draw further recruits.
>   - Lawrence Durrell, Bitter Lemons
>   (emphasis added)

The victims of the first rebel terrorist movements a century
ago were highly visible public personalities assassinated as
"symbols" of the "system's iniquities" and because it was believed their deaths would inspire hopes among the masses that
insurrection was possible. Camus who greatly admired these
Russian terrorists (and abhored all others) characterizes them
in The Rebel as "fastidious assassins"; in his play "The Just
Ones," one terrorist describes his comrades as medieval
knights, "an order of chivalry back to earth," language the
terrorists actually used. The images entail a firm sense of
limits, a belief that only those "worthy" of being attacked
would be.

Can anyone, even ardent sympathizers, describe contemporary terrorists in this way? Terrorist movements today normally avoid assassinating highly placed public figures. In each successive decade, the tendency has been to pick "softer" targets or more defenseless victims, persons who have less and less value as symbols and less and less connection with, or responsibility for, any condition the terrorists are struggling to alter.

The striking differences between the early and the present-day expressions of modern rebel terror lead one to ask whether the two have any spiritual kinship, to wonder if perhaps their connection is really a matter of linguistic accident.(1) The relationship is puzzling, but it helps to remember that the Russians admired their contemporary Sergei Nechaev, whose "Revolutionary Catechism" (its spirit is embodied in the "Document") is generally acknowledged to be the most cold-blooded manual in terrorist history, offering a plan to make government oppress the masses until they could bear it no longer and revolt.(2) No one states either the case for moral limits or its various implications more clearly. Nechaev, furthermore, was imprisoned for organizing a ritual murder of an innocent comrade in order to hold the group hostage to his cause, the chief incident of Dostoyevski's novel the Possessed, and one that seems to parallel Aronson's account of the reasons for Hitler's final solution.

Yet, it is too easy to make Nechaev the link between 19th and 20th century terrorism. The behavior and the writings of the "fastidious assassins" show them desperately concerned with moral questions. Zeev Ivianski, therefore, has wisely chosen to ignore Nechaev in order to develop a very detailed, useful account drawn from primary sources which vividly explain both what the Russians did and the moral quandries that they felt in doing it. Although their own experiences led them in time to sense the direction terrorism was taking them, they failed to discover adequate limiting principles or rules. The view of the world developed to justify and sustain terror contained pressures, Ivianski argues, which created more ruthless revolutionary competitors in their own day, and would, sooner or later, necessarily have created those characteristics which identify contemporary movements.

We will not shed "one drop of unnecessary blood," the "fastidious assassins" said. But when the conventional rules for justifying coercion have been rejected, how does one recognize what is necessary? In the traditional doctrines justifying tyrannicide, the difficulties of finding a limit, though still considerable, were minimized. The victim was always one person who made himself culpable by specific and demonstrable actions. The "right" to assassinate, moreover, was tempered by the requirement that the assailant had good reason to believe that his act would not provoke more violence, or at the very minimum that it would lead to a better state of affairs. But invoking a right to assassinate in order to destroy a <u>system</u> that corrupts many (perhaps all) of its members is another matter. Invariably, culpability gives way to expediency for numerous reasons. The most obvious being that it may be useful to keep the most culpable alive to inflame discontent, just as it could be beneficial sometimes to destroy those whose integrity "masks" the system's evil nature, thereby making that system tolerable. Expediency becomes increasingly important because the assailant knows it is impossible to understand how long it may take the system to collapse, or what it will take to destroy it.

The "boundaries between the permissable and the impermissable become blurred," Ivianski argues, and the history of Russian terrorism shows that the terrorist may know where to begin, but never "knows how or where to finish." There is always a fresh need for more terror, a new reason why it cannot be abandoned. What begins as a tactic for simple insurrection ends by "swallowing everything . . . eats up the entire revolutionary capital." Because he <u>must</u> assume the establishment lacks all morality, the terror<u>ist</u> provides the reason for the opposition to abandon restraint, producing in the real world sometimes the very situation that existed largely in his own imagination before.

Though they did not find a moral limit, the Russian terrorists did demand that the revolutionary pay a moral price, one that established their reputations as truly tragic, even noble figures. One had to accept death, even seek it, to give a life for a life, so that the evil of murder would always be recognized. Thus, the assailants normally used explosives that brought them face-to-face with their victims and often destroyed the assassins as well. One had to acknowledge with dignity the responsibility for actions that were wrong in principle but "forced upon them by the system." Their last act of service to the Revolution, played out first in the court room and then on the gallows, also showed that they understood that while killing hardens, dying may melt resistance.

Ivianski emphasizes themes voiced in preceding essays, namely that the terrorists' justifications and their abilities to demonstrate sincerity though suffering are essential in attracting moral sympathy and political support. But since contemporary terrorists normally choose victims and methods that minimize their own risks (except in unusual cases like that of the hunger strikers in Northern Ireland), justifications become, by that token, even more significant.

Alfred Louch reflects on those issues in his succinct analysis of the most common justifications that terrorists and their sympathizers provide. Are there any known circumstances that might make their arguments defensible or coherent by existing philosophical and moral standards? He concludes that there are none and makes a striking argument that the very idea of terror is inherently an immoral one.

But if this is the case, and if justifications terrorists provide are shabby and necessarily inconsistent, why are terrorist causes able to command our moral sympathies? Louch believes that the problem lies in ourselves, that we suffer from a variety of intellectual, moral, and psychological confusions. In particular, we have lost our ability to distinguish between terror and those forms of coercion that can be legitimized. We suffer also from an inflated and unreal sense of guilt which stems perhaps from the belief that society can be made better and better and, therefore, that existing evils are always felt as a crippling moral burden.

The ability of rebel terrorists to explain their actions in order to manipulate our guilt feelings, or bring them from a latent to an active state, is the focus of Maurice Tugwell's chapter. "Guilt Transfer" offers many historical examples in order to illustrate the various ways and different immediate ends the tactic serves. Ultimately, the end is always the same, to make us feel guilty for the terrorist's outrages, a feeling that paralyzes judgements, gives rise to confused inconsistent responses, and culminates in creating warrants for fresh and much more horrible terrorist outrages. The end is identical with that of "enlightened terror," as the "Document" describes it, except that the state unlike the rebel never identifies itself as an instigating agent, and as a consequence mishaps are likely to be much more disastrous. The fact that every action of the terrorist requires explanation not only underscores the uniqueness of terrorism (as opposed to other forms of violent conflict) but also makes clear why struggles against terrorists do not test a government's military or police strength so much as its legitimacy and its credibility, which ultimately determine whether and in what ways physical strength can be used. In the words of General Grivas, the architect of EOKA's campaign in Cyprus, the aim is to make the enemy suffer a "moral" rather than a "material defeat."(3)

The three remaining chapters deal with appropriate responses to rebel terrorism by communities deeply committed to protecting individual rights. Robert Gerstein reflects on an observation and a question introduced by Louch, who observes that the terrorist is not a criminal so much as he is what used to be called an outlaw, and asks, how are moderns supposed to treat outlaws? Gerstein agrees that the terrorist goes beyond the criminal because his purpose in violating rights is to make everyone's rights insecure, and that his effort to destroy the community of mutual understanding and restraint which rights depend on is often in various degrees successful. Under most conceptions of moral rights, Gerstein acknowledges such behavior would invariably forfeit an individual's claim to the right to have rights.

Still, there are certain rights that belong to persons as humans, and there are others essential to their ability to come back to "a moral" community. The question is whether or not the necessity to protect these two types of rights gives grounds to resist three common practices of democratic governments when dealing with serious terrorist problems; torture, preventative detention, and trials that do not accord full or normal due process. A careful analysis of the practices and the practical and moral reasons for introducing them indicates that each involves a variety of different rights. While some can be forfeited and others may be wrongly but justifiably violated, there still remains a vital core of specific rights that should be protected no matter what the terrorist has done.

While Gerstein reflects on the moral principle that ought to shape our legal rules, Wilkinson's primary interest is in the very important question of whether the domestic or international legal system should have jurisdiction. Ever since the 19th century, most captured terrorists have claimed that we have no right to try them in national criminal courts because they are soldiers, and as such their rights should be respected in accordance with the rules of war, as those rights are defined by international law. The claim has troubled many thoughtful observers who wonder what would happen if we considered it seriously. Could the public ever gain by attempting to "civilize" violence? Wilkinson's response is emphatically no, and it differs from those suggested in two earlier chapters, that of Gregor and especially the one by Dugard.

Dugard observes that international agreements are difficult to achieve because some states want to support terrorist activity and because terrorists so often refuse to accept the obligations that soldiers assume. Nonetheless, Dugard thinks we ought to persist in this effort. Wilkinson cites additional obstacles. The first is that in wars between states the rules are broken regularly, a tendency that necessarily increases as modern technology produces weapons that are more indiscriminate; therefore, efforts to make terrorists abide by conventions which states themselves do not honor in war cannot be morally credible. Secondly, in international law, individual parties bear primary responsibility for enforcing the rules against their own members; but only large and stable organizations like armies can develop adequate discipline, and few if any terrorist groups can meet this condition. Third, rebels now know they can exploit atrocities, and in the foreseeable future the technology available to them will encourage this tendency. In this respect it is significant that although the rules of war have been recently modified to make it easier for terrorists to become guerrillas thereby gaining rights they say they want, few in fact have accepted the opportunities provided. There simply is no reasonable alternative to treating

terrorists as we normally do, as though they really are ordinary criminals.

Although the conclusion that individual states should
continue to decide how they want to deal with terrorists seems
sound, a further question remains which Wilkinson does not
discuss. In what ways should the law distinguish between
rebels, terrorists, and ordinary criminals? Gerstein observes
that sometimes we should, and often we do, recognize that the
terrorists' purpose and effectiveness require us to adopt
measures that are inappropriate for criminals. Yet in a
number of cases the law regards rebels and terrorists simply
as criminals, in spite of the public's different sense of the
matter; the law does this even though unfortunate moral consequences may result.

Take, for example, the ever-increasing terrorist pro-
clivity for assaulting defenseless and/or innocent victims. The
criminal law itself pushes terrorists in that direction, because
in the eyes of the law all lives are equal, except perhaps in
some countries where penalties for assaulting the police may be
more severe. There may be excellent reasons for maintaining
this view when dealing with ordinary criminals, but are they
appropriate for terrorists too? It does seem odd that although
assaults on noncombatants normally generate enormous moral
outrage, those feelings are not incorporated in our law.

The lack of congruity between the moral and legal
spheres creates other problems. When the law does not take
rebels' justification and the character of their violence are not
taken into account, enormous waves of sympathy for them and
revulsion against the government may result. The classic case
is the execution of the leaders of the Dublin Rising in 1916
which Tugwell discusses. He notes that the revulsion created
a climate for the next uprising which was successful, and that
sympathies for rebels occurred because the cause of national
independence had legitimacy in British eyes. There is another
reason which Tugwell does not discuss; the rebels, George
Bernard Shaw tells us, had fought in uniform against soldiers.

> My own view is that the men who were shot in cold
> blood after their capture . . . were prisoners of
> war, and that it was therefore incorrect to slaughter
> them. The fact that (the rebel) knows that his
> enemies will not respect his rights, if they catch him
> and that he must therefore fight with a rope around
> his neck, increases his risk but adds in the same
> measure to his glory in the eyes of his compatriots
> and of the disinterested admirers of patriotism
> throughout the world. It is absolutely impossible to
> slaughter a man in this position, without making him
> a martyr and a hero. . . . I remain an Irishman

> and am bound to contradict any implication that I
> can regard as a traitor any Irishman taken in a fight
> for Irish independence . . . which was a fair fight
> in everything except the enormous odds my country-
> men had to face.(4)

Even Prime Minister Asquith publically acknowledged that by
Britain's own standards the rebels were honorable, that they
"conducted themselves with great humanity . . . fought very
bravely and did not resort to outrage." In view of this
acknowledgement, it was no wonder that the Manchester Guardian declared that the "executions were . . . an atrocity."(5)
     Two more recent, well-known examples illustrate the same
problem. In 1947 three members of the Irgun were hung for
participating in an attack on a police armory, and in Cyprus
(1956) EOKA member Michael Karolis was hung for assasinating
an undercover police agent. The police were considered noncombatants, and the assailants did not wear identifying
emblems or uniforms. (The Irgun members wore British uniforms.) However, these particular violations of the rules of
war (and they were serious violations) in Jewish or Cypriot
eyes did not seem sufficient to merit execution as murderers.
The Irgun hung two sergeants in reprisal, and the ensuing
moral turmoil according to one prominent British military
officer, "did more than anything else to get us out."(6) The
hanging of Karolis provided us with the "first hero of the
revolution," Grivas says. "His execution was condemned by a
large part of world public opinion and led to serious disturbances in Greece (where) 7 people were killed and 200
injured."(7) Lawrence Durrell, a British information officer in
Cyprus at the time, provided a particularly poignant description of the effect of Karolis' death.

> "This is the end of something," (Panos) said, "We
> shall not be able to speak naturally, look each other
> in the eye, for a long time to come. . . . (I)t is
> not Karolis only who will be hanged; the deep bond
> between us will have been broken finally." What he
> meant, I reflected, was that the image of the Eng-
> lishman which every Greek carried in his heart,
> which was composed of so many fused and overlap-
> ping pictures – the poet, the lord, the quixotic and
> fearless defender of right, the just and freedom
> loving Englishman – the image was at last thrown
> down and dashed into a thousand pieces, never
> again to be reassembled. In a paradoxical way they
> were mourning not Karolis but England.(8)

     The particular problem posed by these executions may
have disappeared with the development of feelings against

capital punishment, but as the case of hunger-strikers in
Northern Ireland so well illustrates, the general problem still
persists. There may be no satisfactory way to make the law
conform to the moral sense of the community, and the world
will have to accept the fact that Karolis and the government
are fated to play out their assigned roles.

George Quester's concluding essay displays a very different attitude toward these questions. He chides us for
worrying too much about our failures either to respond successfully to particular incidents and problems or to make some
widespread legal changes that will aid us in coping with the
distinctive qualities of terrorist activity. "Natural forces of
resistance" are being stimulated and are proving effective
without producing in the process either fundamental modifications in the character and laws of democratic states or for
that matter those of the international world too.

Compared to earlier societies, a large portion of our
vulnerability derives from two factors. Specific technological
changes provide terrorists with more physical opportunities to
strike and be noticed. Secondly, increased humanitarianism
offers numerous occasions for moral blackmail. But, Quester
argues, if one examines a variety of specific tactics like
hijacking, hostage taking, etc., it is clear that the novelty
wears off, the public morally and "psychologically" toughens-
up," foreign states begin cooperating, and technical answers
are found for problems technology has created. Insofar as
terrorism can be attributed to these factors, and much of the
phenomena is, it will be contained. The battle may never be
won completely, but terrorism will only be a nuisance which we
will learn to accept in the same way we accept other nuisances
in our life. Quester may be right, but many will not be persuaded.

NOTES

(1) Walter Laqueur notes that the "moral and intellectual
distance" between the first and the latest generation of modern
terrorists "is to be measured in light years"! Terrorism (p.
4).

(2) Nechaev's work is reprinted in my Assassination and
Terrorism. Camus' description of Nechaev's text is worth
quoting at length. "(His) originality... lies in justifying
violence done to one's brothers. . . . He distinguish(es)
between categories of revolutionaries . . . (and gives) the
leaders . . . the right to consider the rest as 'expendable
capital.' All the leaders in history may have thought in these
terms but they never said so. Until Nechaev . . . no revolutionary leader has dared to make this the guiding principle

of his conduct. Up to his time no revolution had put at the head of its table of laws the concept that man could be a chattel. Traditionally, recruiting relied on an appeal to courage and to the spirit of self-sacrifice. Nechaev decided that the skeptics could be terrorized or blackmailed and the believers deceived." The Rebel, p. 162.

(3) The Memoirs of General Grivas ed. C. Foley, (London: Longmans, 1964): p. 204.

(4) George Bernard Shaw, "Letter", Daily News March 10, 1916 quoted by Dorthy Macardle The Irish Republic (London: Corgi Books, 1968): pp. 174-5.

(5) Quoted by Macardle, pp. 174-5.

(6) Menachem Begin, The Revolt (Los Angeles: Nash, 1972): p. 290.

(7) Memoirs, pp. 171-2.

(8) Lawrence Durrell, Bitter Lemons, p. 241.

10 The Moral Issue: Some Aspects of Individual Terror
Zeev Ivianski

THE REBEL'S ANTINOMY - THE LIMITS OF REBELLION

The problem of the limits of the permissible is the central
issue to be faced in any discussion of both revolutionary and
counter-revolutionary violence, in terror and counter-terror,
revolution and counter-revolution.   Some people present it as
the problem of the means and the ends, or as a facet of the
rule that the ends justifies the means.   Nor is it accidental
that in this discussion, which is as old as man's domination
over man, no one has yet arrived at any saving formula.   In
The Rebel, Camus gives expression to one of the central para-
doxes of rebellion, when he points out that the rebel "cannot
turn away from the world and from history without denying
the very principle of his rebellion . . . without resigning
himself, in one sense, with evil"; the rebel who wants to be
consistent to the "bitter end" must "choose history absolutely
and with it murder, if murder is essential to history."   But
rebellion is in its very essence a claim to freedom and "the
most extreme form of freedom, the freedom to kill, is not
compatible with the motives of rebellion."   In any case the
rebel is in a dilemma from which there is no way out: "He
cannot therefore absolutely claim not to kill or lie without
renouncing his rebellion and accepting, once and for all, evil
and murder."   But neither can he agree to kill and lie, since
the inverse reasoning which would justify murder and violence
would also destroy the reasons for his insurrection.   "Thus
the rebel can never find peace.   He knows what is good and
despite himself does evil."(1)   Perhaps it is no coincidence
that Camus can arrive at no clear-cut doctrinal solution but
instead resorts to an example, for example is always the retreat of those who find themselves thus cornered.   And the

example he chooses is taken from the most desperate of all
violent movements, the Russian revolutionary terror movement.
Ivan Kaliayev, who refuses to throw his bomb at the carriage
of the Grand Prince Sergei because it was also occupied at the
time by an innocent woman and her children, and then suc-
ceeds in killing his victim at a second attempt - which was in
fact a suicidal attack - this Kaliayev is Camus' example.
Chernov tells us that Kaliayev thought "far more about how he
would die than how he would kill."(2)   And Camus' comment is
that "faithful to his origins, the rebel demonstrates by
sacrifice that his real freedom is not freedom from murder but
freedom from his own death." By ascending the gallows Kaliayev demonstrates precisely where the limits of terror lie,
"where the honor of man begins and ends."(3)   Yet if Kaliayev
is in fact the archetypal figure who symbolizes an entire
generation of the Russian revolutionary terror movement, the
question still remains: did his behavior mark "the exact limit
where the honor of man begins and ends?"

Trotsky's unfinished biography of Lenin points up the
differences between the two Ulyanov brothers: on the one
hand there is Alexander, the member of the Narodnaya Volya
Terrorist Faction who went to his death on the gallows, and on
the other is Vladimir, leader of the Bolshevik revolution.
Alexander could never tell a lie and when asked what it was
that most sickened him, replied, "Lying and cowardice," to
which Trotsky, defender of the revolutionary lie and later its
victim, comments: "One feels like adding, what a pity. In an
implacable social struggle, such a mentality leaves you politically defenseless. . . . One cannot, by an individual moral
effort, escape from the context of the social lie. In type,
Alexander resembled a knight more than a politician."   (4)
But the conflict between the "knights" of the revolution and
their successors, the politicians, is one of the most tragic in
modern history and one in which all the boundaries are blurred and all the defenses erected to protect the permissible are
destroyed.   "Are we really so sure that no one can go farther?" asks Dora Brilliant, Kaliayev's comrade in the Fighting
Organization and the heroine of Camus' "Les Justes."   "Others
may come who'll quote our authority for killing and will not
pay with their lives." "This will be shameful," Anenkov says.
And Dora Brilliant replies, "Who knows, perhaps that is what
justice is, and then no one will want to look justice in the face
again."(5)

THE "PEOPLE'S WILL EXECUTIVE COMMITTEE" -
THE MORAL IMAGE

Nowhere in the history of revolutionary movements were the problems of morality so relevant and binding as they were in the "People's Will" party, the "Narodnaya Volya" and its descendant, "The Social Revolutionaries." The People's Will partly adopted terrorism at first as a method of political struggle with great reluctance. Their terroristic struggle had been concentrated mainly on the "Blow at the Center," meaning the assassination of Tsar Alexander II, and it lasted till its final downfall, only a few years (1879-1884). The center of all this activity was the executive committee.(6)

Pribyleva-Korba reports the "some called the Executive Committee of the Narodnaya Volya party the finest flower of the burgeoning Russian intelligentsia at the close of the 1870's. This definition is accurate both morally and physically." Its members were experienced and resourceful young people aged between 24 and 30, strong and healthy in body and spirit. All of them, she says, were distinguished for their strong will, their unusual persistence and the tremendous energy they threw into their actions. None of them sought honor or praise.(7) Readiness to sacrifice their lives in action, relinquishing all property and other human "weaknesses" - these were the yardsticks of membership in the executive committee; on the face of it they were Nechayev ground rules, but in effect they were marked by a totally different spirit. The difference, and it is also the quality that distinguishes the Russian revolutionary terror movements in almost all phases in both the "Narodnaya Volya" and "Social Revolutionary" parties, is to be sought in one basic ingredient - the moral check. P. L. Lavrov, who joined the Narodnaya Volya despite his initial opposition to it, put the matter particularly well in his essay on "The Social Revolution and the Tasks of Morality" which was published as a letter to the young membership in the Narodnaya Volya overseas paper, where he primarily addressed himself to the question: "What are the boundaries of the permitted, and where does the border of criminality begin?"

He sets out from two basic premises - the first being the absolute need for a consciousness. "Always and everywhere," he writes, "a man lacking consciousness is a man without morality, a man who does not develop within himself the distinguishing marks of humanity. Always and everywhere, a man who cannot critically examine his views, who has become rigidly dogmatic, has a distorted morality which degrades man's honor." In other words, Lavrov contended that critical thinking was a prerequisite for morality. The second premise of his argument concerned the need for action, or, as he put

it, "Always and everywhere, a man who acts against his
views, or other than in accordance with them, and he who is
incapable of making a sacrifice for his conscience is a miser-
able sinner against morality," and then again "formulate your
viewpoint, develop it critically, carry it out in your life with
all your heart and regardless of the price, for this is the
basis of all morality."(8)

Lavrov's fundamental premises were in effect those which
formed the theoretical background shaping the moral face of
the collective of leaders and fighters known as the executive
committee of the Narodnaya Volya. To them was added another
component - the force of personal example. "It is example
that is needed . . . and not just in name alone, but in action.
We need energetic, utterly dedicated people, prepared to
gamble all, to sacrifice everything. We need martyrs whose
legend is far greater than their real worth and their contribution to the work." Lavrov claims that at a certain stage the
question was posed: "What is a revolutionary's duty when he
finds obstacles in the way of propaganda activities? Is he to
ignore reality? Is he to move aside?" Lavrov's answer is
clear, "It is the obstacle that must be moved away.'" And yet
there is an equally clear qualification laid down: "Unless there
be some extreme need, one has no right to endanger the moral
stance of the socialist struggle." And thus, "Not one drop of
unnecessary blood shall be spilled."

Such, then, were the characteristics of the terrorist
nerve center: moral questioning, an unwilling acceptance of
violence, organization, and discipline that sprang from absolute
necessity alone, and a constant probing of the question as to
the boundaries of what was permitted. The standards were
breached in the hour of the executive committee's decline when
the best of its members had fallen, been imprisoned, or executed, as the broadsheet appearing at the time of the programs proves. The members of the executive committee
drowned their moral hesitations in total self-sacrifice. As
Vera Figner puts it, "Had the demands been less, had they
not made such claims on one's very personality, there would
have been a sense of dissatisfaction." It was this compulsion
that led her to press her claim for being included in the
attacks, and she was then rebuffed and told that all she
sought was personal satisfaction. Yet for all that she did not
give up.(9)

All the letters written by those sentenced to die echo the
same theme - the right to engage in violence was one bought
at the dearest price - the price of their lives. What distinguished the center of the Narodnaya Volya group was that
they imposed this condition on themselves. For the members
of the party center and the general staff were also members
of the fighting organization. This is something that is quite
unusual in the history of the revolutionary movement - a situ-

ation in which authority and mastery go hand in hand with the obligation to act and sacrifice oneself.

THE OBLIGATION TO ACT

Alexander Mikhailov gives the following description of the digging of the tunnel preparatory to mining the Tsar's train: "Those who engaged in this work were like men buried alive and using up their remaining strength in a struggle against death. For the first time in my life, I looked with open eyes at the cold eye of death, and to my amazement and delight, I remained calm."(10) Nothing else characterizes the revolutionary movement of the close of the 1870s so well as this description of the tunneler face to face with death, Mikhailov said. These were the years in which the elite of the Russian revolutionary movement went underground, led by the members of the executive committee armed with the new weaponry of mines and dynamite. Disaster threatened on every side, and it was the general staff which first exposed itself to danger, the entire camp following in its wake. "We may fail," Zhelyabov declared, "but others will take our place." As the March 1, 1881 deadline drew nearer and reinforcements were needed immediately for digging the tunnel, Trigoni, an executive committee member from Odessa, was called upon.

The constitution laid down two basic qualifications for joining the executive committee: "satisfactory moral and intellectual stature" and "participation in revolutionary activity." The numerical strength of the executive committee fluctuated. The activities of the organization and its expansion drew in new people; arrests and the terrible burden imposed meant that the membership had to be filled out anew from time to time. Up to 1882 not one single member disappointed, weakened, or broke under interrogation, in prison or when facing execution. Almost all executive committee members were university graduates or students who had been expelled. Most had begun their revolutionary activities several years before joining the committee.

THE ALEXANDER ULYANOV CASE

The final chapter in the Narodnaya Volya story in fact took place on March 1, 1887 with the attempted assassination of Alexander III, an action that was quite spontaneous and unconnected with any central agency. What gave this event its special importance was the awful isolation in which the group

calling itself the "Terrorist Faction of the Narodnaya Volya"
grew up, the atmosphere of despair in which their action was
carried out, the extreme youth of the would-be assassins, and
the echo that the event itself caused, particularly as regards
the future.   Certainly Lenin's future path must have been
influenced by this event, for his oldest brother, Alexander
Ulyanov, was hanged for his part in it.   By a strange conjunction of historical circumstances, and perhaps by no means
coincidentally, the young Jozef Pilsudski was also involved; he
was later to become the leader of the terrorist struggle in
Poland in the years 1904-1909.   At that point, however, he
drew a five-year term of exile to Siberia; while his brother
Bronislaw Pilsudski was initially condemned to death, his
sentence later being commuted to 15 years imprisonment and
exile.

Born in 1866, Alexander Ulyanov(11) was the representative par excellence of a generation of dreamers.   He came from
a happy home, warm and loving, with a friendly understanding
family atmosphere.   He had intellectual interests and a bent
toward scientific studies, yet for all that, he was greatly
influenced by Russian literature, especially the works of
Pisarev, the impact of which made him leave the church, much
to his father's grief.   At the end of August 1883, when he
was still only 18, he left for St. Petersburg to continue his
studies, having graduated from the local high school in Sim-
birsk with honors.   He made his way into the revolutionary
movement as a result of the student unrest at the university,
his decision to join coming as a result of the violent suppression of a student gathering to commemorate the 25th anniver-
sary of the death of Dobrolyubov on November 18, 1886.   He
published a broadsheet protesting the total alienation of the
tsarist regime from society and calling upon his fellows to
answer the violence to which they had been subjected with
consciousness and the strength of organization.(12)   Already
familiar with Marxist literature and considerably under its
influence, he nevertheless thought that the Russian intelligentsia had no other choice than terror in its fight against the
authorities.

An organization set up in 1886 among the student body in
St. Petersburg (most of its members were 20 or 21) immediately set to work on the practicalities of terror.   The organization was headed by a Polish student from Vilna, Josef
Lukashevich(13), Piotr Sheviryov, Orest Govoryuchin, and
Alexander Ulyanov.   Their achievements were truly amazing:
within a year they had managed to set up an independent
organization that was proof against provocation and included
fighting groups, a laboratory for the manufacture of bombs
and dynamite, a printing press, a "passport table," and a
fund to finance activities that drew its capital from the
contributions of students who were members and supporters of

the organization.(14)   They called themselves the "Terrorist
Faction of the "Narodnaya Volya," although they had no contact with any of the surviving members of the "Narodnaya
Volya," and, according to one of the members, they chose this
name because it "was the most committing."   They could not,
he explained, take the name of the executive committee because
they were acting on their own initiative in St. Petersburg,
without any connection with other political parties and their
splinter groups anywhere else in Russia.(15)

It was Alexander Ulyanov who wrote the Faction's political
program which opened with a pronouncement that bore clear
signs of the increasing influence of Marxism: "In our basic
outlooks we are socialists."   But what distinguished the
statement was the definition of the intelligentsia as "an
independent social unit" whose sole weapon in the struggle for
political liberty in Russia was terrorism.   The statement
claimed that the intelligentsia had no special class character
and thus it could not fulfill any independent role in the
revolutionary social struggle; it could, however, "constitute
itself a pioneer force in the political struggle in the fight for
freedom of thought and speech," and this, indeed, should be
its major role.   With terror as the only possible weapon available to it in the circumstances of Russia's autocratic tyranny,
it was terror that was to be the battleground between the
intelligentsia and the authorities, for the latter had robbed
them of "any possibility of exerting an influence peacefully and
in a cultured manner on the life of society."

Three minimum conditions were laid down for the cessation
of terrorism: full freedom of conscience, expression, assembly,
and organization; a people's assembly called together after
direct general elections; and a general assembly for all political
prisoners of recent time, for "these are not criminals but men
who have done their civic duty."   As for the purpose to which
terror was to be put, it was stated that "recognizing that the
principal importance of terror lies in its being a means by
which to wring concessions from the authorities by way of
systematic disorganization, we nevertheless do not denigrate
its other useful functions."   These latter were formulated in a
manner that borrowed directly from the Narodnaya Volya as
"raising the revolutionary morale of the people, providing
conclusive proof as to the possibility of struggle by shaking
the legend of the government's might and working in a forcefully propagandizing manner upon the masses.   Thus, as we
see it, there is much to be gained both from terror directed at
the central government and from local terrorist protest against
the administrative yoke."   As for centralizing the terror, this
seemed to the group "unnecessary and difficult to achieve.   It
is life itself that will direct it [the terror], that will hasten or
slow down its pace, all in accordance with need."(16)

Discussion within the group opposed isolated attacks along anarchist lines, and instead favored systematic, continuous terror. Thus, they wanted their attacks to demonstrate the character of struggle, i.e., to be carried out by fighting groups who should be equipped with dynamite. Their first such action was intended to be an attack on the life of Alexander III. Ulyanov and Lukashevich prepared the bombs, with the Polish group from Vilna helping by supplying the necessary materials. The attack was planned for the end of February, but after some delay it was agreed that it should take place on March 1, as Alexander III was on his way to attend memorial services for his father.

The group was followed very carefully and finally trapped and caught red-handed preparing for the attack as its members dispersed on the Nevsky Prospect along which Alexander III was shortly to proceed.(17) Their trial took place on April 17 and lasted until May 1, 1887. A special assembly of the senate condemned all 15 conspirators to death.(18) On May 20, 1887, Alexander Ulyanov and four of his accomplices - namely Sheviryov, Osipanov, Generalov, and Andryushkin - were hanged.

The writings of M. Novorusky, one of those who survived Shlisselburg, gives some account of the mood which prevailed among the group. Thus, he writes:

> Ulyanov knew a few moments of doubt and hesitation, although he was thoroughly intent upon terror. Embarking along on such a road did not necessarily mean victory. For victory, if it came, would be reaped by others, while those who had participated in its achievements, those who had trodden his long tortured road, must certainly expect death. And to embark on a road leading to death, at the very dawn of one's life, at the age of twenty-one, when a man is filled with the loftiest ambition and bursting for action, for struggle, for life - but not for death - for this one needs a truly extraordinary power of decision.(19)

Speaking to his comrade Lukashevich, Ulyanov said, "when society's most vital interests are in jeopardy, in a situation of depressing inequality between the rival sides, then the weak side must take to desperate means. The Irish, too, were forced to resort to dynamite."(20)

In a dramatic meeting with his mother in prison, he told her, "The obligation to a homeland that has been robbed of its right and oppressed must come before the obligation to family. It is up to every upright man to engage in the struggle for liberty." And when his mother, agreeing with this, nevertheless protested that the means he had chosen were so terrible, he replied, "What can I do, mother, if there are not other means?"(21)

THE HUMAN PERSONALITY

Among the moral considerations which weighed heavily on the minds of the terrorist revolutionaries in Russia at the close of the nineteenth century and the start of the twentieth, they were particularly disturbed by the problem of setting permissible limits to violence and murder. "Our whole teaching came about, exists and has developed only thanks to the immorality of the old regime; this is first and foremost the logical reaction of man's spirit against lack of morality and social injustice," wrote L. Tikhomirov in an essay entitled "Whose Side is Morality On?" in the second issue of the Narodnaya Volya (October 1, 1879).(22)   These same revolutionaries also pondered over the question of their moral right to resort to violence and murder.   The problem of the "means and the end" plagued the Narodniki from the days of Nechayev onwards. While they arrived at no magic formula in defining the boundary between the permitted and the impermissible as regards violence and terror, nevertheless, looking back from our own vantage point in history today, and especially having regard to the contemporary spread of total terror, one cannot but acknowledge that the Russian terrorist-revolutionary movement did set itself certain standards and that these were related directly to the personalities of those who implemented the terror and to their scale of values.   They demanded a price of their members, they built a dam against the threat of being engulfed by total crime: personal rigor; a sense of commitment and mission; comradeship and brotherhood; a constant acquaintance with death; a commitment that might well demand that they pay with their lives for realizing their goals.   Thus Olga Lyubatovich writes in her memoirs that "the Russian revolutionary of the old Narodniki pattern put moral principles at the head of his personal credo.   . . . He was more to be likened to the mediaeval Christian knights than to the German socialists of Lasalle's time."(23)   Nor is it coincidental that this comparison with the knightly orders returns again and again in the memoirs of those who survived and in the assessment of historians.(24)   J. Kucharzewski rightly points out that the revolutionary intelligentsia resembled political exiles in their own land, weaving an imaginary reality that went far beyond the reality in which they lived: "They lived, as it were, in a political ghetto, surrounded by infidels," and, like the Jews, the Russian intelligentsia also "lived in a world of mean reality, yet in the world of their own dreams and longings.   Man is   thus a citizen of   two powers - on the one hand he is a subject of the Czarist Power, but on the other, he belongs to the power of the revolution which fills his soul and colors his outlook."(25)   Yet the background against which they lived and struggled, the reality within which they conducted their terrorist battle was not the world of dreams, but the world of death.

THE DIALOGUE WITH DEATH

Death stalks perpetually in the wake of the terrorist.   It lies in ambush for him every moment.   The dialogue with death cries out from the letters, the memoirs, and the wills they left behind, for terror is the weapon of weakness and despair.   At times it is a protest against despair, at other times the expectation of the last desperate battle, the courting of death. Aharon Zundelevich writes from prison, where he faces death: "Our trial is studded with crosses, as plentiful as those in the graveyard, and with stars, as plentiful as the stars in the sky."(26)   Alexander Mikhailov writes to his comrades who have been condemned to death: "Friends, I write to you about the last of your social deeds."(27)   And it was death on the gallows that he had in mind.   Sazonov, Plehve's assassin, writing to his comrade in arms, Ivanovskaya, says, "Dying for an ideal in which you believe is tantamount to issuing a call to arms."(28)   Death, a testament and a call to battle, is also the great test, for not all can meet it fittingly.   Yevgenya Figner, Vera Figner's sister, apologizes for having defended herself at her trial, motivated by "a desire to live a little while longer." And she adds: "Continued self-analysis has shaken my faith in my own strength . . . but this should not be interpreted as my having lost any faith in the idea itself. . . . I want to believe, to bear suffering, not to despair, and to hope to the end, for this is the essence of life - and I want to live." Another Narodnaya Volya member, V. Yefremov, apologizes for having put in an appeal for clemency, saying that "he does not feel he is possessed of the strength to ascend the gallows with fitting dignity."(29)
    Yet another theme, proud and unpretentious, is heard in the last letter written by Stepan Shirayev: he takes his leave of his friends saying that he would have wished to continue the battle shoulder to shoulder with them but, "since I have fallen into the hands of the authorities, I can only serve the dearest interests of the party with one last act - by not sparing my skin and by making peace with the necessity of death of the gallows. This is now my only worry."(30)   Death is thus the "last service," the fateful test.   Russia's prison walls heard many a dialogue with death - one of which has survived oblivion, and is perhaps among the most shattering.

In August 1883 an agent of the executive committee, P. Polivanov, found himself the neighbor, in solitary confinement, of
a member of the executive committee, N. Kolodkevich, who was
then imprisoned in the next cell. Polivanov sought to commit
suicide. Kolodkevich, who was deathly sick and paralyzed in
his legs, tried to dissuade him. Later Polivanov was to relate
how their conversation went, all of it carried on in the secret
language of all prisons, the tapping on the wall. The focus of
their talk was the problem of life and death. "I proved,"
Polivanov relates, "that non-being is to be preferred over
being, for this is the only real blessing that is open to man;
that men have to see their hours of deep sleep as the happiest
hours in their lives. . . . in life, men are tossed from
illusion to illusion, all of which are broken on the shoals of
reality. . . . if all men were asked which is better - being
or non-being - all would certainly reply that it would be
better not to be born than to be born." But Kolodkevich,
who was about to die, thought differently: "My reply would be
that it is better to be born than not to be born. As a man
who holds truth dearer than all else in life, I would prefer to
be born in order to know what reality is, what life is all
about; it is better to be born and to know, than not to be
born and not to know."(31)
    Leafing through the literary testament of the Narodnaya
Volya and the Socialist Revolutionaries, one cannot but be
impressed by the unusually high moral level and by the repeated stress put on the reward, the greatest they experienced in return for their sufferings, of working with those
whom they truly felt to be comrades in arms. Thus, A. Mikhailov, condemned to death, writes:

> Despite sorrow at the awful parting, I am tranquil in
> spirit and happy. The past was full to repletion.
> The future is worth fighting for. That life of mine
> that is now past can have had no parallel; I know no
> man to whom fate had given so much joy of action.
> . . . My eyes have witnessed everything that was
> finest in our day. The finest of dreams dreamt for
> many years have come to pass. I was with the best
> of people and I was always worthy of their love and
> their friendship. This is great human happi-
> ness.(32)

Sazonov writes to Ivanovskaya: "When I look around the field of
death that has been strewn with the bodies of those who were
so boundlessly dear and for whose sakes I would have been
ready to die a thousand deaths . . . then sorrow overwhelms
me. But then it seems to me that I have been privileged by a
most unusual life, a wonderful life among people who have no
equals, among those who are in my eyes as giants." Aharon

Zundelewich's previously cited letter contains a last confession
of a Jewish revolutionary who gave his life for a revolution
that was not his own: "As you all know, I never felt any
great enthusiasm for Russia.   I stayed here only out of a
sense of duty to those of my comrades who fell; and now my
duty is fulfilled, for I too am among the martyrs."

THE TRIAL

For the underground fighter, the trial serves as a stage upon
which to justify his actions, to engage in open public confrontation, to take stock of his own actions.   "For many,"
wrote A. Pribylyev," their trial marked the final good days of
what remained to them of their lives."(33)   Trials were occasions for proclaiming the message of the revolution, for
demonstrating its strength and moral superiority.   After the
treachery of Degayev was exposed, Vera Figner wrote that "I
wanted to die.   There was a desire for death, and yet a need
to live.   To live in order to enter the court room - for this is
the final chapter in the story of an active revolutionary."(34)
Writing to those friends due to stand trial, Mikhailov said,
"Your crown, the crown of thorns, is for all that the laurel
wreath of the party, and to you too is due the credit of
having bestowed upon the party a group of totally fearless
martyrs."(35)
      In fact, the show trials that the regime had intended to
use to sully the reputation of the revolutionaries and present
them as criminals became instead the scene of their triumph.
The literature of the period shows the extent to which even
the trial of the Nechayev group, and certainly the trials of
other revolutionaries, acted as a spur to others to join the
struggle.   D. Mirsky correctly points out that what the trials
revealed to everyone was the "height of morality achieved by
their generation."(36)   It was no wonder that Louis Andrieux,
chief of the French police department in the years 1879-1882,
advised Tsar Alexander III against the holding of trials.
Grigori Gershuni, head of the Socialist Revolutionary Organization until his arrest in 1903, vividly describes the atmosphere of the trial: "For a socialist, his first trial may be
likened to the first dance of a young girl of sixteen.   It
matters not to him that his first trial is almost always his last
- he is far removed from the hangman's platform.   You go off
to your trial as if going to war, as if going to a party. . . .
True, the trial itself is pointless, yet for all that one's soul is
afire, eager only to fight.   I fly in thought to that temple
 . . . there I shall tell you publicly that which they did not
wish to hear when we spoke in their ears when we were still
free.   Now we have them in our clutches, we shall force them

to listen! Look, I rise to mount to the accused's box as one
mounts the dais." But these expectations were totally unfulfilled before the real "audience." "The court room was filled
with gendarmes, gendarmes and more gendarmes. Not one
single thinker, not one single glance of empathy, not even so
much as a look of hatred or anger . . . sadness and emptiness
creep into one's soul. That great spiritual exaltation dies
away rapidly. Are these the hated enemy? Is it against such
as these that I shall go out to fight? Shall I prove the justice
of our cause to them?" And yet the severest trial of all still
lies in wait - the dialogue with death: "The tribunal of the
hated is over, now one must stand before the tribunal of the
revolutionary, before which there can be no hypocrisy, from
which one can expect no mercy." "When the spirit of death
hovers before the revolutionary, then there rises up before
him his entire past, demanding to receive an answer: Can you
say you have dealt with me justly and that you can now joy-
fully and with a clearly conscience cross that last great
dividing line that separates you from death?"(37)

THE SUCCESSORS - THE PERSONALITY OF
GRIGORI GERSHUNI

With the crushing of the executive committee and the destruction of the "Narodnaya Volya," the terror continued, brought
back to life by spontaneous forces, fed by the legend of the
destroyed movement, adopting its name and traditions, until
finally at the outset of the twentieth century the Socialist
Revolutionary Organization took its place.
     The story of the rapid rise of this movement from its
establishment in 1901 to its final fall in 1921 is one of the most
dramatic episodes in the history of the Russian revolutionary
movement. It is a tale full of heroism, suffering, audacity,
and self-sacrifice. The history of the influence and achievements of the SRs, the stamp set on the revolution of 1905 and
1917, and the role they played in them has yet to be written.
Founded at the beginning of the century, in 1905 the SRs had
50,000 members and 300,000 active sympathizers, and in 1917
they had an estimated membership of one million. In the
November 1917 elections to the constituent assembly they won a
decisive victory with 22 million votes, gaining majorities too in
the municipal elections, including Moscow and Petrograd.(38)
But the contribution of the SRs to the revolutionary movement
has been consigned to the shades of oblivion, and the spot-
lights have been turned onto the victors who reaped the harvest sown by the heroic deeds and sacrifices of the SRs. The
reason is simple: the latter lost, and history is written by the
winners. The history of the SRs is one of the most inspiring

and also one of the most melancholy episodes in the chronicles of the defeated in history.

In the ranks of the SRs the most outstanding personality in all respects and particularly in his conception of the moral issue was Grigori Gershuni, one of the founders of the SR Party and head of its "fighting organization." Gershuni was the same age as Lenin. He was born on February 18, 1870, the fifth son in a petit bourgeois Jewish family in Lithuania, in the province of Tels in the Kovno district, on the estate of Tavrov where his father worked as the manager of the estate. When he was three years old the family moved to Siauliai (Shavli) and when he was five he was placed in a Heder. The effects of this early Jewish education were not conspicuous but they were nevertheless deep and lasting. From the age of eight until his graduation from the university at the age of twenty-eight, Gershuni's education and environment were Russian. When he was eleven years old and a pupil at a Russian gymnasium in Shavli he wept bitterly when he heard of the assassination of Alexander II, whom he greatly admired.(39)

At the age of fifteen he left the Pale of the Settlement when his pharmacist uncle took him on as an apprentice. Pharmacists were exempt from the restrictions of the Pale of Settlement and during the period of his apprenticeship the young Gershuni moved freely all over Russia. From this date on he also supported himself financially. In 1895, at the late age of 25 he commenced his studies at the University of Kiev in bacteriology and became active in student circles. In 1897 he was arrested for these activities and freed shortly afterwards, and in 1898 he completed his studies and opened a chemical-bacteriological laboratory in Minsk, where his brother, the doctor, Victor Gershuni, also resided. We have no records of his apprenticeship and later work as a pharmacist – a period of about ten years until he started studying at the university in 1895.

Gershuni's entry into the revolutionary movement was not stormy and dramatic; his first steps in the revolutionary movement were rather hesitant and cautious. There is no reason to doubt the honesty of his words to the court which sentenced him to death:

> I commenced my public activities with popular lectures and educational activities. Our reality showed me very quickly that as long as we remained on a legal basis we would never be able to give the people more than the alphabet. In my wish to fulfill my obligations to the people without hypocrisy and compromise, I stepped onto the ground of the revolution.(40)

In his outlook Gershuni was close to the circles which
derived their inspiration from the tradition of the "People's
Will." He seems to have been influenced but not carried away
by the populist ideas, and to have remained quite indifferent
to the cult of the Russian peasant. He was still torn between
sympathy for the Marxist views which were beginning to gain
currency in the circles of the revolutionary intelligentsia, and
his conviction that under Russian conditions terrorism was the
only possible weapon in the political struggle.

In 1898, before the establishment of the SRs, Gershuni
was active and indeed founder of the "People's Party for the
Political Liberation of Russia," a small body which as the name
implies sought to apply a synthesis between the Marxist trends
and the tendency of the "People's Will." His public activities,
personality, and influence over others attracted the attention
of the police, and especially of S. Zubatov. Zubatov, a
former revolutionary who became one of the central figures in
the political department of the police, was at that time
attempting to trap a number of people who were prominent in
the revolutionary movement into founding trade unions patron-
ized by the authorities in order to divert them from the revolutionary and political struggle. Gershuni, who realized all too
well the dangers of this "police socialism," made up his mind
to trick Zubatov. He signed a statement expressing contrition
for his errors - an act for which he was condemned by his
fellow revolutionaries - and embarked forthwith on the terrorist phase of his career.(41) Boris Nikolayevsky, historian
of the Russian revolutionary movement, is of the opinion that
the feelings of humiliation and guilt to which this "confession"
gave rise poured oil on the flames of his hatred for the
regime.(42) Gershuni immediately began to devote his energies
to the creation of the SR Party from all the groups advocating
terrorism in Russia and abroad. First he consolidated all the
groups active in Russia. In November 1901 Gershuni left for
Zurich on behalf of the Russian SR societies; he was accompanied by Azef, in whom he believed to his dying day.(43)

In Switzerland Gershuni succeeded in uniting all the
emigre circles and societies of the SRs into one party. In
January 1902 the third number of "Revolutionary Russia" came
out in Switzerland, under the slogan which Gershuni had coined for the new party: "In struggle you will gain your rights,"
and in the same month he returned to the struggle in Russia.

From this moment Gershuni's history is indistinguishable
from the history of the "Combat Organization" of the SRs,
from its founding by Gershuni immediately upon his return to
Russia at the beginning of 1902 until his arrest on the 18th of
May 1903. Two of Gershuni's letters from that period give a
full expression of his mood, moral considerations, and motivations. They are both addressed to "Olga", then the fiancee
and later the wife of his brother, Victor. In his letter from

the 3rd February 1903 he writes (and it sounds like a testament),

> No one did look more for happiness than I did, until the loss of my senses. That is why my experience may be instructive to others. And I am going to tell you this: If there ever was a time when I was really happy and completely successful, it is now. You will know that I have never been an ascetic type, I am simply unable to renounce the joys of life, but I have never been so overflowed with the full joy of life as I am now. I have never accomplished so much in life, and never had life so precious to me as it is now. Only a scientist who discovers a new law of the universe experiences a similar feeling since this enables him to turn from slave to master of the universe. Such happiness is not a transient one. And I am full of happiness exactly for that reason, for I ceased to be a slave of my own life and became its master.

Then he goes on to explain how much he abhors the routine, empty, boring, and hypocritical way of life of people of "good standing." "One year of my life now," declares Gershuni, "fills me up with satisfaction more than ten of my previous years. . . . Do not think that I deceive myself and that I do not see the unavoidable close and natural end. I also know that I myself shall change nothing and shall probably not live to see any real change. But I do also know that on this path the many will surely ascend, and they will bring about a change." He then discusses the moral degradation into which fell the Social Democrats of the "ISKRA" (naming Lenin and Plekhanov). He concludes:

> We should exclude the arrogant phraseology. Men should be taught not how to yell about service to the masses, but how to serve them in deed. To be revolutionaries not in brochures and leaflets but in deeds. [And he adds] . . . on our revolutionary road we have never permitted ourselves to forget, even for a single instance this fundamental principle: That only a revolutionary party which does not breach the revolutionary morality - the highest morality to be implemented in life - only such a party contains the force of life. That a socialist party can win only by moral integrity not by physical predominance.

In a second letter dated February 19, 1903, Gershuni tells Olga that he could not relieve himself from the painful

experience that he had while visiting the torture chamber of
the inquisition, exhibited in a Budapest museum:

> You could just imagine that man would lose heart
> when only facing those dreadful torture instruments.
> But look how great is human spirit and the man
> beaten and broken and bleeding who has still force
> enough to look the henchman straight in the eye:
> Has he not subdued all the universe to his spirit.
> Did he defeat all the evil throughout. (44)

In an article published in June 1902 in "Revolutionary
Russia," Gershuni deals with the problem of morality in the
spirit of Lavrov's dicta (Gershuni venerated Lavrov).   He
writes that when faced by what he calls the tragic dilemma,
i.e., the necessity to kill for a just cause and the abhorrence
of violence, we must first win the inner personal struggle
within ourselves.   In this struggle, Gershuni continues, "we
must not, out of delicate egoism of fine persons, renounce the
unavoidable choice, for if we do so, we turn to be morally
passive accomplices of the crimes perpetuated around us."   He
then condemns that "other worldly morality" which turns its
eyes from real human suffering; "Man was not created for the
Saturday, but Saturday was created for man."   He exclaims:
"Our morality is terrestrial, it is the science which teaches
how to tread forward a better future for humanity on the hard
thorny road of struggle and toil. . . . Our morality is the
stern morality of <u>duty</u>, which strives to throw a bridge from
reality to the ideal built upon the foundations of our sinful
world." (45)

The heroic legend of struggle and terrorism connected
with Gershuni's name was compressed into less than a year and
a half of feverish activity.   The "Combat Organization" was
the core of the whole party and its crowning achievement, and
Gershuni's days in it were numbered.   The words of Olga
Liubatovich, one of the members of the "Central Committee" of
the "People's Will" come irresistibly to mind: "It is a crime for
a revolutionary to tie himself to a family.   Like fighters under
a hail of bullets, they are obliged, women as well as men, to
enter the battle alone.   But when you are young you forget
that the lives of revolutionaries are numbered in days and not
in years." (46)   On May 18th Gershuni was arrested.   Until
1905 he was imprisoned in the Shlisselberg fortress, where so
many of the fighters of the "People's Will" had been incarcerated and set to their deaths before him.   For nearly a year
he waited first for his trial and then for the execution of the
death sentence, until his sentence was commuted to life imprisonment.   In 1905 when the veteran Shlisselburg prisoners
were freed in a general amnesty, Gershuni was transferred to
Siberia.   From here he escaped in a cabbage barrel in 1906

and took up his position again at the head of the party. On March 17th, 1908 he died in Switzerland at the age of 38. His years of activity in the "Combat Organization" were the crowning glory of his life.

During the period of Gershuni's activity there were no more than 15 people in the Combat Organization and in 1906 their numbers reached 30. Nevertheless, we would be justified in stating that the whole of the SR Party, its thousands of members and sympathizers, its emigre branches and funds were all harnessed to the needs of this tiny nucleus. Gershuni instituted procedures of selection. He interviewed all candidates for membership in the Combat Organization himself and tried to dissuade them from joining. He planned all the terrorist actions in minute detail and was always present at the venue of the attempt himself.

THE "LIBERAL PLUS A BOMB" . . .

Gershuni's terrorist method was based on the meticulous preparation of just and crushing blows, and on rapid and appropriate timing. The choice of target, circumstances, place, and executors was made in strict accordance with the cardinal aims of terrorism as conceived by the Combat Organization. The blow had to be just and appear to be justified in the eyes of the people - an expression of the legitimate wishes of the masses, and a just and lawful act of retribution. The assailant left behind him a letter to his comrades and a formal sentence of death passed by the underground court, both for immediate publication. This was the essence of the mode of terrorism created by Gershuni. Its aim was to arouse the masses and to give expression to their anger and feelings of helplessness. It was intended as a reprisal for arbitrary despotism, brutality, and injustice.

On March 3, 1902, the Minister of the Interior Sipiagin ruthlessly suppressed a student demonstration and ordered the demonstrators to be flogged. On April 15, the student Stefan Balmashev, the only son of veteran members of the "People's Will," disguised as an adjutant bearing an urgent message from the Grand Prince Sergei, assassinated the minister in the name of the Combat Organization. Balmashev was hanged on May 16, 1902 in Shlisselburg. Gershuni saw to it that his speech at the trial was published by the underground press shortly afterwards, together with his letter to his comrades and his picture. The trial was turned into a platform for political propaganda and an accusation of the accusers.

Every SR publication was headed by slogans coined by Gershuni, "In action you will gain your rights," and "According to the deed - the reward." In the leaflet published after the assassination of Sipiagin, Gershuni wrote:

> We the Socialist Revolutionaries think that anyone
> who does not demonstrate opposition to the crimes of
> the regime becomes by virtue of this fact an accom-
> plice in their crimes . . . due to our inability to
> fight these crimes in peaceful ways, we, a con-
> science minority, see it not only as our right but as
> a sacred duty to repay might with might and re-
> venge the spilt blood of the people by shedding the
> blood of their oppressors. Despite the loathing
> which this warfare arouses in us . . . the whistle of
> bullets is the only proper answer which can be made
> to our Ministers, until they are prepared to listen to
> human language and the voice of the entire commun-
> ity. . . .

> The dawn of a great battle is breaking. It threat-
> ens to swallow the whole country in horror and
> terror. There is no way but one to make peace.
> The people must be given the possibility of pro-
> testing freely and by peaceful means against the
> despotism of the authorities. We demand a stop to
> all political persecutions and the release of all
> political prisoners.(47)

Gershuni created a distinctive pattern of terrorism and
terrorist ideology in the Combat Organization, a pattern in
which terrorism was perceived as one link in a broad, general
revolutionary strategy and was founded on a system of moral
prohibitions in the spirit of Lavrov's dictum, "not one drop of
superfluous blood," thus linking it to the terrorism of the
previous generation of revolutionaries in the "People's Will."
Gershuni's terrorism was based on the perfection of techniques
of execution, timing, and propaganda, alongside a system of
self-imposed limitations. The terrorist act was only one part
of the conception as a whole, a necessary evil which was
recognized as such. The other elements were the article
explaining the act in "Revolutionary Russia," the endurance of
the terrorist under interrogation, the trial and sentence, the
terrorist's letter to his comrades, and last, the bearing of the
condemned terrorist in the shadow of the gallows. The Combat
Organization was no more than the "mailed fist" of the party,
but it was never allowed to forget the principle for which it
had come into being - the pursuit of justice.
     The distinctive feature of Gershuni's attitude to terrorism
was the repeated emphasis on his hatred for violence and his
longing for the day when the outrages would come to an end,
when individual liberty and the freedom of expression were
achieved in Russia. Gershuni was described by many of his
critics as a "liberal plus a bomb," and this definition is not

inaccurate. Gershuni's approach was indeed opposed to that
of Savinkov who was influenced by Nietzsche and sunk in the
contemplation of the "aesthetic beauty" of death and struggle
(although Chernov does him an injustice by calling him a
"member of the bloody league whose work gives him .pleasure,"
and who rightly described Gershuni as "a terrorist due to
harsh necessity, waiting for the moment of redemption from
this work of horror").(48)

When the question of putting an end to terrorist activities
arose at the Temefors Conference in February 1907, a number
of members of the Combat Organization, including Savinkov,
came out strongly in opposition, both on the grounds that a
cessation of terrorism would endanger the liberties granted in
the October 17th Manifesto, and because they feared that
without terrorist activities the fighting discipline would be
destroyed, secrecy would be undermined, and the Combat
Organization would collapse. Gershuni took the floor and
defined his own attitude clearly, in the spirit of the principles
of terrorism he had helped to formulate in 1902:

> Since when has SR terrorism been a means in itself,
> good and correct and appropriate in all circum-
> stances and at all times? Terrorism [was necessary]
> when the rage of the people and the hatred of so-
> ciety focus on one of the figures in authority who
> becomes a symbol of violence and tyranny . . .
> when there is no other way to deal with the danger
> he represents, and when the very fact that such a
> person remains alive is like an insult to the con-
> science of society - then the way to terrorism is
> open, in other words, for the execution of the
> sentence which has been passed in the hearts of the
> people. . . . The terrorist act is permissible not
> when it is possible but when it is necessary. [While
> expressing his conviction that all those present are
> ready to die beneath the flag of the revolution
> since] that is why we are revolutionaries. [He
> asserts once more that such readiness is in itself not
> enough:] We must die not only honestly, but also
> wisely, and it is often harder to live and act in all
> conditions than simply to die.(49)

It is thus no empty rhetoric when he reminisces about the 1905
revolution and the "message of freedom" which reached his
cell, and recalls how he reflected:

> Will it really, really be possible to live in Russia?
> Is there really no need to kill? Will no one have to
> murder and be murdered? Is it really possible to
> cast away our pistols and bombs, the terrible in-

heritance of the era of denial of rights, when we
were forced to defend ourselves against tyranny
. . . no need for the meek and loving to take up
the weapon of murderers?

[And he adds, with characteristic pathos] We must
not forget! Let it be recorded in the memories of
the generations to come and written in history in
letters of burning fire, the mark of Cain, the brand
of disgrace and accursedness on the forehead of the
Kingdom of Evil, and let the stain never be removed
so that all men will know: here is the ravening beast
who turned the best sons of Russia into murderers.(50)

THE THIN LINE BETWEEN HEROISM AND TREACHERY

There is surely a considerable discrepancy between the revolutionary personalities revealed to us in the memoirs, the
letters, the court speeches, and even the gallows behavior,
and that which stood revealed in the torture chambers of the
prison, in the total isolation and anonymity of imprisonment, in
the dialogue the prisoner carried on with himself, in that
which was exchanged between him and his hangman, his interrogator, and his gaoler. It is the cruel tension of the
struggle between the revolution and the regime that distinguishes the hero from the coward, the martyred from the
saint, the deserter from the deviationist. This was a point
well understood by those revolutionaries who had themselves
borne the test of suffering. Tyrkov, who caught a glimpse of
Rysakov's wrung-out and tortured state(51), when he pleaded
for his life when on trial for assassinating Alexander II,
queries not his betrayal, but rather his suffering. Zundelewich and Kvyatkovsky urged from the depths of their prison
cells that Goldenberg - the informer - should not be regarded
as a traitor, despite the damage he had done.
    Gregory Goldenberg (1855-1880) is one of the tragic
figures in the story of the revolutionary terror movement in
Russia. Born to a family of Jewish merchants in Kiev, he
joined the revolutionary movement in the south in 1873-1874,
was arrested and exiled to Arkhangelsk from which he managed
to escape in June 1878. Throwing himself heart and soul into
the wave of terror, he struck Mikhailov as a "straight, sincere
man" who was entirely at the mercy of his emotions. On February 9 he assassinated the governor of Kharkov, Prince
Dmitri Kropotkin, in reprisal for his cruel treatment of
prisoners. Arriving in Petersburg in March 1879 he pressed

his claim to be allowed to attempt the assassination of the tsar. Apparently Zundelewich's warning of the danger that he would bring upon the Jewish population in general served to check him. At Lipetsk he emerged as one of the most extreme in pressing for terrorism and the murder of the tsar. He later took part in all the preparations to blow up to the tsar's train, in digging the tunnel and in supplying the dynamite. He was arrested carrying dynamite from Petersburg to Alexanderovsk. Both in prison and under interrogation he was a special focus of the finest interrogators (including Dobrinsky). Exploiting his extreme sensitivity, his desire to be involved in some "great act," his revolutionary egocentricity, working long and hard, exerting all sorts of mental pressure (including bringing his parents to visit him and having his mother sleep in his cell), they finally wrung from him a frank "confession" that was intended to put an end to the spilling of blood and "to provide the regime with an opportunity to mend its ways from the top." Loris-Melikov was among those who visited him in prison, carefully fostering his pride to the point at which Goldenberg began to see himself as possessed of a mission to bring together those "men of good will" within the administration with the revolutionaries. As proof of his sincerity, he revealed all he knew. When he finally learned what had happened to his comrades he commited suicide by hanging himself in his cell. Tikhomirov, in his pamphlet on Zhelyabov, said of him: "He was no traitor for he was a brave man and had no fear of the gallows. He devoted himself entirely to the cause for which he sacrificed both himself and his wife whom he loved dearly." Tikhomirov was convinced that he became mentally unbalanced owing to his solitary confinement. When everything had been wrung from him, Goldenberg warned his interrogator not to harm a hair of the heads belonging to those of whom he had spoken so frankly. "Their hair will come to no harm," he was told, "but as to their heads . . ."(53)

Vera Figner prefers Tikhomirov, the deviationist living the life of a dog, over N.K. Mikhailovsky, the writer who was such a staunch supporter and who had been so beloved of the revolutionaries but who for all that looked on from the sidelines.(54) History loves heroes, but the dividing line between heroism and weakness is often thin and wavering.

T. Mikhailov, brought to trial with the assassins of Alexander II, had left his post on March 1, 1881, overcome by a last minute fear that he would not be able to throw his bomb. But he ascended the gallows with the bearing of a hero and supported Sofya Perovskaya, who trembled as the moment of death approached.(55) The Goldenberg and Tysakov episodes, Okladsky and Degayev, Tikhomirov and Romanenko(56); the repeated episodes that marked the years of Socialist Revolutionary, Anarchist, and Maximalist terror during and after the 1905-1907 revolution; the riddles posed by Bagrov,

Stolypin's assassin and "Mortimer" Ryss, the Maximalist leader, who maneuvred between "collaboration" and revolutionary fervor and ended his life as a hero on the gallows(57) - all those involved walked the tightrope between betrayal and dedication, all present us with yet another facet of the problem posed by determining the limits of the permitted as it relates to violence and revolution. The worker Okladsky (an agent of the executive committee and a member of the team that participated in the tsar's assassination), proclaimed in court that he would regard it as an insult if he were not condemned to death, yet a short while later, he turned around and acted as informer against the best members of the committee.(58)

Instructive and tragic is the case of the two bomb throwers, the assassins of Alexander II, Nicholay Rysakov and Ignacy Hrinevitski. A member of the battle battalion of the Workers' Section of the Narodnaya Volya, Nicholay Rysakov was chosen by Zhelyabov to take part as a bomb thrower in the March 1, 1881 assassination. He was then nineteen. Caught immediately after he had thrown the first bomb, and hearing the tsar say that he was, "thank God," still alive and well, Rysakov shouted after him that "it's too early yet to thank God!" The bomb then thrown by Hrinevitski, which in fact ended Alexander's life, was by way of an echo to the youngster's words. After his arrest, Rysakov was handed over to Dobrinski who had been Goldenberg's interrogator, "a consumate soul destroyer." Afraid of dying, cut off from his surroundings, and shocked by the fact that his hero and leader had fallen captive to the authorities, Rysakov was totally unable to put up any resistance. His interrogator managed to make him feel that his behavior under cross examination would influence the regime's future path and hence the fate of all others who sought the good of the people, and that stripping his soul and revealing his ideas were of the most political importance. The result was the document known as the "Rysakov Confession," a confession wrung from a young terrorist who was squeezed to the last drop (in fact he was scarcely let alone up to the moment of his execution). Thus, on March 8, Rysakov delivered his ideological credo, in effect mirroring all of Zhelyabov's attitudes. He describes terrorism as a merely defensive instrument designed to build up and develop strength and the legend of strength.

Next Rysakov expounded the inevitability of terror in the Russian reality. "It was not we who prepared the ground for terror," he claimed. As he put it, the Goldenberg episode merely proved just how baseless were the hopes of arriving at an accommodation with the authorities. The expectation of change from above amounted to reconciling oneself to unbearable conditions. Yet in his later confessions, he follows Goldenberg, saying that he, Goldenberg, the experienced terrorist, was right in changing his attitude. Terror was

useful to the party. But it should not have attached itself to
the sole aim of killing the tsar. Here he takes issue with
Zhelyabov's stand, although without mentioning him by name.
As for the March 1 assassination, it had one clear purpose:
"To put an end to terror and bring about a real improvement
in the lives of the peasants and workers." As for himself,
said Rysakov, "I never saw the attack as a murder. Never in
my life did I envisage myself face to face with blood, the
groans of the wounded, and such like; as I saw it, the attack
would be a marvellous act that would lead society into a new
life." Under Zhelyabov's influence, he saw himself as a
partner in the attainment of the good, even being happy to
sacrifice his life to this end. Then he adds, "Even as I threw
the bomb I felt no hatred of the Czar."(59)

Thus, here in the confession of the young assailant whose
spirit was broken by interrogation, the whole tragedy of
individual terror is expressed. The second assailant, Hrinevitski, also left a confession, in the form of a will prepared
before he set out. Thus, again speaking in the spirit of
Zhelyabov, Hrinevitski says, among other things:

> Alexander II has to die. His days are numbered; I
> or someone coming after me, must be charged with
> dealing the final awful blow which will echo, like
> thunder, throughout all Russia, even as far as its
> furthest corners. This the near future will prove.
> The Czar will die and with him - we, ourselves, his
> enemies, his murderers. This act is essential for
> the cause of freedom, for it will deal a mighty blow
> to that system which some sly souls term "absolute
> monarchy" and we ourselves term tyranny. . . . I
> shall not be privileged to witness the last battle.
> Fate has decreed me an early passing and thus I
> shall not see the victory, shall not feel, not even
> for as little as a single day, a single hour, the
> hours of the glorious festival. Yet, for all that, I
> feel convinced that in my death I shall be doing all
> that I have to do, and more than that no man can
> ask. A revolutionary party must devote itself to
> igniting the glowing tinder, setting the spark to the
> gun-powder, taking all steps to ensure that the
> movement which serves as redeemer shall also reap
> the victory and not end with the destruction of all
> the best of the country's sons.(60)

Rysakov and Hirinevitski are widely separated in revolutionary legend, but the two friends set out together and it
was but chance that decreed that one should ascend the gallows with the taint of betrayal marking him while the other was
to die in the bomb attack that killed the tsar, leaving poster-

ity to judge him a hero.   The thin line between hero, martyr,
and traitor became even more blurred in the torture cellars of
the Gestapo and the NKVD.   Solzhenitsyn, who brings us the
message of the individual standing firm against the crushing
might of the totalitarian state machine, calls more with the
voice of despair than with that of consolation.

THE FRUITS OF VIOLENCE

In the course of the struggle between the terror and the
counter-terror, it transpires that the human element, which is
at the same time the source of strength on which revolutionary
violence is built and also its limiting factor, is nevertheless
insufficiently armed against moral inroads.   The recourse to
terror has to be based on the assumption that the opposite
side lacks all morality, and in its turn this assumption negates
all reservations, and pioneers the way for total terror and
counter-terror.   The techniques of modern counter-terror have
discovered how to corrupt the revolutionary movement, even if
this has meant corrupting the entire society - for provocation
destroys brotherhood, faith, and comradeship.   The torture
cellars and the interrogation techniques have eroded heroism.
The totalitarian states have usurped the limelight and the
stages from which the revolutionaries were formerly able to
preach the justice of their cause.
      In   Savinkov's   self-searching,   indeed   generation-
searching, novel, That Which Was Not, he presents us with
the antimyth of terror.   "Everything is permissible," he
states, "almost everyone thinks this way.   Violence?   Even
violence is permissible if it is for the good of the people.
Lies?   For the sake of the revolution, lies too are permissible.
Cheating?   In the name of the party, this too is permissible.
And yet now," he continues, he sees that "it is not as simple
as all that. . . . true, one has to lie, to cheat, to murder,
but one should not claim that all this is permissible, that it is
justified, that it is good; one should not claim that by lying
one is sacrificing oneself for the sake of the revolution, that
by murdering one is doing one's moral duty . . . no.   One
must have the moral strength to admit that all this is foolish,
cruel, terrible. . . . The Narodnaya Volya left us a legend;
Zhelyabov, Perovskaya, Kibalchich, Mikhailov, all were heroes.
They were certainly heroes, but why did they hide from us
the fact that terror is not only sacrifice, but also lies, blood,
and shame?"(61)
      In his innermost heart the terrorist knows that in taking
upon himself the right to violence to murder, even within
self-imposed bounds, at the same time he removes all restrictions from the system he combats.   In arrogating to himself

the right to murder, he in fact buys but one right that no
force or tyranny can take away from him: the right to become
a victim. The trial, the gallows, the stage of history, all
these form the day of doom from which he will emerge either
as victor or as vanquished. His victory on the gallows is his
victory over fear, over submission to evil and tyranny, for all
tyranny exists by virtue of the fear it instils. But this
victory is dearly bought not merely because the revolutionary
pays for it with his life, but also because its price involves
the removal of all restraint from challenged social orders,
rulers, or regimes. Thus the revolutionary's freedom to carry
out his ideas may endanger the freedom of society. As put by
a recent writer: "The menace of these revolutionaries is not
that they will succeed in destroying our lives, but that they
will drive us towards a destruction of our own liberties."(62)

WINNERS AND LOSERS - THE LEGEND

Legend marks the true culmination of the terror campaign.
Historical perspective blurs the distinction between victors and
vanquished; in the light of historical events even the victory
of the police machine seems doubtful, for in the end its victims
are rehabilitated. Those who survive the cruel struggle are
the debased, the treacherous, the great provocateurs - a
Fouche, a Degayev, and an Azef; they are the ones who truly
perceive the terror weapon for what it is, who plumb its
almost unlimited secret depths and build upon them to their
own ends. They represent history's scorn of the "knights" of
history, of their vain pretensions and lofty ideals. They are
the great gamblers, they are those who adopt as their own the
satanic logic that underlies the terrorist war of destruction in
its lack of choice as regards the means, in its blurring of the
boundary between the permissible and the forbidden, between
crime and exaltation, and they are the ones who win the big
prize - for they survive. The crown of thorns goes to the
men and women who fight the campaign, who are its victims,
the St. Justs, the Robespierres, the Zhelyabovs, the Mik-
hailovs. This is their moral victory, theirs is the Pantheon of
those temporarily rejected, of the crucified, of the stigmatized.
And this is history's other mockery, for it extends immortality
to those who ascended the gallows at its command. But when
one penetrates beyond the myth, can one clearly determine to
whom the victory belongs? There is no doubt but that the
terrorist duel produces clear losers - those who ascend the
gallows, Louis XVI and Robespierre, Alexander II and Zhelyabov. But in the long range even the victory of those who
hold on to their power is a pyrrhic victory. Ruler and revolutionary alike, neither can change their stripes; the tsar

cannot grant a constitution for by doing so he will cease to be the tsar; the revolutionary cannot compromise without ceasing to be a revolutionary. One of the dilemmas of the situation obtaining between the regime and the revolution lies in this that while, personally, the tsar may be able to abandon his crown, and the revolutionary to abandon the path of revolt, yet as the tools of history they are condemned to be what they are.

Who, then, are the victors, if indeed there be any? There are the seeming victors, ending their lives in the halls of splendor, at a ripe old age, the shekels hidden in their homes. There are the Thermidorian victors, whose victory reveals itself in retreat or historical truce. And there is the victory won by the sons, the descendants. Whether or not the Bolsheviks were ideologically, tactically, or organizationally the descendants of the Narodnaya Volya is not relevant here; in any event, they were their heirs, those who reaped the fruits of their labor and their sacrifice; it was the Bolsheviks who emerged from that state of confusion into which both regime and revolution alike had fallen.

SUMMARY

A study of terror suggests that there is an internal logic governing its appearance and its development. Peter Lavrov's words, in the debate with Tkachev in 1874, while they relate to the dangers inherent in an intoxication with the might of force in revolution, apply equally well to the problem of terrorist violence: "History has shown, and psychology convinces us, that every unlimited power, every dictatorship, demoralizes the best of men. . . . One can dream about the abandonment of a dictatorship which has been forcibly set up by some party or other, only before this seizure of power; in the party's struggle for power, in the agitation of intrigues both open and clandestine, every moment gives rise to a fresh need to retain power, a fresh reason why it cannot be given up."(63)

He who embarks on terrorism, like he who clings to power, knows where he begins but never knows how or where to finish. The terrorist dream of a final, redemptive blow, the dream of both totalitarian and individual terror is a false dream. "Do not rush to proclaim the terror," says the Nestor of the Russian Revolution, Mark Nathanson, "the hour of its birth is never the right hour. This right to have recourse to terror must be confined to those who have explored all other avenues. . . . unjustified terror is terror that condemns itself to suicide. Further, once embarked upon, terror cannot

be brought to a halt, for it does not move forward, it re-
treats."(64)   Terror flourishes in a step-by-step struggle,
whether it is embarked upon as a stage in some overall, long-
term strategy, or perceived from the outset as a sole and total
weapon.   The history of the Narodnaya Volya, of the Socialist
Revolutionaries, of the Fighting Organization of the Polish-
Socialist Party all prove that terror swallows everything -
effort, might, and means; it eats up the entire revolutionary
"capital" even where it is perceived as but one link in the
general strategy.

A further lesson that emerges from the study of terror
movements is the rise and fall of such movements in a wavelike
curve.   The terrorist wave is the work of a generation trapped in despair, as a result of some profound historical shock,
feeling that it has no way out.   The generation of the terror
destroys itself, has no direct continuation, yet the tradition
renews itself in later waves of violence.   If Marcuse found it
necessary to declare that "in the course of a revolutionary
movements, hatred may naturally be transformed into cruelty,
bestiality and terror" and "that the line between the two is
very thin," and if, on the other hand, he comforted himself
by saying that "in a true revolution ways and means will
always be found to prevent the excesses of terror," one
should heed the message of cruelty and bestiality, for no
comfort can be found in the promise of "means that may be
found."(65)

When radical intellectuals try to justify and praise the
violence of the "Third World," of the "Black Panthers," of
"Black September" and other such organizations in which one
can see a "new proletariat," it is then that freedom-loving
people must be on guard, knowing that the licensing of violence, its cult, and the spread of its message all preceded the
horrors of our own day.   Some of the theorists of individual
terror saw in it much more than a breakthrough - they
thought it spelled the end of tyranny.   It was thus that N.
Morozov, member of the People's Will executive committee,
perceived "permanent terror" and the terror of the intelligentsia as an alternative to revolution itself.   I believed that
this claim is baseless since one of its possible outcomes is the
removal of all restraints from both sides, and the corruption of
society at large.   Revolutionary terror paves the way for a
terror far more powerful: the counter-terror of the totalitarian
state.(66)   Terrorist strategy has sought to make use of the
latest in technological advances ever since the advent of
dynamite.   In our day, this means the danger of terror armed
with the atomic bomb.

Yet another lesson to be learned from the history of
individual terror is the decisive role played by society in
its prevention and eradication.   Society must live up to its
responsibilities even when this involves abandoning its tranquil

ways and its illusions of safety. The danger of terror plus
the atomic bomb is one that should sound the alert and awaken
society to just this degree of responsibility. But the prevention of such a horror cannot be left to the "technicians."
There can be no substitute for society's own critique, for its
own treatment of its ills. It is a moral struggle which must be
waged fearlessly and to the very end.

The question of tyrannicide is still with us, as is the
problem of political murder. Is one not duty bound to destroy
those who let loose the wars and the holocausts? I believe
that one cannot but answer this question in the affirmative.
But what limits are to be set to this right, what is to be its
price, and from where is it to derive its authority? Karl
Popper argues with some medieval and Renaissance Christian
thinkers who taught the admissibility of tyrannicide, "that
there may indeed, under a tyranny, be no other possibility,"
but grants the right to use violence to "all loyal citizens"
confronted with a "government which attempts to misuse its
powers and to establish itself as a tyranny," since citizens
have then "not only a right but also a duty to consider the
action of such a government as a crime, and its members as a
dangerous gang of criminals."(67) We come back to the arguments of a John Salisbury and a George Buchanan.

Victor Chernov quotes Gregorii Gershuni on the terror
and the question of means and ends, stating that means that
do not befit the aim can pervert that aim forever, and this
being so, one must treat terror as a drug that, while it can
cure, may also kill. "Only he who has vanquished the anguish
of terror and revolution, only he who knows the fateful moral
contradictions inherent in them, is armed against slipping and
falling."(68)

The means and their realization must be determined by
humble and critical attitudes toward the aims. Aims cannot
justify all means. We must not abandon the balancing of means
against ends, but this balancing must be free of religious
fanaticism and rigid dogmatism. Only thus will we prevent
moral degeneration and universal horror. Even though war
and violence cannot be entirely eliminated, it is still possible
to reduce them and restrain them. The real danger lies in abstract goals, in impatient messianism, for they are responsible
for peoples, races, and classes becoming the targets for
extermination; their roots, the soil on which they grow, exist
as much in the world of the spirit as in the instincts of men.

NOTES

(1) A. Camus, The Rebel, (London; 1967 Penguin), pp.
248-251.

(2) V. M. Chernov, Pered Burey (Chekov: 1953) [Reminiscences] (New York: 1953), p. 188; B. Savinkov, Vospominanya Terrorista [Memoirs of a Terrorist], (izd. Proletariy, 1926), pp. 47-50, 96-7; Ivan Kaliayev (1877-1905), member of the "Combat Organisation" of the "Social Revolutionaries Party"; he went out to assassinate the Grand Duke Sergey (cruel governor of Moscow and Tzar Nicolas' II uncle) on February 15, 1905, but when he noticed that in the carriage the Grand Duke's sister-in-law and her two children were also present, he could not bring himself to throw the bomb, thus endangering all his group. Two days later he threw the bomb in completely different circumstances, when it was a suicidal act. He was executed after trial on May 10, 1905. On Kaliayev's biography, see I.P. Kaliayev, booklet ed. by the S.R. Party, 1905. (In Russian).

(3) A. Camus, The Rebel, p. 250.

(4) Cited in Bertram D. Wolfe, Three Who Made A Revolution, (Boston: Beacon Press, 1955), p. 57. On Alexander Ulyanov and "The Terrorist Faction," see pg. 233-237.

(5) Albert Camus, "The Just Assassins," Caligula and 3 other plays, (New York: Vintage, 1958) p. 296ff; "Les Justes," Teatres, Recits Nouvelles, bibl. de la Pleiade. (Paris: Gallimard, 1962), pp. 323, 324, 339, 384.
Dora Brilliant (1880-1906), member of the "Fighting Organisation," who participated in the assassination of V. Plehve, then minister of the interior, could not stand the strain and committed suicide. See Savinkov, Memoirs of a Terrorist, pp. 48-49. In an obituary of Dora Brilliant, Savinkov relates how when they were strolling through the streets and heard the newspaper vendors proclaiming the grand duke's death, Dora Brilliant started to cry, exclaiming "But I wanted to die, not to kill." Znamya Truda, Dec. 1907, N8, pp. 10-11.

(6) Vera Figner points out in her memoirs that the name "terrorist" was affixed to the "Narodnaya Volya" later "because of one obvious characteristic that emerged from its activities, but terror was never, in and of itself, an aim of the party." Vera Figner, Polnoye Sobranye Sochinenyj, T. I. Zapechatlennyj Trud, (Complete Works) (Moskva: izd. Politkatorzhan, 1932), p. 80; This is also the essence of the claim made by A. Zhelyabov in court, Byloye, (3), 1906, p. 630.

Vera Petrovna Figner (1852-1941), one of the leading members of the People's Will Party; arrested in 1883 she spent 20 years in Schlisselburg prison, exiled in 1904 to Archangel Siberia; 1906-1915 in Western Europe worked with Social-Revolutionaries. In Soviet Russia she was active in relief work among political exiles.

The terms "terrorist struggle" and "terrorism" are employed by Plekhanov in his controversy with the Narodnaya Volya; the term "Individual Terror" doesn't occur there. V.I. Lenin uses it only twice; in an article of 13 (26) September 1905, "From the Defensive to the Offensive, "Collected Works, Vol. 9, (Moscow: Foreign Language Pub. House, 1962), p. 283; and in his essay "Left Wing Communism - An Infantile Disorder," 1920, Collected Works, Vol. 31, (Moscow: Foreign Language Pub. House, 1966), p. 33.

In a letter to Franz Koritschoner of October 25, 1916 dealing with Fredrich Adler's assassination of the Austrian Prime Minister Karl Sturgh, Lenin writes (in English; emphasis in original): "Killing is not murder, wrote our old Iskra about terrorist acts; we are not at all opposed to political killing . . . but as revolutionary tactics individual attacks are inexpedient and harmful. . . . Only in direct, immediate connection with the mass movement can and must individual terrorist acts be of value." V.I. Lenin, Collected Words, Vol. 30, (Moscow: Foreign Languages Pub. House, 1973), p. 238.

(7) A. P. Pribyleva Korba, "Ispolnitenyj Komitet" 1879-1881g. Kat. i Ssylka (24), 1926, pp. 27-31.

(8) P. Lavrov, "Sotsyalnaya Revolutsya i Zadachi Nravstvennosti," Vestnik Narodnoy Voli No. 3, 4, god Pervyj, Volnaya Russkaya Tipogr. Zheneva 1884. See in part. N.4, pp. 51-57, 44, 45; N. 3, pp. 32, 56.

(9) V. Figner, Polnoye Sobranye Sochinenyj, pp. 183, 184.

(10) A. Mikhailov by A. P. Pribyleva-Korba, V. N. Figner, (Leningrad-Moskva: 1925) pp. 137-140.

A. D. Mikhailov (1857-1883), member of the executive committee, considered by later renegade L. Tikhomirov as the most outstanding personality in People's Will Party. He organized and took part in many of the terroristic attempts of the N. V. Arrested November 1880. Died in prison in 1883.

(11) On Alexander Ulyanov, see B. S. Itenberg i A. Ya. Chernyak, Alexander Ulyanov 1886-1887, Gosud. izd. (Moskva: 1957), J. Lukashevich, Vospominanya 1 - go Marta 1887 (Rememberances of March 1, 1887) (Peterburg: 1920), Zhizn' Kak Fakel, (Moskva: 1966).

(12) Zhizn' Kak Fakel, pp. 264-267.

(13) Josef Lukaszewich was sentenced to death penalty, changed to life imprisonment in Shlisselburg. In 1905 he was released. He finished as professor in the Polish Yagellonian University in Vilno. The brothers Pilsudski were involved in that affair through Lukaszewich. Of the Vilno group were also Leon Jogiches (future friend and husband of Rosa Luxembourg), and Dembo Brinstein, killed later in a bomb explosion in Switzerland.

(14) J. Lukashevich, Vospominanya, pp. 22, 23; Zhizn' Kak Fakel, p. 286.

(15) Zhizn Kak Fakel, p. 291.

(16) Ibid., pp. 294, 303. The program was composed by A. Ulyanov and typed in B. Pilsudski's apartment.

(17) See detailed story of the attempt in W. Pobog Malinowski, Josef Pilsudski 1867-1901. 2 tomes (Warsaw: 1935 W. Podziemiach Kospiracji, Nakl. Geberthnera i Wolfa,) (Warszawa: 1935), pp. 82-105. Itenberg and Chernyak, Alexander Ulyanov, pp. 129-133.

(18) See procedures of their trial and Ulyanov's speech in Zhizn Kak Fakel, pp. 427-460.

(19) Ibid., pp. 459, 460.

(20) Ibid., pp. 287, 288.

(21) Alexander Ulyanov, p. 144.

(22) Literatura V. N. ed. by S.R.s (Paris: 1905), p. 94.

(23) O. Lyubatovich, "Dalekoye i Niedavnoye", Byloye, (5), 1906 pp. 238, 239.

(24) I. Berlin "A Marvellous Decade," I. Encounter, June 1955; S. R. Tompkins, The Russian Intelligentsia, Makers of the Revolutionary State (Norman: University of Oklahoma Press, 1957), pp. 100, 101; S. Stepnyak, (Kravchinski), Podpolnaya Rossiya (Underground Russia) (Petersburg: 1920) pp. 18, 19.

(25) Jan Kucharzewski, Od Bialego Caratu do Czerwonego (From the White to Red Czarism) (Warsaw: 1933), T. VI, pp. 399, 400.

(26) His letter from 1.11. 1880. Arkhiv Zemli i Voli i Narodnoy Voli, p. 249.

(27) Ibid., p. 258.

(28) Pr. S. Ivanovskaya, "Delo Pleve," Byloye (23), 1924 p. 188.

(29) Arkhiv Z. i. V. iN.V. Moscow 1930, pp. 255-257, 284-285. (Archive of the "Land and Liberty" and of the "People's Will," ed. S. N. Volk).

(30) Shirayev's letter of October 29, 1980, Ibid, p. 258. Stepan Grigorievich Shirayev (1857-1881) of peasant stock, member of the executive committee of the N.V., and one of its dynamite experts, participated in the attempt on Tsar Alexander II's life near Moscow. Arrested in December 1879, imprisoned with Nechayev and won his confidence, in the Peter and Paul Fortress. Died there August 1881.

(31) Schegolev S. G., "Nechayev v Alekseyevskim Ravel-inye," Krasnyj Arkhiv, (VI), 1924, pp. 111, 112.

(32) A Pribyleva Korba, Vera Figner, A. Michailov, p. 197.

(33) A. Pribylev, "Protsess 17-ti Lits v 1883 godu," Byloye (11), 1906, p. 225.

(34) V. Figner, Zap. Trud, p. 356.
Sergey Petrovich Degayev (1854-1921), artillery officer, member of the Center and one of the main organizers of the military organization of the Narodnaya Volya. In August 1882 Vera Figner co-opted him to the executive committee. On his arrest he started to collaborate with G. Sudeykin, then head of the Political Police Department, gave out his friends, including Figner when Sudeykin organized his fictitious escape. Then reported and organized the assassination of Sudeykin himself. Died as Professor Alexander Pell in Vermont, South Dakota, in January 26, 1921.
On the Degayev Episode, see Z. Ivianski, "Provocation at the Center," Terrorism 4, 1980: pp. 63-69.

(35) "Arkihv Z. i V. i N.V.," p. 258. In the original words, "bestowed martyrs" has been erased. Mikhailov realized that this was "too much" to say to comrades facing the gallows.

(36) V.K. Debagori Mokryevich, Vospominanya, (Remembrances) (Petersburg: 1906), pp. 64, 65; V. Burtsev, "Borba Za Svobodnuyu Rossiyu" (Struggle for Free Russia) (Berlin: 1924), p. 20; D.S. Mirksky, Russia, A Social History (London: The Cresest Press, 1931), pp. 261, 262; Shebeko, Khronika Rev. Dvizhenya (Chronicles of the Revolutionary Movement) (Moskva: 1906), p. 104.

(37) G. Gershuni, Iz Nedavnogo Proshlogo, pp. 27, 27, 58, 59.

(38) See B.D.H. Radkey, The Agrarian Foes of Bolshevism (New York: Columbia University Press, 1958), pp. 63; 236-245; also by the same author The Sickle Under The Hammer (New York: Columbia University Press, 1963), pp. 281, 282.

(39) V.A. Gershuni "Die Ershte Trit." Griguri Gershuni, ed. Arbeiter Ring (in Yiddish) (New York: 1934), p. 83.

(40) Grigori Gershuni Speech in court, Ibid., p. 324.

(41) See on this episode, D. Zaslavski "Zayavlenya Gr. Gershuni Zubatovu," Byloye, 9, March 1918 N (3), pp. 129-136; Also Z. Ivianski, "The Zubatov System," Provocation in the Center," pp. 69-73.

(42) B. Nikolayevski, Istorya Odnogo Predatelya (History of One Traitor) (Berlin: 1932), p. 51-52.

(43) Yevna (Yonah) Azef was Gershuni's successor in command of the "Fighting Combat Organization." He turned out to be one of the greatest double-faced agents-provocateurs in history. Gershuni believed, up to his last minutes, in his innocence as is disclosed in his letter to Azef of March 2, 1908, two weeks before his death; see letter to Azef, Hoover Institution Archives, Nicolaevsky Collection, container No. 125, item 13.

(44) Hoover Institution Archives, Nicolaevsky Collection, No. 7, Box 5, item 95.

(45) G. Gershuni "Vynuzhdonnoye Obyasnenye," (Necessary explanation) Revolutsyonnaya Rossiya N7, June 1902, pp. 7ff.

(46) Olga Liubatovich, "Dalekoyei Nedavnoye," Byloye (6), 1906, p. 13.

(47) The first proclamation of the "Combat Organization" (written by Gershuni) in Grigori Gershuni, pp. 306-309.

(48) V. Chernov, Grigori Gershuni, pp. 40, 41.

(49) "Speech on SR Conference." Temerfors, Finland, February 1907. Grigori Gershuni, pp. 365-367.

(50) Grigori Gershuni, Iz Niedavnogo Proshlago, Reminiscences. izd. C.K. Partii SR (Paris: Tribune Russe, 1908), pp. 152, 153.

(51) Tyrkov Arkadi Valdimirovich (1860-1925) was a member of the Scouting Party for the attack of March 1, 1881. Arrested shortly afterwards he suffered a nervous breakdown in prison and was transferred to Siberia. Amnestied 1905. After the revolution he was alloted a pension by the Soviet government. See Tyrkov's Reminiscences of March 1st, 1881, in Byloye, (5), 1906, pp. 141-163; Ibid. on Rysakov, pp. 154-156.

(52) Zundelevich Aaron Isakovich (1855-1923), of poor Jewish parentage, who dreamt in his youth to become a Rabbi, turned revolutionary and became one of the pillars of the executive committee until his arrest in October 1879. Sentenced to hard labor for life, he was released in 1905. He then settled in London where he died in 1923. On Zundelevich, see A. Litvak "Aron Zundelevich" Royter Pinkes, Vol. 2, (Warsaw: 1927) (in Yiddish). Lev Tikhomirov, in "Teni Proshlogo" (Shades of the Past) Katorga i Ssylka (25), 1926, p. 175, names him as one of the six most outstanding personalities of the People's Will. Kviatkovski Alexander Alexandrovich (1853-1880), member of the executive committee and one of the founders of the People's Will, was arrested January 1880, hanged November 1880. See his speech in court in Narodnaya Volya Pered Tsarskim Sudom (Moskva: 1903), pp. 49-52.

(53) A. Zhelyabov, (Geneve: Carouge, 1899) (biography written by L. Tikhomirov), pp. 31, 33. A. Mikhailov, pp. 31, 33. See Goldenberg's heartbroken confession in "Ispoved' Grigorya Goldenberga," Krasnyj Arkhiv (30), 1928, pp. 117-181.

(54) Lev Tikhomirov (1850-1922) One of the main ideologists and leaders of the People's Will; escaped abroad in 1882; recanted in 1888 and subsequently amnestied and returned to Russia where he became a prominent anarchist and right-wing journalist. See his most interesting reminiscences and diaries edited in Soviet Russia. Vospominanya L'va Tikhomirova (Moskva-Leningrad: 1927).
         N. K. Mikhailovski (1842-1904), journalist, sociologist, populist theoretician. Editor of progressive Otechestvennye Zapiski, he also wrote for the underground People's Will literature and had a great influence on revolutionary youth. Vera Figner protested against exaggerated importance attributed to Mikhailovski by S.R. historian, D. Kuzmin. See V. Figner's critical notes in D. Kuzmin, Narodovolcheskaya Zhurnalistka (Moskva: 1930), p. 256.

(55) Sofya Perovskaya (1854-1881), daughter of one-time governor-general of Petersburg, member of executive committee of the NV. She assumed charge of the bombing attack on March 1 1881. Arrested March 3, 1881. Tried and executed April 1881.

(56) Romaneko Gerasim Grigorievich (1885-1928), member of the People's Will, published a pamphlet in London 1880, Terrorism and Routine, advocating the terrorist struggle. He returned to Russia in 1881 and was co-opted to the executive committee. Before his arrest in November of that year he published the infamous call to pogroms against the Jews. In prison he was treated leniently and got a five year term of exile to Turkestan. Permitted to return to his native Bessarabia in 1887, he "turned his coat" and became a convinced monarchist serving as advisor to the notorious progrom instigator Krushevan.
         The proclamation of some of the epigons of the People's Will in favor of the pogroms is a painful episode, showing that even an organization which tried to stick to moral standards was not immune to moral degradation. Romanenko, who was not alone in his assessment, saw the pogroms against the Jews as "a purely popular movement." If the movement understood the reasons for violence it would develop an "anti-Jewish" character. He cites the Russkiye Vedomosti which claimed that the Jews were the focus of attack not out of any principle, but simply because they presented "the weakest form of resistance." Romanenko goes even further, claiming that the landowners in the south were an anachronistic force, and that "in the eternal struggle for a crust of bread" the masses no

longer saw them as the main enemy. Their whole attention was
turned to the "new exploitative force": the shop-owners the
inn-keepers and the usurers - i.e., the Jews. His long article on the subject, appearing in Narodnaya Volya, No. 6,
October 1881 (Literatura Narodnaya Voli, pp. 419-439), still
shows a reluctance to take up the cudgels on behalf of the
pogromists in any open manner. Discussing the horrors of
revolution, he asks whether Robespierre, St. Just, and Des-
moulins should have surrendered their roles in the history of
France because of the extremist acts perpetrated by the masses. (Ibid., p. 438-489). Shortly thereafter he wrote the
infamous pogrom broadsheet in the name of the executive committee, despite its prominent members' objections. Vera Figner
tore her copy to shreds when it reached her in Odessa and
Tikhomirov wrote an article condeming the progroms in Nar.
Volya, No. 10, September 1884. See S. Valk, "G. G. Roman-
enko" Katorga i Ssylka, (48), 1928, pp. 36-58. Litertura
N.V., pp. 674, 675. Further, on the pogroms it is worth
noting that it was in the Narodnaya Volya that there first
appeared the formulation permitting attacks on "Jews" while at
the same time protesting hatred against "Hebrews" (a later
version made it permissible to attack "cosmopolitans," "Zionists," etc., while pronouncing that this in no way expressed
hatred for Jews as a whole). "One must distinguish between
"Yevreys," as a depressed national group, and "Zhids," as the
representatives of the exploiting classes, and hence as those
who are to be attacked," proclaimed the Listok Narodnoy Voli
in issue no. 1, July 1883 Lit. Nar. Voli, pp. 622-628).
Further, it was not merely the French Revolution that served
in this case as an excuse; Marx, too was cited: "the Jews, as
a people that has been pursued thoughout history, sensitive
and nervous, hold up the mirror as it were, to all the per-
versions of the regime," and thus "when an anti-semitic movement starts one can be certain that in its wake will come a
more profound move against the regime." Ibid.

(57)   The Maximalists group headed by Mikhail Ivanovich Sokolov named "Medved" (Bear) split from the SRs in the course of
the year 1906. They advocated an industrial and agricultural
terror, meaning sabotage and killing of brutal industrialists
and landowners. To finance their activity they perpetrated
many desperate expropriations, i.e., robberies, in which a
great number of their best men were killed. Most of them
were caught and executed, including Sokolov. Solomon Yakov-
levich Rys "Mortimer" (1876-1907), son of a wealthy Jewish
family, studied engineering and philosophy. Joined the SRs in
1904. In October 1905 his younger brother, aged 13, was
killed in a pogrom perpetrated by the "Black-Hundreds." This
painful experience made him join the Maximalists and become
one of their most active members. When he was caught on
June 9, 1906 in the course of a robbery ("expropriation"), he

tried to outwit the police by offering "collaboration." The police department then organized his fictitious escape so that he could serve them as a double-agent. Instead he began to organize the remnants of the Maximalists. He was then caught and executed.

On Ryss and his controversial personality, there is an extensive literature. See "Delo S. Ryssa" Byloye (9-10), 1909, pp. 237-244; V. Burtsev "Rys i Ego Snoshenya S. Dep. Politisii," L'Avenir (14) Paris Dec. 31, 1911; I Zhukovski-Zhuk, "In defence of Mortimer," Katorga i Ssylka, (49), 1928, pp. 28-61.

A somewhat similar case is that of Dmitri Bogrov (1887-1911), born to a respectable family of converted Jews. He got mixed up with the SR and anarchist circles and served also as an informer of the police department. To exonerate himself he single-handedly assassinated the minister of the interior, P.A. Stolypin on September 1, 1911. See G. Tokmakoff, "Stolypin's Assassin" Slavic Review 24 (June 1965): 314-321.

(58) Ivan Okladsky, tried on October 16, 1880, showed great pride during the trial and requested that he not be granted a pardon since he would regard this as a disgrace. He was sentenced to death but in fact pardoned. In June 1881 his life imprisonment was converted to a sentence of exile to Western Siberia and later still in November 1882 to exile in Caucasus. Immediately after sentence had been pronounced he began to make those revelations which were subsequently to bring disaster upon the executive committee. Thus at his door must be laid the arrests of Friedenson, Barannikov, Kolodkewich, Kletochnikov, Zlatopolsky, Trigony, and Zheliabov. Frolenko, Aronchik, Isayev, and Kibalchich were probably also the victims of his indiscretion. Subsequently, and until 1917, he served as a police agent, but after the revolution his treachery was revealed and he was tried and executed. See P. Schegolev, "K. Delu 1-go Marta," Byloye, (10-11), 1918, pp. 12, 13; F. Kon, "Okladski Kak Predatel i evo Povedene na Sude," Kat i Ssylka, (15), 1924, pp. 47-193; N. Tyuchev, "Sud'ba I. Okladskova," Byloye, (10-11), 1918, pp. 221-226.

(59) See Rysakov's Confessions in "Pokazanya Pervomartovtsev," Byloye, (10-11), 1918, pp. 230-311; This document was disclosed only in 1917; also P. F. Schegolev "Strakh Smerti-Posldneye Priznanye Rysakova" (Fear of Death, Last Confession of Rysakov) Okhranniki i Avantyuristy, (Moskva: 1930), pp. 5-12.

(60) Lit Nar. Voli, p. 971.

(61) V. Ropshin (Savinkov), To Chego Nye Bylo, (Moskva: 1914), pp. 210, 211.

(62) William Deeds, Intro. to Ian Greig, Today's Revolutionaries, (Richmond: Foreign Affairs Publishing Co., 1970) p. 11.

266 THE MORALITY OF TERRORISM

(63) P. Lavrov, "The the Russian Social Revolutionary Youth," 1874. Izbrannoye Sochinenya Lavrova (Lavrov's coll. works) (Moscow: 1934), pp. 360-361.

(64) V. M. Chernov, Pered Burey, p. 207.

(65) Herbert Marcuse, La Fin de L'Utopie, (Paris: 1967); Symposium on the "End of the Utopia" held in West Berlin on July 10-13, 1967, pp. 33, 123-24. It should be noted that Marcuse's stand on terrorism is vague and ambivalent. In Counterrevolution and Revolt, (New York: Beacon, 1972), pp. 52, 53, he writes: "The desperate act doomed to failure, may for a brief moment tear the veil of justice and expose the faces of brutal suppression. It may arouse the conscience of the neutrals; it may reveal the hidden cruelties and lies. Only he who commits the desperate act can judge whether the price he is bound to pay is too high. . . . Any generalization would be ambivalent, nay profoundly unjust. It would condemn the victims of the system to the prolonged agony of waiting to prolonged suffering." But then he adds, already in a different vein, "The desperate act may have the same result perhaps a worse result. . . . Action directed towards vague general, intangible targets is senseless, it augments the number of adversaries" (emphasis added).

(66) It was in face of the excesses of Red counter-terror that Maria Spiridonova of the left SRs exclaimed at her trial, "These nightly murders of fettered, unarmed, helpless people, these secret shooting in the back, the unceremonious burial on the spot of bodies . . . often still groaning . . . what sort of Terrorism is this? In the course of Russian revolutionary history the word terrorism did not merely connote revenge and intimidation (which were the very last things in mind). No, the foremost aims of Terrorism were to protest against tyranny, to awake a sense of value in the souls of the oppressed, to rouse the conscience of those who kept silence in the face of this submission. Moreover, the Terrorist nearly always accompanied his deed by a voluntary sacrifice of his own liberty or life. Only in this way, it seems to me, could the Terrorist acts of the revolutionaries be justified" (emphasis added). Cited in L. Steinberg, Spiridonova, Revolutionary Terrorist (London: Methuen, 1935), pp. 236-237.

On the tragedy of the last SRs who continued to proclaim the right to individual terror and revolted against the terror of the revolutionary government, see B.D. Henry Radkey, The Sickle under the Hammer, pp. 152-162.

(67) K. R. Popper. The Open Society and its Enemies, Vol. 2 (London: Routledge, Kegan & Paul, 1966), pp. 151-152.

(68) Cited in V. Chernov. Grigori Gershuni, pp. 33, 34.

11 Terrorism: The Immorality of Belief
Alfred Louch

Are there actions so abominable that no reasons could justify or contexts excuse them? Answers, I suppose, may differ. My list would include torture, killing for the fun of it, and blowing up the innocent in order to demoralize those one supposes guilty. Others will say, the first two surely, the Shah of Iran and Charles Manson, but the third, in spite of the apparent atrocity of it, is after all the response to atrocity. The innocent suffer and that is unfortunate, but their death and dismemberment are stages in a radical social surgery. At the end of that process is the millenium, when repression and exploitation will cease.

If we believe that only terror can bring about the millennium, we will be well on the way toward admitting its necessity. Even so, we may find it hard to shake off a rather different impression of the terrorist - the person who carries out the ghastly assignment. This may be so for two related reasons. First, terrorists, like kidnappers, put us in the unenviable position of acceding to their illegitimate demands or becoming accessories to their atrocities. If we comply we only make further demands more likely; if we refuse we feel a joint responsibility for the fate of their victims. Rage is the natural response to this dilemma, and rage does not exactly diminish feelings of moral, as well as personal, distaste.

Second, it is cowardly to attack the defenseless. It speaks of an indifference to violence that is not suitable psychological material for the millennium. Most of all, terrorists are arrogant, acting on beliefs about social causality that the available evidence does not license. Their moral perceptions are equally dulled, since they seem quite unable to distinguish between the repressiveness of totalitarian regimes - Hitler's, Amin's or Stalin's - and those, like the Western democracies, that, even if they limit human freedom, do so within recogniz-

constraints on political or economic power, and in an atmosphere that allows for some freedom of opinion. They are, in
short, fanatics, and fanatics are not part of the good society.
They are the effluvia of social unrest, ambition, frustration,
and hatred. Even if we allowed that only through fanaticism
are great social objectives ever attained, we would still be
repelled by the fanatic.

Are we hypocrites if we tacitly approve the consequences
while condemning the doer and the deed? It has been suggested to me by my friend and former student, Professor Keith
Quincy, that morality has to do with what is done, not with
the agent who does it. So we might consistently approve a
deed and condemn the doer - approve terror and condemn the
terrorist. On the face of it, this distinction amounts to a
utilitarian account of action. Of the act we ask: does it
result in a balance of good over evil? Of the person: is he or
she someone we could like, trust, or regard as a friend? But
if we reject a utilitarian calculus - as unworkable or as false
to our moral intuitions - we might believe that the judgments
about persons are a better index of the morality of actions
than the consequences that issue from them. If, along these
lines, we saw that only a repulsive character could perform
certain acts, we should find this a reason to condemn them.

And this applies to jailers, secret agents, soldiers,
informers, and all sorts of people whose business and talent it
is to do violent, sordid, and unpleasant things, as well as to
terrorists. But most of us acknowledge the necessity of nasty
functions, and try not to think about the agency of them,
even while comdemning noninstitutionalized terror. Are we in
the position of Bolingbroke? -

> They love not poison that do poison need,
> Nor do I thee: though I did wish him dead,
> I hate the murderer, love him murdered.
>   Richard II; vi. 38-40.

So the first question is: do we have a leg to stand on in
condemning terror?

Another question arises also from our equivocal attitude
toward violence. We don't condemn all instances of random or
sudden violence. We applaud the act, and from a distance
admire the actor, where terror is directed against regimes so
hideous and oppressive as Nazi Germany. Many, though obviously not all, will feel similarly equivocal about the methods of
internal warfare employed to bring down Chiang Kai-shek,
Batista, or Somoza, or to establish the state of Israel. We say
that the evil against which we fight is both serious and powerful; only by fighting fire with fire can we hope for a remedy.
If at the same time we condemn the PLO, the Red Brigade, the
IRA, or the SLA, it must be because we think the targets of
these groups are neither evil enough nor powerful enough to
warrant such extreme measures. Or we may feel rather more

fastidious than they about targets - it is one thing, we say, to blow up dictators, banks, or bridges, quite another to plant bombs in supermarkets where the victims are innocent. We must then ask, is our condemnation of terrror selective? And if so, does our distinction between allowed and disallowed forms of terror rest on an assumption that Western societies are really not so bad? We shall doubtless feel at least some-what tepid about this assumption - embarrassed, perhaps, at finding it in our ideological baggage. This is a second chal-lenge to the moral condemnation of terrorism.

Finally, we shall need to face up to the moral strains under which terror places us. What are we to think of ter-rorists, and how are we to respond to them? Terrorists com-mit us to a response which is itself violent, for they are outside the reach of law because they do not acknowledge its authority. They are thus outlaws. But we have few, if any, instructive precedents for dealing with outlaws. This is perhaps the most important dimension of terrorism, but I have, alas, the least to say about it.

I.

Are we hypocrites in condemning terror? Or without sin in casting stones? Suppose we draw the following distinction: there is all the (moral) difference in the world between public institutional sanctions and random individual reprisals. The difference is that the first commands community consent and gives advance warning of the consequences of acting in certain ways. The second raises an idiosyncratic conception of the good, or the just, above the consensus, and applies sanctions without warning. In a community dominated by terror, there is no way that citizens could know their guilt or how to avoid it. In contrast, settled communities have at least in-stitutionalized their barbarities (allowing for the sake of argument that all forms of force applied by the state on individuals are barbaric). An individual has grounds for predicting the state's use of force, and knows how to act in order to avoid it.

Now terrorists say the distinction is meaningless. Law and authority are illusions that tempt the imperceptive to cooperate in their own exploitation. It is odd that this argument has so often paralyzed moral judgment, for it is the most transparent instance of a tu quoque. We don't appeal to examples of admitted wickedness as models and justifications of our own conduct. Corporations, banks and the democratic process, in their various ways, may be instruments of exploitation and coercion; for that very reason they hardly serve as an excuse for greater violence. That would be like using the existence of capital punishment in one jurisdiction as a motive for another to resort to torture.

But to construe the argument this way is to miss its effect. Political societies are described in the language of exploitation not to license violence but to paralyze the will of those who give at least tepid allegience to such societies. We bourgeois feel, hearing the charges, the twinge of guilt at our own practices or those in which we have acquiesced. We are people in glass houses, and that is a frame of mind in which we lose our grip on the important distinction between practices admittedly needing improvement or rectification, and those that are incorrigibly evil.

Nonetheless, here is a sketch of an attempt to maintain that distinction. Unless we are fanatics, we don't believe that a perfect society is possible. Bourgeois regimes, which are so often villified by revolutionaries as the paradigms of exploitation and repression, are marked by severe disparities of advantage and opportunity and by obstacles to legitimate pursuits and the airing of righteous grievances. Nonetheless, some mitigation of these evils is better than none. A state in which, for example, it is possible to appeal through the courts to win relief from police misconduct has to be preferred to one in which the police are wholly immune from citizen complaints, and brutality and torture are the rule. We shall not, having made that judgment, justify the brutality of our own police, or fail to take note of gross injustice, to which venality or race or class consciousness of public officials exposes us. But we will argue that a system like ours, with its partially working constraints on police power, is immensely to be preferred to one in which torture or imprisonment without trial are accepted practices. We don't want to be complacent about our faults, but neither do we want to obliterate the distinction between capricious and lawlike exercises of the police function, simply because both rest on coercion. The policeman's even reluctant reading of the Miranda warning to the quaking suspect is not to be compared to the interrogations of a secret police or the staged executions of terrorist justice. If we cannot find it in our hearts to condemn the terrorist because the police carry guns and sometimes use them too rashly, we evidently believe that violence is evil. Otherwise the example of police brutality would not embarrass us. If we do believe thus, we should be able to distinguish greater and lesser degrees of violence, or greater and lesser control over it. I therefore see no reason to suffer paralysis of judgment on account of tu quoque arguments. Let us agree: the act of terror is evil.

II.

If anything more is to be said, it must be by way of extenuation. The terrorist's reasons, or the context of his
action, must make a difference. And here, I think, the
friends of terror say one of two things. First, they say, you
must sometimes fight fire with fire, a slogan designed to show
that violence is the only means to a worthy or a necessary
end. Second, they complain that systematic (and cunningly
disguised) repression prevents legitimate points of view from
being heard; violence is the only remaining way to express a
certain range of beliefs about politics and society. Let us look
at these apologies in turn.

  1. If the fighting-fire-with-fire principle applies,
terrorists must have good reason to believe either that worse
things will happen unless he throws his bombs, or that a more
than offsetting good will be brought about, and can only be
brought about, in this way. Terrorists seldom trouble themselves about the eventual good; their future extends only to
the destruction of present institutions. So we and they don't
know what positive qualities of life the destruction of society
aims at. To kill in the name of unspecified and unspecifiable
benefits is to kill for no reason at all. This is gratuitous
violence, for which no extenuation is produced or sought. It
is an immorality of thought as well as act.

  Terror as preventive action may seem more promising.
Most of us allow that violence might be necessary in self-
defense, or to subdue a madman, or to assassinate a tyrant.
These cases sometimes - even in the critical light of hindsight
- warrant violence. Hitler and Amin are not open to persuasion or vulnerable to other lawful pressures. We know, moreover, that they will certainly commit further atrocities if we
fail to kill them. If we are lucky, a single bullet may put an
end to the imminent evil. But usually the method is more like
war. There will be regretted casualties, as war always brings
in its wake; but still more will die, and still more rot in
prisons, if the chance isn't taken.

  The argument is not unpersuasive. But before it can be
assessed to help the terrorist, distinctions must be made. The
assassin and guerrilla soldier kill so that atrocities may cease.
They may be mistaken, but it is at least plausible to believe
that on occasion they are not. It is possible that the evidence
supports their actions and excuses the suffering they cause.

  But are guerrillas soldiers or terrorists? I have no zeal
for definitional disputes, but a matter of importance hangs on
the answer to this question. Terrorism, guerrilla warfare and
assassination share a form of extenuation. Bloody work is
done to prevent bloodier consequences. But in attempting
wicked things for virtuous ends, stronger than usual evidence

is required to show that the work will indeed bring about the
desired future, that it will not have unforeseen effects that
cancel out the accomplished good, and that other options for
action are unavailable.   The Vietnam War protester who sits on
the White House lawn may or may not have adequate grounds
for his views about the evil of the war or the consequences of
withdrawing from it, but because his action is not itself
morally momentous - causing at most minor inconvenience to
public officials and passersby - we do not oblige him to prove
his case beyond the shadow of a doubt.   He is, we say, entitled to his opinion.   But the assassin who supposes a president must die to end the conflict, or the terrorist who sees
the war as a symptom of social malaise and, attempts to destroy society by random violence, cannot claim immunity because
these are privately held opinions.   Can an assassin ever be
sure that with the death of his or her target evil will cease,
or that it will not bring other unforeseen evils in its wake?
Rarely, we say.   And those cases for which we may find the
grounds sufficient are tyrannies in which present evils are so
frightful that our inability to rule out untoward consequences
of tyrannicide simply cannot matter.   Can the terrorist's
theories of social repression ever offer grounds for capricious
violence?   Here, I think, the answer is that the antibourgeois
terrorist cannot profit by sharing a common label with the
guerilla or the assassin of lunatic despots.   Those who rail
against bourgeois society and attempt to bring it to its knees
by leaving bombs in supermarkets cannot claim to be frustrating demonstrable and about to be committed evils.   They
do not know what specific evils they are preventing; the
rhetorical flourishes of repression and exploitation do not
serve to identify the alleged evils.   They have no evidence to
show that the social structure will crack under the pressure of
their sporadic violence.   And nothing, surely, is more horrifying than the use of tendentious slogans of social theories
as bills of indictment against individuals.   Yet this is the
proposed extenuation offered on behalf of terrorists in the
Western world, in Ireland, or in Palestine.   No greater atrocity will be prevented by their exploding bombs.   Such reasons do not mitigate violence, but simply make light of it.

   2.   Sometimes terrorists are described as seeking an
audience for their views in the only way open to them.   We
cannot therefore accuse them of doing terrible deeds on the
merest pretext of evidence as to their efficacy, because
efficacy is not part of the terrorists' immediate intention.
Rather, their bombs dramatize their condemnation of the social
order.   I find this idea bewildering.   The message of dis-
membered housewives is at the very least unclear.   By what
twisted reasoning can it be supposed that the exploitation of
persons will succeed in stating a message about exploitation?

Should I be awakened to my status as a wage slave or a mani-pulated consumer by contemplating this ultimate use of people as means? Why should I not learn instead the lesson that my current exploited state is much to be preferred to the ex-ploitation I may expect at terrorist hands? Those who can say that terrorists are only expressing opinions they have a right to hold and express have failed to appreciate what the ex-ploitation of persons means. They can demonstrate it in their social theories, and fail to notice it in dreadful fact. These are threadbare defenses indeed.

One last effort at extenuation. Sometimes it is argued that no man is innocent, therefore the terrorist is not guilty --or at least not of slaughtering the innocent. This argument shifts the grounds of mitigation from the reasons for acting to the context in which it takes place. But what can that mean? Not, surely, some Kafka-like eschatology, which when applied to practical affairs converts killers into agents of divine retribution, even though an element of just such madness can be detected in the minds of many terrorists. In a more mun-dane spirit, one might suppose that the loss of the status of being innocent means only that a state of total war exists. Many who could not be connected positively to the war effort died at Dresden and Hiroshima, but their presence there made them accidental victims of a strategy with a rightful cause, the defeat of the Axis powers. So terrorists are at war with society, fighting for its demise through tactics imposed on them by the logic of the situation. To argue in this way, whether about bombing Hiroshima or the Bank of America, sidesteps the issue as to whether the probabilities of good results can justify such atrocities. We might answer - as many friends of terrorism would - that we lacked such warrant in Dresden or Hiroshima. What, then, would lead us to sup-pose that the terrorist declaration of total war is any differ-ent? Indeed, it is ludicrous to suppose that a half-dozen self-appointed rescuers of humanity are in any position to declare war, total or otherwise, or to appoint themselves just executioners of the wicked against a nation of 50 or 250 million people. Such a defense is just another instance of banal reasons thought adequate for the commission of violent crimes.

It is, of course, part of the terrorist's eschatology to believe that citizens of modern states are hopelessly corrupted by their affiliation, and by their exploitation. To say no one is innocent may mean just this - some are exploiters and die for that, others are exploited and are thus past saving. So in pulling down prisons as centers of repression, guards should die as agents of repression, and the prisoners as victims of it. Such a bloody salvation can only be self-immolating; terrorists must be victims of the social order also. At least they do not, as far as I know, come down from the sky, though some of them, or their defenders on university campuses, may appear to have come up out of the earth.

III.

So much for extenuation. But what of us? Terror is a fact of life to which we must respond somehow or other. Terror tempts us to violent reprisal because it strikes us as irrationally violent. By the same token, we want to say that terrorists are mad. And so our minds are diverted to thoughts of therapy and commiseration. This response is self-deceiving, unless we remember Conrad's remark in Lord Jim: "how much certain forms of evil are akin to madness, derived from intense egotism, inflamed by resistance." On the other hand, a violent response to violence caters to the propaganda of terror. Our violence supports the terrorist's otherwise shabby case, or seems to do so for many. And so we seek accommodation, which appears as a sign of the success of terrorist methods. In the end, we must reluctantly admit that the terrorist's uncompromising position makes it impossible to treat him or her as other than the enemy – as an outlaw. Except in war we lack the conventions of violent reprisal. And even in war we maintain the minimum conventions of civility; we recognize that our enemies hold other, but still plausible, allegiances. Men and women who blow up supermarkets and glory in their deed have moved beyond the reach of that courtesy. But what it means to treat someone as an outlaw is a matter on which I fear I have no more to say, except to say that it is what we ought to think about.

12 Guilt Transfer

Maurice A.J. Tugwell

During Easter Week 1916, about 1,250 Irish rebels in Dublin seized a number of key buildings, important symbolically or tactically or both, and challenged the might of British rule. By the end of the week some 300 men and women were dead - 56 rebels, 120 police or military, the remainder uninvolved civilians. Nearly a thousand people were wounded. Damage to the city by fire, bombardment and looting amounted to nearly one-third of Ireland's total annual revenue.(1) This uprising occurred in the middle of the first Great War, in which a quarter of a million Irishmen were fighting in the British ranks, and the rebels received little support from the Dublin population, who jeered the survivors as they were marched away into captivity. The Irish Times wrote: "The rapine and bloodshed of the past week must be finished with a severity which will make any repetition of them impossible for generations to come."(2) Yet, within months it was the British who had begun to feel guilty about the Easter Rising, while Irish nationalists glorified the deed and its martyrs, and invested both with symbolic significance for the future. Guilt for the bloodshed and violence had been transferred from the shoulders of the rebels and their supporters onto those of authority and its constituency - the British government and people.

Guilt transfer is a very old technique of propaganda which is perhaps more in use today than ever before. It involves a switch of public attention away from the embarrassing acts of its originator toward the embarrassing acts of the adversary, so that the former may be forgotten or forgiven while the latter erode the confidence and legitimacy of the other side. Sometimes it is necessary to rely on diversion of attention, by simply drowning out the protests against the sponsor's action with some new allegation. But at peak performance, guilt transfer goes further - it justifies the original

275

act, turning it from a psychological liability into an asset, while simultaneously stripping the opponent's actions of moral righteousness and practical utility.

In the aftermath of the Dublin rising, it was by any nation's standards a perfectly reasonable thing for authority to bring the rebel leaders to trial. Given that the death penalty was enforced against soldiers in France who lost their nerve and fled, or who slept at their posts when on sentry,(3) it was no more than appropriate that those held responsible for 300 deaths and for "stabbing the Empire in the back" in time of war should receive the same punishment. Perhaps it was lenient that only 15 prisoners suffered this fate. But this is not the verdict of history, either in Ireland or in Britain. These executions are recorded as vindictive, cruel, stupid, and provocative, and counter-productive to the British cause.(4) Perhaps it should be added, looking behind the facade of history to the inventive and dedicated Irish nationalists who fashioned it, that propaganda was the real determinant of our present perceptions. It was the propaganda exploitation of these executions which made them counter-productive for Britain, more than the punishments themselves.

The martyr theme was supported by the skillful exposure of every illegal or vindictive act by British troops during the suppression of the rising, and by allegations that undue force had been used in the operation. The 300 who died in the rebel-inspired conflict were quickly forgotten - even the boy, the unarmed police, and the old men shot in cold blood - because all attention was focused on the victims of a mad(5) British captain, who murdered four, and on alleged trigger happiness by unidentified members of the South Staffordshire Regiment during costly street fighting.(6) These themes fortified Irish nationalists and troubled the consciences of English liberals. At the latter, another psychological blow was struck at home. On May 10th George Bernard Shaw wrote to the London Daily News asserting that "an Irishman resorting to arms to achieve the independence of his country is doing only what Englishmen will do if it be their misfortune to be invaded and conquered by the Germans in the course of the present war."(7) This argument threw into question the whole legal and moral basis of British rule and Britain's role in suppressing the rising, and hence in executing ringleaders. Meanwhile the Irish were treated to the verses of William Butler Yeats, glorifying violence and martyrdom, and justifying revolution. British policy as well as British performance in the execution of policy were now under fire, and the fire was effective because the rebellion awakened in the English all the latent guilts of centuries of Irish misrule and neglect, and perhaps because the uniformed rebels unlike the shadowy Fenian assassins, touched cords of sympathy in a country where David had always been more popular than Goliath.

Propaganda is a neutral agent, capable of use in good causes as well as bad, and its role in converting the 1916 rising from an utter shambles into a great mobilizing victory does not detract from that victory. Students of irregular warfare may admire the Irish nationalists more if their skill in this field is recognized. The British, however, wished to forget, and the Irish wished to glorify, so little if any analysis was done in the British Isles. Those students who did take the trouble to study the psychological aspects of the 1916 rising and the subsequent Irish independence struggle were for the most part contemplating similar rebellions against colonial rule. One such was Menachem Begin.(8)

In July 1946 the British government made public a collection of intercepted telegrams between the Jewish Agency in Jerusalem and Zionist leaders in London. These exposed the agency's control over the United Resistance Movement (Tenuat Hameri), composed of the Haganah, Begin's Irgun Zvai Lemui, and the Stern Group.(9) A few days earlier, the Irgun had blown up part of the King David Hotel in Jerusalem, which housed the government secretariat, killing 91 people. The link between this outrage and the top political leaders of Zionism and the Yishuv seemed in the circumstances proven beyond reasonable doubt, as indeed was the case, but it would never have done for the agency to admit responsibility while simply pointing out that the casualties were unintended. Guilt had to be transferred, and quickly.

The agency condemned the attack, disclaimed any responsibility, and blamed the Irgun for operating independently. By joining the British mandatory authorities in the chorus of indignation, the Agency sidestepped some of the blame. The Irgun, left to bear the invective, sought to transfer guilt to its victims. A warning, it said, had been telephoned to the hotel, but through alleged arrogance and inefficiency, this had not been acted upon.(10) Neither of these maneuvres, however, could bring the 91 victims back to life, and although some audiences may have been confused, most remained stunned with horror.

Then a mistake by the authorities provided the agency and its worldwide propaganda apparatus with the means of creating a diversion. A document came into their hands which urged British troops to make Jews "aware of our feelings of contempt and disgust at their behaviour" by boycotting Jewish restaurants, cafes, shops, and places of entertainment in order to "punish the Jews in the manner this race dislikes most; by hitting them in the pocket."(11) Published in angry haste by the general officer commanding, General Sir Evelyn Barker, the order was immediately denounced as "anti-Semitic." An historian of the period has written: "these foolishly ill-considered orders of General Barker were blown up into atrocity proportions by skilful propaganda manoeuveres. In

Palestine, Europe and America the orders were given well-planned publicity which resulted in Barker's minor misdemeanour completely overshadowing Irgun's one."(12)   Here was guilt transfer by confusion, the shouting down of an embarrassing message by a relatively weak counter, which nevertheless was used with some degree of success.

The Algerian independence struggle took political, military, and economic forms and certainly amounted to what Marxists might call a war of national liberation.   Terrorism was part of this war from the outset, used against Muslims to enforce obedience and support, and against the French to invite overreaction with its polarizing side-effects.(13)   It was, however, in the Battle of Algiers that the Front de Liberation Nationale (FLN) made terror their prime weapon. The city commander, Saadi Yacef, was ordered by the FLN to "kill any European between the ages of eighteen and fifty-four.   But no women, no children, no old people."(14)   Between June 21 and 24, 1956 Yacef's killers accounted for 49 civilians.   The limitations on targeting were removed after French counter-terrorists blew up a number of houses in the Casbah, killing 70, including Muslim women and children. Thereafter the FLN used random terror against targets in the French sectors of the city, mainly by time-delay bombs planted in milk bars, cinemas, and other crowded places.   The indiscriminate killing and maiming shocked Dr. Pierre Chaulet, a FLN sympathizer who was sheltering one of its leaders, Ramdane Abane.   The latter, however, remarked coldly: "I see hardly any difference between the girl who places a bomb in the Milk-Bar and the French aviator who bombards a mechta or who drops napalm on a zone interdite."(15)   His host was made to share the guilt.

The FLN terrorists in Algiers were hunted down and killed or captured by General Massu's 10th Parachute Division. The French tactics - like all appropriate counter-terrorist tactics - relied on intelligence as the key to success.   But because they were impatient, angry, and conditioned by long years of frustrating combat, the paras took a shortcut to ensure a swift intelligence flow: they tortured suspects. Nothing was done by the French high command to stop this practice because the ends seemed to justify the means.   The information did flow, and in a remarkably short time the FLN grip on the Casbah had been broken.   Thus, if ethical considerations were for a moment set aside, the French reasoning seemed justified.   The greater evil of rampant terrorism had been contained by the seemingly lesser evil of selective torture.   The FLN, however, understood how this sort of logic could be stood on its head and turned to their own advantage in the wider war for national independence.   French rule in Algeria would end when sufficient French men and women ceased to support the war.   They would not support for long a campaign which relied for its operational effectiveness on practices abhorrent to all civilized people. French recourse to torture provided opponents of the war in France with precisely the weapon they needed in their expanding struggle to turn mainstream French opinion against the struggle. FLN propaganda agents made sure that all necessary evidence reached such activists. In particular, a European communist, Henri Alleg, wrote a book(16) describing his experiences under interrogation and torture, which he suffered because Massu's men suspected him of terrorist links. Once the story of institutionalized torture spread across France, other witnesses, including young officers who had been forced to participate, broke their silence. The Church condemned such policies. France was fatally divided. This transfer of guilt from the defeated terrorists to the sponsors of successful counter-terrorism was made relatively easy because, in this case, the agents of authority had undoubtedly committed acts unacceptable to most Frenchmen. Nevertheless, the FLN were able to erase most if not all of their own guilt by this process, simply because it is virtually impossible for an observer to feel angry about one set of outrages if he is overwhelmed with guilt about another series for which he feels responsible. Ends did justify means, but in the sense opposite to that anticipated by the paras: the end was Algerian independence, the means, terrorism. Immediately after the French withdrawal, the victorious FLN butchered all Muslims suspected of having cooperated with the French, the toll being estimated variously between 30,000 and 150,000. Many were tortured atrociously; army veterans were made to dig their own tombs, then swallow their decorations before being killed; they were burned alive, or castrated, or dragged behind trucks, or cut to pieces and their flesh fed to dogs. Many were put to death with their families, including young children.(17) Yet the consciences of the liberal West are untroubled by these events, and no one has felt inspired to make a prize-winning film documentary to record them.

It might be thought that the anticolonial struggles of the 1940s, 50s, and 60s provided unique conditions that favoured guilt transfer. Often, the colonial power had lost the sense of imperial mission, and conducted counter-insurgency operations with nagging doubts about the moral basis of the campaign. Yet the end of colonialism did not attenuate guilt transfer, which has been made to serve today's terrorists in spite of the relatively isolated political position of many such groups.

Perhaps they are assisted by the spirit of our age, by the "new morality."(18) Terrorists are apt to be half-revolutionaries and half-exhibitionists. They frequently attract sympathy from the radical chic, who in turn lead the attack on conventional moral standards. Another group, the socially committed reformers, are apt to see morality in absolute terms, to reason that because all is not perfect, all must be lost and in need of revision. In another setting, the Vietnam War proved how fertile a ground these new values provide, and the modern terrorist has developed the technique of guilt transfer to suit his case.

Before a West German court on November 28, 1967, Fritz Teufel, a radical German student, was asked to explain a previous conviction for theft. He replied by naming it a "Mammon-possession-equalizing experiment." He had taken what he wanted, he explained, because he considered that "with the present system of utilizing the means of production it was the right thing to do."(19) This relatively harmless attempt to transfer guilt from the individual thief onto an allegedly corrupt society typified what was to follow in the rise and fall of the Baader-Meinhof gang, which called itself the Red Army Faction. One year later Thorwald Pohle refused to defend himself at his trial for arson, arguing that authority was fascist, capitalism was fascist, the court was fascist, and the four accused were heroes of the resistance.(20) These events preceded the bombings and murders that made the gang notorious. When the killing was done, and the culprits were awaiting trial, the guilt transfer technique was stretched to its limit.

The gang's lawyers, many of whom were terrorists too, launched a campaign to protest against the holding of Baader-Meinhof prisoners in separate cells, claiming that this amounted to torture. Pressures generated by this propaganda led to the prisoners' receiving specially privileged conditions. They had books, journals, televisions, record players, and other comforts, so much so that other prisoners complained - rightly - of inequity. But these concessions were insufficient. The lawyers wanted the German government and people to feel guilty for the way these poor souls were being treated. They encouraged hunger strikes among the gang members and, in February 1973, seven lawyers staged a four-day hunger strike themselves. Dressed in the robes which they had tried to avoid wearing in court, they carried banners outside Federal High Court in Karlsruhe reading:

> BGH [Federal High Court] - brown Nazi gangster-
> band. BGH is reprehensive. One, it's shit, and
> two, expensive. Stop the murder of legally deprived
> groups.(21)

In 1974 Jean-Paul Sartre visited Andreas Baader in Stammheim jail. Questioned afterwards on the ethics of violence, the philosopher explained: "In 1943 every bomb against the Nazis was legitimate because mankind had to be freed from the Nazis."(22) Sartre knew all about guilt transfer. He had written the preface to Henri Alleg's book and, besides condemning torture, he had gone on to justify Algerian terrorism.

Suicide, whether by hunger strike or other means, is a useful tool in this technique. Irish nationalists have always put great store by the martyrdom that is involved and the opportunity to focus hatred against authority while obliterating revolutionary guilt.

But the desperate systematic campaign of hunger strikers which began in the spring of 1981 is quite unprecedented, and has revived the flagging reputation of the IRA when the organization seemed finally to be on the verge of collapse.

In Germany suicide took another form. On the night of Saturday, May 8, 1976 Ulrike Meinhof ceased typing political tracts in her prison cell. She put the mattress from her bed on the floor against the wall under the window and stood her chair on it. She tore her towel into strips to make a rope, knotting a noose at one end. By standing on the chair, she was able to tie the other end to the crossbar of her window. She placed the noose around her neck and jumped.(23) She was found the next morning, dead. At noon a post morten was performed by two state-appointed specialists. They found that Meinhof's death was suicide by hanging.

The RAF lawyers were not content to turn Meinhof into a martyr simply by praising her courage and sacrifice in the just cause. Perhaps they were aware that too few Germans saw their cause in such a light. Instead, they decided that the girl's death could be utilized to transfer guilt in another way: it would be alleged that she had been murdered by the authorities, which illustrated the gang's rhetoric about "fascist repression" and "resistance." As in many such allegations against authority, all that the terrorists had to do was to cast a shadow of doubt: the news media would do the rest.

Klaus Croissant, one of the "committed" lawyers, told reporters that "there was no crossbar on her [Meinhof's] window." This was untrue. But true or false, here was a story. The suggestion that the state had committed murder made the story sensational. It was seized upon by the foreign press. Some English newspapers aired the proposition of a clumsy state cover-up of murder as "a perfectly plausible and even preferable alternative to suicide."(24) Student riots broke out in Frankfurt and other German cities, as well as in France and Italy, to protest against the "state murder" of Ulrike Meinhof. At her West Berlin funeral, four thousand left-wing sympathizers came to endorse the RAF's murderous campaign, an endorsement made possible by the unfounded but comforting theory of "state murder." Although acceptable only to the fanatical fringe of the European left, this transfer of guilt from terror group to state justified, in their minds, more terrorism to revenge her death, and this was to be forthcoming soon.

In Northern Ireland, terrorists of the Provisional IRA have used guilt transfer as a standard operating procedure since the shooting began in 1970. Their purpose has been not so much to rid themselves of responsibility (although this has happened) as to deprive the security forces (police or army) of credit for successful operations and to leave them, instead, smarting in the face of public accusations. An important theme of revolutionary propaganda is that of inevitable victory. The attempts of authority to erode the terrorists' capability or to undermine their base of public support have always to be shown to fail. In time, these themes may lower morale in police and army ranks and inspire the uncommitted members of the public to throw in their lot with the winning side, that is to say, the terrorists.

Using friendly journalists, gullible priests, and other supporters as their spokesmen, the Provisionals drilled the Catholic population in their areas to cover up whenever security forces shot a terrorist. Almost invariably such an event set in motion the same procedure. The man's weapon was spirited away. The victim was taken where he could be cleaned of any forensic or other evidence that might indicate that he had used a firearm. Then "eye witnesses" would be briefed, usually from one of the categories mentioned, and presented to news reporters and television. "Evidence" hardly ever varied: the civilian had been unarmed, innocent of any offense, and the soldier's shot had been unwarranted. In short, the army or police was guilty of murder. By the evening's television news, an event which in reality amounted to a minor success for authority was often portrayed to the general public as a confused and hotly contested incident. By the nature of electronic journalism, the wrap-up would frequently tend to cast doubt on the security force version of events, especially as the "witnesses" provided by the IRA were often superb actors. One journalist has admitted:

> I speak as someone of Irish extraction on both sides, yet even I am surprised on occasions at the instant and expert mendacity to which journalists and no doubt other interested parties such as the police and security forces are treated in episodes of this sort.(25)

General allegations of security force misbehavior, from ill treatment of suspects, "harassment" of the local population, "torture" of suspects and the elimination of gunmen by "Special Assassination Squads" served a multitude of propaganda and operational purposes, but overall and over a long period their intended effect was to cause confusion and anxiety in liberal hearts in England. The idea that there is "no smoke without fire" provides a useful point of entry for propaganda since, as in the Meinhof case, all that is needed is a shadow of doubt. The policy of administrative internment of suspected terrorists, with its worrying moral implications, was a great vehicle for generating guilt. Investigative journalists, some of them politically biased against authority, were provided with "evidence" and enabled to write lucrative stories, and this type of informal alliance between terrorists and news reporters, which keeps both in business, is a worrying feature of modern terrorism, rare though it may be. Sometimes, of course, the British and Northern Irish authorities committed follies deserving of criticism, and every police force or army has idiotic and malevolent individuals. The task of distinguishing between the genuine complaint, which deserves immediate action to remedy the grievance and, where appropriate, to punish the offender, and the bogus propaganda story is difficult. Terrorists wish to keep it difficult, since it is to their advantage if, by failing to deal fairly with the sincere petitioner, authority becomes weighed down by guilt.

In November 1979 Iranian militant students seized the United States embassy in Tehran and held the staff hostage. Contravening all norms of international law and usage, and posing a violent threat to innocent lives, this action outraged American and Western public opinion. When the Iranian authorities endorsed the event, indignation rose still higher and people became aware that modern terrorism was passing out of the exclusive hands of covert, underground groups, into those of a maverick state. Nevertheless, efforts began at once to transfer guilt for the hostage seizure away from the Iranian government and people onto the backs of the American president and his administration.

One of the first statements in support of this theme came from Moscow. A Farsi radio broadcast said: "The anger of the Iranian nation and its youth, who ask that a stop be put to U.S. imperialist interference in the country's affairs, is totally understandable and logical."(26) It was certainly understood by Mohammed Javad Bahonar, an Iranian spokesman, who explained:

> The United States insulted the Iranian national honor and the Islamic revolution by giving the deposed Shah a visa. The ex-dictator represents all the pain, torture, humiliation, deprivation and repression suffered for decades by our nation . . . you trigger a new revolution, and then you hide behind your customary legal nitpicking. . . . The Revolutionary Council did not do it. You deserve the credit for unleashing this rebellion [the hostage taking].(27)

When, after two weeks, eight black men and five white women were released from the embassy, Alvin Poussaint, a black psychiatrist at Harvard University said: "The Iranian regime is calling attention to the world that there is racism and sexism in the US."(28)   Closer to the party line, an Iranian student group in America claimed that the Shah's "crimes and atrocities are well documented by the thousands of graves of innocent children, youths and adults and by the scars from torture borne by countless individuals still among the living who lost feet, hands and eyes in his brutal torture chambers."(29)   Ayatollah Khomeini added: "he roasted your young people in boiling pots, charred them on fire and cut their limbs."(30)   In Tehran, CBS television producer Don Hewitt succeeded against intense competition in obtaining a full-hour Mike Wallace interview with Khomeini, on the under-standing that it would be featured on "60 Minutes," a program which evidently stood high in the Ayatollah's estimation.(31)

These early themes, concentrating on the Shah's injustice and America's role in keeping him in power, were in due course sharpened by the story that the CIA was deeply impli-cated in SAVAK's torture program.   A Canadian author, Robin Woodsworth Carlsen, visited Tehran in March 1980, and during his travels he met Bill Blakemore of ABC Television who was asking the Iranian government for permission to do an investi-gation of SAVAK, particularly in terms of its assistance from CIA officials.(32)   "Blakemore had contracted with Carl Bern-stein of Watergate fame to put together a devastating expose on the CIA and SAVAK."(33)   He had already broadcast a radio report that "indicated how seriously and injuriously America had interfered in the affairs of Iran, how such in-terference . . . was at the heart of the present crisis and how it was only natural and appropriate that his country apologize for its 'crimes' against the Iranians."(34)   One of President Banisadr's aides, Farhad, told Carlsen that the techniques of torture (roasting in boiling pots, amputation of limbs, putting out of eyes?) had been taught by CIA special-ists to SAVAK pupils at a Washington police academy.(35)

These examples have numerous companions, and the out-lets for the themes have been expanded to include Iranian demonstrators inside the United States and a former United States attorney general in Tehran.   Fifty students went so far as to stage a hunger strike in Washington, illustrating the international popularity of this technique.   Another report(36) claimed that at least $5 million had been smuggled into the United States to support Iranian protest and propaganda.   The guilt transfer campaign lost much of its fire when Iraq at-tacked Iran.   Perhaps the Ayatollah and his followers found it difficult to continue to operate in the abstract when confronted with concrete problems that would not wait.

The technique of guilt transfer relies for its effectiveness upon audience susceptibility.   An ideal target audience for a revolutionary propagandist might be a weak government with heavy pretensions toward morality.   Some readers might think that such an arrangement favored the Iranian Islamic revolutionaries in their dealings with the United States. If this ideal audience is unavailable, at least there must be a government that is sensitive to public criticism of its conduct, where this strays outside the bounds deemed acceptable by domestic or international opinion. These bounds vary between cultures, and are affected by social, ideological, and religious factors. In the examples given in this essay, the domestic audiences to which efforts were made to transfer guilt were all steeped in the Judeo-Christian tradition and therefore vulnerable to allegations relating to human rights, cruelty, or bad faith. A regime outside this tradition might be susceptible to internal critics, if allegations were made of deviance from accepted ideological or religious principles. Even if such a government were oppressive and forbade criticism, the technique might still work, using bureaucratic channels, innuendo, and guarded metaphors. Probably, it would become very difficult. So far as the writer is aware, any attempts to transfer guilt into the Soviet Union for its actions in Hungary, Czechoslovakia, and Afghanistan have not succeeded. Perhaps this is because all these actions were or could be represented as being in accordance with Soviet ideological principles and not therefore a matter for regret. No one in Britain felt guilty about imperialism so long as the flame of that concept burnt brightly. Seeds of doubt are perhaps a necessary precondition for guilt transfer.

International criticism may influence governments indirectly because such censure is often followed by political isolation and economic sanctions, as in the case of South Africa. To be effective, the technique has to be modified for each and every audience. For the most part this happens instinctively, as the skilled communicator tunes his message to his audience's wavelength.

A revolutionary movement working within a nation or a society may use a mixture of violent, psychological, economic, and political means to achieve power. The activist aims not so much to overwhelm the regime's armed forces as to render that power irrelevant by winning the battles for credibility and legitimacy. Credibility represents a proven ability to achieve stated aims, creating a bond of trust between the actor and the audience. It is reinforced by a reputation for truthfulness, by reliability, and by the appearance of knowing the final destination and how to get there. Legitimacy relates to the focus of group allegiance, which may not correspond to legitimacy in legal terms. It reflects the group's verdict on an assumed right to govern. The accumulation of these assets by the rebels can only be at the government's expense: once the balance has tipped in favor of the revolutionaries, they may be close to victory. This explains why guilt transfer is so important in revolutionary warfare and terrorism. It provides one means of conveying legitimacy and credibility, particularly the former, from regime to rebel.

When guilt for the 1916 Easter Rising was transferred from the Irish rebels to the British authorities several purposes were achieved. The revolutionary fighters who had killed police officers and military personnel were <u>relieved of the moral consequences of murder because,</u> as soldiers in a <u>just cause, they had</u> by the new interpretation merely carried <u>out lawful orders.</u> Within a deeply religious society, such exoneration is <u>important to morale</u> and recruiting. In a retrospective way, the transfer justified the rising itself. Most importantly, it legitimized the revolutionary ethos at British expense, thus creating a reserve of mobilizing propaganda to be drawn upon in 1919. The success of the technique can be measured by the remark of the Irish Catholic Bishop O'Dwyer, who led the Church into its new position behind the revolution. Speaking of the executed leaders, he claimed they "had been shot in cold blood."(37) The success of this operation undoubtedly owed much to growing liberalism in England and Britain's shameful past record in Ireland. Combined, these factors created psychological conditions which only needed to be scratched to produce guilt.

The French recourse to torture in Algeria exposed them to this danger too, and the existence in the mind of the regime and its supporters of genuine reasons for guilt, whether arising out of ancient deeds or the immediate incident, obviously strengthens the technique. We may feel that liberal democracies that offend their own ideals must feel guilt; they would not be liberal or democratic otherwise. In our other examples, however, guilt transfer was attempted under less promising conditions. The Zionist need in the aftermath of the King David tragedy was to sidestep. Here the revolutionaries felt real guilt for an event which had gone astray. Their impromptu attempts at transfer were designed to protect their reputations before world opinion, rather than to gain legitimacy. Tactical in nature, and relying on diversion, the exercise could only be partially successful. The Provisional IRA attempted to saddle authority with guilt for the deaths of their gunmen by portraying all shooting incidents that resulted in such deaths as unlawful, sectarian, and oppressive acts of cruelty. Buried within the scores of allegations there were undoubtedly a small number of cases that deserved rebuke. For the rest, the technique depended on "instant mendacity" and for that reason was open to defeat by intelligent counter-propaganda. Nevertheless, the security force did lose credibility through the consistent application of this method, since it seemed to British audiences that nothing their soldiers ever did was above criticism or fully successful.

Some interesting parallels can be drawn between the political philosophy of New Left terrorists in the West and

Islamic fundamentalists of the Middle East. Each, it would seem, promotes action above achievement, and turns means into ends. They share the view of a world so corrupt that nothing less than root and branch transformation can effect a cure. The ideal may be vague and its attainment uncertain, but its strength justifies any actions on the part of true believers. Moreover, the suffering inflicted by the powers of evil, whether this be the consumer society or a United States - supported imperial regime, should create so severe a sense of guilt among all those responsible (a broadly defined group) that these people should accept almost without complaint the vengence of Marx or Mohammed. The guilt transfer technique in such cases as the Baader-Meinhof group and the Iranian government resembles a fast-moving B movie, where the improbable nature of the story-line is submerged in the effective skills of editing and presentation. And like the B movie, this often works, at least to the point where authority is forced onto the defensive when circumstances might warrant righteous indignation. Within these examples we see martyrdom, whether by the hand of authority or by suicide, as a particularly effective tool. And since other elements in revolutionary propaganda will deny the state its legitimacy, such deaths will always be presented as murder.

In the campaign to discourage and contain international terrorism, as well as in the East-West struggle, the liberal democracies cannot afford to operate under the handicap of what lawyers call mens rea - the guilty mind. Contemporary society seems particularly vulnerable on account of its confused attitudes and lack of moral reference points. Part of the answer must lie in political leadership and part in a better-informed and more responsible news media. But the best defense would be a public that understood the technique and was therefore able to reject fraudulent appeals directed at their consciences.

NOTES

(1) See Warre B. Wells and N. Marlowe, A History of the Irish Rebellion of 1916 (Dublin: Maunsel, 1916).

(2) Quoted in Owen Dudley Edwards and Fergus Pyle (eds.), 1916 The Easter Rising (London: MacGibbon & Kee, 1968).

(3) Some 300 British and Empire troops were executed after trial by court martial in the 1914-18 War.

(4) See, for example, Constantine Fitzgibbon, Out of the Lion's Paw; Ireland Wins Her Freedom (London: Macdonald, 1969).

(5) Captain Bowen-Colthurst was examined by two Dublin doctors. Their evidence at his court martial brought in a verdict of "guilty but insane."

(6) London Public Record Office file 79/Irish/493. WO032-9510.

(7) Quoted in Dorothy Macardle, The Irish Republic (Dublin: Irish Press, 1951).

(8) J. Bowyer Bell, Terror Out of Zion (New York: St. Martins Press, 1978), p. 106.

(9) UK government, Palestine, Statement of Information Relating to Acts of Violence, Cmd 6783, (HMSO, July 1946).

(10) There was indeed a warning, but according to subsequent police investigation, it was given too late to be acted upon. The telephone operator at the King David Hotel was informed two minutes prior to the explosion. As he was passing the message to the hotel manager, the explosion took place. J.P.I. Fford, CID Report on King David Outrage, 16 August 1946, P.R.O. C0537/2290.

(11) Quoted in Begin, The Revolt (Los Angeles: Nash, 1948), p. 221.

(12) Christopher Sykes, Cross Roads to Israel (London: Collins, 1965), p. 359.

(13) See Alf Andrew Heggoy, Insurgency and Counter-Insurgency in Algeria (Bloomington: Indiana University, 1972).

(14) Quoted in Alistair Horne, A Savage War of Peace (London: Macmillan, 1977), p. 184.

(15) Quoted in Horne, p. 186.

(16) Henri Alleg, La Question, (Paris: Les Editions de Minuit, 1958).

(17) Horne, p. 535.

(18) See Clare Booth Luce, Is the New Morality Destroying America? (Washington, D.C.: Georgetown University, 1978).

(19) Quoted Jillian Becker, Hitler's Children: The Story of the Baader-Meinhof Terrorist Gang (Philadelphia and New York: Lippincott, 1977), p. 45.

(20) Ibid., p. 88.

(21) Ibid., p. 267.

(22) Ibid., p. 272.

(23) Ibid., p. 281.

(24) Ibid., p. 282. See also Gerhard Lowenthal, "Political Violence and the Role of the Media: The Case of West Germany," in Political Communication and Persuasion, An International Journal, 1, 1 (1980): 92.

(25) Tony Geraghty, quoted in "Terrorism and the Media," in Ten Years of Terrorism, (London: Royal United Service Institute, 1979), p. 108.

(26) Quoted by US News and World Report (November 26, 1979).

(27) Quoted in Time (November 26, 1979).

(28) Quoted in US News and World Report (December 3, 1979).

(29) Ibid.

(30) Ibid.

(31) Newsweek (December 3, 1979).

(32) Robin Woodsworth Carlsen, Seventeen Days in Tehran (Victoria, B.C.: Snow Man Press, 1980), p. 45.

(33) Ibid., p. 45.

(34) Ibid., p. 46.

(35) Ibid., p. 127.

(36) Guardian (London: August 17, 1980).

(37) Letter from Bishop O'Dwyer to General Maxwell, quoted in M. O'Dubhghaill, Insurrection Fires at Easter Tide (Cork: Mercier Press, 1966), p. 318.

13 Do Terrorists Have Rights?
Robert S. Gerstein

This is an essay in the moral foundations of the law. It starts from the assumption that our fundamental legal rights - rights to life, liberty, privacy, and moral and physical integrity - have a moral basis, that we establish these legal entitlements mainly in order to give protection to the underlying moral entitlements we believe people have to these things. It considers some of the ways in which individuals might lose these underlying moral entitlements. This discussion naturally proceeds on the level of morality, but also has great relevance for the law. If our legal rights are largely founded on moral entitlements and we lose our moral entitlements, the major argument for retaining our legal rights will have been lost as well. There is then no longer any moral objection to depriving us of our fundamental legal rights, and it may even be morally objectionable to allow us to retain them.(1)

It is the specific purpose of this chapter to explore the limits of the idea that people may forfeit their rights through wrong-doing. The case of the terrorist puts the issues involved most powerfully because the terrorist himself explores the outer limits of wrong-doing. He not only violates the rights of others by violence, but he does so with the purpose of making everyone's rights insecure. The terrorist seeks to destroy the community of understanding and mutual self-restraint upon which the existence of rights depends. If anyone could forfeit the right to have any rights at all, it would be the terrorist.

But I shall contend that not even the terrorist forfeits all of his rights. This is not because there are no good arguments for such a forfeiture. I shall examine various arguments that can be made for forfeiture of rights, even of all rights, by terrorists, and conclude that they are generally sound. Finally, however, I shall argue that there are some rights which are so essential to being a person that no amount of wrong-doing could lead to their forfeiture. These are the rights which protect our <u>capacity</u> to become individuals and to maintain our individuality: to be people who understand ourselves to have the moral title to shape our own values and the capacity to do so. Such people have the opportunity to be morally autonomous; that is, to make decisions on the basis of values which are truly their own, chosen by them rather than imposed upon them by coercion or conditioning.

The chapter begins with a sketch of what is intended to be the extreme form of a terrorist campaign. It then continues to articulate an answer to the question: what rights, if any, are retained by the people who carry on such a campaign?

THE TERRORIST CAMPAIGN

A terrorist group sets out systematically to alienate a population from its government. This it does through a series of bombings in public places, through kidnapping, and brainwashing members of the populace, and by making it clear that it will continue to commit such atrocities without any regard for the normal standards of decency until they have brought down the existing regime.(2)

The group does succeed in creating a general sense of insecurity among the populace and in provoking the government into generally repressive measures, including the round-up and detention of all those suspected of complicity with the terrorists. Pressure on those detained results in information leading to the capture of a number of the leading terrorists. Those captured are sentenced to death and are systematically tortured while awaiting execution (though neither of these measures is prescribed by law as punishment for the offenses they have committed).

The terrorists protest this treatment, arguing that their rights as citizens and human beings are being violated. They argue in fact that this way of dealing with them, in disregard of established legal standards, is a denial of all rights. Ought their protests to be attended to?

THE TERRORIST AS CRIMINAL

The terrorists have committed the crimes of murder, kidnapping, and destruction of the property of others. The first question is whether the acts lead to a forfeiture of rights which would affect the terrorist no more and no less than it would anyone who engaged in them, without regard to motive.

I should say that a forfeiture of rights is always attached to such acts.(3)   The terrorist makes himself vulnerable, as does any wrong-doer, to being treated as badly as he has treated others, in that he loses the moral title to complain of such treatment.   Having a right consists precisely in having the title to command respect for our demands that others act or refrain from acting in particular ways toward us, and for our complaints when they fail to do so.   The assertion of this title is inconsistent with the position into which the terrorist has put himself to the extent of his wrong-doing.   For him to claim that his rights remain intact in spite of the harm he has done to others is for him to claim that he deserves to be left in a better position than his victims, and the unfairness of such a claim seems clear.   In general, the wrong-doer cannot fairly demand respect for his claim not to be treated as he has treated others.   This does not mean that he is vulnerable only to precisely the same harm he has meted out to others - maiming for maiming - but rather that he cannot complain of treatment which is no worse than what he has done to others, where the standard for comparison is that which is accepted as reasonable within his society.   Thus, we would regard imprisonment as not at all excessive for a bombing in which people were maimed, but would consider the death penalty clearly excessive for a bombing which destroyed only property and did not endanger lives.

Further, it must be remembered again that the forfeiture of rights only makes the terrorist or other criminal vulnerable to being treated in this way because he has lost his title to complain of it.   There is still a question of whether the punishment to be inflicted upon him can otherwise be justified.   To say that the terrorist has no right to resist some harsh treatment is not yet to say that the government has a right to inflict it: the forfeiture of the right removes one objection to such treatment, but it neither provides in itself a positive justification for such treatment nor does it remove all possible objections.   Thus, a terrorist who shoots people in the leg would lose the moral title to complain if he were shot in the leg, but such treatment might still be wrong, not because it would violate the terrorist's right but because it is always wrong to be cruel.

But I contend that there are limits upon the forfeiture of rights even for the worst criminals.   The terrorists have undoubtedly lost all of the rights which a human being can lose through their conduct.   They have murdered, tortured, and in every respect violated the human dignity of their victims.   Still, I believe that they retain those rights that are inseparable from the humanity which they have violated in others.(4)

Even the terrorist would have a right to protest the destruction of that capacity which is at the core of humanity:

the capacity for autonomous choice. This would mean that even the terrorists who brainwashed their captives could rightfully protest if they were subjected to brainwashing. Any effort forcefully to control the formation of their values or to dictate the expression of their beliefs would be a violation of this indefeasible right.(5)

This does not mean that a punishment such as imprisonment, which limits the terrorists' present opportunities to develop and communicate their values, must violate their rights. Imprisonment does undoubtedly pervasively limit such opportunities, but it leaves the capacity to develop and communicate one's own values intact, and does not challenge the right to remain sovereign over that development.

It is one thing to limit freedom of movement, and quite another to destroy the capacity to decide autonomously what one's movement will be. Having a capacity for autonomous choice is central to the idea of rights. It is difficult to see what the point would be of having any rights at all if we lost control over our capacities to shape our own values. Rights are important because they give each of us the capacity to decide how and to what extent we want to defend our own interests. They are worthy of respect precisely because they support the individual ability to make choices as to what is important. Beings incapable of shaping their own values would have no basis for making claims of right. If we are to have any rights at all, therefore, the rights necessary to maintain the capacity for autonomous choice must be among them.(6)

What of the other forms of suggested punishment? Does the terrorist who kidnaps and tortures others lose the right to protest if he is tortured? If what is meant by torture here is any very harsh or cruel treatment, I should say that he does, though it must be remembered that it would probably still be wrong to use torture on grounds of humanity.(7) If, however, what is meant is the infliction of pain of such a character that the convicted terrorist's capacity of autonomous choice might be permanently impaired, then the answer must clearly be that he does not lose the title to protest it.

Further, the infliction of torture without limit could always be protested, even by a terrorist who has made use of it. Anyone who can be subjected to unlimited pain by his tormentor has his rights utterly disregarded. He is placed entirely at the mercy of another person and is treated as one who has no rights whatever that need be respected. The horror of such a position lies precisely in the sense that a person in it simply will not be listened to, no matter how urgent his cries for relief, or how terrible the treatment inflicted. To deny thus entirely the status of the terrorist as a holder of rights is again to deny his humanity, and therefore to violate rights which he necessarily retains.

Would similar reasoning lead to the conclusion that even a person who has cold-bloodedly blown innocent people to bits may still claim a right not to be executed? If so, it would not be because one who is executed has his capacity for autonomous choice extinguished, and execution must therefore be treated as brainwashing. The evil involved in brainwashing is that of destroying the capacity of a living person to develop and adhere to his own autonomously established values. A dead person is not a person who cannot choose his values freely, but rather not a being for whom questions of free choice arise at all. Rather, it could be argued that the process of imposing capital punishment as currently practiced involves the loss of the right to have rights: it is a process in which the person to be executed will ultimately be stripped of all dignity, and treated as a disposable animal.(8) On the other hand, it must be said that execution need not have this character. In fact, it is precisely people like the politically motivated terrorist who still may think of an execution as a kind of martyrdom to be chosen with pride, and a martyr clearly retains human dignity.

BEYOND CRIMINALITY

But the terrorist is something more than a common criminal. He not only violates particular rights, he also rejects the principles on which rights rest, and aims at destroying the capacity of the government to protect them.(9)
Once the terrorist is seen not simply as a common criminal, but as an enemy of rights in general, an argument can be made that he has forfeited all of his rights.(10) How can one who actively engages in a campaign aimed at destroying the effectiveness of the rights of all others in society now come forward and coherently ask that any of their rights be respected while still maintaining that he need not respect the rights of others? He is simply in no position to make claims of right.(11)
A terrorist might respond that he is not the enemy of rights at all, but the only effective proponent of them against a corrupt and illegitimate system. His contention would be that those who acquiesce in the corruption of society forfeit their rights, so that he can deny the legitimacy of their claims of right without forfeiting his own.(12) In making such an argument, however, the terrorist still cannot legitimately expect respect for his claims from those to whom he makes them, for he is exempting himself from the rightless status to which he would relegate all others purely on the basis of his self-appointment to the position of purifier of the society, an appointment which is not founded on any common understanding that need be respected by others in the society.(13)

The argument that terrorists forfeit in this way all of their rights is a powerful one. Why should we have to respect the claims of someone who continues to insist that he is under no constraint to listen to our claims? To do so could be seen to be not simply unnecessary but wrong, for it is a response which seems to legitimate the claim in spite of its moral incoherence. I again contend, however, that some claims even of the terrorist can and should be responded to in spite of this. No matter what his conduct or his attitudes toward the rights of others, he retains that which is required to demand respect for his right to maintain his capacity for moral autonomy, just because he has (at least potentially) that capacity. No more than this is required as the basis for the assertion of these rights, and nothing can justify their forfeiture if it is present.

In arguing that terrorists have rights, I have argued not only that the government cannot mete out to them the harsh treatment intended for them, but also that it must stay its hand in response to the terrorists own assertions of their claims that it is wrong to treat them so harshly. This latter point may be the hardest to take.

Is that much respect really required for those whose words and actions reflect no respect for others? Why would it not be enough simply to refrain from the harsh treatment planned for the terrorists and to justify this leniency on the basis of the duty we have to be humane to any sentient being, no matter how degraded?

The answer to this contention is that you cannot respect the rights of another person simply by obeying the demands of humanity; the duty of any human to act humanely does extend to his conduct toward any sentient being, but respect for rights requires a recognition of the special quality that is imparted to our relationships with other people by their humanity.

The government might go one step further and still sustain its refusal to listen to the terrorist. It might, for example, agree that it cannot brainwash him because we have a duty not to destroy his capacity for moral choice, but still insist that we need pay no attention to his claims for the respect of this or any other right. Such a stance seems just the appropriate one to take toward one who, though still human and entitled to respect for his rights, has forfeited respect for any assertion he would make of those rights. Wouldn't this be sufficient respect for their rights under the circumstances?

My response to this would be to insist on the tight connection between the idea of having rights and the idea of being allowed to assert them. The essential way to show respect for a human is not simply by refraining from interfering with his interest by respecting his rights, and the essential way of respecting rights is by attending to their holder's assertion of them. It is in listening to a person's own articulation of what is owed to him and making that the basis for our conduct toward him that we show our respect for him as a person. It is this that establishes that we regard him as a being capable of making his own choices among values, rather than as a mere object of benevolence.(14)

THE USE OF TORTURE IN INTERROGATION

Torture is a practice that is universally condemned, but it is also one of the most prevalent responses of governments to terrorism. The major justification for its use is the need for information, and this justification requires separate treatment from that which was given to torture as a kind of punishment.(15)

The argument for the use of torture to get information about terrorist activity is a variant on the argument for the use of force in self-defense. If we imagine that the government has captured a terrorist who has set a bomb which will go off and kill people unless we can get him to reveal where it is and disarm it, the analogy to the clear case of self-defense seems clear. For both cases an individual makes it impossible for us to refrain from harming him except at the expense of innocent lives, our own or others. In such a case it seems clear that the individual forfeits his right to the extent necessary to protect the life or lives of those he is threatening. He has created the situation in which the terrible choice must be made, and he cannot complain if the choice is made to sacrifice him for the sake of innocent life. An innocent person who happened to find out where the bomb was hidden might legitimately protest if he were tortured to extract the information from him, but, the argument would run, not the terrorist himself.

The argument is a sound one in form. People should in general be understood to forfeit rights to the extent that they create situations in which they make it too costly to others for those rights to be vindicated. The only question is whether the right involved here is one that can be forfeited. It is not the right to withhold the information that is being dealt with here. I assume that there would be nothing wrong with imposing a duty upon anyone who has such information to come forward and disclose, with punishment for those who fail to do so. What we are dealing with here is the right not to be tortured into disclosing the information. When a person is ordered to talk and threatened with punishment if he fails to do so, he may choose to remain silent and take the consequences. He may not be either legally or morally at liberty to remain silent. In a case like the present he is in fact presumably under a moral as well as a legal obligation to tell where the bomb is hidden. But to be placed under an obligation to speak is still to have the choice of not speaking. Significantly, a person who felt himself under an obligation of personal loyalty not to speak might believe that this obligation would override the obligation to save lives by speaking. Such a person could make his own choice between conflicting obligations.

Where torture is applied, however, the situation is no longer one in which a price is imposed on one of the alternatives that can be chosen in order to prevent its being chosen. Rather, the method used is directed at destroying the capacity for choice. Gradually escalating torture is not like a fine which is increased over time in order to gain compliance with a court order. The infliction of excruciating pain is not simply an element of persuasion: it can literally destroy the capacity to resist in a way that other sorts of pressure cannot.

In fact, the same argument can be made against techniques used to break the will of persons interrogated even if they do not involve inflicting severe pain. This is true, for example, of the techniques of sensory deprivation once used in the interrogation of IRA suspects in Great Britain. Interrogated suspects were hooded, subjected to continuous monotonous noise, deprived of food and sleep, and required to stand at arms length against a wall for prolonged periods.(16) The Commission of the European Human Rights Convention found that these techniques fell within their definition of torture because "the will to resist or to give in cannot, under such conditions, be formed with any degree of independence."(17) Torture of this sort may of course work long-range or permanent impairment of the capacity for choice,(18) and to the extent that it may do this, the right to resist it would clearly not be subject to forfeiture. But even if the effect is only temporary, the use of power to break the will and compel disclosure is inconsistent with respect for the individual capacity for autonomous choice.

Torture intended to gain information would therefore always be a violation of the rights of the person tortured. Does this mean that the practice could never be justified? This is not necessarily true. The first question is whether it is ever justifiable to violate rights. I should say quite clearly that it is.(19) Unfortunately, the world is not so organized that we can avoid conflicts between rights, or between rights on the one hand and other sorts of needs on the other. The only way to argue away the conflict would be to understand rights as having built-in escape clauses, always giving way whenever there seems to be strong enough reason for overriding them. But while some rights do seem to give way before the circumstances in this way, others do not. When free access to public buildings is restricted owing to terrorism, for example, there is a derogation from the right to move about freely, but not a violation of that right. This is because there is no absolute right to go wherever you choose, but only a right to freedom of movement subject to reasonable restrictions. This flexibility is part of the definition of the right. It is for this reason that restricting access to public buildings may be an inconvenience, but is not in itself a violation of any right.

But the right not to be tortured into submission does not have such an escape clause. It is not a right not to be tortured unless there is good reason for doing do. Whatever the reason for the torture may be, the reason for protesting it remains the same, and remains equally forceful. It is always a severe violation of the integrity of individual autonomy. (20)

Can violation of this right ever be justified? At least it must be said that the possibility cannot be ruled out. If the stakes were sufficiently high and the facts sufficiently clear, most people would probably come to agree that it is justifiable. But there is more to the problem than the question of whether the right of a particular individual should be violated in a particular case where the justification is extremely strong. If a practice of torture is established, it is very likely to be abused. It is likely that innocent people will be caught up in it, that people will be tortured who do not in fact have the information in question, and it is likely that those doing the torturing will become brutalized and use torture where it is not required at all. The needs of the particular occasion must thus be considered not only in relation to one person's rights, but also the evils that are likely to result from establishing the precedent. It would therefore have to be a very extreme case indeed that would justify resort to torture. (21)

DETENTION

The roundup and detention of those suspected of association with terrorism is another typical response to terrorist campaigns. The argument for taking this measure is that the conditions created by the terror make it flatly impossible to treat the terrorists like common criminals and subject them to the normal processes of trial and punishment. Witnesses cannot be expected to testify against those who are part of a movement that effectively terrorizes society, nor can juries be expected to convict them. If they are to be incapacitated as public safety requires, therefore, they must be imprisoned without trial. (22)

Does such detention violate the rights of those interned? Certainly it denies them the right not to be imprisoned except on the basis of proof of particular act of wrong-doing, and this is a right which is central to the affirmation of individual autonomy. But perhaps the terrorists have forfeited this right. Certainly the terrorists have brought their imprisonment upon themselves. They made it impossible for the government to treat them in a way that is consistent with due process of law. They cannot now complain if they have left the government with no alternative for self-defense except detention of all of those associated with the terror.

Detention is not regarded as a punishment for the offense of belonging to a terrorist organization in such an argument. Rather, the association is seen as placing the member of a terrorist organization into a status different from that of other citizens. He becomes, in this respect, like the hostile soldier. Because of the danger he presents, he is subject to being captured and held prisoner without regard to his responsibility for particular acts of violence.(23) His commitment to the terrorist group justifies the reversal of the usual presumption and warrants his imprisonment because he will do harm if left free.

The problem with this argument is that it assumes that those interned have decisively identified themselves as enemy soldiers. This is generally not the case, however. Unlike soldiers, they generally do not wear uniforms, nor do they openly proclaim themselves as enemies when caught. Their identification as members of the terrorist group is frequently controversial, based upon a variety of indications which may be ambiguous, like informal associations with those known to be terrorists; or unreliable, like the testimony of anonymous informants.(24) In the absence of open identification with the terrorist cause, therefore, the process takes on a very different character. Rather than the taking of prisoners in wartime, it comes to resemble the use of preventive detention against those whose character or background seems to make them more unreliable than others.(25) To restrain people on such ground is clearly not to respect their capacity for autonomous choice; it is to treat them as something less than competent human beings. Certainly it cannot be justified on the basis of any forfeiture of the rights of those subjected to it, because they have not been reliably proven to have forfeited their rights by their actions or commitments.

The most that could be said for such a system of detention is that it honestly aims at removing all of those suspected of terrorist involvement from the streets until the danger can be ended, and that it must do this because it is impossible under the circumstances reliably to separate those who have committed offense from those who have not.(26) The question, then, is not one of whether particular individuals have lost

their rights through their conduct or character, but whether
the rights of the populace as a whole have been diminished
because of the exigent circumstances. The question is whether the right not to be imprisoned without trial (except for a
brief period while awaiting trial) is operative only when it is
practicable to try people.

The plausibility of this position rests upon the fact that
this is a right which depends on the existence and operation
of particular institutions: the courts. If the courts cannot
operate, would not the rights connected with their operation
cease to exist?

I would respond that while procedural rights which arise
from the structure of a particular system of courts would be
rendered inoperative if the courts were inoperative, human
rights which should be and are generally protected by courts
do not cease to exist when they cannot be protected in the
normal manner. People ought to have the protection of the
courts for their rights, and those who lose that protection can
rightfully complain about its absence.

The right not to be imprisoned without proof of individual
responsibility for wrong-doing is not a right which arises out
of the procedural niceties of some particular system of courts.
It is a right which is essential to the protection of the
capacity for autonomous choice under any system. That this
is so can be seen from a consideration of the violation of this
right by detention from the point of view of one subjected to
it. Indeed, it is a system which depends for its operation
precisely on not having entirely satisfactory requirements for
reliable determination of the subject's wrong-doing or for the
subject's effective participation in determining his fate or any
predetermined limit on loss of freedom.(27) It thus renders
his life completely uncertain and takes its control entirely out
of his hands. The person is treated not as a responsible
subject, taking part of the process by which his fate is
determined, but as an animate object, to be dealt with according to estimates of the likelihood that it will threaten or
endanger society if it is free. It is clearly inconsistent with
treating him as an autonomous person.(28)

Detention does, therefore, violate the rights of those
subjected to it. If the conditions of fear created by an
effective terrorist campaign require such a system to be
established it must be regarded as a violation of rights. This
does not mean that it cannot be put into operation, but that
the dilemma created by the need to do so should be faced.
The government which adopts such a plan must accept responsibility for violating rights, though the violation is forced
upon them by the terrorists.(29) Those detained are wrong-
ed, though justifiably so, and are deserving of some compensation when they are released. The terrorists are ultimately
responsible for the wrong done to them, but the government

cannot entirely escape responsibility for the choice forced upon them.

If detention violates rights, then when may it be justifiable? The formula of the European Convention on Human Rights is a plausible one: it speaks of an emergency which threatens the life of a nation, and requires that the derogations from rights be only those that are strictly required to meet the emergency.(30)   It is reasonable to think of sacrificing even those rights essential to the affirmation of autonomy where it is necessary for the survival of the system of rights as a whole.   In the context of terrorism, the critical thing is that the very aim of the terrorist is to destroy the capacity of the government to protect the rights of those who live under it, and that an effective terrorist campaign can render the machinery of government directed to the protection of rights inoperative.   Where this occurs, there seems to be sufficient reason for detention even though rights are violated by it.   This seems to be true for two reasons.   First, because among the rights rendered defenseless by successful terrorism will be some, such as the right not to be willfully killed or maimed, which seem to have a more pressing claim upon us than the right to move around freely, and secondly because the general insecurity of rights will as a practical matter bring in its wake a paralysis which will make it impossible to meet the vital needs of many people.

I should emphasize that I do not take these arguments to be of the sort which balance rights off against rights, preferring those which have greater weight, and therefore lead to the conclusion that no wrong is done to those who are interned. Which rights people have depends on what they as individuals deserve as a matter of justice.   Certainly those who take part in creating the threat which deprives people of the things they have a right to themselves forfeit the right to complain of deprivations of freedom.   But those innocent people who are bound to be caught up in the dragnet of detention do not lose their rights just because the operation by which they were unfortunate enough to be caught is a necessary one.

CUTTING BACK THE RIGHTS OF THE ACCUSED TERRORIST AS CRIMINAL DEFENDANT

Aside from detention without trial, there is a whole range of derogations from normal due process which governments may adopt to deal with terrorists.   The experience of Northern Ireland offers two examples of this, both arising from the Diplock Report.   One seems a sort of hybrid case, a procedure which blurs the distinction between detention and imprisonment as punishment.   The Diplock Report described it as "depriving

THE MORALITY OF TERRORISM

a man of his liberty as a result of an investigation of the facts which inculpate."(30)   It was admitted, however, that the procedure was, though in some sense fair, so deficient as not to meet the minimum standards established for criminal trials by the European convention.(31)   The presumption of fairness rested on the fact that the detainee had to be shown to have been personally involved in terrorist activity to the satisfaction of an impartial tribunal.(33)   The principal deficiency involved the fact that the tribunal could and generally would make its decision on the basis of information not available to the suspect, making the presentation of any substantial defense impossible.(34)

The other sort of derogation, resulting from the recommendation of the Diplock Commission involved the institution of a special procedure by which crimes likely to be committed by terrorists were to be tried in the regular courts of justice.   In trials of these offenses the normal right to trial by jury was not available, the statements of those dead or otherwise unavailable at time of trial were made admissable in contravention of the normal rules of hearsay, and confessions were admitted provided only that it was shown on the balance of the probabilities that they were not obtained by torture.(35)

The question raised by these two processes is whether the rights which shape the procedure by which a criminal defendant is found to have forfeited the right to be free are on a sliding scale, so that it is acceptable to allow a loosening of the procedures under increasingly difficult and threatening circumstances.   Clearly there is considerable variation in procedure between various jurisdictions, and there can be few absolutes.   If, then, there is a range of justified procedure, why should it not be possible to adjust the rights to be allowed within that range according to the circumstances, lowering the requirements where, as was arguably the case in Northern Ireland, the intimidation of the population made it very difficult to convict terrorists?

Again, this is not a question that can be dealt with wholesale.   The nature of the individual right in question must be examined in order to determine whether it can be subjected to the sliding scale or not.   The answer to the question must depend, I believe, not on whether there is universal agreement on the necessity of a certain procedural right among various systems, but on what sort of significance the right is understood to have within the particular system being considered. Does it simply involve the legislative establishment of a particular point at which the interests of individual and authority are to be accommodated to one another, when another point could also have been chosen, or does it embody this particular society's understanding of the way in which people must be treated?   The basic values of humanity are expressed in a variety of ways in different societies.   No doubt there are fundamental rights which would be common to all developed societies and their legal systems. But there are also fundamental rights, like those involved in the adversary system of justice embedded in the common law, which affirm a particular kind of society's view of what is essential to humanity. Respecting rights is a matter of being true to the human values of the particular society in which the rights are asserted. To allow for the diminution of rights which affirm the particular society's view of what is essential to humanity is to be unfaithful to the most important values of that society.(36)

It is apparent from what has already been said that the process by which detention was authorized by quasi-judicial tribunals was a violation of rights. Whatever might be thought of the fine points of the common law adversary process, there can be no doubt that the denial of any effective participation by the defense, including even the denial of any effective notice of the charge and evidence against the suspect, cannot be regarded as an acceptable derogation from rights. Detention on this basis means imprisonment of indefinite duration, for reasons necessarily made vague, on evidence which will not be made available to the suspect. The point is the same as that already made for detention without trial: to be deprived of freedom unexpectedly for an indefinite period of time with no opportunity to know or contest the precise basis of the deprivation is not to be treated as one who has a capacity for autonomous choice. Such procedure must always be a wrong to the person who is subjected to it.(37)

As to the changes made in the normal trial process for terrorist offenses, the outcome is less clear. The provision of trial by jury, while it has been held to be a fundamental right in American constitutional law,(38) does not seem so fundamentally connected with the conception of humanity of this or any society to warrant saying that it violates the rights of those tried under emergency circumstances to deny it to them.(39) So too, the hearsay rule, though it connects up with the more significant right to confront witnesses against one in criminal law,(40) does not seem so intrinsic to our conception of how people must be treated in the criminal process that we must rule out the limited derogation from it approved by the Diplock Commission. The change in the law regarding confessions is more perplexing. The question here is whether the rule prohibiting the admission of coerced confessions is a utilitarian means of ensuring a fair trial, or an essential protection of moral autonomy. This is a question on which there is considerable dispute in Great Britain itself,(41) and the question of whether this change is to be regarded as an acceptable derogation from rights or a violation of them depends upon giving the right answer to it. This makes it clear that the question of just how a particular right

may be dealt with may be a controversial one. What it requires is a grasp of the nature of the particular right as it
exists in the operative political theory of the particular
system.

CONCLUSION

Do terrorists have rights? I have come to the conclusion that
they do. But this conclusion has not been reached by rejecting the contrary assertions as no more than rhetoric. The
arguments for denying rights to terrorists are good ones.
They rest upon the perception that claims of right are grounded in a relationship: the relationship between people who have
a shared understanding of what they owe to one another as
people. It makes sense to argue that terrorists have forfeited
the right to have rights because they have by word and action
made clear their complete rejection of that shared understanding, destroying the relationship of which they now wish to
take advantage by making claims of right.

The response I have argued for comes to this: that while
the terrorist by his acts and words has certainly damaged that
relationship, and has lost the capacity to make some claims he
could otherwise have made, he has not and could not destroy
the relationship entirely. Because he retains the distinctively
human capacity for autonomous choice, we continue to have a
relationship with him characterized by a duty to respect him as
one who has that capacity, which means respecting his claims
to keep that capacity intact.

It is true, then, that the terrorist deserves to be treated
as an outlaw if anyone does; but finally I assert that no one
can be treated as an outlaw. A terrorist can and ought to be
punished, but the punishment must remain within the limits set
by our common humanity.

NOTES

(1) Of course this does not necessarily mean that we must
lose our legal rights. There may still be reasons of expediency for allowing us to retain our legal rights. Thus, you
might believe that people who torture others lose the moral
title to complain when they are tortured by prison guards, but
still maintain that they should have the legal right not to be
tortured, because allowing them to assert that right is the
best way to ensure that prison guards do not acquire an excessive amount of power, which they might then abuse in their
own interests.

(2)   This picture of the nature and purposes of a terrorist campaign is admittedly the most extreme case.   I use the most extreme case because it is the most effective test for questions about assertions of rights: if these people can still make claims of rights, then those involved in less extreme wrong-doing must be able to.   It is molded on Rapoport, "The Politics of Atrocity," in Terrorism: Interdisciplinary Perspectives, ed. Y. Alexander and S.M. Finger (New York: John Jay Press, 1977), pp. 46-57.

(3)   I have found Morris, The Status of Rights (unpublished paper), esp. pp. 13-15, helpful on this aspect of forfeiture.

(4)   See Joel Feinberg, Social Philosophy, pp. 84-97, esp. 96-97 (Englewood Cliffs, Prentice-Hall, 1973).

(5)   Ibid.

(6)   Ibid., pp. 58-59.

(7)   See Morris, The Status of Rights.

(8)   I have developed this approach to capital punishment further in "Capital Punishment - 'Cruel and Unusual'?: A Retributivist Response," Ethics 85, 75 (1974).

(9)   This means, for one thing, that in addition to his other crimes he is guilty of making what the Model Penal Code calls "terroristic threats," threats of crimes of violence made with the purpose of terrorizing another or causing serious public inconvenience.   Model Penal Code Section 211.3.   See California Penal Code Section 422.5.

(10)   The forfeiture described here is different from that which arises from the doing of an injury to another, described above.   One who has done an injury to another has forfeited the right to claim better treatment than he has given even if he has now repented his offense.   The forfeiture described here arises not from the commission of the particular act but from the continuing attitude of rejection of all rights.

(11)   This is, I think, the basis for Louch's conception of the terrorist as outlaw.   See "Terrorism: The Immorality of Belief," Chapter 11 in this volume.

(12)   Ibid.

(13)   See Rawls, A Theory of Justice, 213 (Cambridge, Harvard, 1971), where the argument is made that liberty should be limited "only by reference to common knowledge and understanding of the world."

(14)   See Feinberg, Social Philosophy, pp. 58-59.

(15)   See Henry Shue, "Torture," 7 Philosophy and Public Affairs 7 (1978): 124.

(16) Report of the Enquiry into Allegations against Security
Forces of Physical Brutality in Northern Ireland Arising out of
Events on the 9th of August 1971, Cmnd. No. 4823, pp. 15-17
(1971) (The Compton Report).

(17) Ireland v. United Kingdom, Report of the European
Commission on Human Rights (January 25, 1976), p. 402.

(18) See Report of the Committee of Privy Counsellors appointed to consider authorized procedures for the interrogation
of persons suspected of terrorism, Cmnd. 4901 (1972) (The
Parker Report) 20 (Minority Report of Lord Gardiner).

(19) Morris, The Status of Rights, p. 18.

(20) See Feinberg, Social Philosophy, pp. 87-88.

(21) See Shue, "Torture," pp. 137-39.

(22) See Report of the Commission to consider legal procedures to deal with terrorist activities in Northern Ireland,
Cmnd. 5185 (hereafter cited as the Diplock Report), pp. 9-10,
14-17 (1972); Report of the Committee to Consider, in the
Context of civil liberties and human rights, measures to deal
with terrorism in Northern Ireland, Cmnd. 5847 (hereafter
cited as the Gardiner Report), pp. 41-43 (1975).

(23) See the Gardiner Report, p. 42.

(24) On detention in Northern Ireland, see Spjut, "Executive
Detention in Northern Ireland," The Irish Jurist, (1975), pp.
277, 286; David Lowry, "Internment: Detention without Trial in
Northern Ireland," Human Rights 5 (1976): 297-301.

(25) Tribe, "An Ounce of Detention," Virginia Law Review 56
(1970): 371. The classic precedent is the Law of Suspects,
passed by the revolutionary government of France on September 17, 1793. The law authorized the internment of "those
who, either by their conduct, relationships, suggestions or
writings, have shown themselves to be partisans of tyranny."
See Carter, "The French Revolution: 'Jacobin Terror'" Chapter
6 in this volume.

(26) See Diplock Report, pp. 14-16.

(27) Ibid.

(28) See Lowry, "Internment," pp. 275, 289-90, 305.

(29) For this general view that violation of rights may be
justified but must still be regarded as violations of rights, see
A.I. Melden, Rights and Persons (Berkeley, U. of Cal. Press,
1978) and Morris, The Status of Rights.

(30) The European Convention on Human Rights, Article 15.

(31) Diplock Report, p. 14.

(32)   Ibid., pp. 8-9.

(33)   Ibid., p. 14.

(34)   Ibid.

(35)   Ibid., pp. 25-34.

(36)   See, generally Ronald Dworkin, Taking Rights Seriously (Cambridge, Harvard, 1977).

(37)   See supra, pp. 387-88.

(38)   See Duncan v. Louisiana, 391 U.S. 145 (1968).

(39)   See Justice Harlan's dissent in Duncan, 391 U.S. at 171.

(40)   See Pointer v. Texas, 380 U.S. 400 (1965).

(41)   See my "Self-Incrimination Debate in Great Britain," American Journal of Comparative Law 27 (1979): 81.

14 The Laws of War and Terrorism
Paul Wilkinson

INTRODUCTION

Terrorism by rebel factions of every ideological hue has become the characteristic mode of conflict in our time.(1) The international law of war has been developed primarily to suppress or at least to curb terroristic usages of war between states. If twentieth-century experience of law of war teaches us anything it is that the whole noble Grotian project of humanitarian restraints or limits on the conduct of international war has become almost impossible to implement and sustain in a period of such dramatic enhancement of weapons of mass destruction, and when ideologies and strategies of total war have increasingly conspired to obliterate the distinctions between combatant and noncombatant, military and civilian, neutral and belligerent. It is true that the frightfulness of most recent and somewhat misleadingly termed "limited international wars" has been ameliorated to a small yet significant extent by at least partial observance of the Geneva Convention code, for example, in the care of sick and wounded enemy personnel and the taking of prisoners. Nevertheless, when one considers the large gaps in the law of war - above all its failure to deal with the question of nuclear weapons - one is forced to conclude that the whole effort of humanitarian restraints on the conduct of war is not only very sick, it is at death's door.

In order to appreciate why the laws of war regime is not merely hopelessly inadequate to constrain terrorism by factions, but also entirely inappropriate, the peculiar status and inherent problems of developing and applying the laws of war and the special characteristics of terrorist crimes need to be properly understood. This chapter will deal first with the special nature of factional terrorism as a mode of violence and its integral relationship to criminality. It concludes by considering the reasons why the international laws of war, already under severe challenges in their applicability to other forms of conflict, appear particularly inadequate and indeed inappropriate in constraining factional terrorism.(2)

THE NATURE AND IMPLICATIONS OF TERRORISM AS A MODE OF VIOLENCE

Terrorism is a form or mode of violence, and therefore it is first necessary to define the latter.(3) Although the long-standing philosophical debate about the force/violence dichotomy is by now rather sterile, the attempt to make the two terms interchangeable is surely a mistake. It is valuable to distinguish the legitimate use of force by the state and its agencies to prevent, restrain, or punish breaches of the law, from violence which both lacks the legitimation of constitutional and legal sanction and is therefore essentially arbitrary. Accordingly, I shall persist in maintaining this distinction. I believe, however, that the report of the National Commission on the Causes and Prevention of Violence(4) made a valuable move to greater precision by its insistence on defining violence as direct or threatened injury or damage. In sum, I wish to define [violence] as the illegitimate use or threatened use of coercion resulting or intended to result in the death or injury, restraint or intimidation of persons or the destruction or seizure of property. This definition has several advantages: it does not confuse the capacity to inflict violence with its actual use, and it clearly distinguishes violence from the impassioned rhetorical and figurative use of the term to describe, for example, poverty or discrimination. If social scientists join the ideologues in abusing the canons of established usage in this way they will surely confuse public discourse unnecessarily and render serious investigation and theory far more difficult.

Can we distinguish terrorism from other forms of violence - whether criminal, psychopathological, civil, or international - which it so often accompanies? I believe this is possible provided we can avoid the Scylla of blind nominalism and the Charybdis of reification. The nominalists want to deny that there is any particular violence which is terrorist in nature, modus operandi, and sociopsychological affects. For this school, "terrorism" is merely a pejorative for "guerrilla" or "freedom fighter." Others have fallen into the error of identifying a single locus, agent, or context of terrorism with terrorism per se. Some equate it with certain criminal and psychopathological manifestations.(5) Many assume it to be purely a mode of urban insurrection(6) and thereby ignore whole aspects of the history of terrorism in rural conflicts in, for example, the Balkans, Indo-China and Ireland. Commoner still is the attempt to restrict the "terrorist" designation to acts of nongovernmental movements and individuals.(7) Yet this is to turn one's back on the ghastly facts of the systematic use of repressive terror by states, such as that employed by the revolutionary regime in France 1792-1794, by the Bolsheviks in Russia after 1917, by the fascist regimes, and by numerous imperialist and colonial regimes. Nor should we ignore the growing propensity of states to sponsor, arm, and plan proxy terrorism as a form of coercive diplomacy and subversion against allegedly hostile states. Of course, it is true that many acts of state violence have been clothed in the legitimacy of positive law or raison d'etat, but many would argue with Arendt(8) that such acts can be shown to violate the more fundamental norms of moral and natural law. This chapter is primarily concerned with revolutionary terrorism by nongovernmental groups, yet I wish to make clear my agreement with the other contributors to this volume who argue that the all-important questions of justification and legitimacy must be posed concerning acts of states as well.

Political terrorism of all types has certain common features:

1. It is the systematic use of murder, injury, and destruction, or threats of murder, injury, and destruction to realize a political end such as repression, revolution, or a change in the policy of a regime;

2. As a means to their end, terrorists seek to create an atmosphere of fear, despair, and collapse among their target group in order to coerce, intimidate, or blackmail their targets into succumbing to the terrorist demands;

3. Terrorism is inherently indiscriminate in its effect. This is partly a consequence of the nature of much terrorist weaponry (bombs, land mines, etc.) and the frequent, deliberate terrorist attacks on the civilian population and public facilities. But is it also inherent in the objective of spreading terror. As Aron has noted, "an action of violence is labelled 'terrorist' when its psychological effects are out of proportion to its purely physical result. . . . the lack of discrimination helps to spread fear, for if no one in particular is a target, no one can be safe."(9) Even if terrorists claim to "select" individual or group targets (for instance among government officials, police, or members of a rival ethnic or religious group), their acts of assassination are inevitably planned in secret and appear entirely arbitrary to the communities in which they occur. It has been suggested that in an age of bureaucracy the classic mode of assassination of tyrants and its justification by the doctrine of tyrannicide has been rendered obsolete and has been replaced by terrorism;(10)

4. Terrorism can therefore be defined as a peculiarly unpredictable form of tyranny in which the individual is unable
   to do anything to avoid destruction at the hands of terrorists acting on the basis of their own idiosyncratic code;
5. Terrorists recognize no rules or conventions of war, and
   no distinction between combatants and noncombatants.
   They regard anyone and everyone of their victims as expendable in the interests of their cause. In the Manichean
   world of the terrorist no one has the right to be neutral.
   One is either with them or against them;
6. Terrorism involves particularly barbaric methods and
   weaponry. This is true even in preindustrial and relatively primitive communities.(11) Modern technology has
   greatly increased its repertoire of instruments of torture,
   death, and destruction;
7. Politically motivated terrorism is generally justified by its
   perpetrators on one or more of the following grounds:
   (a) any means are justified to realize an allegedly transcendental end (in Weberian terms "value-rational"
   grounds); (b) terrorism can be shown to have "worked" in
   the past, and is held to be either the sole remaining or
   best available method of achieving success. This is in
   Weber's terms an instrumental-rational attitude to terrorism; (c) the morality of the just vengeance, or "an eye for
   an eye and a tooth for a tooth"; and (d) the theory of the
   lesser evil: greater evils will befall us or our nation if we
   do not adopt terror against our enemies.
      Political terrorism becomes international in the strict
   sense when it is (a) directed at foreigners or foreign
   targets, or (b) concerted by the governments or factions
   of more than one state, or (c) aimed at influencing the
   policies of a foreign government or the international
   community.

    Some other preliminary points must be made about this
general concept of terrorism as a mode of violence. It is vital
to recognize the distinction between terrorists who are politically motivated and who, by definition, evince some degree
of rationality and political idealism, and those who are merely
criminal or criminally insane. A major difficulty arises at the
borderline of these categories when basically criminal or
psychopathic individuals clothe themselves in the rhetoric and
crude ideology of the political terrorist. Was De Freeze of the
Symbionese Liberation Army more criminal than revolutionary
or vice versa? It may be relatively straightforward to resolve
such a problem in an extreme case such as that of the Manson
family, who claimed political motivation at their trial. But
in organizations such as the Baader-Meinhof, the FLQ, and the
Weathermen, revolution and criminality are found to be inex-
tricably intertwined. It is the main thesis of this chapter that

there is a special syndrome of factional-criminality which characterizes certain extremist movements and factions, especially those of the nihilist and anarchist tendencies, and that it is movements such as these that show the greatest propensity for international and transnational terrorist operations. If we wish to understand the nature and causes of international terrorism and to consider the most appropriate means of dealing with it, it is vital that we should first understand something of the factional-criminal mentality and the movements that are its main manifestation and carriers.

There is, however, another crucial preliminary distinction to be made which has been rightly emphasized by some of the pioneering scholarly analyses of terrorism,(12) the distinction between terror and terrorism. Many major eruptions of intraspecific violence such as international war and revolutionary civil war are inevitably accompanied by spasmodic, random acts of sanguinary terror, and, because of the high intensity of violence and the relatively large number of armed participants and sophisticated destructive weaponry generally involved in such conflicts, the casualties and social destruction caused may reach catastrophic proportions. That is to say that many eruptions of war, terror, and outbreaks of the mass terror or revolutionary insurrection are essentially epiphenomenal and uncontrolled. Terrorism, on the other hand, is a deliberate policy of waging terror for political ends: it is the systematic and calculated use of terrorization and is explicitly rationalized and justified by some philosophy, theory, or ideology, however crude. It is not difficult to find examples of polemics prescribing, justifying, and acclaiming the use of terrorism:

> Les prévaricateurs des administrations seront fusillés.
>
> — Saint-Just(13)

> The revolutionary [terrorist] despises all dogmas and all sciences, leaving them for future generations. He knows only one science — the science of destruction. . . . the object is perpetually the same: the quickest and surest way of destroying this whole filthy order. . . . For him, there exists only one pleasure, one consolation, one reward, one satisfaction, the success of the terror. Night and day he must have but one thought, one aim, merciless destruction.
>
> — Nechayev(14)

> Long live death
>
> — Spanish Anarchist rallying cry

But the revolution does require of the revolutionary
class that it should attain its end by all methods at
its disposal - if necessary by an armed uprising: if
required by terrorism.
                                        - Trotsky(15)

Violence is a purifying force. It frees the native
from the inferiority complex and from despair and
inaction. It makes him fearless and restores his
self-respect.
                                        - Fanon(16)

We have to form groups and to settle accounts, once
and for all, with the whole gang of those damned,
heartless exploiters. . . . There is enough dynamite in Quebec to blow up all of them. It will be
the turn of the millionaires and militarists to taste
blood - their own blood. After all, guns can be
used for something else but hunting.
                                        - Vallieres(17)

TERRORISM AND CRIMINALITY

It is precisely because terrorists by definition follow a
systematic policy of terror that their acts are analogous to
crimes. The very notion of crime, even in the most primitive
legal systems, implies the moral responsibility of individuals
for their actions, and hence for any violations of the legal
code. We cannot make a general rule that terrorists are to be
exempted from criminal responsibility unless we are either
prepared to plead their irresponsibility on grounds of insanity
or are willing to allow the whole moral and legal order to be
undermined by deferring to the terrorist. In most legal
systems the typical acts of terrorist groups (such as bombings, murders, kidnapping, wounding, and blackmail) constitute serious criminal offenses under the prevailing codes.
Without exception murder is punishable under the legal codes
of all states. As terrorism involves systematic, cold-blooded
murder, it is particularly repugnant to all societies deeply
infused with humanist values.
    It is still widely held that the divine injunction against
killing (the sixth commandment) is an absolute imperative
which allows only four special exceptions: (1) necessary killing
committed in the course of a legitimate war (a pacifist would,
of course, object to this exception and to exception 3);
(2) execution in punishment for the crime of murder or treason
(an opponent of capital punishment would deny this ground);
(3) necessary killing committed in the course of a just re-

bellion against tyrannical rule or foreign conquest: and ④ in
individual self-defense against violent attack. Clearly there is
a world of difference between justification for specific acts and
justification for a systematic policy of indiscriminate killing as
a means to a political end. Even if the terrorists claim, as
they commonly do, that they are waging a just war or a just
rebellion in terms of the classical criteria laid down by
theologians and moral philosophers,(18) they do not thereby
succeed in providing ethical justification for their deliberate
choice of systematic and indiscriminate killing as their sole or
principal means of struggle.

It would be a logical absurdity to try to justify terrorism
in terms of an ethic founded on the sanctity of individual
human life. Hence, terrorists claim to act according to a
higher "revolutionary morality" which transvalues everything
in terms of the revolutionary struggle. This terrorist revolutionary morality takes many different forms and is informed by
a confusing and often self-contradictory collection of self-
justificatory beliefs, myths, and propaganda.

The point I wish to establish here, however, is that if we
attach any meaning and value to our Western Judeo-Christian,
liberal, and humanist values, and to the ethical and legal
systems shaped by this tradition, we must logically recognize
the criminal nature of terrorism.

Terrorism is more than simply a manifestation of psycho-
pathology and more than a symptom of social discontent, oppression, and injustice - though it may be both of these
things as well. It is also a moral crime, a crime against
humanity, an attack not only on our security, our rule of law,
and the safety of the state, but on civilized society itself.

Terrorists speak a different language of justification, and
for them the arguments from ethical and humanitarian principles are dismissed as sentimental and bourgeois irrelevancies.
Defiantly and proudly they place themselves outside and
"above" the law. Hence, as we shall observe later, the apparently close bonds between terrorists and bandits (whom Bakunin regarded as the natural and original revolutionaries).
Hence also the intimate organization, financial, and logistic
links between terrorist movements and criminal subcultures.

Yet there remains a significant difference between them in
that the terrorist, unlike the criminal, insists on the revolutionary legitimacy and historical necessity and significance of
his acts. If captured and brought to trial the terrorist thus
typically refuses to recognize the legitimacy and legality of the
courts. In his eyes the judiciary is simply the contemptible
creature of an irredeemably rotten order. There can thus be
no meaningful dialogue between them. As we shall observe,
terrorists generally claim that their owns acts dispense justice
and punishment according to a higher law of revolution: the
terrorists claim to extirpate the crimes of the state.

Revolutionary terrorists make war on legality and their "criminality" is therefore an essential part of their self-definition. They regard the law and its agents as both symbol and embodiment of the "oppressions" and "injustices" they wish to remove. Echoing Kropotkin, they would claim "everything is good for us which falls outside legality." Yet the awesome consequence of this nihilistic rejection of all ethical and legal constraints is that the professional terrorists become totally corrupted and criminalized by their obsessive absorption in assassination, massacre, and destruction.

CAN LAWS OF WAR HELP IN CONSTRAINING TERRORISM BY FACTIONS?

A fundamental premise of the laws of war is that states are entitled to employ war as a rational instrument of policy to serve limited and clearly defined ends. It is therefore in the perceived interests of all governments to uphold some basic humanitarian restraints on the conduct of war in order to ensure that the fabric and functioning of society is not irreparably damaged, and to provide some possible basis for eventual peacemaking between the states at war with each other. In an age which has seen the development of the doctrine and practice of total war, demands for unconditional surrender, and an arms race with nuclear weapons capable of destroying not only the populations of the superpowers but also much of the rest of the planet, it is all too obvious that this basic assumption of rationally limited war, and indeed the very feasibility of the whole humanitarian project of the laws of war, is in question.

It is of course the case of nuclear war which totally undermines the last shreds of credibility of the laws of war regime. In a conventional war reprisals are permissable under certain circumstances as a response to illegal acts by the other side, but only as a warning to the enemy and to compel them to conform thenceforward to the laws of war. But in a nuclear war reprisal attacks on the enemy's civilian population centers, technically illegal under the laws of war, would be designed to defeat the enemy by inflicting irreparable damage on his economy and military capabilities. Modern nuclear weapons, and indeed many so-called conventional weapons, have such awesome capacities for mass destruction that the traditional laws of war distinctions between combatants and noncombatants, military and civilians, and neutrals and belligerents, become inevitably obliterated. The fact that nuclear weapons have totally undermined the laws of war doctrine of limiting methods of destruction is clearly recognized by most international lawyers. For instance, the report of 50th Conference of the International Law Association, Brussels 1962,

recorded the view of the preponderance of legal opinion that
the effects of nuclear radiation are "akin to those inflicted by
the use of poison and poisoned weapons. . . . Thus, in
principle, the use of such weapons is illegal." It is clear that
the outbreak of nuclear war would involve not only the breakdown of mutual deterrence but also the collapse of the whole
fragile construct of laws of war. What would be the point in
establishing a war crimes tribunal to discuss questions of
culpability and possible punishments in a world reduced by the
superpowers to a thermonuclear wasteland? What use would
there be in discussing claims for compensation or reparations?
What would be the good of mobilizing world public opinion
against aggression when it is too late?

Even if we exclude the case of nuclear war, it became
quite evident even before World War II that the development of
laws of war already lagged so far behind the development of
military technology and tactics that the civilian population
could no longer look to international law for real protection
against the terrorist practise of modern war. At the heart of
this weakness is the failure of the Hague Conventions and
successive conferences on laws of war to limit armaments. The
1899 Hague Convention succeeded in forbidding the use of
asphyxiating gases and expanding bullets (dumdums), but both
were used in World War I. There has never been an international convention covering laws of war in the air, and hence
civilian populations had no international legal protection against
the massive saturation bombing offensives against major cities
in World War II and in more recent conflicts.

It is true that some significant progress was made on
agreeing upon conditions for the care of prisoners of war, the
sick and wounded. Reciprocity was undoubtedly an important
inducement here. But some other law of war provision, such
as those included in the 4th Geneva Convention, 1949, in the
light of the disregard for international law principles in World
War II, appear to be statements of noble intent rather than
practicable or viable international law. For instance, the
Fourth Geneva Convention specifically forbids, inter alia, the
deportation of individuals or groups, for whatever motive, the
taking of hostages, outrages upon personal dignity, torture,
collective punishment and reprisals, unjustified destruction of
property, and discrimination on the basis of race, religion,
nationality, or politics. Yet we all know that these prohibitions have been more honored in the breach in the whole history of international conflicts since 1949. The key problems
are: how can the international community possibly ensure that
such prohibitions are enforced and, where they are not observed, how can offending states be punished?

However admirable the intentions of the designers of the
laws of war codes, the harsh fact is that their main significance is more symbolic than practical. The Geneva Conven-

tions, with their additional protocols (1977), and the Nuremburg Principles of 1946 do at least constitute important statements of moral principle, norms commended to the international community for the protection of human rights. But such documents, in common with other noble pronouncements - such as the Universal Declaration on Human Rights and the Covenants on Civil, Political and Economic, Social and Cultural Rights - can, by the very nature of international politics, only have the most marginal effect on the <u>practice</u> of states. For when there is no world sovereign legal authority capable of enforcing such codes, they remain mere embryos of a global human rights regime in a more ideal world. Hence, for this reason alone, those who put their faith in the present laws of war regime as a foundation for restraining or suppressing terrorism by factions are building on sand.

Perhaps the most obvious reason for the inappropriateness and inadequacy of the laws of war regime as a means of curbing terrorism by factions is the practical argument that terrorist movements generally lack any territorial jurisdiction or juridical framework for applying international laws. While it is true that there have been frequent cases of terrorist organizations "disciplining" their members by means of summary punishments, it is clear that such groups lack true judicial procedures or processes. It is not merely of course that such movements are generally on the run, without any permanent base, and lacking in the resources and expertise either to participate in the development of such international conventions and rules or to enforce them. The faction or movement conducting a campaign of pure terrorism without any concomitant broader struggle of guerrilla war or revolutionary insurrection is usually no more than a network of tiny cells, constantly on the run from the authorities, entirely lacking in democratic or constitutional legitimacy, and is generally opposed as a matter of principle to all existing systems of national and international law. Thus, even if one were to decide that, in principle, terrorist movements should be allowed to become parties to international conventions on the law of war, in practice they exclude themselves for three main reasons: (1) as they are already <u>hors la loi</u>, it would be very difficult to identify them and their leaders; (2) it is impossible to know who or what such movements would represent; and (3) most of the revolutionary factions devoted entirely to using the weapon of terrorism reject the political and legal order from which the laws of war are derived.

The argument of the "pure terrorist" would be that the doctrines of humanitarian and legal restraints on the use of violence are sheer hypocrisy and "bourgeois sentimentality" designed to serve the repressive "imperialism" of states. Moreover, he or she would claim that conformity to the laws of war would deny them the weapons of maximum terror and vio-

lence which they invariably claim are the only means available
to them for defeating the tyrannical oppression of the regimes
ranged against them. The dedicated terrorist really believes
that his ends justify any means and, in common with tyrannical
rulers who employ terror as an instrument of rule, they simply
cast aside all arguments about respect for human rights and
international law as just so much bourgeois sentimentality.

    Yet another insuperable obstacle to encompassing terror-
ism by factions under the laws of war regime derives from the
deep division in the international community on the question of
terrorism.   The laws of war are codified and applied by the
global community of states. Yet many of these states - including the Soviet Union, Cuba, North Korea, Libya, South
Yemen, Iraq, and Iran - have actually championed and promoted terrorist movements as proxy weapons to subvert other
regimes.   These states have given sanctuary, training, cash,
diplomatic assistance, weapons, and many other forms of aid to
their protégé terrorist movements.   It is naive, to say the
least, to expect such states to cooperate in formulating or
implementing a law or war code that would in any way inhibit
the operations of their covert murder squads.   As long as
these states continue to promote terrorism and the rest of the
world community refuses to penalize them for doing so, perhaps because of lack of unity and will or because they have
been blackmailed by threats to their oil supplies, there is no
real hope of getting an effective set of international legal
constraints on terrorism agreed upon or enforced.

    The ambivalence of the international community concerning
terrorism is all too clearly reflected in the contradictions
inherent in United Nations principles. (19)   On the one hand,
the United Nations Declaration on the Principles of International Law and the Conduct of Relations between States enjoins
them to refrain from "organising, assisting, or participating in
acts of civil strife in another state."   On the other hand, a
later United Nations resolution proclaims that "States have a
duty to promote . . . realisation of self-determination" and to
refrain from any 'forcible action' against 'national liberation
movements.' It also pronounces that peoples engaged in such
struggles are "entitled to seek and receive support."   Because
the criteria for defining a bona fide national liberation
movement are nowhere properly defined in international law, it
is possible for any state to define its terrorist proteges as
national liberation movements, thus legitimating its action in
terms of United Nations principles! It is important to emphasize the distinction between the irregular guerrilla fighter of
partisan resistance or liberation in a war or movement against
the the armed forces of an adversary, and the use of terroristic attacks against innocent civilians, such as the placing of
bombs to cause mass slaughter in public places, hostage tak-
ings, and murders.   In the case of the former, the clear case

the case of the former, the clear case of partisan or guerrilla warfare, international laws of war rightly accord some protection, and this has recently been considerably increased by the insertion of national liberation movements in the 1977 Protocol I of the Geneva Convention, according them full belligerent status under certain conditions.(20) It is worth noting, however, that the new rules have been "bent" slightly to accommodate the national liberation movements (accorded observer status at the conference on the laws of war). National liberation movement guerrillas are now only required to carry arms openly at the moment of attack, and are no longer required to wear distinctive badges or other distinguishing marks.

Guerrilla partisans have often been treated with great ruthlessness by orthodox army commanders. It is true that the 1974 International Conference at Brussels provided a formula for the recognition of irregulars as lawful belligerents. To obtain this status they had to be answerable to a specific commander, wear a distinctive badge, carry their weapons openly, and, during operations, conform to the laws and customs of war. With a few minor modifications these criteria were incorporated in the 1899 and 1907 Hague Conventions and the Geneva Conventions of 1949. It is one thing to arrive at abstract legal formulas, but, of course, quite another matter to put them into practice effectively. There were three major obstacles to the observance of this formula. First, many national liberation and partisan resistance movements tend to be loose coalitions of factions or local groups operating semiautonomously. As the weapon of terrorism became more widely known and apparently successful as propaganda of the deed and in achieving other tactical objectives, so it became increasingly popular as the resort of the weak and the desperate. It is well nigh impossible to find a twentieth-century national liberation or partisan resistance struggle in which there has been no use of systematic terrorism by at least one faction in the struggle. Yet, in order to achieve the full status and benefits of a lawful belligerent, a national liberation movement has not merely to eschew terrorism: under the new protocols it has the duty to discipline its own forces to suppress such acts. In practice, few national liberation movements have sufficiently cohesive centralized or authoritative political leadership and command structures to enforce such discipline.

Second, many national liberation movements and resistance movements lack the desire or the will to abandon the use of terrorism as a "weapons system." They argue that performance of the laws of war would effectively nullify the considerable propaganda and tactical advantages reaped by terrorism.

ed a blind eye to executions of guerrillas without trial, and to torture.(21)   In such circumstances an awful cycle of terror and counter-terror is begun; guerrilla fighters who are unlikely to receive just treatment tend to be more ready to carry out acts of terrorism.   It is often hard to discern who instigated the cycle of terror - the guerrillas or the repressive forces of the state.   It is clear that the majority of movements and factions engaged exclusively in terrorist campaigns in the developed countries would not begin to qualify for lawful belligerent status even if they wanted to.   Protocol II, 1977, covering internal wars, applies only to situations of conflict between the armed forces of a government and a dissident armed group under a responsible military commander and in such control over part of the state's territory as to enable them (1) to carry out sustained military operations, and (2) to meet the obligations of implementing the detailed provisions of Protocol II.   Very few currently active national liberation movements meet these criteria.(22)   The nationalist movements fighting the Muzorewa-Smith regime in what was then Rhodesia only just succeeded in achieving that degree of control over very limited areas during the war, and even they depended heavily on sanctuaries and bases across Rhodesia's borders.(23)   It is highly doubtful whether they ever achieved sufficient centralized control and communications to fulfill the second requirement.   The Polisario guerrillas in the Western Sahara have undoubtedly taken firm control of large parts of the desert, but this is because of the liberal external military support they are able to call upon, and the weaknesses of the Moroccan forces.   The pure terror groups, such as the Red Brigades or ETA-Militar, do not really come within the orbit of the laws of war, even if one takes into account the implications of the 1977 Protocols.   The provisions of Protocol II would not begin to operate in these cases unless or until they developed into full-scale civil wars, and this is yet another incentive to governments to deal speedily and effectively with such challenges, for no government welcomes the international and legal complications which follow from invoking the laws of war regime.

     For all the reasons adduced above, it is clear that in the overwhelming majority of cases terrorists must be dealt with under the domestic laws of states.(24)   From an international lawyer's point of view this is obviously untidy, and in some respects unattractive.   International judicial cooperation in dealing with terrorism is undoubtedly infinitely complicated by the multiplicity of different systems of jurisdictions, criminal codes, judicial procedures, and traditions.   Naturally these different national traditions express widely variant underlying legal and political values.   In some states those who would be charged and convicted of terrorist crimes elsewhere are treated as national heroes and freedom fighters.   Even among Western

democracies who share a common antipathy to terrorism there
appear to be irreconcilable differences over the vexing question of extradition of those claiming a political motivation for
their crimes.(25)   There is no easy way to avoid these judicial
conflicts. Indeed, what is really worth marking is the extraordinary degree of international cooperation against terrorism
that Western states have been able to develop, not only in the
form of useful conventions like the Council of Europe Convention on the Suppression of Terrorism (1977), but also in the
more practical form of mutual assistance and bilateral and
multilateral cooperation at the more practical levels of
intelligence and police work. We are a long way from achieving a global international law consensus on methods of dealing
with terrorism, but this does not mean that all paths to
improved international cooperation are blocked.   Moreover, the
recent tendency toward greater convergence in the area of
human rights law, as illustrated by the development of the
European Convention and Commission on Human Rights, helps
to smooth the way for more effective cooperation in other
matters of urgent international judicial concern.

Experience indicates that any progress made will be by
inching forward in one or two areas at a time, often while
simultaneously suffering setbacks in international cooperation
and understanding in other areas.   The most solid achievements in international cooperation against terrorism have been
piecemeal and pragmatic, concentrating on specific limited
aspects such as aircraft hijacking or border cooperation in
policing.

With regard to the laws of war, it should be self-evident
that acts of calculated and systematic terrorization are a
flagrant violation of its basic principles. As this chapter has
argued, however, the contemporary international regime of
laws of war has proved piteously inadequate in attempting to
inhibit terrorist practices in war by the armed forces of
states. Indeed it has been argued that if we compare the
doctrine of laws of war to the practice of states involved in
international conflict, one is forced to conclude that even
though the laws of war are not yet entirely defunct, they are
so gravely debilitated as to be in danger of expiry. In any
event, we have seen that by their very nature, the laws of
war are quite incapable of controlling or curbing the terrorism
of factions which has been a particular plague to the Western
democracies in recent years.

As for the insertion of the national liberation movement in
the 1977 Protocol I, I have suggested that its overall effect is
unlikely to reduce the terrorism of factions. A few national
liberation movements may manage to meet the criteria, but
many violent factions will have no wish to do so. Most terrorists will continue with "murder as usual." In any case, the
prospects of the international community as a whole adhering

to the laws of war regime appear somewhat remote, barring changes of a revolutionary nature in the international system. Just as we must face the possibility that terroristic regimes will only be restrained from abusing the rules of war in international conflict by the victory of superior force, so the terrorism of factions is more likely to be effectively suppressed by the superior will, determination, and professionalism of national governments and security forces than by the introduction of complex additional national legislation, and Utopian redesigns of international law.

NOTES

(1) For inventories and chronologies of incidents, see, for example Lester A. Sobel, ed. Political Terrorism (New York: Facts on File, 1975); Brian Jenkins and Janera Johnson, "International Terrorism: A Chronology, 1968-1974" (Santa Monica: Rand Corporation R-1597-DOS/ARPA, March 1975); and "International Terrorism: A Chronology, 1974 Supplement" (Santa Monica: Rand Corporation R-1909-1-ARPA, February 1976); and Edward F. Mickolus, Transnational Terrorism: A Chronology of Events, 1968-1979 (London: Aldwych Press, 1980).

(2) For the contrary view, cf. Paul A. Tharp, "The Laws of War as a Potential Legal Regime for the Control of Terrorist Activities," Journal of International Affairs, 32, 1 (1978), pp. 91-100.

(3) For a discussion of the definitional problem, see Paul Wilkinson, Political Terrorism (London: Macmillan, 1974), pp. 9-44; and Terrorism and the Liberal State (London: Macmillan, 1977), pp. 47-80.

(4) J.F. Kirkman, S.G. Levy, and W.J. Crotty, eds., Assassination and Political Violence; A Report to the National Commission on the Causes and Prevention of Violence, Vol. 8 (Washington, D.C.: U.S. Government Printing Office, 1969).

(5) For example, D.V. Serge and J.H. Adler, "The Ecology of Terrorism," Encounter 40, 2 (February 1973): 17-24.

(6) For example, Robert Moss, Urban Guerrillas (London: Maurice Temple Smith, 1972); Anthony Burton, Urban Terrorism: Theory, Practice and Response (New York: Free Press, 1975).

(7) For example, Brian Crozier, The Rebels: A Study of Post-War Insurrections (London: Chatto and Windus, 1960), and Theory of Conflict (New York: Scribner, 1975).

(8)   Hannah Arendt, Eichmann in Jerusalem: A Report on the
Banality of Evil (New York; Viking Press, 1965).

(9)   Raymond Aron, Peace and War (London: Wiedenfeld and
Nicholson, 1966), p. 170.

(10) Bernard Crick, Political Theory and Practice (London:
Allen Lane, 1972), p. 233.

(11) See J.S. Roucek, "Sociological Elements of a Theory of
Terror and Violence," American Journal of Economics and So-
ciology 21, 2 (April 1962): 165-72; and Eugene V. Walter,
Terror and Resistance: A Study of Political Violence (New
York: Oxford University Press, 1969).

(12) J.B.S. Hardman, "Terrorism," Encyclopaedia of the
Social Sciences, Vol. 14, ed. E.R. Seligman (New York: Macmillan, 1937), pp. 575-79; and Eugene V. Walter, "Violence
and the Process of Terror," American Sociological Review 29, 2
(Spring 1964): 248-57.

(13) Quoted in Andre Malraux, Le Triangle Noir (Paris: Gallimard, 1970), p. 123.

(14) Sergey Nechayev "Catechism of the Revolutionist," 1869,
reprinted in Michael Confino, ed., Daughter of a Revolutionary
(London: Alcove Press, 1974), pp. 221-230.

(15) Leon Trotsky, Terrorism and Communism (Ann Arbor:
University of Michigan, 1963), p. 58.

(16) Frantz Fanon, The Wretched of the Earth (Harmondsworth: Penguin, 1967), p. 74.

(17) Pierre Vallieres, quoted in Gustave Morf, Terror in
Quebec (Toronto: Clarke Irwin, 1970).

(18) See discussion in R. Tucker, The Just War (Baltimore:
The John Hopkins Press, 1960); M. Walzer, Just and Unjust
Wars (New York: Basic Books, 1977); J.R. Pottenger, "Libera-
tion Theology: Its Methodological Foundation for Violence,
supra Ch 5 and J. Dugard, "International Terrorism and the
Just War," supra Ch 4.

(19) For a fuller discussion of the contradictions inherent in
United Nations statements, see Paul Wilkinson, Terrorism:
International Dimensions (London: Institute for the Study of
Conflict, 1979) pp. 14ff; Robert Friedlander, "Introduction,"
in Terrorism: Documents of International and Local Control,
Vol. 1 (New York: Oceans Publications, 1979); and L.C.
Green, "Double Standards in the United Nations: The Legal-
ization of Terrorism," in Archiv Des Volkerrechts, ed., H.
Schlochauer, 18 Baud, 2 Heft (Tubingen: Mohr, 1979).

(20) A cogent case against the national liberation movement
insertion in the 1977 Protocol is made in G.I.A.D. Draper,

"Wars of National Liberation and War Criminality," in Restraints on War: Studies in the Limitation of Armed Conflict, ed., Michael Howard (Oxford; Oxford University Press, 1979), pp. 135-162.

(21) Some of the worst historical instances are mentioned in Walter Laquer, Guerrilla (Boston: Little, Brown & Co., 1976); and E. Kossoy, Living with Guerrillas: Guerrilla as a Legal Problem and a Political Fact (Geneva: Droz, 1976).

(22) The Johannesburg Star reported in November 1980 that the South African National Congress (ANC) signed Protocol I of the Geneva Convention of 1949. In the light of this development, the director of the Centre for Legal Studies in South Africa, Professor John Dugard, stated that guerrillas of the ANC should henceforth be recognized as prisoners of war.

(23) See Anthony Wilkinson, "Insurgency in Rhodesia, 1957-1973: An Account and Assessment," Adelphi Papers (London: IISS, 1973); and Anthony Wilkinson's contribution to Basil Davidson, J. Slovo, and A. Wilkinson, Southern Africa, (Harmondsworth: Penguin, 1976).

(24) The case for this general approach is comprehensively discussed in Alona Evans and John Murphy, eds., Legal Aspects of International Terrorism (Lexington: D.C. Heath & Co., 1978); and Paul Wilkinson, Terrorism and the Liberal State.

(25) For differing perspectives on extradition of terrorist suspects, see contributions by Robert Linke, "International Co-operation in the Struggle Against Terrorism," and Paul Wilkinson, "The Problems of Establishing a European Judicial Area," in Report of the Conference on The Defense of Democracy against Terrorism in Europe (Strasbourg: Council of Europe, 1980).

15 Eliminating the Terrorist Opportunity
George H. Quester

Some portions of the phenomenon of terrorism are clearly explained by the frustrations and injustices of our society and by the sociology or psychology of the individuals then driven to enlist in terrorist groups. Other portions of terrorist activity stem from technological or social changes which make terrorist attacks easier or harder.

I am more interested in the latter than the former. This may simply be my personality or it might reflect my contention that opportunity plays an underrated role here, while the values and grievances of the rebel have drawn disproportionate attention. At a slightly different level, the working premise, regardless of whatever causes terrorism, is that the opportunities provided by technological change are more manipulatible and controllable than the plane of value preferences; it will be easier to lock up the boarding areas of airports than to change the feelings of the would-be skyjacker, or to attend to his grievances which sometimes are quite bizzare, Moreover, whatever the current significance of personal motivation or physical opportunity in the explanation or control of terrorism, the trend over time may have to be toward the control of opportunity, as some very significant and dangerous avenues of attack are opening by which the terrorists can make his mark on society.

WHAT IS THE PROBLEM?

Most of us are appalled by terrorism. Yet our reasons may differ substantially when we are forced to explain them. Some would be quick to note the unnecessary human suffering caused by attacks on airliners or by the dynamiting of tourist attractions. Yet the human suffering caused by terrorism has not yet even begun to match that caused by automobile accidents, accidents whose frequency might be substantially reduced if a still lower limit were legislated and enforced.

Others might then state a much more serious objection to terrorism, in the threat it poses to all of law and order and legitimacy in society. If felons can be released from prison simply because their friends have seized an airliner, is there any end to all of this? Or will all of society be compromised and forced to submit to a blackmail of the most fundamental sort? Most of us thus share a sense of dismay and humiliation at seeing bank robbers leave the scene of a crime with hostages as their shield, having been given safe conduct to some unknown destination. Even when the hostages are released unharmed, the worry of how in the future we will ever be able to deter or apprehend bank robbers assails us.

The novelty of some terrorist tactics has thus suggested open-ended possibilities of success, and it may be this open-endedness in particular that dismays the ordinary citizen. It is one thing for such forces occasionally to get away with the holding of a hostage and the dictating of terms to a government, as long as one can see some definite limit to how much the state is willing to concede in such a case. If a period of time must elapse, however, before this limit is identified, doubts will arise as to whether the state will even be able to thwart physically such attacks or to reject them when they have become contests of resolve.

If ambassadors are the objects of kidnapping attempts abroad, is there anything that the government can do to shield them more effectively against such imprisonment in the first place. Or will all bodyguard arrangements ultimately be breached? If such important persons are taken hostage, will there be any circumstances in which the state can at last reject the demands made in exchange for the hostages release, so as to avoid encouraging still more such kidnappings?

A "solution" of simply tolerating and "living with" such terrorist tactics will not strike most citizens as bearable. If we simply decided to "grin and bear it," huddling out of the line of fire of terrorist offensives, life might become altogether constricted, and law and order too confined. Rather, the sense of most people is to look for as early a reassurance as possible that such terrorist attacks are being hemmed in and contained.

Society could, of course, reduce the incidence of terrorism simply by giving up the parts of technology that have proven most vulnerable to the attacker. Yet the price of this would also strike many as altogether too great in terms of material sacrifice.

Additionally, we could consider a redistribution of wealth and political influence so that the grievances of society were more evenly spread, so that the poor would not feel driven to such tactics by their resentment of the rich. Again, the vested interests would oppose the material sacrifice, but this is not the only problem. I believe that such redistribution could not by itself stamp out terrorism. Deprivation is not the only motive which has driven people throughout history to try to impose their will upon the rest of society by threats of physical violence. Recourse to terrorism reflects a combination of motives and opportunities.

The motives thus might never be totally eliminated, no matter what the reform of society, the opportunities for terrorism, if anything would threaten to increase. And as if the array of weapons currently at the terrorist's disposal is not fearsome enough a future wave can be visualized that may be a quantum jump more terrifying. What will the world be like if nuclear weapons slip into the hands of groups with similar motivations? Even short of this, what can we expect when modern precision guided missiles (PGM) appear more and more into the catalogues of weapons sold to substate political movements? It is on these possibilities that an individual might perhaps want to base a bet that opportunities rather than intentions may be more determining in the future than in the present.

Is there any society in the world that even today would not have to fear the uses to which dynamite, letter bombs, high-powered rifles, and hand grenades might be put, if they were not forbidden or countered? As one ranges from the United States to Sweden to Albania to Cuba to Vietnam, or to anywhere else, the threat of terrorism that springs from such simple availability weapons remains. The police states of this world (some of which also purport to be the most egalitarian of societies) in the end solve their terrorism problem by making the possession of guns and bombs more difficult.

Why then have we seen a particular upsurge of terrorism since 1960? An observer of a theoretical bent different from my own would point to the boiling over of the frustrations and social injustices that had remained from before World War II, indicating that the world was overdue for revolution. The approach here, in explaining the current wave of terrorism as well as some earlier waves would point rather to the increasing fragility of many of the physical arrangements upon which we depend. The mere invention of dynamite facilitated and thus set the stage for the earlier waves of terrorist attack, and the dissemination of the pistol made assassinations easier. Airplanes today are more fragile and vulnerable than buses, and thus lend themselves more to hijackings and seizures of hostages. The improvement of rifles with telescopic sights, and the continued development of smaller and smaller explosive devices, deliverable by mail, continues the trend. The increasing dependence of society on electricity generated in fragile power plants and transmitted on vulnerable lines offers a further target for attack.

The vulnerability of society is also expanded by social and political developments, as the respect shown for human life has indeed increased for much of the Western and industrialized world. The greater investments we make in medical devices keeping patients alive illustrate this, as does the abolition of the death penality in large segments of our society. This concern for human life obviously handicaps a regime when bargaining with anyone threatening such life. The new ability of the news media to transmit a direct view of the plight of such hostages, and of the anxiety of their relatives, makes it all the more difficult for a state authority to pretend to be indifferent to hostages' safety. And the absence of the death penalty conversely suggests that a convicted terrorist will always then serve as an incentive for his comrades to capture new hostages somewhere else, in a campaign to release him.

SOME ISSUES OF DEFINITION

Most discussions of terrorism thus far have pertained to individuals and underground groups, operating from the position of guerrillas against a more powerful state authority. Yet many students of the subject would see moral or definitional reasons to expand the term to include state terror as well.

What would be the advantages, or disadvantages, of including "state terror" in our concept of "terrorism"? Some advantages are clear. We do not wish to seem morally disapproving only of underground terrorism, while sanctioning the activities of the Gestapo in Nazi Germany. The word "terror" (as apart from "terrorism") has indeed been used quite often to refer to the techniques used by the Nazi regime, or by Stalin in the same years, or by Pol Pot or the Brazilian regime in more recent times, or by Robespierre almost two centuries ago. Terror is a straightforward enough word denoting fear, and political movements, government or underground, are prone to apply fear. The American and British bombings of World War II and the earlier German bombings were widely interpreted as intended to instill such terror.

Yet it will be argued here that "terrorism" is something more special. If a friend had asked me a year ago for the principal news item of the day and I had wanted to tell him that the feature story concerned the techniques of the Pol Pot regime in Kampuchea, I would have been misleading him by responding that "there's a lot of terrorism in the news," for he would immediately have concluded that something else had happened, something involving an underground group rather than a regime in control. This would not have reflected any moral judgment on his part, for we both might have disapproved more of the Pol Pot performance than of any underground bombings or skyjackings. It would simply have shown that we had identified a discrete phenomenon, one that has its own reasons for increasing or decreasing in volume, one that should not be confused with some other things that also worry us.

The following stricter, and narrower, definition is proposed as indeed according with our intuitions. It will be aligned with two distinctions.

All of warfare, of any form, can usefully be characterized by what is attacked, on a spectrum from "counter-force" to "counter-value" operations. The former are operations solely or primarily intended to cripple an enemy, to attack and eliminate his ability to fight. The latter are primarily intended to inflict pain on an enemy, to make him sorry he is in the war and reluctant to continue, even if his physical ability to fight is in no way impaired by the attack. The distinction between counter-force and counter-value applies currently to targeting doctrines for a nuclear war, it has applied to land and naval warfare in the past, and it will refer to what we now mean by terrorism.

All of warfare can also be distinguished by whether or not something is being defended. Ordinary warfare sees a military force throwing up a line and declaring that the enemy "shall not pass," so that what is behind that line will be kept under one's own sovereignty, with its economy functioning along normal lines. Guerrilla warfare, by contrast, dispenses with this defense, thereby losing the ability to maintain a national capital, to receive a diplomatic corps, to maintain hospitals and power plants, but gaining the advantage that the enemy does not know at whom to shoot. At sea, submarine warfare has been of the guerrilla mode, as was pirateering and piracy in the past.

What, then, is terrorism in terms of these distinctions? It is the confluence of the two, being a counter-value campaign in terms of what is attacked (things that hurt rather than things that incapacitate), and a guerrilla campaign in terms of what is being defended (for the moment, nothing).

Guerrilla operations can be conducted in a rural or in an urban environment. Some people believe that guerrillas are tempted to shift more and more into counter-value attacks (into "terrorism") as they move into the urban sector. The guerrilla ambush in the countryside can often have counter-force success in suddenly outnumbering and incapacitating a government battalion, etc. In the built-up areas of an industrialized society, however, the opportunities to win such military results in a guerrilla campaign are more limited. Assassinating a president or a key police chief or blowing up an army munitions dump would belong in this category, crippling the regime's ability to function, but success will more often go to the guerrillas by attacks designed to inflict pain rather than to disable, to inflict pain and thereby win concessions from the regime.

In implying a criticism of such tactics, we always risk sounding as if we were morally endorsing the law and order of all existing regimes. Without writing a continually balanced essay on "eliminating the terrorist opportunity and the tyrannical opportunity," it is hard to avoid such accusations.

It should be clear, however, that some of the examples of terrorism cited will have been carried out by forces with which the author or the reader indeed sympathizes, whether they comprise individuals trying to escape the Soviet Union or Cuba by hijacking an airliner, or showing their disapproval of a tyrannical government elsewhere in the world by detonating a bomb to discourage tourism. Consequently, terrorist tactics are hardly limited to the service of causes of which we disapprove. Yet the difficulty may also be that they are not limited to the causes we favor.

One kind of objection to terrorist methods would thus pertain to any form of military operation that threatens to be, or is, counter-value in that the damage to bystanders and nonmilitary targets in such a campaign is substantially increased. One does not know how much to make of this objection, however, for it applies equally to a great deal of warfare, to aerial bombing campaigns, to blockades, etc..

A second objection might be more serious, namely, that terrorist methods may become materially too easy, may require too little in the way of national backing or popular support to be deployed. If too many different groups can use such approaches, sometimes with two or more opposed groups applying such techniques quite effectively in the same space at the same time, we then have a mode of violence which enfranchizes even the most marginal group that is discontent with the peace of the status quo.

As is also true with guerrilla warfare more generally, even the types which are more typically counter-force out in the countryside, it might be a great mistake to exaggerate the degrees of popular backing and popular discontent that are required for (and thus proven by) such terrorist campaigns. To leave a bomb in La Guardia Airport may show little or nothing about how the residents of New York feel about their government, and it may mainly show that bombs are becoming too easy to acquire or make.

SOME HOPES FOR CONTAINMENT

Bombs left randomly in market places, diplomats held for ransom, and hijacked airliners, all basically fall into this counter-value, "terrorist" category. The concessions we make to free hostages, or to put an end to bombings may sometimes seem minor but they may indeed become quite major if they help erode the entire structure of society's commitments to rules and regimes.

Yet even as things stand, the picture for our society may never be quite as hopeless as all this sometimes suggests. The terrorism of hostage taking does not sweep all before it outmoding all laws and taking over governments. There are definite limits to how much society must give in to these tactics as they are introduced. The goal of the remainder of this chapter is thus to explore the nature and explanation of these limits as they take effect.

Some tendencies toward terror clearly stem from example, as the first group to use a new tactic demonstrates to others how it is to be applied. The past waves of bombings or of assassination attempts on statesmen, and the more recent waves of skyjackings, thus may not really show any particular groundswells of discontent, since the incidents were obviously not independent of each other, stemming only from a single basic source, but were rather inspired in a series, as the example of the first was reported around the globe.

It is important that we in the West remember when the precedents for some terrorist tactics were set. The first bombs dispatched by mail in the Middle East conflict were not directed against supporters of Israel, but were mailed by supporters of Israel to German scientists working for Nasser in Cairo. The first skyjackings involving Cuba did not come from people wanting to go to Havana, but from those wanting to escape Castro's regime who forced Cuban airliners to come to New York.

Once the idea for a good terrorist approach is known, it can be applied anywhere on the globe where similar situations of vulnerability exist. It will then take some time for counter-ideas to be developed to blunt such attacks and to be similarly spread around the world.

As social scientists we may even have occasionally felt an injunction to hold back speculation about techniques in this area, lest we create a problem without first developing an antidote. Some arms-control analysts in the 1950s apparently hit upon the idea of skyjacking, and decided to avoid publishing discussions of it lest their analyses become self-confirming. Discussions of terrorism utilizing nuclear weapons were under a similar sort of injunction until five years ago.

As the new technological possibilities of terrorism spread, with the prospect that any successful attack will be publicized and soon replicated elsewhere, where is the counter-wave of innovation to come from? It is probably not beyond reach.

We are hardly alone in worrying about the possibilities of terrorism. Whatever the faults of any particular society, there are enormous numbers of people in every society who welcome some regularity and law and order in their lives, who also have a vested interest in seeing these tactics of the terrorist offensive not become so powerful.

Not the least of these with a vested interest in blunting this offensive are, of course, the police officers of the world, whose horror at the prospect of terrorism is reinforced by the bureaucratic career-promotion incentive. Policemen, in effect, sell a service called law and order. To sell it, they must demonstrate that it can still be indeed delivered. We allocate tax monies to those segments of the public sector that seem to have demonstrated and proven themselves. Whatever ingenuity the terrorists thus put into their campaigns will at least call forth some counter-ingenuity by those whose whole professional status and way of life is threatened.

If we have established that we will hardly be alone in our alarm about the potential power of terrorist blackmail, what assurance do we have that the counter-terror coalition will have any means of containing this menace? After viewing one blatant example after another of terrorist or guerrilla tactics embarrassing the government forces, of terrorist demands being cravenly surrendered to, where indeed are the lines of the new firebreak, the lines to which we can retreat for some security?

ORDINARY PHYSICAL PRECAUTIONS

The first part of a logical response to terrorism might of course simply be to fall back on the physical structures that make kidnappings and assassinations and skyjackings and bank robberies less possible. The police have all along been urging us to install better locks, as have the companies that produce the locks, and we as consumers may feel impelled now to accept this advice. Terrorism and criminality may come and go in waves, matched by waves of defensive investment and relaxation, but some kinds of protection, once installed, will remain in place for good. As a most dramatic illustration of this straightforward "physical" approach, we see the devices now installed at airports of the world to keep weapons from being brought on board aircraft. Another example is the Secret Service protection given American presidents, reluctantly accepted at first, now a standard operating procedure.

Beyond better locks and barricades, of course, police
forces have also been investing in better "offensive" weapons
for the hostage situation. They have particularly devoted
more effort to training sharpshooters who might, when the
opportunity arises, kill or incapacitate the hostage taker with
relatively low risk to the hostage. Hostages are undeniably
exposed thereby to some danger but the danger is still much
less than if the police were to take no notice of the hostages'
plight while apprehending the criminals involved.

Such physical safeguards may work imperfectly, but they
will still impose uncertainties on potential attackers which will
often deter terrorist attack. Can terrorists know for sure
that there will be hostages they can seize in a bank robbery if
the police should appear? Enough can still go wrong with this
possibility so that bank robberies will not become ridiculously
simple, so that the entire financial and political structure will
not be toppled. Similarly kidnappers still inevitably run some
chance of being caught, even when the police are bound not to
begin their pursuit until after the victim has been released.
Part of our prescription for a response to terrorism will thus
just be "more of the same" in police protection and physical
safeguards. This will hardly eliminate terrorism altogether,
but it will serve as part of the explanation as to why terrorism is not simply an open-ended ticket to financial or
political success.

PSYCHOLOGICAL TOUGHENING-UP

But our hopes are not limited to the random possibility of
something "going wrong" in a terrorist plot, for we have not
yet really begun to probe the inherent logic of the kinds of
blackmail which now plague society. Society cares a great deal
about human life; the political kidnapper plays on this by
pretending to be indifferent to the welfare of the diplomat or
bank patrons or planeload of passengers he or she holds.

Can society simply eliminate this advantage for the
terrorist by quickly "toughening up" and brainwashing all of
us to become more indifferent to the lives of these innocent
persons? The answer, happily, is no. Most of us would
worry about a society in which the regime could so easily
reverse major moral trends. Our increasingly humane concerns
for the welfare of helpless individual hostages may be a
problem in repulsing terrorists, but these concerns nonetheless
reflect a trend toward greater decency in general, a trend we
would not want reversed.

Yet again the outcome is not that society is endlessly
vulnerable to the exploitation of its decency. Even if we at
times cannot see the limit, there is most probably a limit to the

political concessions any society will be willing to make for the
safety of hostages. As the demands of terrorists increase, the
public begins to attach more significance to precedent, and
less to the safety of the immediate victim.

We are all human beings, humane, but we are also subjective and fallible. We grieve more about a hostage than about
someone already murdered, if only because our attention is
captured for a longer time in the continuing case of the
hostage. Even here some of our moral concern is less logical
than psychological. A part of our attentiveness, moreover,
also depends on the sheer novelty of the hostage situation.
What if such crimes occurred with the frequency of auto accidents, which also often cause death, which also are often the
direct result of crimes? Our attention, and the attention of
the news media that reflect our attentiveness, would fade soon
enough, and with it some of the psychic costs of the hostage's
fate.

Moreover, long before a society's willingness to capitulate
has been exhausted some other basic strategic steps tend to be
taken. Societies, like individuals, can cultivate a false
impression that they are tougher and less susceptible to
pressure than they really are. If the regime and the police
force cannot brainwash the general public into becoming truly
indifferent to the plight of hostages, there can nonetheless be
a societal conspiracy to make the concerns less obvious, to
match terrorist threats and terrorist bluffs with societal
threats and bluffs.

Police officials can, moreover, be clever and innovative in
setting up new sets of alternatives, so that the hostage taker
can no longer be so sure that society will always want to make
concessions. For a first illustration of all such tendencies,
one can look at the practice of a number of American police
departments in hostage situations. The practice now is neither
to attack the building in which the hostages are being held
nor to allow the criminal to depart with them, but merely to
wait out the criminal in a state of siege. Hostages held by
terrorists or bank robbers are then, in effect, a wasting
asset. Do the terrorists dare let the cumulative damage,
physical and psychological, to their hostage become so great
that the terrorists lose their ability to deter the police? Or
must they surrender before that, to escape the hail of bullets
of a final police assault on the building? The police assuredly
are taking risks and playing games with the safety of the
hostages in these circumstances. Yet the public tolerates it
because of its incremental nature, because there is no clear
police initiative in itself posing a direct threat to the hostages'
well-being.

MANAGING THE NEWS

Our generation grieves more than earlier ones would have for
hostages, we are more "humane" about their welfare; this is
why the taking of such hostages is "news." As in the case of
political demonstrations and urban riots, some would blame the
news media for inducing the events in the first place, by
serving as vehicles for attracting attention. Suggestions have
been offered for forbidding the publications of news on politically inspired kidnappings and highjackings. In a nation
that prides itself on its freedom of the press, such restrictions
would be a very dear price to pay for the reduction of terrorist leverage over society. A free press cannot remain free
if it is used by terrorist groups to convey anti-government
slogans.

However a free press is not likely to become a tool of
terrorists: perhaps the public's and press's attention can now
be exploited in 20 hostage situations a year, but it cannot be
exploited in 60. Familiarity breeds disinterest. Taking press
coverage alone, one might predict a stable but contained level
of political violence, beyond which the returns of attention of
political influence would quickly begin to diminish.

One sees a powerful argument for an unhampered press in
the experience of some Latin American countries; diplomats
have been kidnapped simply to force the government to publish
the revolutionary manifestos that could not otherwise have
been printed. Where criticism of the government is more
generally legal and possible, the incentive to resort to
terrorism for this specific purpose fades considerably.

Society's resistance rebuffs terrorist attacks by exploiting
the real limits of its concern for hostage safety in some cases,
and by feigning an indifference to such safety in others. A
valuable example can be extracted from the construction of a
new bank in southern California. All communication between
customers and tellers in the new building is now by closed
circuit television. For all the customer or would-be bank
robber knows, the tellers could be miles away in a different
building, hence making the dynamiting of a bank a less-potent
threat, since no bank personnel are obviously at hand to be
threatened by the explosion. But what if the threat is simply
redirected at some innocent depositors who unfortunately happen to be in the bank at the time of the robbery? The bank
has an answer for this, too. As soon as a robbery is announced, all the lights and television screens are turned off,
creating the impression that the management has lost all
interest in, and information about, what is occurring at its
bank. If in truth the cameras are still recording the fate of
the innocent hostages, the hostage takers for the moment have
no way of verifying this.

Quite apart from bank managements, the political leaders of countries have historically proven themselves adept at "tuning out" in a similar way when their concern would prove to be a bargaining handicap if visible to the opponent. Governor Rockefeller's decision to stay some distance away from the prison riot at Attica was clearly an effort to avoid strengthening the hand of the prisoners who were holding the prison guards as hostages. Kaiser Wilhelm's decision to go ahead with his yacht cruise in the summer of 1914 may have been a similar ploy during the crisis prior to World War I.

If we all disapprove of any state efforts to control or suppress the information media during a terrorist maneuver, the state can at least avoid allowing itself to become a tool of the terrorists via the media. News should not be suppressed but it should not unnecessarily be made either.

THE CONTEST OF MOMENTUM

An important part of any such contest of resolve between government and terrorists depends on who will be bluffing most demonstrably. Each side may for the short time have to do things it would prefer not to do to avoid giving the other opportunities to exploit preferences to its advantage. Not only will there be pretenses of indifference to the costs of the contest, but even retaliations that are like "cutting off your nose to spite your face," to impose the desired responses on one's adversary. An important part of such a game will depend on whether either party can communicate a sense of momentum, a sequence of some earlier steps that prove malicious retaliatory propensities in the latter stages.

For example, holding a plane full of hostages on the ground may give a terrorist much more leverage than planting a radio-controlled bomb to be detonated when the plane is airborne. In the latter case, if the terrorist's bluff is called, the game is over either way; he can carry through with this threat to blow up the plane, and collect no ransom, or he can fail to carry through with it. In the former case (as happened once with a plane sitting on a runway in Tunisia), the terrorist might kill one passenger first to prove his resolve, and then a second passenger, and so forth still leaving enough hostages unharmed to continue as the focus of the government's anxieties.

As a parallel case, it might do little good for a terrorist group to acquire one atomic bomb; having several, though, it could detonate one if the government had decided to take its chances by ignoring the demands, and then presumably could begin winning concessions when the government saw the inexorable trend of events. As a demonstration of the reasoning that may make a repeat capacity crucial for this kind of nuclear terrorism, apparently there have already been a number of nuclear threats directed against various cities in the United States. In every case, the demand for a cash ransom payment was ignored. In every case, apparently, the threat was a hoax. One might also recall that two atomic bomb attacks were required to drive Japan to surrender in World War II, not one.

Yet it is obviously not only the terrorist who might be capable of aligning some resources to present a continuing and repeatable threat, i.e., to develop some momentum. All in all, the state will be far more capable of this since it has more resources to deploy. Law, after all, may be nothing more than the state doing for the short run what it doesn't want to do as part of developing a pattern of predictable responses that deter for the longer run.

Where the process is orderly enough, the credibility of the state in this mode of behavior has been fairly high. The state is not always being simply vindictive, of course, for to lock up confirmed criminals is to shield oneself against further crimes, and to collect traffic fines may help balance a small town's budget. Yet many of the penalties imposed amount to an immediate loss of public utility, as when a father of five children must be sent to jail after having been convicted of embezzlement. Here there is no need to jail the individual to protect society, and society would draw greater material profit if the man were allowed to take on some other job to support his family. Rather, the state is acting punitively against the man and against itself as a method to establish a deterring precedent for future crimes.

THE THRESHOLDS OF RESOLVE

Recent events have produced expressions of nostalgic fondness for an earlier day when states supposedly displayed a steely moral resolve and never paid blackmail to shield privileged humans. Frederick the Great's instructions were indeed quite categorical that no ransom was ever to be paid if he should be taken prisoner, a practice in striking contrast to the concessions made to the Baader-Meinhof Gang after the 1974 kidnapping of the CDU candidate for mayor in West Berlin. Japan's attitude toward the fate of any Japanese soldiers taken prisoner during World War II may have approached this, again in contrast with the much greater and more obvious concern for the safety of Japanese diplomats falling into terrorist custody today.

Perhaps this simply shows that rulers and diplomats are more valuable today than before, as the election process

results in persons with mandates clearer than that of Frederick
the Great. Governance in the days of monarchy was by proprietary right, with a well-established succession following the
terms of the proprietary arrangements; taking one's chances
under such circumstances might simply reflect fulfilling
obligations to the family, with little damage to the workings of
the state. Quite apart from this, of course, Germany has
become more generally humane a place in the era of Baader-
Meinhof, and Japan confronting the Red Army Faction in 1975
has become more humane than it was in 1941. At the same
time kidnapping and associated terrorist tactics have become
more prevalent than at any recent time in the past; as a
relatively "new thing," such kidnapping may not yet have
betrayed the counters to which it is vulnerable.

One country attempting to maintain the older standard is
Israel, which has repeatedly and fairly consistently risked the
lives of hostages to set the grander precedent of giving no
encouragement to the hostage takers. Israel may be more
humane than Frederick's Prussia, but at the same time it is
more clearly threatened on the foreign policy front, with the
final outcome producing the same state tactic.

Some commentators have similarly proposed the passage of
general laws forbidding anyone to pay ransom to kidnappers,
by anyone, no matter what the situation. Not all laws are
enforced, of course, and the risk is great that the first
violation of this law in seemingly compassionate circumstances
would go unprosecuted. However much such a statute might
contribute to discouraging kidnapping, the costs of seeing
worried parents punished in such a case would probably be too
much for a society to bear. But surely if the number of
"ordinary" kidnappings for simple monetary ransom were to
double or triple, society's attitudes on such a law would
change quickly enough, such that payers of ransom would
indeed begin to be prosecuted. There is a finite and limited
amount of kidnapping that society will tolerate before it begins
to strike a new balance in its humanistic equation.

Society has long faced similar problems in combatting the
technique of the hunger strike, in which the political activist
in effect uses himself as the hostage. In some instances, the
state has been clever or diabolical enough to devise methods of
force-feeding, which keep the adversary from committing the
suicide he seeks and turn the technique of political endurance
totally around, as the hunger striker is shown to be incapable
of fulfilling his threats. When such force-feeding techniques
are not possible, the state, of course, might yet steel itself to
the sacrifice of letting some hunger strikers die, in hopes that
the precedent would discourage the tactic soon enough to keep
the losses from becoming politically and socially unbearable.

A parallel choice appears in the all-night gas stations
where employees immediately deposit all receipts in vaults that

cannot be opened until morning. If a gunman threatens to kill the attendants unless money is handed over, there will still be no way for anyone to give in to the threat. Perhaps a few attendants will be killed as the gunmen vent their frustration and rage, but not many will be, and the number of holdups goes down.

PACTS NOT TO BE HONORED

A substantially different range of tactics for the state emerges when one begins to question the state's obligation to keep any pledge it makes while under the duress of the hostage situation. We normally wish our governments and rulers to keep any promises they offer in public; much of what is regular in law and order depends on this.

What the state can nonetheless do is categorically announce in advance that it will never consider itself bound by any promises made under the kinds of duress implicit in the hostage situation, i.e., that it will make every promise demanded but not necessarily keep any of them. If thus denied the option of relying upon the government's habit of keeping its word, the hostage taker will be forced to hold on to his hostages in all situations until he can receive "payment in advance" on his demands; this will increase the discomfort and peril to the hostages in many situations, but at the same time it is likely to make the technique of hostage taking seem less effective. As noted earlier, the hostage is a wasting asset while held in captivity in a position of deteriorating health and well-being. In some cases, this technique will produce an earlier surrender by the kidnappers, lest the fate of the hostages come so much into doubt that the police are no longer deterred from storming the place in which they are held.

When we revert to discussing the status quo, many might note that police behavior is already employing this type of deception. In the tragic incident of the Israeli athletes at Munich, for example, the German government had brought sharpshooters to the Furstenfeldbruck Airport despite an implicit promise that the Palestinian terrorists would be allowed to make their escape holding their hostages. Yet the position of the state on these matters might well be clarified in both directions. Rather than allow the public to think of their police in general as increasingly duplicitous, it might be well for the state clearly to delineate the ordinary circumstances under which its word is to be taken seriously, and the terror-hostage situations in which it will not feel bound. The police should establish a clear precedent and habit of "promise them anything" in the hostage situation, with no link between this and the solemnity of the ordinary true promise.

As with the other techniques discussed, this avenue will complicate the task of those who care only about saving the lives of the hostages; yet the point here is again that more complicated motives will take hold soon enough, indeed have already taken hold, with the likelihood that the impact of terrorists' tactics will be circumscribed.

FORCING SYMMETRY ON TO THE TERRORIST

Some people argue that the terrorist group can counter the "broken promise" ploy easily enough simply by demanding secure access to the ultimate point of sanctuary before releasing the hostages. Yet even here the state will win some important points, if it in the process constrains the terrorists to identify openly the territory to which they must "belong." Simply disappearing into the depths of a city is much safer than having to find a home in Cuba or Libya or Yemen. The country that offers sanctuary must accept that its territorial identity lays it open to various kinds of retaliation, not excluding terrorism, as a counter-weapon. The absense of a populated territory with which one is identified (the absence, in effect, of some vulnerable hostages for counteraction) has been all along an important asset for guerrillas and terrorists. When they are forced to fall back on the prop of the sanctuary, some of this asset has been whittled away.

When groups want only to win the trappings of statehood, as may be true with the Palestinian desires for sovereignty over "Palestine," we can hope that the terrorists might thus be domesticated soon enough, as a consequence of winning their major demands. It is less clear, however, what "sovereignty" groups like the Baader-Meinhof gang aspire to; granting them access and control over any piece of territory might not end their felt need for terrorist activity, and it might indeed be an embarrassment for them. It is precisely this kind of embarrassment that state tactics can most profitably try to impose on such groups not by granting them territory, but by forcing them to need the amenities and protections that only territory can offer.

Some might argue that the concessions currently made to convicted PLO terrorists simply amount to the "exchange of prisoners of war" or "diplomatic immunity" to which we are accustomed in the normal international scene. Yet the exemptions and privileges of formalized diplomacy are much more symmetrical in style and impact than what we seem to be witnessing between the British Army and the IRA, or between the French government and the PLO. When both sides have territory there will be symmetry. If Libya repeatedly offers itself as comfortable sanctuary for those seizing diplomats, Libya after all has some diplomats of its own out on the international circuit. One would not have to see the Jewish Defense League as a conscious arm of Israeli policy to conclude that terrorism against Arab or Cuban officials is not an impossibility.

TRANSFERS OF MONEY

Anonymity has generally helped the guerrilla and the terrorist, while any need for openness and publicity sometimes hurts. Terrorists need money, and here again the forces of society have begun to make some changes in regular practices that can frustrate terrorist activity and diminish its appeal as a tactic.

Even when the leverage of the terrorist seems enormous, there may still be problems, for example merely in delivering the huge ransoms. If the ransom is to be a huge amount in cash, the payment may simply be too bulky to facilitate anonymity and escape. Much more clearly this is true if any resort has to be made to banking systems as the mode of payment. The classic anonymity of the Swiss bank account was introduced in the 1930s to help Jewish refugees escaping from Hitler's Germany. More recently, such accounts have been used to shield the holdings and operations of criminal syndicates such as the Mafia. Whether the Swiss would long tolerate this criminal use of their system, [should organized crime begin operating within Switzerland itself] is open to doubt. Similarly in doubt is whether the Swiss would tolerate accounts by political terrorists in the wake of the operations that have plagued the world's airports, and whether outside powers would allow Switzerland to maintain such a system.

This must all be considered together with a larger-scale trend whereby the state harnesses computers and other intrusions into privacy to collect more and more information about all aspects of daily human life. Without for a moment denying that the latter "big brother" effect is largely undesirable per se, its seemingly inexorable growth again suggests some counter to the growth of terrorist power.

The terrorist organization can of course dispense with trying to collect monetary ransoms for itself, instead demanding a transfer of wealth to some worthy charity or to the poor at large. This was the approach of the SLA (Symbionese Liberation Army) after the kidnapping of Patricia Hearst, and it has also been used in the case of Argentinian kidnappings. Here, the state may find itself even more threatened and frustrated, since the diffusion and anonymity of such a "class action" will make it difficult to find targets against whom to retaliate.

At some outer extreme, the state might feel driven to legislate against such transfers of wealth, again parallel to

laws against the more straightforward payment of ordinary
blackmail, again quite difficult to enforce unless and until the
hostage-taking menace becomes more serious. Yet even if such
tactics and payments cannot be outlawed, the power impact for
the terrorist movement involved is not nearly as powerful as
when the cash is transferred directly into its hand. If the
poorer people of California welcomed the goods distributed as a
result of Patty Hearst's plight, they surely were astute
enough, given the common knowledge of the possibilities of
crime and extortion, not to attach very much broad political
and sociological significance to the coerced transfer. They did
not pledge their services and allegiances to the SLA. The
SLA surely would have extracted a greater punch from collect-
ing the cash itself; its subsequent decision to undertake
several bank robberies clearly illustrates how it would have
liked to acquire more direct control over monetary resources.

UNAVOIDABLE RISK SHARING AMONG VICTIMS

What amounts to a marginal concession by one government
could of course be a central push to surrender or defeat for
another. States look after themselves; the United States might
wash its hands of a regime in Vietnam while France or Austria
might feel no commitment to Israel. A policy of beggar-your-
neighbor, or of making concessions without concern for a
weaker member of the system, will hardly be aesthetically
attractive, but it shows up in politics often enough. It can be
condemned as immoral, but is not prima facie irrational. If
freedom is no longer thought to be indivisible, resistance to
terrorist attack may not be all of one piece either.
        Yet what does the weakest or most friendless state in the
system then do to keep itself from going under? We have
noted that Israel is more firm than other states in rejecting
concessions for hostage situations. It is simultaneously no
surprise that some of the fears concerning the open-ended
concessions we have discussed here are articulated more often
by Israelis, with particular reference to the attacks launched
by the PLO. It might be easy to document that Zionist terrorists once were engaged in similar activities. Yet, that is
well back into the past. Today it is easy to document that
French and other governments are making concessions to Arab
terrorist groups that Israel would not make itself, concessions
that might well be seen as establishing a threat to Israel's
continued existence.
        What can a country like Israel do to avoid bearing an
unfair share of the burden of terrorism? It can remonstrate
with the governments of West European countries as to the
shallowness of their morality where law and order are con-

cerned. If realpolitik governs international behavior as much
as many of us fear, however, this will only have some marginal
effect. Much more promising are the developments that naturally force the other governments of the world simply to share
the burdens of terrorism, and thus to allocate additional
resources to resisting and combatting it, whether they want to
or not.

Perhaps the Palestinian terrorist at the Rome airport will
desire to inflict damage only on airplanes bound for Tel Aviv.
But his example may embolden someone else to inflict similar
destruction on planes bound for Belgrade, or for Milan.
Although generalized morality might not spare Israel from
suffering by itself, generalized vulnerability may yet find
allies for Israel - reluctant allies, but allies nonetheless. The
Paris and Zurich airports may have been forced to become
armed camps because of the Palestinians, but they will notably
be compelled to remain so in the future because of some other
group.

In this connection, it may be very important for Israelis
and others confronted by terrorist attacks to remember that
they have a natural ally in the police forces of the world. All
such forces are upset and embarrassed by the incidence of
terrorism. In terms of simple bureaucratic politics, an
acceptance of terrorism is a menace to their careers. If the
Israeli government feels tempted to resort to extralegal means
of retaliation, perhaps with terrorist strikes of its own in the
cities of Europe and America, it loses itself a powerful source
of support, for it then begins to pose the same menace that
the PLO poses to police respectability. Even if European
governments bend over backwards at the cabinet level to avoid
seeming too pro-Israel, the officials who run their police forces
will for the moment have to be functionally pro-Israel, in the
very nature of being antiterrorist.

INTERGOVERNMENTAL ACCORD

Terrorism, like guerrilla warfare in general, requires a
sanctuary, or a secure rear area to which the insurgents can
flee when superior forces are pursuing them. A clear avenue
of solution might therefore be to try to get every country on
earth to join in opposing such tactics, on the premise that all
of law and order is threatened at once when terrorism is not
rebuffed and convincingly punished.

In some sense we might be quite impressed with the degree of international consensus that has been achieved here.
The Chinese, who might have passed for the most radical
regime on the globe 15 years ago, made it clear very early
that they would not be hospitable to skyjackers bringing

344 THE MORALITY OF TERRORISM

captured aircraft to Chinese airports, sometimes forcing the skyjacker to apologize to the passengers involved and then giving him a tour of hard labor in the countryside.

Showing great fear of what terrorist tactics might achieve in the context of the ethnic and political dissent within its own area of control, the Soviet regime has similarly shown a general disapproval of such tactics, but with some occasional slips. One might venture the guess that the KGB is able to escape central control about as much as our own CIA is, thus remaining free to dabble from time to time with some of the less predictable and acceptable political factions of the world. Any secret intelligence service worth its name is likely to invite every new political force to dinner on occasion, just on the possibility that there may be a payoff of information or influence over the longer run. The reports that Soviet money found its way to the Baader-Meinhof gang and that Italian terrorists have spent time in Czechoslovakia probably prove no more of a departure than this from the general Soviet aversion to terrorism.

The Castro regime, after long tolerating the skyjacking of airliners by American dissidents coming to Cuba (perhaps understandably in terms of the original precedents for this technique), then changed its stance dramatically, possibly because the international image of such tolerance of terrorist tactics was becoming very negative. Similarly, Algeria went through a phase of serving as a haven for such terrorists and then became less supportive in light of world attitudes.

The impact of only one or two holdouts, however, illustrates an important technological point here, namely that the increased range of transport aircraft has left the terrorist free to exploit sanctuary possibilities at very long distance. It may consequently take "only one rotten apple to spoil the bunch," to upset future efforts to stamp out terrorism by international agreement.

The governments and citizens in the West are also periodically embarrassed to discover that people with whom we very much sympathize can use the same skyjacking tactic to try to escape from the Soviet Union and other Marxist-governed regimes. (Again, we must remember the original Cuban linkage to this tactic.) What are we to do when a young Russian or Czech seizes control of an airliner to make his escape to Munich or Stockholm? Can we be content with a simple response of returning him to the tender mercies of the Soviet or Czech police?

For one apparent solution, we have developed the formula of "extradite or imprison." Rather than send these fugitives from Communism back to a Communist-governed country, we might show our displeasure with the means used for this escape by sentencing them to some reasonable term in a prison in West Germany or Sweden. While this solution might strike many as reasonable, some important flaws remain in it, stemming from the elementary differences between the societies on the two sides of the iron curtain.

First, would a Russian really be deterred by the prospect of serving time in the Swedish prison system, the model for the world in terms of humane treatment and of serious effort to rehabilitate rather than simply to punish? If word about this got back to the Soviet Union, serious problems could arise: life in a Stockholm prison might well look nicer to the Soviets than life in the USSR in general. Yet we surely cannot ask the Swedes, as a matter of their international duty to law and order, to reintroduce an element of sadism into their penal system.

Second, the very reasons for skyjacking from the Soviet side will make some of us inconsistently sympathetic to the tactic when used by refugees from Communism. A dissident in West Germany or the United States or Japan does not need to threaten the passengers of an airliner to reach China or the USSR or Algeria or anywhere else, for he or she is altogether free to travel. It is mostly in the Communist countries that the right to show disapproval by emigrating is routinely denied.

SOME CONCLUSIONS

In all of its ramifications, the problem of terrorist challenge and state response is probably too often portrayed as a once-and-for-all moral contest. "Either a state proves it has moral backbone, or it fails." So the logic would go. The argument here has been quite different. States and societies do what they want to do, which often enough will displease social commentators or neighboring states, but which at the same time may hardly spell ultimate doom or ultimate surrender in all subsequent contests of resolve. If Chancellor Kreisky's closing of the camp for Jewish emigrants from the USSR signalled a willingness to give in to terrorism, we do not yet know that this willingness will extend to the very heart of law and order and civilization in Austria in general. Most probably it will not. Some surrenders to threat are total, as was the failure of Czechoslovakia to resist the Russian invasion in 1968; others are less than total, as fences are mended, and new firebreaks are cut.

We should return then to our basic question at the start. "Why be so appalled at terrorism?" Perhaps the reason to be appalled is indeed not that society and law are in danger. We roll with the punch of terrorist attacks, and society carries on. If assassination threatens our presidents, we make do by setting forth the succession to the office more carefully and explicitly. Some good men are scared away from seeking the office, but other good candidates remain. If prisoners must occasionally be released because of an unusual sensitivity in a hostage situation, we toughen up to avoid having to release prisoners the next time. Perhaps the real cause for worry is much more analogous to the auto accidents to which comparison was made. It is simply a major nuisance to have to dodge bombs or to have to fear kidnapping.

It is true that the physical destruction incurred on the highways of Israel or the United States remains far greater than that caused by terrorists of any denomination. For perfectly rational explanations, however, the fear surrounding terrorist possibilities has to be greater than that of auto accidents. We are not confronted by calculating antagonistic human beings who want to have accidents; but our adversaries in terrorist cases indeed mean to do us harm.

Terrorism is thus a major nuisance rather than a minor one. As with other nuisances, the purpose of social policy will be to see that it is contained. If the costs of tolerating the terrorist possibility become too high, other costs will be paid to reduce the risk. It may never be reduced to zero, but a reduction to zero is not possible with any of the other nuisances either.

Selected Bibliography

Alexander, Yonah. The Role of Communications in the Middle East Conflict: Ideological and Religious Aspects. New York: Praeger, 1973.

Alexander, Yonah, Browne, Narforie Ann and Names, Allan S., eds. Control of Terrorism. New York: Crane, Russak, 1979.

Alexander, Yonah, Carlton, David, and Wilkinson, Paul, eds. Terrorism: Theory and Practice. Boulder: Westview Press, 1979.

Alexander, Y. and Finger, S., eds. Terrorism: Interdisciplinary Perspectives. New York: John Jay Press, 1977.

Ali, Tariq, ed. The New Revolutionaries: A Handbook of the International Radical Left. New York: William Morrow, 1969.

Arendt, Hannah. Eichmann in Jerusalem: A Report on the Banality of Evil. New York: Viking Press, 1965.

_____. On Revolution. New York: Viking Press, 1963.

_____. On Violence. New York: Harcourt, Brace, 1969.

_____. The Origins of Totalitarianism. New York: Harcourt, Brace, 1951.

Aron, Raymond. Peace and War. London: Weidenfeld and Nicholson, 1966.

Avineri, Shlomo, ed. Israel and the Palestinians: Reflections on the Clash of the Two National Movements. New York: St. Martin's, 1971.

Avrich, Paul. The Russian Anarchists. Princeton: Princeton University Press, 1967.

347

Bassiouni, M. Cherif, ed. International Terrorism and Political Crimes. Springfield, Ill.: Thomas, 1975.

Becker, Jillian. Hitler's Children: The Story of the Baader-Meinhof Terrorist Gang. Philadelphia: Lippincott, 1977.

Begin, Menachem. The Revolt. Los Angeles: Nash, 1972.

Bell, J. Bowyer. The Secret Army: The IRA 1916-1974. Cambridge: MIT, 1974.

_____. On Revolt. Cambridge: Harvard University Press, 1976.

_____. Terror out of Zion: The Irgun, Lehi, Stern and the Palestine Underground. New York: St. Martin's, 1977.

_____. A Time of Terror: How Democratic Societies Respond to Revolutionary Violence. New York: Basic Books, 1978.

_____. Transnational Terror. Washington, D.C.: American Enterprise Institute, 1975.

Baumann, Bommi. Terror or Love? Bommi Baumann's Own Story of His Life as a West German Urban Guerrilla. New York: Grove Press, 1979.

Bienvenu, Richard T. The Ninth of Thermidor: The Fall of Robespierre. New York and London: Oxford University Press, 1968.

Billington, James H. Fire in the Minds of Men: Origins of the Revolutionary Faith. New York: Basic Books, 1980.

Black, Eyril E., and Thornton, Thomas P. Communism and Revolution. Princeton: Princeton University Press, 1964.

Bonino, Jose Miguez. Doing Theology in a Revolutionary Situation. Philadelphia: Fortress Press, 1975.

Brandon, S.G.F. Jesus and the Zealots. Manchester: Manchester University Press, 1967.

Brown, Robert McAfee. Theology in a New Key: Responding to Liberation Themes. Philadelphia: Westminster Press, 1978.

Brownlie, Ian. International Law and the Use of Force by States. Oxford: Clarendon Press, 1963.

Burton, Anthony M. Revolutionary Violence: The Theories. New York: Crane, Russak, 1978.

Butterfield, Herbert, and Wight, Martin, eds. Diplomatic Investigations. Cambridge: Harvard University Press, 1966.

Camara, Dom Helder. Revolution Through Peace, trans. Amparo Mclean. New York: Harper & Row, 1971.

_____. Spiral of Violence. Danville, N.J.: Dimension Books, 1971.

Camus, Albert. Caligula and Three Other Plays, Translated by Stuart Gilbert. New York: Vintage, 1958.

_____. Neither Victims Nor Executioners. Chicago: World Without War, 1968.

_____. The Rebel. New York: Vintage, 1954.

Canadian Council on International Law. International Terrorism: Proceedings of the Third Annual Conference Held at the University of Ottawa, Ottawa, Canada, October 18-19, 1974. Ottawa: Faculte de Droit de L'Universite d'Ottawa, 1974.

Chailand, Gerald. The Palestinian Resistance. Baltimore: Penguin, 1972.

Comblin, Jose. The Church and the National Security State. Maryknoll, New York: Orbis Books, 1979.

Conquest, Robert. The Great Terror: Stalin's Purge of the Thirties. New York: Macmillan, 1968.

Cranston, Maurice W. The New Left: Six Critical Essays on Che Guevara, Jean-Paul Sartre, Herbert Marcuse, Frantz Fanon, Black Power, R.D. Laing. New York: The Library Press, 1971.

Crelinsten, Ronald S. (Danielle, Denis, Laberge-Altmeja Szabo, eds.) Terrorism and Criminal Justice. Lexington: Lexington Books, 1978.

Crozier, Brian. Theory of Conflict. New York: Scribner, 1975.

Dallin, A. and G. Breslauer. Political Terror in Communist Systems. Stanford: Stanford University Press, 1970.

Davies, J.G. Christians, Politics and Violent Revolution. Maryknoll, N.Y.: Orbis Books, 1976.

Debray, R. Revolution on the Revolution. New York: Monthly Review Press, 1967.

DeQuincey, Thomas. Works. Boston: Houghton, Mifflin & Co., 1877.

Devlin, Bernadette. The Price of My Soul. New York, Knopf, 1969.

Dobson, Christopher. The Terrorists. New York: Facts on File Publications, 1979.

Draper, Theodore. Castro's Revolution: Myths and Realities. New York: Praeger, 1962.

Durrell, Lawrence. Bitter Lemons. London: Faber & Faber, 1957.

Dworkin, Ronald. Taking Rights Seriously. Cambridge: Harvard University Press, 1977.

Eckstein, Harry. Internal War. New York: Free Press of Glencoe, 1964.

Eliade, Mirea. Myth of the Eternal Return. New York: Pantheon, 1959.

Ellul, Jacques. Violence: Reflections From A Christian Perspective. New York: Seabury, 1969.

Essien-Udom, Essien. Black Nationalism: A Search for Identity in America. Chicago: University of Chicago Press, 1962.

Ettinger, Leon, and Strom, Axel. Morality and Morbidity After Excessive Stress. New York: Columbia University Press, 1976.

Evans, Alona and Murphy, John, eds. Legal Aspects of International Terrorism. Lexington: D.C. Heath & Co., 1978.

Evans, Earnst. Calling a Truce to Terror: The American Response to International Terrorism. Westport, Conn.: Greenwood Press, 1979.

Fanon, Frantz. The Wretched of the Earth. Harmondsworth: Penguin, 1967.

Farmer, W.R. Maccabees, Zealots and Josephus. New York: Columbia University Press, 1956.

Ferrero, G. Principles of Power. New York: G.P. Putnam's Sons, 1942.

Fierro, Alfred. The Militant Gospel: A Critical Introduction to Political Theologies. Translated by John Drury. Maryknoll, New York: Orbis Books, 1977.

Fleming, Marie. The Anarchist Way to Socialism. Totowa, New Jersey: Rowman and Littlefield, 1979.

Frank, Gerold. The Deed. New York: Simon and Schuster, 1963.

Friedlander, Robert. Terrorism: Documents of International and Local Control, Vol. 1. New York: Oceana Publications, 1979.

Gaucher, Roland. The Terrorists: From Tzarist Russia to the O.A.S. Translated by P. Spurlin. London: Secker and Warburg, 1968.

Giap, Vonguyen. People's War, People's Army: The Viet Cong Insurrection Manual for Underdeveloped Countries. New York: Praeger, 1962.

Gibellini, Rosino, ed. Frontiers of Theology in Latin America. Translated by John Drury. Maryknoll, NY: Orbis Books, 1979.

Gillo, M.E. The Tupamaro Guerrillas. New York: Ballantine, 1970.

Gross, Feliks. Violence in Politics Terror and Political Assassination in Eastern Europe and Russia. The Hague: Mouton, 1972.

Guevara, Ernesto. Che Guevara on Guerrilla Warfare. Translated by Harries-Clinchy Peterson. New York: Praeger, 1961.

Gregor, A.J. The Ideology of Fascism. New York: The Free Press, 1968.

Grivas, George, Ed. Memoires. C. Foley. London: Longmans, 1964.

Guillen, Abraham. Philosophy of the Urban Guerrilla. Translated by D.C. Hodge. New York: Morrow, 1973.

Gunnemann, Jon P. The Moral Meaning of Revolution. New Haven: Yale University Press, 1979.

Hacker, Frederich. Crusaders, Criminals and Crazies. New York: Norton, 1976.

Halperin, Ernst. Terrorism in Latin America. Beverly Hills: Sage, 1975.

Hildebrand, Klaus. The Foreign Policy of the Third Reich. London: Batsford, 1973.

Hodges, Donald Clark. National Liberation Fronts 1960-1970. New York: Morrow, 1972.

Hodgson, Marshall. The Order of Assassins. Gravenhage: Mouton, 1955.

Hoffer, Eric. The True Believer: Thoughts on the Nature of Mass Movements. New York: Harper and Row, 1951.

Honerich, Ted. Political Violence. Ithaca, New York: Cornell University Press, 1977.

Horne, Alistair. A Savage War of Peace: Algeria 1954-1962. New York: Viking, 1978.

Horowitz, Irving Louis, ed. The Anarchists. New York: Dell Publishers, 1964.

Howard, Michael. Restraints on War; Studies in the Limita-
    tions of Armed Conflict. Oxford: Oxford University
    Press, 1979.

Hutchinson, Martha Crenshaw. Revolutionary Terrorism: The
    FLN in Algeria 1954-1962. Stanford, California: Hoover
    Institution Press, Stanford University, 1978.

Jonas, Hans. The Gnostic Religion. Boston: Beacon Press,
    1963.

Josephus, Flavius. Works. Translated by H. St. J. Thacker-
    ay and Ralph Marcus. Loeb Classical Library. London:
    Heineman, 1926, 8 Vols.

Kohl, J. and Litt, J. Urban Guerrilla Warfare in Latin Amer-
    ica. Cambridge: MIT Press, 1974.

Kossoy, E. Living With Guerrillas: Guerrilla as a Legal
    Problem and a Political Fact. Geneva: Droz, 1976.

Laqueur, Walter. Terrorism. Boston: Little, Brown, 1977.

_____. Guerrilla. Boston: Little, Brown, 1976.

Lambrick, H.T. The Terrorist. London: Rowman, 1972.

Leach, Edmund Ronald. Custom, Law, and Terrorist Violence.
    Edinburgh, University Press, 1977.

Lefebvre, Georges. The Great Fear of 1798: Rural Panic in
    Revolutionary France. New York: Pantheon, 1973.

Levi-Strauss, Claude. Myth and Meaning. Toronto: Univer-
    sity of Toronto Press, 1978.

Lewy, Gunther. Religion and Revolution. New York: Oxford
    University Press, 1974.

Mallin, Jay, ed. Terror and Urban Guerrillas: A Study of
    Tactics and Documents. Coral Gables, Fla.: University of
    Miami Press, 1970.

McDonald, Lawrence Patton. Trotskyism and Terror: The
    Strategy of the Revolution. Washington D.C.: ACU Edu-
    cational and Research Institute, 1977.

McKnight, B. Mind of the Terrorist. London: Michael Joseph
    Ltd., 1974.

MacStiofan, Sean. Revolutionary in Ireland. London: G.
    Cremonesi, 1975.

Mannheim, Karl, Ideology and Utopia. London: Routledge,
    1955.

Marcuse, Herbert. Eros and Civilization. Boston: Beacon
    Press, 1955.

_____ . One Dimensional Man: Studies in the Ideology of Advanced Industrial Society. Boston: Beacon Press, 1964.

_____ . An Essay on Liberation. Boston: Beacon Press, 1969.

_____ . Five Lectures. Translated by Jeremy J. Shapiro and Sherry Weber. Boston: Beacon Press, 1970.

_____ . Counter-Revolution and Revolt. Boston: Beacon Press, 1972.

Marighella, Carlos. For the Liberation of Brazil. Harmondsworth: Penguin, 1972.

Martic, Milos. Insurrection: Five Schools of Revolutionary Thought. New York: Dunellen, 1975.

Melden, A.I. Rights and Persons. Berkeley: UC Press, 1977.

Melzer, Yehudi. Concepts of Just War. Leyden, Netherlands: A.W. Sijthoff, 1975.

Mickolus, Edward F. The Literature of Terrorism: A Selectively Annotated Bibliography. Westport Conn.: Greenwood, 1980.

Minh, Ho Chi. On Revolution. New York: Praeger, 1967.

Moltmann, Jurgen. Theology of Hope: On the Ground and the Implications of a Christian Eschatology. Translated by James W. Leitch. New York: Harper & Row, 1967.

Moore, John N., ed. Law and Civil War in the Modern World. Baltimore: Johns Hopkins University Press, 1974.

Moss, Robert. Urban Guerrillas. London: Maurice Temple Smith, 1972.

Mosse, G.L. Nazism. New Brunswick: Transaction, 1978.

National Advisory Committee on Criminal Justice Standards and Goals: Task Force on Disorders and Terrorism. Disorders and Terrorism. Washington D.C.: National Advisory Committee on Criminal Justice Standards & Goals, 1967.

Nomad, Max. Aspects of Revolt: A Study in Revolutionary Theories and Techniques. New York: Noonday Press, 1959.

Norton, A. International Terrorism: An Annotated Bibliography and Research Guide. Boulder, Colorado: Westview Press, 1980.

O'Ballance, Edgar. Language of Violence: The Blood Politics of Terrorism. San Rafael: Presidio Press, 1979.

Oppenheim, L. International Law. 7th ed. London: Longmans, Green & Co., 1952.

Payne, Pierre Stephen Robert. The Terrorists: The Story of the Forerunners of Stalin. New York: Funk and Wagnals, 1967.

Pompe, C.A. Aggressive War: An International Crime. The Hague: Mouton, 1953.

Radkey, B.D.H. The Sickle Under the Hammer. New York: Columbia University Press, 1963.

Rapoport, David C. Assassination and Terrorism. Toronto: Canadian Broadcasting Corporation, 1971.

Ramsey, Paul. The Just War: Force and Political Responsibility. New York: 1968.

Rawls, John. A Theory of Justice. Cambridge: Harvard University Press, 1971.

Reitlinger, Gerald. The Final Solution. London: Valentine, 1961.

Rhodes, James M. The Hitler Movement: A Modern Millenarian Revolution. Stanford: Hoover Institution, 1980.

Rubin, Jerry. Do It! New York: Simon & Schuster, 1970.

Sale, Kirkpatrick. S.D.S. New York: Random House, 1973.

Schleuns, Karl E. The Twisted Road to Auschwitz. Urbana: University of Illinois Press, 1970.

Scholem, G. The Messianic Idea in Judaism. New York: Schocken Books, 1971.

Schonfield, Hugh J. The Passover Plot. New York: Random House, 1965.

Schreiber, Jan Edward. The Ultimate Weapon: Terrorists and World Order. New York: Morrow, 1978.

Scott, James Brown. The Spanish Origin of International Law: Francisco de Vitoria and His Law of Nations, Oxford: Clarendon Press, 1934.

Segundo, Juan Luis. The Liberation of Theology. Translated by John Drury. Maryknoll, New York: Orbis Books, 1976.

Shaw, Jennifer, ed. Ten Years of Terrorism: Collected Views. London: Royal United Services; New York: Crane Russak, 1979.

Smallwood, E.M. The Jews Under Roman Rule. Leiden: Brill, 1976.

Sorel, Georges. Reflections on Violence. Translated by T.E. Hulme and J. Roth. Introduction by Edward A. Shils. New York: Collier Books, 1950.

Steinberg, L. Spirndonova, Revolutionary Terrorist. London: Methuen, 1935.

Sterling, Claire. The Terror Network; The Secret War of International Terrorism. New York: Holt Rhinehart, 1981.

Strange, S.M. Reason and Violence: Philosophical Investigation. Totowa, New Jersey: Littlefield, Adams, and Co., 1974.

Thrupp, Sylvia L. Millennial Dreams in Action: Essays in Comparative Study. The Hague: Mouton, 1962.

Tomekins, S.R. The Russian Intelligentsia Makers of the Revolutionary State. Norman: University of Oklahoma Press, 1957.

Torres, Camilo. The Complete Writings and Messages of John Gerassi. New York: Random House, 1971.

Trelease, Allen W. White Terror: The Ku Klux Klan Conspiracy and Southern Reconstruction. New York: Harper & Row, 1971.

Trotsky, Leon. Terrorism and Communism. Ann Arbor: University of Michigan Press, 1963.

Trujillo, Alfonso Lopez. Liberation or Revolution?: An Examination of the Priest's Role in the Socioeconomic Class Struggle in Latin America. Huntington, Indiana: Our Sunday Visitor, 1977.

Tucker, R. The Just War. Baltimore: Johns Hopkins Press, 1960.

Turney-High, H.H. Primitive War: Its Practices and Concepts. 2nd ed. Columbia, S.C.: University of South Carolina Press, 1971.

Tuveson, Ernest L. Millennium and Utopia: A Study in the Background of the Idea of Progress. Berkeley: University of California Press, 1949.

Vekeman, Roger. Caesar and Gold: The Priesthood and Politics. Maryknoll, N.Y.: Orbis Books, 1972.

Walter, Eugene V. Terror and Resistance: A Study of Political Violence. New York: Oxford University Press, 1969.

Walzer, Michael. Just and Unjust Wars. New York: Basic Books, 1977.

Wasserstrom, Richard, ed. War and Morality. Belmont, Calif.: Wadsworth, 1970.

Wilkinson, Paul. Political Terrorism. London: Macmillan, 1974.

_____. Terrorism and the Liberal State. London: Mac-
millan, 1977.

                      SELECTED ARTICLES

Bainton, Roland. "Congregationalism: From the Just War to
    the Crusade in the Puritan Revolution." The Andover
    Newton Theological School Bulletin 35 (April 1943): 1-20.

Brandt, E.B. "Utilitarianism and the Rules of War." Philoso-
    phy & Public Affairs (hereafter P.P.A.) I, (Winter 1972):
    145-164.

Dodson, Michael. "Liberation Theology and Christian Radical-
    ism in Contemporary Latin America." Journal of Latin
    American Studies 2 (May 1979): 206.

Hardman, J.B.S. "Terrorism." In Encyclopaedia of the Social
    Sciences, (hereinafter ESS) ed. E.R. Seligman. New
    York: MacMillan, 1933.

Hare, E.M. "Rules of War and Moral Reasoning." P.P.A. I
    (Winter 1972): 166-181.

Kohn, Hans. "Messianism." ESS. New York: Macmillan,
    1933).

Lerner, Max. "Assassination." ESS. New York: Macmillan,
    1933).

Lowry, David. "Internment: Detention Without Trial in North-
    ern Ireland." Human Rights (1976): 297.

Nagel, Thomas. "War and Massacre," P.P.A. I (Winter 1972):
    123-165

Rapoport, David C. "The Politics of Atrocity." in Y. Alex-
    ander and S.M. Finger, eds., Terrorism: Interdisciplin-
    ary Perspectives. New York: John Jay Press, 1977.

Romero, Oscar A. and Arturo R. Damos. "The Church, Politi-
    cal Organization and Violence," Cross Currents 39
    (Winter 1979-80): 385-408.

Shue, Henry. "Torture" P.P.A. 7 (1978): 114-34.

Talmon, Yonina. "Millenarianism," ESS. New York: Macmillan,
    1968.

Walzer, Michael L. "Puritanism as a Revolutionary Ideology."
    History and Theory III (1963): 59-90.

Index

About the Contributors

YONAH ALEXANDER is professor of International Studies and Director of the Institute for Studies in International Terrorism at the State University of New York. He is also a staff associate of the Center for Strategic and International Studies, Georgetown University, and fellow, Institute of Social and Behavioral Pathology (Chicago). An author, editor, and co-editor of fifteen books, Dr. Alexander is editor-in-chief of Terrorism and Political Communication and Persuasion, both international journals.

MOSHE AMON studied history at the Hebrew University of Jerusalem and received his Ph.D. in political philosophy from Claremont Graduate School, where he studied with Herbert Schneider and Leo Strauss. He taught history, philosophy, and Judaic studies in different universities in the United States and is currently Assistant Professor of Religion at the University of British Columbia.

SHLOMO ARONSON, associate professor of political science at the Hebrew University of Jerusalem, has served as radio and television correspondent in Germany, head of news for Israeli television and commentator for BBC, London and PBS, Washington, DC. He has published extensively on Nazi Germany, European politics and the Middle-East conflict.

MICHAEL P. CARTER, formerly professor in the history department at Dartmouth College, teaches at Stanford University while acting as director of the Instruction and Research Information Systems division of its Center for Information Technology. He has written and lectured for years on the period of the terror in France, and served for a time as a consultant on terrorism to the Senate Foreign Relations Committee.

JOHN DUGARD is Professor of Law in and director of the Centre for Applied Legal Studies of the University of the Witwatersrand, Johannesburg, South Africa; Visiting Professor of Public and International Affairs, Princeton University, 1969; Visiting Professor of Law, Duke University, 1974-75; Visiting Professor of Law, Boalt Hall School of Law, University of California, Berkeley, 1981. B.A. 1956, LL.B. 1958, University of Stellenbosch; LL.B, 1965, LL.D 1980, Cambridge University. His publications include The South West Africa/ Namibia Dispute (1973), and Human Rights and the South Africa Legal Order (1978).

ROBERT GERSTEIN received his bachelor's degree in political science from UCLA in 1961, his law degree from Harvard in 1964, and his Ph.D. in political science from UCLA in 1967. He taught at the University of Minnesota for one year, and has been a member of the UCLA department of political science since 1967. He has published a number of articles on self-incrimination, privacy, and the nature of the law in such journals as Ethics, Law and Society Review, and the UCLA Law Review. He is also an active member of the bar, specializing in criminal appeals.

A. JAMES GREGOR is Professor of Political Science at the University of California at Berkeley and a senior fellow at the Institute of Advanced Studies at Hebrew University in Jerusalem. He is the author of ten books and many articles and a former Guggenheim fellow (1974).

ZEEV IVIANSKI, Ph.D., lectures at the Hebrew University, Department of General History and Russian Studies. He is the author of Individual Terror, Theory and Practice (1977) and numerous articles including "Individual Terror: Concept and Typology" (Contemporary History, 1977); Provocation at the Center: A Study in the History of Counter-Terror" (Terrorism, 1980); and The Blow at the Center: The Concept and its History (Proceedings of the Conference on Terrorism, Tel-Aviv, 1979).

VYTAUTAS KAVOLIS is Charles A. Dana Professor of Comparative Civilizations and Professor of Sociology at Dickinson College. He is author of Artistic Expression - A Sociological Analysis (1968) and History on Art's Side: Social Dynamics in Artistic Efflorescences (1972); editor of Comparative Perspectives on Social Problems (1968) and of the journal, Comparative Civilizations Review; and president of the International Society for the Comparative Study of Civilizations.

ALFRED R. LOUCH is chairman of the philosophy department, Claremont Graduage School, Claremont University. He received his Ph.D. at Cambridge (1956), has published Explanation and Human Action (1966) and numerous articles on action theory and political and legal philosophy.

JOHN R. POTTENGER is a Ph.D. candidate in political science at the University of Maryland, College Park. His dissertation is on the methodology and political ethics of a radical Christian philosophical movement in Latin America - liberation theology - and how it is applied in political practice. Mr. Pottenger's other research fields include political economy, traditional and contemporary political and moral philosophy, and modern social theory and its methods.

GEORGE H. QUESTER is a professor of government at Cornell University, and has served as director of its Peace Studies Program. His major research interests concern military strategy and arms control, and his most recent book is Offense and Defense in the international system.

DAVID C. RAPOPORT (Assassination and Terrorism, Toronto, 1971 and "Politics of Atrocity," 1977) is professor of political theory at UCLA and has published a variety of essays on military conspiracy and the concept of corruption. His most recent publications are "Moses, Charisma, and Covenant" (1979), and "The Praetorian Army: Insecurity, Venality, and Impotence" (1982).

MAURICE A.J. TUGWELL, (Ph.D., King's College, University of London, 1979), is director of the Centre for Conflict Studies at the University of New Brunswick, Canada. He is the author of The Unquiet Peace (1957), Airborne to Battle (1971), Arnhem, A Case Study (1975), and Skiing for Beginners (1977), as well as many articles.

PAUL WILKINSON was appointed to the new chair of international relations at the University of Aberdeen in 1979. He was formerly reader in politics at the University of Wales. His published works include Social Movement (1971), Political Terrorism (1974), and Terrorism and the Liberal State (1977).